Management Accounting

A Business Planning Approach

Second Edition

By Noah P. Barsky and Anthony H. Catanach, Jr.

Villanova University

cognella® | ACADEMIC PUBLISHING

Bassim Hamadeh, CEO and Publisher
Kassie Graves, Director of Acquisitions and Sales
Jamie Giganti, Senior Managing Editor
Jess Estrella, Senior Graphic Designer
Mieka Portier, Senior Field Acquisitions Editor
Sean Adams, Project Editor
Luiz Ferreira, Senior Licensing Specialist
Christian Berk, Associate Editor

Cover image copyright © Depositphotos/nmarques74.
            © Depositphotos/akomov.
            © Depositphotos/Ozerina.

Printed in the United States of America

ISBN: 978-1-5165-0628-6 (pb) / 978-1-5165-0629-3 (br)

Brief Contents

Contents

Chapter 2

The Business Value Chain

Chapter 3

Evaluating Financial Performance

Chapter 4

Business Processes and Risks

Chapter 5

Planning Profitable Operations

Chapter 6

Forecasting Tools and Techniques

Chapter 7

Budgeting Fundamentals

Chapter 8

Analyzing and Using Budgets

Chapter 9

Performance Evaluation and Decision Making

Chapter 10

Analyzing Costs at the Customer and Process Level

Appendix

Preparing and Presenting the Business Plan

Preface

To successfully compete in today's dynamic business environment, both graduate and undergraduate students must appreciate the role that accounting information plays in business decision making. The primary goal of this introductory accounting text is to help students gain an appreciation for the *value of managerial accounting information*. This text also encourages students to think about business problems in a structured and organized manner, and actually motivates more advanced coursework in a variety of business disciplines. Our unique approach inspires students to acquire the knowledge and develop the skills they will need in business. Additionally, we find that these materials can be used effectively in both graduate and undergraduate management accounting classes.

A Business Planning Approach

Our business planning approach integrates traditional managerial accounting topics with current business themes, proposed by academics and the profession, by simulating the actual strategic planning, resource management, and performance measurement activities commonly found in business enterprises. To accomplish our goal, i.e., developing student appreciation for the value of managerial accounting information, we rely on three educational objectives:

- Introduce students to strategy and its impact on process and performance.

- Provide students with an understanding of basic business processes and their inherent risks.

- Emphasize the role of managerial accounting information in making decisions about strategy, process, and performance.

To accomplish these goals, we rely heavily on Kaplan and Norton's Balanced Scorecard philosophy, and we have organized our materials to parallel the sequence of events found in the *business planning* process. We find that this context adds a realism that not only gives students a first-hand glimpse of what accounting professionals do in today's marketplace, but also stimulates student demand for managerial accounting information. Each chapter is built around the "real-world" business problems and information needs faced by a fictitious service enterprise. Students follow this business from its inception through the first three years of operations, witnessing increasing complexity in its operations that provides ideal contexts in which to introduce managerial accounting topics. Such a delivery structure also allows students to integrate and gradually build upon fundamental concepts introduced in earlier chapters. Additionally, we have carefully tailored end-of-chapter exercises, problems, and cases to reflect business environments with which students have experience and can readily identify.

Unique Text Features

Each chapter includes several special features that complement the delivery of topical content. These include:

C&F Enterprises, Inc. In each chapter, we use the unfolding story of a landscaping business to demonstrate the importance of managerial accounting information in a student-friendly context. Our C&F example integrates chapter material, highlights the complexity of running a business, and reinforces the value of information to business decisions, all in a setting that students understand and appreciate.

Business Beacons. These illustrations motivate and link each chapter's managerial accounting topics to interesting, contemporary examples found in practice. For example, the AICPA's Information Value Chain illustrates the importance of information. We rely on a variety of respected publications to confirm the relevance of each chapter's discussion and related examples.

Net Gains. Where relevant, we have provided a section that directs students to free online resources that enrich chapter material by providing links to high-quality electronic spreadsheets and other tools that perform many of the most common, traditional management accounting computations. Using these links allows more classroom time for discussion and development of analytical skills.

Mini-Cases. Located at the end of each chapter and complete with discussion questions, these cases promote critical analysis and the development of high-level decision-making skills. They are also excellent classroom exercises that promote and encourage team learning.

Business Planning Application. Each chapter includes an *optional* module that allows students to engage in a semester-long business planning simulation. These exercises reinforce chapter content and further demonstrate the very real role that management accounting information plays in business decision making.

Management Accounting: A Business Planning Approach

Effective Chapter Organization

Our text delivers much of the technical content contained in most introductory managerial courses, but differs from traditional texts in several ways. First, since we rely on a broader business perspective (e.g., balanced scorecard) to motivate the need for management accounting information, we include much more material on strategy, risk assessment, and basic business processes than is found in most introductory texts. Additionally, the text does not cover topics that the profession (i.e., IMA's Practice Analysis) finds to be less important to current practice, or that are commonly addressed in other accounting or finance courses (e.g., transfer pricing, cost accounting, capital budgeting). Instead, the text specifically links a firm's business strategy with the value chain activities necessary to carry it out. By doing so, students learn just how important management accounting information is to business planning and decision making.

Chapter 1: Business Strategy and Management Accounting

Chapter 1 examines why businesses exist and the purpose of strategy. Students gain an appreciation for the competing information demands of various stakeholders. We introduce the fundamental strategic planning process, including the importance of business vision, the mission statement, and goal setting. C&F Enterprises, Inc. begins operations, and its owners struggle with formalizing their business strategy and the basics of planning and running a business. End-of-chapter exercises and problems require students to use the Internet to explore what type of information is available about products and services, strategy, and so on. A Mini-Case asks students to consider what management accounting information a bookstore needs, as well as what role they believe that their intended business major plays in resolving the bookstore's business issues. If instructors choose to assign the Business Planning Application in Chapter 1, student teams will develop an initial idea for a new, start-up business.

Chapter 2: The Business Value Chain

Chapter 2 identifies forces affecting businesses (e.g., technology and globalization), gives an overview of customer value creation, and describes how companies implement business processes (i.e., the Value Chain) to execute strategy. Together with Chapter 1, Chapter 2 emphasizes the critical role that planning and information play in managing business processes. This chapter introduces students to the "real world" in which they will compete. C&F Enterprises, Inc. begins to address customer-focused market issues like product offering, pricing, and delivery. In end-of-chapter exercises and problems, students now use the Internet to look for information on how companies deal with technology and globalization or address the customer value proposition. A Mini-Case requires student "consulting" teams to visit a local business and gather basic information about strategy, business process, and performance measurement. If instructors elect to use the Business

Planning Application in this chapter, student teams will analyze the market and competition for a new, start-up business.

Chapter 3: Evaluating Financial Performance

Many students leave their introductory financial accounting course with the perception that financial statements are simply a high-level aggregation of transactions captured by a bookkeeping system. Therefore, Chapter 3 actually links business processes to financial performance outcomes. Specifically, this chapter reviews how managers and financial analysts use ratios to evaluate firm operations. This discussion reminds students that financial data can be used to evaluate the effectiveness of business processes. We have used the operating data from C&F Enterprises, Inc.'s first complete year of operations for ratio analysis. End-of-chapter exercises and problems require students to find and download financial data from the Internet and perform limited analysis. A Mini-Case requires students to use a transaction processing spreadsheet to prepare a balance sheet, income statement, and statement of cash flows. The optional Business Planning Application asks students to visit their college or university library to determine what industry performance ratios and services are available to assist them in preparing a formal business plan.

Chapter 4: Business Processes and Risks

Having established a foundation for discussing basic business processes and their role in creating firm value, we introduce students to basic business risk in Chapter 4. The chapter begins with a discussion of how business activities *drive* financial results. Students then learn how to systematically identify and assess the risks that underlie these processes. This risk assessment chapter helps students to see the value of information in managing the risks that all businesses face. Throughout each chapter, we present specific examples of the value delivered by accounting professionals and their associations (e.g., the AICPA and IMA, among others). C&F Enterprises, Inc. provides examples of business processes and risks that are discussed throughout the chapter. End-of-chapter exercises and problems give students practice in identifying business processes and risks in a variety of contexts. One Mini-Case shows students how process affects performance, and another allows students to assess their individual tolerance for risk. If assigned, the Business Planning Application in this chapter has students evaluate the most relevant risks facing the start-up business for which they are preparing a business plan.

Chapter 5: Planning Profitable Operations

Once managers define strategy, identify core business processes, and assess risk, the next step is to create profit plans. Chapter 5 introduces students to cost behavior, cost-volume-profit (CVP) concepts, and breakeven analysis. Students are exposed to these topics in the context of managing business processes. C&F

Enterprises, Inc. encounters an unforeseen environmental shock, a major new competitor, which motivates the need for more sophisticated cost analysis and profit planning. End-of-chapter exercises and problems give students practice in cost identification and classification, CVP and breakeven calculation, and basic profit planning strategies. One Mini-Case is devoted to cost classification issues and another to breakeven analysis and CVP analysis. If instructors choose to use the Business Planning Application in Chapter 5, student teams will identify costs and perform a preliminary breakeven analysis for their planned business venture.

Chapter 6: Forecasting Tools and Techniques

After they have learned how business processes affect costs and profits, Chapter 6 introduces students to revenue and expense forecasting techniques that managers use in the planning process. This chapter illustrates how common statistical methods, such as correlation and regression analysis (readily available in Microsoft Excel) can be used to perform CVP analysis and predict operating results. Chapter 6 also highlights qualitative factors managers must consider when using sales and cost forecasts, and it concludes with a brief discussion of the effects of learning on cost behavior. C&F Enterprises, Inc.'s first-year operating results are disaggregated to illustrate how customer demand and price affect revenue forecasts. End-of-chapter exercises and problems provide students practice in discussing cost drivers, collecting cost data from publicly available resources, and applying statistical analysis to cost data. A Mini-Case asks students to perform statistical analysis and incorporate their results in a profit planning exercise. If assigned, the Business Planning Application in this chapter asks student teams to create a sales forecast and cost estimates for their start-up enterprise.

Chapter 7: Budgeting Fundamentals

Chapter 7 demonstrates how companies create and use budgets to communicate business strategy, allocate resources, and create pro forma financial statements. Drawing upon the forecasting chapter, Chapter 7 illustrates how the sales budget drives the start-up budget, operating budgets, and pro forma financial statements. In addition to introducing budgeting techniques, this chapter also discusses the advantages and limitations of budgeting. C&F Enterprises, Inc. recognizes the need for a formal budget to guide its operations for the coming year. Chapter 7 describes the master budget in detail using C&F as an example. End-of-chapter exercises and problems require students to discuss the benefits of budgeting in a variety of business contexts, and to forecast sales and related contribution margins. A Mini-Case is devoted to preparing an operating budget, a cash flow budget, and financial statement budgets for a donut shop. If instructors choose to assign the Chapter 7 Business Planning Application, student teams will prepare a start-up budget and an operating budget for their new business venture.

Chapter 8: Analyzing and Using Budgets

Chapter 8 extends the previous chapter's budgeting discussion by demonstrating how budget credibility can be tested using a rigorous sensitivity analysis. This chapter also shows how budget data are used in flexible budgeting and variance analysis. Since C&F Enterprises, Inc. has just completed its second year of operations, the chapter uses C&F operating data to illustrate how variance analysis can provide insights into a company's business practices and processes. End-of-chapter exercises and problems require students to prepare flexible budgets, calculate variances, and explain potential reasons for observed variances. A comprehensive, two-part Mini-Case evaluates students' abilities to integrate CVP and breakeven analysis with budgeting and variance analysis. If assigned, the Business Planning Application in this chapter helps student teams perform both a sensitivity analysis and a ratio analysis on their start-up's budget numbers to evaluate the credibility of their financial projections.

Chapter 9: Performance Analysis and Decision Making

Chapter 9 illustrates the value of managerial accounting information in a decision-making context. A review of the balanced scorecard integrates previous chapter coverage of strategy, process, risk, and resource management issues, and it sets the stage for discussion of financial and nonfinancial performance measures. This chapter also introduces responsibility centers and explores performance evaluation in a divisional setting. Common management accounting topics such as make-or-buy decisions, special orders, partnering, and outsourcing decisions also are addressed. Now two years old, C&F Enterprises, Inc. provides a rich setting in which to evaluate past financial and nonfinancial performance, and to conduct cost-benefit analyses on potential future operating alternatives. End-of-chapter exercises and problems ask students to create financial and nonfinancial performance measures for a variety of business contexts. Students also are required to evaluate responsibility center performance and conduct cost-benefit analyses under several operating scenarios. A Mini-Case also assesses students' ability to perform cost-benefit analysis in the context of a local pizza parlor. If instructors decide to assign this chapter's Business Planning Application, student teams will carefully evaluate their plans for potential partnering or outsourcing opportunities. Student teams are also encouraged to prepare a formal written and oral presentation of their business plans.

Chapter 10: Analyzing Costs at the Customer and Process Level

Chapter 10 is an optional chapter for those accounting programs whose students require a manufacturing and cost accounting perspective in the introductory managerial accounting course. This chapter introduces types of manufacturing costs, and discusses both job order and process costing. Activity-based costing and its role in business reengineering is addressed, as are reengineering management topics such as continuous improvement, total quality management, and knowledge management. C&F Enterprises, Inc. begins its third-year operations by confronting service pricing issues that require a more detailed analysis of costs at the customer level. In this context, manufacturing cost topics are further explored. End-of-chapter exercises and problems ask students to compute manufacturing costs in a variety of settings. A Mini-Case requires students to compare product costs using activity-based costing with product costs calculated using traditional overhead allocation techniques.

Appendix: Preparing and Presenting the Business Plan

An appendix summarizes the business planning process discussed in the ten chapters of the text. It also provides specific examples of each element found in a market-quality business plan. The appendix concludes by detailing presentation guidelines that students can use to effectively communicate business plans to interested parties.

Management Accounting: A Business Planning Approach offers a fundamentally new approach to help students gain an appreciation for the value of information. This guiding principle uses business planning as a context to highlight the relevance of management accounting topics. The creation of a business plan serves as a realistic mechanism to introduce students to the competitive market in which they will compete. Through this experience, students gain a first-hand appreciation for the challenge and value of transforming data into information. Our students have responded most positively to this approach and these materials. We sincerely hope that this text provides your students with a similarly meaningful learning experience.

Acknowledgements

We gratefully acknowledge and thank the following individuals for their suggestions, recommendations, and insightful comments that made this and previous text editions possible:

Jeffrey Archambault	*Marshall University*
Deborah Beard	*Southeast Missouri State University*
Barney Cargile	*University of Alabama*
Deb Cosgrove	*University of Nebraska, Lincoln*
David Dearman	*University of Arkansas at Fort Smith*
Lou Fowler	*Missouri Western State College*
Larry Hegstad	*Pacific Lutheran University*
Robert Holfreter	*Central Washington University*
Mohamed Hussein	*University of Connecticut*
Larry Killough	*Virginia Polytechnic Institute and State University*
Leslie Kren	*University of Wisconsin, Milwaukee*
Scott Lane	*University of New Haven*

Kate Lancaster	*California Polytechnic State University at San Luis Obispo*
Thomas Largay	*Thomas College*
Michael Licata	*Villanova University*
Anne Lillis	*University of Melbourne*
Garry Marchant	*University of Melbourne*
Richard Newmark	*Northern Colorado University*
Chei H. Paik	*George Washington University*
Paige Paulsen	*Salt Lake Community College*
Sandra Pelfrey	*Oakland University*
Roy Regel	*University of Montana*
Shelley Rhoades-Catanach	*Villanova University*
Gina Sturgill	*Concord College*
Walter Smith	*Marshall University*
Steve Wells	*Alcorn State University*
Loren Wenzel	*Marshall University*

The authors also gratefully acknowledge the financial support provided by the Institute of Management Accountants Faculty Development Grant Program, as well as the feedback received from presentations at Marshall University, the University of Melbourne, the University of Nevada–Las Vegas, the University of Western Ontario, the Boston Accounting Research Colloquium at Bentley College, the Colloquium on Change in Accounting Education, and the American Accounting Association's 2001 Southwest Regional and Annual Meetings. This publication would not have been possible without the wonderful editorial guidance and assistance of Jessica Carlisle, Sarah Jane Shangraw, Claudine Bellanton, and Lydia Haas.

About the Authors

Noah P. Barsky
Ph.D., CPA, CMA

Noah P. Barsky is an accounting professor in the Villanova School of Business at Villanova University. He earned undergraduate and masters degrees in accounting at the Pennsylvania State University and his Ph.D. from the University of Connecticut. He is a Certified Public Accountant and Certified Management Accountant. Dr. Barsky has authored five books and published over fifty articles in academic and professional journals, including *Advances in Accounting Education, Commercial Lending Review, Corporate Finance Review, Issues in Accounting Education,* and *Strategic Finance.* He has received multiple teaching excellence awards and has been recognized with national and international awards for scholarly writings. He was a co-recipient of the Innovation in Accounting Education Award from the American Accounting Association for his work on the Business Planning Model. Dr. Barsky is a member of the American Institute of Certified Public Accountants and the Institute of Management Accountants.

Anthony H. Catanach, Jr.
Ph.D., CPA, CMA

Anthony H. Catanach, Jr. is a retired professor of accounting in the Villanova School of Business at Villanova University. He obtained his undergraduate and masters degrees in accounting from the University of New Mexico and his Ph.D. from Arizona State University. He has received numerous national and international awards for his teaching and scholarly activities, and has twice received the American Accounting Association's Innovation in Accounting Education Award—once for his work on the Business Activity Model, and again for his efforts on the Business Planning Model. He also has authored over fifty articles on accounting and management issues in such journals as *Advances in Accounting, Accounting Horizons, Bank Accounting & Finance,* the *Commercial Lending Review,* the *Journal of Managerial Issues,* and *Strategic Finance.* He is both a Certified Public Accountant and Certified Management Accountant, as well as a member of American Institute of Certified Public Accountants and the Institute of Management Accountants.

Chapter 1

1. Define and describe a business.

2. Identify and describe the stakeholders of a business.

3. Explain the relationship between strategy and profitability.

4. Describe the strategic planning process and its results.

5. Identify barriers to successful strategic planning.

Business Strategy and Management Accounting

This chapter explains the fundamentals of business strategy and the strategic planning process. Understanding business strategy is essential to helping a business meet the expectations of customers, investors, and other stakeholders. This knowledge also highlights just how important information is to managers in making business decisions. In fact, businesses reward business professionals who can create and execute effective strategies based on financial information. To serve companies in this way, individuals must develop the skills and experience necessary to formulate strategy, assess risk, and make business decisions. Most importantly, business professionals need a thorough appreciation for what their company or client does: *They need to understand the overall strategy of the business.*

Managing a business can be very complex. Today's businesses continually attempt to manage a variety of competing demands such as creating value for owners, satisfying customers, developing and retaining employees, and complying with regulatory requirements. However, addressing these challenges requires a wealth of timely, meaningful, and relevant information that managers can use in making their daily decisions. Such information is called **managerial accounting information**. It is the primary focus of this book. **Management accounting** is that body of knowledge that captures the concepts, theories, tools, and techniques by which company performance data are transformed into information that managers can use to create and execute strategy.

To better explain the factors that affect management decision-making in a business context, this chapter introduces a simulated company, C&F Enterprises, Inc. This company's operations will provide a recurring illustration throughout the text that will show how managers use information to operate their business. The start-up company's story follows.

C&F Enterprises, Inc.: Making a Dream Reality

For several years, Keith Cummings and Dale Fisher, two close friends, had discussed the possibility of providing landscaping services to both commercial and residential customers in a growing suburban market area. Keith had recently completed an undergraduate mechanical engineering degree at a local university and was anxious to apply his newly acquired skills in the business world for both "fun and profit." Dale, a high school graduate, had worked several years with a residential construction company building single-family homes. Both Keith and Dale were convinced that changing market forces and consumer demographics had created a demand for a full-service landscaping business in their area.

Recently, Keith had received a modest inheritance from his uncle. With this newly acquired wealth, the possibility of pursuing this business venture became more real. To identify potential customers and businesses currently providing landscaping-related services, Keith and Dale consulted both the local telephone book as well as Internet resources. The study's results were promising, and preliminary negotiations resulted in several new commercial lawn maintenance contracts. So, Keith and Dale decided to incorporate a new company, C&F Enterprises, Inc., that would provide a full range of lawn services including mowing, trimming, weed control, tree and shrub care, aeration, and mulching.

Given the start-up nature of its operations, C&F would require its clients to provide the materials, such as seed, fertilizer, and weedkiller, used in their maintenance services and operate with two rented trucks. Both Keith and Dale also planned to play an active role in the management and delivery of landscaping services. Students would assist them during the summer months. A steady supply of local agricultural workers would support the business during the fall and spring seasons. Staffing requirements were expected to be minimal during the winter, although Keith and Dale had not discounted the possibility of supplementing their landscaping services with snow-removal services during these months. Initial financing for the company came from Keith's inheritance as well as from friends and family who purchased an ownership interest in their venture. A local accounting and business advisory services firm helped C&F set up an accounting information system and also recommended a local bookkeeper, Frances Chan.

What, Exactly, Is a Business?

Learning Objective 1
Define and describe a
business.

A **business** is an economic entity that aims to create wealth for its owners by using financial, human, and physical capital to deliver products or services that the market demands. This profit motive distinguishes a *business* organization from a nonprofit entity such as a church, school, government, or charity. C&F Enterprises, Inc. employs all three types of capital in delivering landscaping services to its customers. As with most new enterprises, C&F initially had to attract cash funds that could be used to acquire the assets that would ultimately be used to deliver services. These start-up monies are called **financial capital**, and in C&F's case, they include the cash received from Keith's inheritance, as well as the funds invested by family and friends. Since landscaping services require individuals to mow lawns, trim trees, and perform similar services, Keith and Dale used some of their financial resources (that is, cash) to employ student and part-time farm workers. These employees represent the **human capital** in C&F's operations. However, C&F's workers also needed lawn mowers, trimmers, and other equipment to do their jobs. So, financial resources also had to be used

Figure 1.1
**Customers and employees are
important business stakeholders. A business cannot
survive without its customers,
and employees run daily
operations.**

to buy the company's equipment and tools. Such assets are frequently referred to as physical capital, the equipment and property that employees use to create a product and/or deliver a service.

The rest of this chapter illustrates how strategic planning, a critical business activity, transforms data into information that managers and other financial professionals can use to guide a business to its goals. You will learn about the various constituencies that businesses serve, the link between strategy and profitability, and the fundamentals of the strategic planning process.

Stakeholders and Their Interests

Several economic parties inside and outside the firm take an interest in the success of the business. These parties frequently are called stakeholders, as they have a "stake" in or in some way depend on the firm for economic benefit. These stakeholders often have competing interests. However, once a business decides to deliver a product or service, it must consider the interests of its various stakeholder groups. The stakeholder web depicted in Exhibit 1.1 summarizes the many constituencies that a business must serve in order to succeed.

Learning Objective 2
Identify and describe the
stakeholders of a business.

Customers

Customers should be the primary focus of any business. No business can survive if it does not deliver what its customers want. Historically, businesses have relied on

Exhibit 1.1
A Web of Relationships:
A Company and Its
Stakeholders

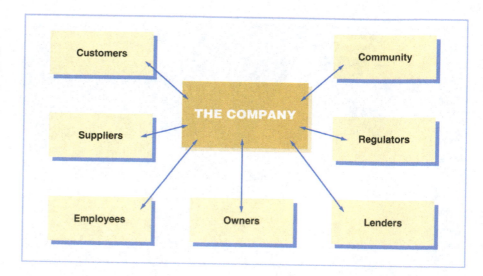

advertising or a product's unique reputation to attract and retain their customers. Because so many products are becoming harder to distinguish from one another, many companies now use a variety of techniques to differentiate themselves and foster customer loyalty. For example, American Airlines and many of its competitors rely on frequent flyer programs to enlist customer allegiance by offering "free" tickets for flying a certain number of miles or flights. Most airlines also offer accelerated boarding privileges and first-class upgrades as well as reduced-fee memberships to their "member only" lounges for loyal frequent flyers. These are just a few of the techniques that companies use to keep customers interested in their products and services.

Suppliers

Businesses must develop relationships with suppliers to obtain the necessary inputs or resources to deliver quality products and services to customers. Suppliers include vendors that supply inventories, as well as capital asset providers that furnish buildings, equipment, and other physical assets. The importance of a reliable vendor relationship can be seen in troubles once encountered by Ford Motor Company with its primary tire supplier, Firestone. Ford alleged that Firestone supplied defective tires to the manufacturer for its Explorer model vehicles and that these tires led to a significant number of automotive accidents and deaths. These allegations terminated a buyer-vendor relationship that had lasted for decades and created consumer concerns about the safety of Ford products.

Employees

Firms rely heavily on people to run daily business operations. Consequently, companies must develop ways to recruit, train, and retain the "right" people to manage the core processes used by the business to achieve its goals. Since

4

employees deliver labor services, businesses must offer competitive salaries. In addition to regular wages, companies often reward employees with cash bonuses, stock ownership and profit-sharing arrangements, and other employee benefit plans. Favorable workplace environments and advancement opportunities also are critical for recruiting and retaining qualified, high-performing individuals. Alternatively, well documented corruption, fraud, and incompetence at Veterans Administration (VA) hospitals resulted in poor medical care for military veterans, negative media reports, lawsuits, reputation impairment, and waste of scarce resources.

Owners

Owners also demand significant attention, since they provide the financial capital that starts and sustains operations. Today's global economy offers these stakeholders a wide range of investment choices. If not adequately compensated for the capital they provide, these stakeholders divert their investments to other opportunities that better meet their expectations. Consequently, managers must pay great attention to attracting and retaining these capital providers by ultimately delivering a consistent record of earnings growth and/or dividend payments that investors can rely

Regulatory Watchdogs Protect Investors

The U.S. Securities and Exchange Commission files enforcement actions against companies for overstating revenues, understating expenses, and improper accounting for assets. These cases have raised serious concerns about the integrity of corporate financial reporting and have dramatically affected the public's willingness to invest, thereby adversely impacting stock markets.

To restore public trust in the capital markets, the U.S. Congress passed the Sarbanes-Oxley Act of 2002. The act focuses on preventing corporate governance failures of the type recently witnessed in publicly traded companies. Executives now must implement safeguards against conflicts of interest, personally sign and certify periodic financial statements, and report on internal control procedures designed to prevent fraud. The act also established the

Public Company Accounting Oversight Board (PCAOB) to develop and enforce new oversight rules affecting companies and their executives, accountants, financial analysts, and other related parties. For example, a company's external auditors now are required to register with the PCAOB and to comply with new standards relating to work quality, business relationships with clients, and ethical standards. In addition, financial analysts are now subject to stricter compensation and review standards to prevent them from unfairly influencing their firms' lending activities to clients. Such regulatory oversight is intended to improve the quality of financial reporting and promote investor confidence. The Sarbanes-Oxley Act of 2002 is a example of the prominent role that regulators play in our economy.

upon to meet their capital appreciation or cash flow requirements. Businesses also must provide these stakeholders with accurate, timely, and relevant information that can be used to monitor the risks and rewards of their investment.

Lenders

Lenders do not have an ownership stake in the business, but they provide financial capital to the firm—usually on a temporary basis. These creditors expect timely payment of interest on the monies borrowed by the firm, as well as an eventual return of the borrowed capital. There are many different types of lenders and creditors. They include financial institutions such as banks, savings institutions, and insurance companies, as well as suppliers who may extend to a business short-term credit to pay for inventory, capital asset purchases, or other services. These creditors earn interest on the credit they supply to compensate them for the cost of allowing another party to use their money and the risk of the borrower failing to repay its loan.

Regulators

Firms also must adhere to the laws and regulations of the locations in which they conduct business. Governments are actively interested in business operations and regularly monitor tax collection, employee safety, environmental protection, hiring practices, consumer interests, and a variety of other public interest issues. Regulators can dramatically affect the nature of business processes, quality standards, competition, and even investment decisions. For example, the United States government recently battled technology companies over data encryption and privacy in criminal and terrorist investigations. Airline mergers have drawn increased scrutiny as consumers worry that fewer air carriers might lead to higher ticket prices and a decline in service to smaller communities.

Community

Businesses also strive to protect the communities in which they operate. Communities can exercise great influence over a company's advertising practices, its use of physical assets, and its customers. In fact, businesses expend significant resources to build and maintain their community image. For example, most firms participate actively in local chamber of commerce activities and sponsor charitable fundraising events. Some also spend heavily on advertising and promotion of local cultural and sporting events.

Learning Objective 3
Explain the relationship between strategy and profitability.

Business Strategy: The Link to Profitability

All businesses strive to make a profit. Therefore, revenues from goods and services sold to customers must exceed the costs needed to produce and supply those

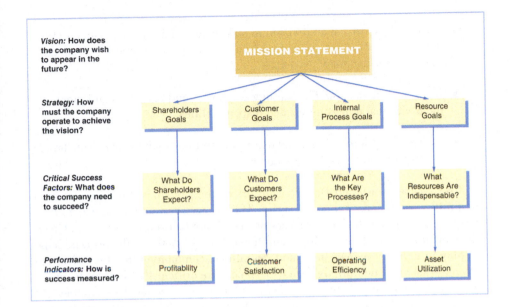

Exhibit 1.2
A Strategic Planning
Framework

goods and services. Yet, such profitability does not occur accidentally. Success means generating sales and controlling costs, usually in a competitive marketplace. Consequently, a firm's managers develop and execute strategies that enable the business to succeed, *to profit*. Essentially, a business strategy is an action-oriented, master plan that guides the business to profitability by successfully accomplishing its missions and achieving its goals. A sound business strategy also shows how an organization meets its customers' needs while differentiating itself from its competitors. Today's business environment is characterized by dramatic technology changes, aggressive competition, and globalization. To profitably operate in such a climate, companies must define exactly how they intend to compete. *In short, what is the business strategy?* Exhibit 1.2 illustrates the relationship between a company's mission, strategy, critical success factors, and performance indicators, one of which is profitability.

In smaller companies, the sole owner/manager's expectations generally shape strategy. In larger organizations, high-level committees staffed by the company president, other senior executives, and professional corporate planners usually are involved in developing this master plan. As companies grow in complexity or size and ownership becomes more distant from those who manage the company, it is particularly important for managers to:

- Evaluate critically the basic assumptions on which a business is built and encourage new ideas and information to help identify growth opportunities.

- Develop a compelling vision of the company's future that is shared by stakeholders.

- Communicate this shared vision to stakeholders and inspire collaboration. Meetings, newsletters, posters, and slogans are tools often used by managers to spread the company's vision.

- Invest in human capital by training employees and managers and providing them with real opportunities and responsibilities.

- Recognize both individual and team contributions to the vision. This builds team spirit and cements commitment.

In C&F's case, Keith and Dale's vision drives their business strategy: creation of a full-service landscaping enterprise. The primary assumption on which they base their venture is the local market's need for more landscaping services. Given the start-up nature of the business and the active role both Keith and Dale hope to play in its daily management and operations, communicating their vision to others is not an issue initially. It may become more critical should their business grow quickly, forcing them to rely more on others to execute their strategy. As might be expected in any new business, Keith and Dale's initial focus is short term: their first year of operations. But without a solid plan, their first year could be their last.

The Balanced Scorecard: The Link Between Strategy and Profit

The balanced scorecard is a popular performance measurement framework used by hundreds of global businesses to communicate strategic goals to employees. This contemporary management tool translates an organization's strategy into a comprehensive set of measures that provide feedback on how well the company has performed in meeting its goals. The balanced scorecard addresses four important questions that directly affect profitability:

- *Financial Results*: To succeed financially, how should the company appear to its stakeholders?

- *Customer Satisfaction*: To achieve its strategy, how should the company appear to its customers?

- *Business Processes*: To satisfy its customers, at what business processes must the company excel?

- *Learning and Growth*: To achieve its strategy, how will the company sustain its ability to change and improve?

A company's strategy must answer each of these four questions: successfully achieving the strategy generally results in financial success. Exhibit 1.3 illustrates the cause-and-effect relationship among the four dimensions of the balanced scorecard. A trained workforce results in effective business processes that satisfy customers, and satisfied customers lead to revenues and profits.

The balanced scorecard's contribution to strategic planning and performance measurement is explored more fully in Chapters 3 and 9.

Planning for the Future

Successful companies plan for their future. Almost all businesses plan for at least the next year using a budget. While a necessity, a single year's financial budget does not fully recognize the opportunities and risks of longer-term business commitments. Consequently, many institutions, particularly larger ones, engage in long-term planning. Strategic planning is an ongoing, continuous process in which a company determines what the business will be in the future. For example, Shake Shack, which started in Madison Square Park in New York City became a public company and expanded across the United States and overseas. This decision required its managers to project future store openings during the next five to ten years. As Exhibit 1.2 and the foregoing example suggest, strategic planning involves developing a set of attainable goals and the means to achieve them. This process addresses what the business should do *today* to achieve its objectives in an uncertain *tomorrow*. Consequently, strategic planning deals with the present, *not* with *future* business decisions.

Strategic planning addresses four fundamental questions:

1. *Where is the company now?* Do the products and services offered meet customer expectations? Is the business successful? Are the owners and other stakeholders satisfied with the firm's performance?
2. *What do senior managers want the business to look like in the next one-, five-, or ten-year period?* What is the company's mission? Is this vision consistent with that of other stakeholders?

Learning Objective 4
Describe the strategic planning process and its results.

FINANCIAL RESULTS	Improved products and services lead to satisfied and loyal customers, which lead to increased revenues and profits.
CUSTOMER SATISFACTION	Improved processes lead to improved products and services for customers.
BUSINESS PROCESSES	Skilled, creative employees work to improve business processes.
LEARNING & GROWTH	Employee training and investments in technology develop skilled, creative employees and form the foundation for learning and growth.

Exhibit 1.3
Linking Strategy to Profitability

Exhibit 1.4
The Business Plan: Evidence
of Strategic Planning

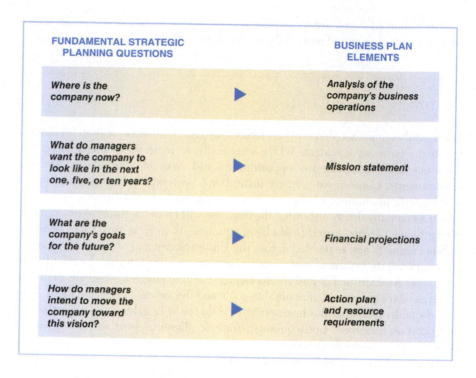

3. *What are the company's goals for the future?* What potential factors will impact current business operations? How will these affect the company's ability to execute its strategy?
4. *How will the company move toward this vision?* What is the plan?

The answers to these questions are generally documented formally in a **business plan**, which is comprised of the following five parts:

1. An analysis of the company's current and future business operations
2. A mission statement that describes company goals
3. An action plan
4. A description of resource requirements
5. Financial projections.

Exhibit 1.4 illustrates how the business plan documents senior managers' answers to fundamental strategic planning questions. Throughout the rest of this chapter, each of these strategic planning issues will be examined in the context of C&F's operations.

Analyzing the Business

In reviewing the company's business, managers must evaluate the current state of the company's operations as well as its future prospects.

Current Business Operations. The first step in strategic planning is to critically review the company's stakeholder relationships with an eye to external and internal opportunities the company may have. A manager must consider if there are any external opportunities, for example:

- Have new markets developed?

- Does the competition have any weaknesses that can be exploited?

- Are consumers calling for new products and services?

- Does the local community provide any new opportunities on which the business can capitalize?

- Are there any new laws and regulations that might favorably affect the company?

Keith and Dale of C&F Enterprises, Inc. recognized that existing landscaping services could not adequately meet the demand of commercial and residential consumers in a rapidly growing suburban market. This led to their incorporation of their business to provide a full range of lawn services to this developing market.

A manager must also identify internal opportunities:

- Can the company's existing organizational structure and business processes be improved?

- Does the company have adequate information to meet current and future opportunities?

- What are the major factors affecting the company's revenues and costs?

In C&F's case, opportunity lay in the delivery of quality landscaping services to a growing and potentially underserved market. Since C&F is a start-up company, Keith and Dale have the opportunity to create completely new service delivery or business processes. They clearly recognize the importance of cost control by their planned reliance on students and migrant workers to staff their operations. They also realize that the seasonal nature of their landscaping business provides opportunities for them to enter other markets such as snow-removal services. The company's installation of an accounting information system and the hiring of a bookkeeping service suggest that Keith and Dale appreciate the importance of management information in the execution of their business strategy.

Next, managers should identify those factors that are absolutely essential to the company's long-term profitability: **critical success factors**. Often, a critical success factor is simply the ability to identify change and meet future expectations. In

Exhibit 1.5
C&F SWOT Analysis

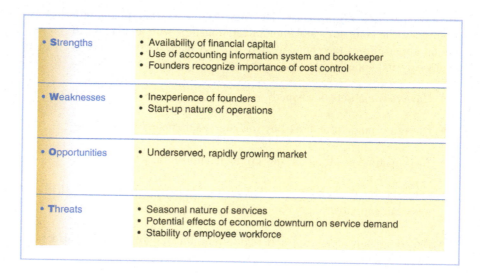

• **S**trengths	• Availability of financial capital • Use of accounting information system and bookkeeper • Founders recognize importance of cost control
• **W**eaknesses	• Inexperience of founders • Start-up nature of operations
• **O**pportunities	• Underserved, rapidly growing market
• **T**hreats	• Seasonal nature of services • Potential effects of economic downturn on service demand • Stability of employee workforce

addition to evaluating the needs of customers, particular attention should be paid to the *competition's* strengths and weaknesses. Managers must honestly evaluate whether the factors responsible for the company's own current success are likely to remain the same in the future.

As with most start-up businesses, C&F Enterprises' long-term success hinges on two considerations: the availability of sufficient market demand for landscaping services, and Keith and Dale's ability to provide quality services that earn a profit. The preliminary market analysis performed by Keith and Dale suggests the need for another landscaping service provider in their target area, and the early negotiation of several new commercial lawn maintenance contracts validates this excess demand. Keith and Dale appear reasonably cost conscious given their intent to be actively involved in the business, their planned reliance on low-cost labor sources, their use of rented vehicles instead of purchased ones, and their reluctance to hold inventories of landscaping supplies.

Finally, managers should realistically assess the organization's own strengths and weaknesses in the current environment. Such a review is frequently referred to as a **SWOT analysis** by practicing financial professionals since it identifies the company's strengths, weaknesses, opportunities, and threats (SWOT). SWOT analysis usually describes the firm as it *currently* exists, discussing those factors that influence the organization's long-term profitability. Firms often rely on business consultants to perform this objective analysis and critique of current operations. These consultants also can help determine whether the strengths and weaknesses identified will be relevant in the future. In short, they help management answer the question, how can the company capitalize on its strengths and eliminate its weaknesses? Since C&F has not yet begun operations, a SWOT analysis based on its *current* business is not possible.

Management Accounting: A Business Planning Approach

Future Business Operations. Managers also must define the environment in which the company expects to operate in the future. To do this, they observe the current business environment and estimate just how it will react to governmental regulations, technology developments, social and economic conditions, and other market changes.

After expectations for the future environment have been defined, *potential* opportunities, threats, and risks to the company's business can be identified. This essentially is a SWOT analysis with a *future*, rather than a current, orientation. Managers use this analysis to determine how they will operate should their assumptions, expectations, and forecasts become reality.

While C&F's current prospects seem bright, unforeseen and unexpected developments could significantly hamper Keith and Dale's ability to have "fun and profit." For example, a sudden economic downturn in the targeted market area due to a recession could severely reduce the demand for both commercial and residential landscaping services, as companies close, new residential home construction slows, or existing homeowners cut back on their spending. Such occurrences would make it virtually impossible for C&F to attain its first major success factor: sufficient market demand for landscaping services. Alternatively, what if the economy is expected to be so healthy and business so robust that employee shortages arise? At a minimum, these labor shortages might drive up costs. In more severe cases, C&F may lose customers because it simply cannot find employees to provide the services required. This scenario could impair C&F's ability to achieve its second major success factor: quality services that earn revenues in excess of delivery costs. Clearly, managers like Keith and Dale cannot ignore the potential effects of future environmental changes on the long-term success of the business. Keith and Dale's SWOT analysis for C&F for the early stages of their business is presented in Exhibit 1.5.

The Role of Economic Data in Strategic Planning. Economic forecasts provide a reality check in the strategic planning process. Economic, demographic, and business environment data are particularly useful. These data can be obtained from a variety of sources including consultants, research organizations, trade magazines, and government agencies. Increasingly, accurate, reliable economic data is provided at little or no cost. Industry market data can often be easily downloaded from an Internet trade publication.

C&F might use industry data to help to identify market trends and plan their operations. These data could also provide Keith and Dale with insight into how their business will perform relative to its industry.

Core product data is available in almost every industry. Exhibit 1.6 shows recent trends in craft brewing that have changed consumer markets and posed threats to legacy companies. Assume that you have decided to open a sports bar and grill or have been hired to provide consulting services to one that is struggling. A restaurant can use these data about beer trends to develop a menu that has the greatest appeal to its customers.

A company often uses economic data to answer the following questions, which typically arise in the strategic planning process:

- *How fast can or will the company's revenue grow?* The growth rate of a company's product or service sales affects its ability to increase profits and depends on many broad economic factors. For example, both the number of new houses under construction and home sales data are essential in forecasting revenue for products like appliances and home loans. If these data indicate that the housing market is growing, this will likely indicate an increase in demand for housing-related products and services. Managers need to plan accordingly.

- *What company costs are likely to increase in the near future?* Are changes expected in the cost of inputs such as wages, raw materials, and utilities? Forecasts of inflation and interest rates may be very useful in forecasting increases in input cost. Additionally, unexpected increases in the minimum wage may increase the cost of labor for companies with many workers in that particular pay range. Likewise, a drought may affect the supply of fruits and vegetables and cause a restaurant or supermarket to re-evaluate the price of its products. In some states, due to energy shortages, many hotels have added electricity surcharges to guests' bills during hot summer months to help to offset rising utility bills. Managers must understand how changes in certain costs in the market affect their profits.

- *How large will the company's market be and what level of penetration can it expect over the next five years?* Industry publications like those shown in Exhibits 1.6, business newspapers, and magazines can be useful in evaluating both actual and planned changes in local markets by competitors. Firms should be careful to identify the cause of any changes in market competition. Are they caused by new products, new technology, changes in customer behavior, or some other factor? For example, Southwest Airlines competes as a low-cost, no-frills provider of flights. In recent years, it has expanded its service markets to include service to many airports in the Northeast and Midwest regions. Southwest's entry into these markets has forced other carriers to reconsider and, in some cases, reduce their pricing on many routes. Managers must recognize how increased competition and new products affect their share of a market's total revenue.

- *What consumer trends will affect the company's current products?* Changes in consumer attitudes can affect product demand. One such trend is the increasing length of the work week. Another is the growing number of two-income families. Such trends may lead to greater demand for timesaving products and services such as Internet shopping, concierge services, and child care. In recent years, grocery stores have added prepared meals to their product offerings. These ready-to-heat dinners save working families' time and allow them to eat nutritious meals during busy weeks. Grocery store managers must identify which communities are most likely to demand these prepared foods and effectively plan their resource use to hire cooks,

Management Accounting: A Business Planning Approach

Exhibit 1.6
The Rise of Craft Brewing

The Rise of Craft Brewing

One of the fastest growing markets in business is the rise of craft brewing over the past two decades. The Brewers Association (BA) reported that, as of 2015, small and independent craft brewers now represent 12 percent market share of the overall beer industry on a volume. In 2015, craft brewers produced 24.5 million barrels, and saw a 13 percent rise in volume and a 16 percent increase in retail dollar value. Retail dollar value was estimated at $22.3 billion, representing 21 percent market share on a dollar value basis.

Additionally, in 2015 the number of operating breweries in the U.S. grew 15 percent, totaling 4,269 breweries—the most at any time in American history, exceeding a level last seen in 1873.

Small and independent breweries account for 99 percent of the breweries in operation, broken down as follows: 2,397 microbreweries, 1,650 brewpubs and 178 regional craft breweries. Throughout the year, there were 620 new brewery openings and only 68 closings. One of the fastest growing regions was the South, where four states—Virginia, North Carolina, Florida and Texas—each saw a net increase of more than 20 breweries, establishing a strong base for future growth in the region. Combined with already existing and established breweries and brewpubs, craft brewers provided nearly 122,000 jobs, an increase of over 6,000 from the previous year.

As an example, Evil Genius Beer Company of Philadelphia started when its founders, Luke Bowen and Trevor Hayward, met in an accounting course in the MBA program at Villanova University. Realizing that their job prospects were limited due to an economic recession, they decided to follow their passion and start their own brewery. With limited capital, they enlisted contract brewers in Indiana, New York, and Connecticut to transform their recipes into product. After partnering with Thomas Hooker Brewing Company to brew and

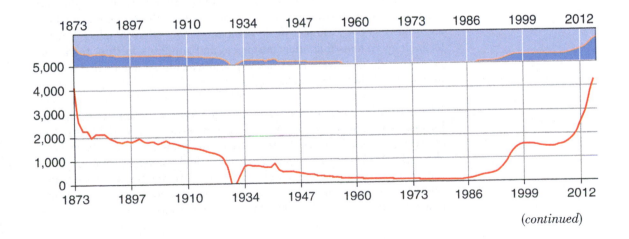

(continued)

help distribute their line of beers, they purchased a property in Philadelphia to house their brewery, grow their production, and become a destination for loyal and new customers.

"For the past decade, craft brewers have charged into the market, seeing double digit growth for eight of those years," said Bart Watson, chief economist, Brewers Association. "There are still a lot of opportunities and areas for additional growth. An important focus will remain on quality as small and independent brewers continue to lead the local, full-flavored beer movement."

These market trends present some incredible opportunities and intense competitive challenges in the decade to follow. Owners and managers in the industry will monitor trends closely to help craft both their beer and business plans.

Sources:

http://www.evilgeniusbeer.com/story.html
https://www.brewersassociation.org/statistics/number-of-breweries/
https://www.brewersassociation.org/press-releases/small-independent-brewers
-continue-grow-double-digits/

coordinate work shifts, purchase the proper inventory, acquire equipment, and dedicate floor space to prepared foods.

- *What business trends will affect the company's products?* Rapid technological change is having profound effects on how business is being conducted. Businesses expect an increasing number of their routine transactions to be processed using technology. For example, overnight delivery companies like Federal Express and United Parcel Service now compete with free, instantaneous electronic delivery of documents. E-mail replaced the need to send many documents via overnight delivery. In turn, overnight delivery firms must develop strategies to grow the business through other products and services. For example, these companies now offer complete Internet technology systems that allow customers and suppliers to ship, track, and pay for goods. Managers must develop and execute strategies that address new business trends and technologies.

- *Who lives in my company's market and is the market growing or shrinking?* Lists of households and businesses, as well as a variety of census data, are provided and/or shared by many vendors. State and local governments also sell lists of professionals, organizations, and companies that they have captured from license and tax rolls. Companies frequently buy these lists to generate targets for direct marketing. For example, home sales registrations in local county offices often lead to new homeowners receiving "welcome" offers from local businesses for new customer discounts on painting, carpentry, banking, dining, and carwashes. Likewise, new businesses receive promotions and offers for business products (for example, office supplies, computers) and services (for example, accounting, legal, technology). These solicitations originate from mailing lists triggered by the company's incorporation or license registration. Clearly, market data is useful to managers in their short-term and long-term planning.

Managers must be able to use economic data to analyze issues in a company's strategic plan. While care is needed in the selection and interpretation of such data, strategic plans that use this external input are likely to be more realistic and achievable. Again, the insight of business professionals is needed to transform such data into *information* that managers can use to make decisions when running the business.

Statement of Mission and Goals

With the analysis of the company's current and future operations complete, the company next must define its future vision by explicitly stating its mission and the goals needed to achieve it (see Exhibit 1.2). In doing so, the company should carefully consider the needs of its various stakeholders.

The Mission Statement. As illustrated in Exhibit 1.2, a mission statement is intended to clearly document a company's vision for the future. It should be the focal point for all planning activities in the organization. Without clarity and focus, building a consensus on future directions to pursue and priorities to establish will prove difficult for a company. Good mission statements are the product of the many different perspectives that stakeholders can provide. This diverse group can improve a company's mission statement because each individual stakeholder views the ultimate mission of the organization differently. A good mission statement should possess the following characteristics:

- It serves as a guide to management decision making.

- It is understandable: simple, clear, concise, and free of jargon.

- It defines the business the company *wishes* to pursue, not necessarily the business in which the company is *currently* engaged.

- It differentiates the company from others in the "same" business.

- It identifies broad objectives and directions for the long term.

- It is relevant to the interests of all stakeholders.

A quality mission statement provides managers and employees with a clear and unambiguous set of standards and values to guide them when they make complex decisions for the firm. Most businesses view their mission as to increase owner wealth over the long term by providing a reasonable rate of return to investors, quality service to customers, and a favorable work environment to employees.

Mission Statement for C&F Enterprises, Inc.

C&F Enterprises, Inc. seeks to be a leading provider of commercial and residential landscape services in the local market area. The Company commits to providing timely, responsive, and high-quality services to all of our customers, while earning an above-market return for our shareholders. C&F recognizes that its employees are critical to achieving this vision and pledges to provide them with a safe, friendly, and economically satisfying environment.

In C&F's case, Keith and Dale appear to have crafted a reasonable mission statement for their start-up enterprise. Their simple statement is easy to read and clearly outlines the major business in which the company intends to operate: landscaping services. More importantly, the statement suggests that C&F intends its "timely, responsive, and high-quality service" to be what distinguishes the company from its competition. Finally, the mission statement clearly identifies its primary stakeholders as its customers, shareholders, and employees and describes how it intends to meet their needs.

Starbucks Coffee Company's mission statement is typical of that found in a major international corporation. See Exhibit 1.7.

Starbucks Coffee Company's mission statement succinctly defines the company's line of business and identifies the interests of its major stakeholders in clear, simple language. These values provide managers with usable standards that will guide decision making.

Goals. Once the company's mission is clearly established, managers can define the goals needed to support the stated mission. These goals must be realistic and achievable given the resources that are available to the organization to address the previously forecasted opportunities, threats, and risks. Particular care must be taken to ensure that the goals are:

- Specific

- Time-based with target dates

- Measurable with quantitative or numerical targets where possible

- Applicable to all areas of the company including marketing, human resources, finance, data management and processing.

Exhibit 1.7
Starbucks Coffee Company
Mission Statement

Starbucks Coffee Company Mission Statement

To inspire and nurture the human spirit – one person, one cup and one neighborhood at a time.

Starbucks Coffee Company is the leading retailer, roaster and brand of specialty coffee in the world. The company has the following mission statement:

Establish Starbucks as the premier purveyor of the finest coffee in the world while maintaining our uncompromising principles while we grow.

The following six guiding principles will help us measure the appropriateness of our decisions:

Provide a great work environment and treat each other with respect and dignity.

Embrace diversity as an essential component in the way we do business. Apply the highest standards of excellence to the purchasing, roasting and fresh delivery of our coffee.

Develop enthusiastically satisfied customers all of the time. Contribute positively to our communities and our environment. Recognize that profitability is essential to our future success.

Source: Starbucks Coffee Company, "Mission Statement," http://www.starbucks.com/about-us/company-information/mission-statement. Copyright © 2017.

Goals guide the company in its pursuit of specific business initiatives and actions. For C&F Enterprises, Inc. to accomplish its mission, it must create goals that bring its vision to life. For example, Keith and Dale might view being the "leading provider" in terms of market share. In this case they could set specific growth goals like the number of commercial and residential customers or the level of revenue to link the mission to the realities of business. As for C&F's commitment to "timely, responsive, and high-quality service" delivery, Keith and Dale must decide what outcomes constitute such service and design goals and related measures that will result in such service. In the case of "timeliness," the company might set a goal of strictly adhering to service schedules. This could be measured by customer satisfaction surveys as well as by monitoring customer complaints.

Exhibit 1.8 illustrates how Starbucks Coffee Company uses specific expansion goals to accomplish the growth dimension of the mission statement shown in Exhibit 1.7.

Statement of Action Plan

After documenting the company's mission statement and goals, managers must develop a *detailed* plan to take the company from where it is currently to where it would like to be in the future. This is referred to as the action plan. The action plan outlines specific activities and tasks that help the company allocate resources

Starbucks Coffee Company Goals

Starbucks Coffee Company's mission statement calls for the company to be *"the premier purveyor of the finest coffee in the world while maintaining our uncompromising principles while we grow."* To support its commitment to growth, company management sets specific, time-based, measurable goals for company expansion (in terms of the number of new stores worldwide). These targets provide expectations against which company performance can be evaluated.

For example, the company's 2015 Annual Report stated:

> Today, Starbucks occupies a front-row seat at the intersection of the physical and digital worlds. Our social, digital, and mobile applications are a strategic advantage as they extend our reach, strengthen our connection with customers, and drive profitability. In October 2015, mobile pay accounted for 21 percent of all transactions in our U.S. company-operated stores, just incredible, and we're seeing a pattern of swift adoption as we roll out Mobile Order & Pay at participating stores across the U.S., the U.K. and Canada. From payment to original content, Starbucks will maintain our lead by continuing to innovate ahead of expectations.
>
> Digital and mobile innovations also fuel the success of our powerful loyalty program, My Starbucks Rewards (MSR), which has 10+ million members in the U.S., up 28 percent from FY14, Card loads in the U.S. and Canada alone totaled $5.1 billion in fiscal 2015, up

Exhibit 1.8
Starbucks' mission is all about a quality product, excellent customer service, and taking care of its employees. The company now operates coffee shops at over 23,000 store locations, including this one in Beijing, China.

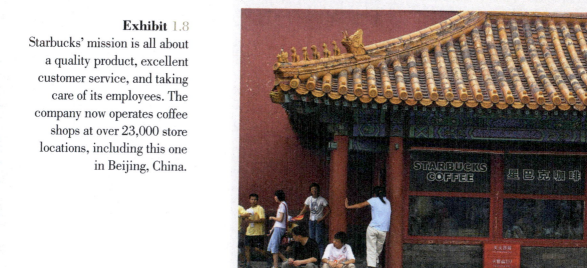

Management Accounting: A Business Planning Approach

19 percent year over year. During holiday in calendar 2015, MSR members enjoyed a chance to win Starbucks for Life.

In our expanding beverage business, we're seeing ongoing success of our Teavana brand of handcrafted teas, which in fiscal 2015 generated nearly $1 billion of sales throughout our U.S. stores, up 12 percent over the last year. And, we're just getting started as we plan to bring Teavana to the China /Asia Pacific and EMEA regions. By applying our unique assets and innovative muscle to the tea category, we will continue to tap tea's tremendous global opportunity. Our diverse food program is transforming Starbucks into a destination for meals, snacks, and sweet treats. Revenue from food grew 19 percent in the fourth quarter of fiscal 2015 alone, led by our breakfast sandwich platform, which has doubled in size from just three years ago. We also completely reimagined holiday in fiscal 2015, a transformation we continued through the most recent holiday season with solid red cups, a beautiful Dot Collection of serveware, and the Gift Card mall.

Constant innovation and a commitment to playing the long game let us make the big bets that are essential for growth. But today more than ever, we know that growth for growth's sake cannot be our company's only goal.

Our commitment to ethical sourcing and supporting farmers was further advanced as we announced critical advancements in research and transparency benefiting the entire specialty coffee industry, and verified that 99 percent of Starbucks Coffee supply chain is ethically sourced. With seven farmer support centers, and an eighth in Mexico scheduled to open in 2016, we continue to promote sustainable, best-farming practices and augment our comprehensive approach to ethical sourcing. To date, more than 1 million farmers and workers on four continents have benefited from our support program, and in 2015 we proactively sought to address a significant threat to coffee farmers—coffee rust, a plant fungus that damages millions of coffee trees per year—by committing to plant one new tree for every bag of coffee purchased in a U.S. store.

in order to meet its goals. To make the action plan viable, a manager should divide it into discrete projects, with each project addressing the following three issues:

1. *Purpose.* What is the project intended to accomplish?

2. *Scope.* How will various departments/functions within the company be affected by or involved in the project? How will other projects be impacted by this particular project?
3. *Contribution.* How will the project advance the goals outlined in the strategic plan?

After assigning priorities to the action plan projects, managers can begin implementing the individual action plans. In C&F's case, Keith and Dale require an action plan to address potential growth goals associated with being the "leading provider" of landscaping services. *How specifically do they intend to accomplish this?* One action plan project might initially focus on aggressively promoting their services to increase market share. This probably will require both Keith and Dale to actively solicit new customers through personal visits. The action plan project might also call for the development of print ads that could be distributed physically, listed in telephone books, or published in newspapers and other periodicals. Whatever marketing approach they use must be evaluated for its success

C&F Enterprises, Inc. Promotion Action Plan

Project Description:
To develop and execute a plan that will communicate the availability of C&F's landscaping services to the local area market.

Scope:
This project should address three specific approaches to marketing C&F's services:

1. Personal visitation: Target select commercial clients for solicitation visits by Keith and/or Dale. Criteria for selection should include such factors as size, service need, and financial stability. Create a formal "call program" in which Keith and Dale systematically and periodically visit potential clients to inform them of C&F's services.
2. Flyers and brochures: Design, print, and deliver advertising materials to potential commercial and residential customers. How these materials will be distributed must be decided first, since delivery cost may impact the content and form of the promotional items. At a minimum, include a discount coupon with such materials to promote feedback on the effectiveness of this means of advertising.
3. Internet advertising: Determine the need and extent to which this form of advertising should be relied upon to promote C&F services. If used, establish a monitoring mechanism to determine how many customers learned about the company through this medium.

Contribution:
If successful, this plan will provide C&F with a steadily increasing stream of customers, allowing it to execute its business strategy.

in achieving the "growth" goal and ultimately the mission of being the "leading provider" of landscape services. Had Keith and Dale committed their promotional action plan to writing, it might have looked like the following:

Milestones and timetables that managers can use to monitor implementation are important parts of the action plan. Milestones can be both quantitative and qualitative in nature. Quantitative measures are those that can be expressed in numbers, like revenues or the number of new customers. Qualitative measures, on the other hand, cannot be expressed numerically, only in words. Examples of factors that are measured qualitatively are customer satisfaction, product quality, employee morale, and customer perceptions. Whatever measures or milestones are used must be designed so that the company can evaluate its progress toward achieving goals and objectives. Timetables for achieving the milestones should be realistic and adjusted as operating conditions require. Any deviations from the implementation timetables should be reported regularly and corrective action should be taken to get the company back on track if necessary.

Resource Requirements

The next component of the strategic plan is a listing of the financial, human, and physical resource requirements needed to deliver products and services to customers. To begin operations, businesses first must obtain resources from lenders and investors. Most investors and lenders require a clear explanation of how the financial capital they are asked to provide will be used. Therefore, businesses must develop plans that address what resources are needed and how they will be used by the company in executing its strategy. Resource questions that business managers typically face include:

- What mix of people, machines, and technology will the company's major business processes require?

- How much physical space is necessary to produce products or deliver services?

- What are the necessary educational backgrounds and skills expected of employees?

At a minimum, human capital, physical capital, and financial capital need to be addressed in any discussion of resource requirements. In C&F's case, Keith and Dale used an inheritance as well as monies invested by family and friends to start their business. These funds then were used to purchase the equipment and hire the people needed to deliver landscaping services to their customers.

Financial Projections

The final component of the strategic plan is a set of projected financial statements. These financial projections often are referred to as pro forma financial statements. These pro forma projections provide interested stakeholders with a quantitative representation of the strategic plan and typically include detailed

balance sheets, income statements, and statements of cash flows for the next one-, five-, and ten-year periods. The format of these projections usually is consistent with that used to prepare periodic financial statements for a company's stakeholders. If the projected financial performance is acceptable given the company's goals, then the strategic planning process is complete. However, if the forecasted results are not acceptable, managers must modify the action plan projections, *not the goals,* until the pro forma financial statements reflect the desired outcomes.

Creating pro forma financial statements and other types of financial projections requires the knowledge of key managerial accounting techniques and skill in their application. A detailed discussion of pro forma financial statements is presented in chapter 3. The remaining chapters of this text will introduce you to managerial accounting tools and techniques and a semester-long business planning simulation that will give you practice in their application.

Learning Objective 5
Identify barriers to successful strategic planning.

Successful Strategic Planning

As noted in an earlier section, strategic planning is an ongoing, continuous process in which a company decides what its business will be in the future. As Exhibit 1.2 illustrates, this process requires companies to document their future vision in a mission statement and outline their strategy in a set of specific goals. Strategic planning can be a very difficult process, particularly for larger entities. Large companies often suffer the consequences of a myriad of mistakes when engaging in these exercises. Some companies never adopt such a long-term planning perspective, choosing instead to focus solely on the next twelve months. While understandable

Management Accounting: A Business Planning Approach

for a start-up enterprise like C&F, mature companies that ignore the long term will find themselves *reacting* to market developments, rather than creating market opportunities.

Failure to identify critical success factors can create problems for many businesses. Exhibit 1.2 clearly indicates the impact that these critical success factors have on goal attainment. How can a company improve its business processes if it does not know what its processes are or what key attributes drive its operations? Or, if faced with a mandate to cut costs, how will a business know which costs to reduce? If a service company eliminated its key employees in an attempt to reduce costs, the economic consequences could be catastrophic to the business.

One of the most common strategic planning errors is the failure to allocate sufficient time for the strategic planning process. As this chapter has illustrated, planning is a complex process that requires research, data, insight, communication, and unity. Unlike the ingredients in a milkshake, these factors cannot be quickly blended in a day- or week-long planning session. Rather, they are like the soil, fertilizer, water, and sun in a well-tended garden that requires season-long care and attention to generate a good harvest. Strategic planning is a time-consuming, continuous process critical to successful strategy execution.

Sometimes companies ignore what is happening outside the company, choosing to focus exclusively on what is happening internally. In these cases, companies often are blindsided by unexpected environmental factors like new laws and regulations or market issues, such as new technologies and competition. These factors make it either more difficult or impossible to achieve their strategies, no matter how efficient their internal operations happen to be. Take the case of small businesses that operate as sales forces for larger companies in the insurance, securities, or travel services industries. In the past, these "brokers" focused almost exclusively on building customer relationships and providing quality service to achieve their business strategy. However, the Internet has virtually eliminated the need for these businesses as consumers now can purchase these products directly from the company offering the service, both at a lower price and at a high level of customer service.

Also problematic is the failure of a company to develop achievable and realistic goals. It does little good for a company to set expectations that cannot be met given the resources that are available to it. After all, how can one expect to get a specific job done without the proper tools? In fact, when this occurs, the resulting employee dissatisfaction often contributes to poor operating performance in the company.

Stakeholder buy-in is critical to the strategic planning process. All interested stakeholders should be given the opportunity to provide input during this process, either formally or informally, and their long-term commitment to the plan is critical. After all, it is the stakeholders and their relationships that make up a company and contribute to its ultimate success (see Exhibit 1.1).

For a strategic plan to succeed, senior managers must be willing to make the difficult decisions that are necessary to implement it. Whether creating a new product or improving an existing one, the use of financial, human, and physical capital requires difficult choices. These may not be popular or acceptable to all stakeholders. For example, some strategic directives may require job cuts, never a well-liked alternative. However, once stakeholders agree and are committed to a plan, managers are often asked to sacrifice popularity for successful plan execution.

Nowhere is the "keep it simple" approach more appropriate than in the strategic planning process. The more complex and intricate the plan, the harder it is for stakeholders to understand it and remain focused on its execution. Complicated strategic plans have a higher likelihood of failure. Avoiding planning blunders similar to those outlined above can dramatically increase the chances that strategic planning will succeed.

Summary

This chapter introduced you to the fundamentals of business strategy and strategic planning. An effective strategy is necessary to meet the interests of customers, owners, and other stakeholders in the business. To achieve their strategy,

Strategic Planning Resources on the Web

An incredible amount of data and resources are available on the Internet about various business topics. In each chapter, the Net Gains section will provide you with links to and descriptions of websites that directly relate to the content of that chapter. You should visit these websites to gain an appreciation of the types of data available at no cost and to enhance your understanding of the chapter's focus. The following Internet sites have resources about strategic planning:

- **Planware (http://www.planware.org/).** Planware offers downloadable software to help businesses develop a strategic plan. For example, their On-Line Strategic Planner is a step-by-step guide for creating a three-page strategic plan. The site also offers a business plan template and development guidelines (downloadable in Microsoft Word format).

- **EDGAR: A Database of Information About Public Companies (http://www.sec.gov/edgar/searchedgar/companysearch.html).** The U.S. Securities and Exchange Commission's EDGAR website hosts a database of various required filings of publicly owned companies. One of the most detailed reports about a company is known

as the Annual Report or Form 10-K. To access a company's 10-K, log on to the link listed above and type (in the box labeled Company Name) the name of a company of interest. Select Find Companies. A new screen will appear—click on the ten-digit CIK (Central Index Key) number that appears to the left of the name of your selected company. A chronological list of recent filings will appear in the new screen. Scroll down until you find the most recently filed 10-K report. Click on HTML or TEXT to read the 10-K in the format you prefer. This resource will help you to learn about different companies and to complete many assignments in this text.

- **What Works And What Doesn't (http://www.apqc.org/).** The American Productivity and Quality Center is a research group that is funded by large, well-known companies to conduct studies about contemporary business topics. This website includes research reports, PowerPoint presentations, and news articles about strategic planning.

Collectively, these resources will help you to gain insight into successful strategic planning through examples and case studies from well-known businesses.

businesses rely on managers to develop mission statements, long-term goals, and action plans that guide employees and enable the company to satisfy customer needs and generate profits.

To participate in the strategic planning process, managers must be able to effectively collect, analyze, and interpret data from sources inside and outside the company. With the application of the necessary insight, these data provide the foundation for credible plans and goals. This valuable managerial accounting information sets the course that managers follow when pursuing strategy in day-to-day business operations. Analyzing a business for strategic planning purposes requires a thorough review of both current and future operations. However, such an analysis requires a keen awareness of what market forces have the potential to affect a business and its operations. The next chapter examines current business forces that managers must consider when developing strategy and implementing business processes.

Summary of Learning Objectives

1. **Define and describe a business.** Businesses attempt to create wealth for their owners by using their resources to deliver products or services that their customers demand. Doing this means managing the competing demands of their stakeholders.

2. **Identify and describe the stakeholders of a business.** Several economic parties inside and outside the firm, known as stakeholders, take an interest in the success of the business. Common stakeholder groups are customers, suppliers, employees, owners, lenders, regulators, and the community.

3. **Explain the relationship between strategy and profitability.** Business strategy describes how a company plans to position itself in the marketplace to meet the needs of customers, while delivering returns on the investments of owners. Profitability is an integral part of most business strategies, and generally does not occur accidentally. Therefore, managers create strategies that allow a company to generate sales and control costs in competitive markets.

4. **Describe the strategic planning process and its results.** Strategic planning is an ongoing and continuous process in which companies determine what their businesses will be in the future. It involves defining a mission and outlining its strategy in a set of realistic goals and the action steps needed to achieve them. The process results in a formal document that: (1) analyzes the company's current and future business operations to identify potential opportunities and risks, (2) defines the company's mission, (3) details specific goals and related action plans to execute strategy, (4) lists the resources required by the action plans, and (5) presents projected performance reports that reflect the outcomes expected of the business strategy.

5. **Identify barriers to successful strategic planning.** Strategic planning can be hindered by a number of common oversights, including the failure to identify critical success factors and set achievable goals, not setting aside enough time for the planning process, or neglecting to focus both externally and internally. Careful consideration of such factors increases the likelihood that a strategic plan will succeed.

Glossary of Terms

Action plan A detailed plan composed of discrete projects specifically designed to promote achievement of the company's goals. This plan helps the business allocate its resources.

Balanced scorecard A popular performance measurement framework used by hundreds of global businesses to communicate strategic goals to employees. This contemporary management tool translates an organization's strategy into a comprehensive set of measures that provide feedback on how well the company has performed in meeting its goals.

Business An economic entity that aims to create wealth for its owners by using financial, human, and physical capital to deliver products or services that the market demands.

Business plan A formal written document that defines a specific business idea and provides a thorough description of the actions and resources needed for successful implementation, including forecasted financial results.

Business strategy An action-oriented master plan that guides a business to profitability, creates value for customers, and differentiates the company from competitors in the marketplace.

Critical success factors The environmental and/or operating conditions of the business that are absolutely essential to its long-term profitability.

Financial capital The monies invested in a business by its owners and creditors that allow it to acquire the human and physical capital needed to operate.

Human capital The personnel resources acquired by a business that are needed to bring a product or service to market.

Management accounting The concepts, theories, tools, and techniques by which company performance data are transformed into information that managers can use to create and execute strategy.

Managerial accounting information Timely, meaningful, and relevant information that managers use in making their daily business decisions.

Mission statement A clear, concise definition of a company's broad business purpose that is the focal point for all other planning activities in the organization, including strategic planning.

Physical capital The equipment and property acquired by a business that are needed to bring a product or service to market.

Pro forma financial statements Financial projections that provide interested stakeholders with a quantitative representation of the strategic plan. They typically include detailed balance sheets, income statements, and statements of cash flows for the next one-, five-, and ten-year periods.

Stakeholders Economic parties that have an interest in the success of the business. They include customers, suppliers, employees, owners, lenders, regulators, and the community.

Strategic planning An ongoing process in which management prepares a plan to guide the organization's operations during the next five to ten years. This exercise should result in a set of attainable objectives and the means to achieve these results.

SWOT analysis A review of a company's strengths, weaknesses, opportunities, and threats that describes the business as it currently exists, discussing those factors that influence long-term profitability.

Chapter Review Questions

1. What is a business?
2. List and define the three types of capital that businesses use to deliver products and services to their customers.
3. What is management accounting?
4. What is a stakeholder?
5. List the seven types of stakeholders common to most businesses and describe why they are each interested in the success of the company.
6. Define business strategy and describe how it is linked to profitability.
7. Describe what is meant by strategic planning and list the five components that comprise a strategic plan.
8. What is SWOT analysis? Why is it useful in the strategic planning process?
9. How are economic data used in the strategic planning process?
10. What are the six characteristics of a "good" mission statement?
11. How do a company's goals differ from its mission statement?
12. What is an action plan? What must a manager do to make an action plan viable?
13. What three project-related issues should be addressed when developing an action plan?
14. What specific resource requirements should be addressed in a strategic plan?
15. What purpose do pro forma financial statements serve in the strategic planning process?
16. List the most common mistakes companies make when conducting strategic planning exercises.

Exercises and Problems

1. Classify each of the following items as financial capital (FC), human capital (HC) or physical capital (PC).
   a. A company's computer system
   b. Employees
   c. A corporate checking account
   d. Inventory
   e. Automobiles owned by a car rental agency
   f. Company borrowings
   g. A factory
   h. Shelving in a retail store

2. For each of the following businesses, identify a specific example of financial, human, and physical capital that the company would need to run its business.
   a. Sports bar
   b. Miniature golf course
   c. Bakery
   d. Auto parts shop
   e. Computer consulting company

3. Identify the stakeholder group to which each of the following parties most likely belongs:
   a. A government tax agency
   b. A person who invests in a business
   c. A bank that lends money
   d. A local Little League team that receives sponsorship
   e. People who work for a company
   f. People who buy products from a store
   g. Companies that produce and sell goods to other companies

4. For each of the following businesses, identify (1) its stakeholders and (2) the *specific* types of information in which each party would be interested.
   a. Pizza parlor
   b. Bowling alley
   c. Flower shop
   d. Hardware store
   e. T-shirt print shop

5. Review a recent copy of *The Wall Street Journal* or your local newspaper. Identify a news article that discusses how the local, state, or federal government has affected a company or industry. Based on the article, address the following questions:
   a. Which company (or industry) was affected?
   b. Which government agency was involved?
   c. What action (or intended action) was taken by the government?
   d. What was the purpose of this action?
   e. How will this government action affect future business conducted by the company or industry?
   f. Do you think such action on the part of the regulators was appropriate? Why or why not?

6. Discuss the critical success factors essential to each of the following companies' long-term profitability.

a. Sandwich shop
b. Professional sports team
c. Grocery store

d. Furniture store
e. Auto body shop

7. List several sources of economic data that each of the following businesses might find useful to its strategic planning process.

a. Gourmet restaurant
b. Private country club
c. Convenience store

d. Automobile dealership
e. Shoe repair service

8. Using the criteria outlined in this chapter, prepare a mission statement for each of the following businesses.

a. Sports bar
b. Movie theater
c. Technology retailer

d. Clothing store
e. Home construction company

9. Identify a major local company or use one that your instructor has selected, access its website, and address the following requirements:

a. What products and/or services does the company deliver? Be specific.
b. Who are the company's stakeholders? Support your answer with references (either direct or implied) from the company's website.
c. What is the company's business strategy? How does the company intend to meet its customers' needs while differentiating itself from its competitors?
d. What kind of information is provided to stakeholders and other interested parties about the success of the firm in achieving its business strategy?

10. Identify a major local company or use one that your instructor has selected, access its website, and prepare a SWOT analysis to address the following questions:

a. What are the company's strengths?
b. What are its weaknesses?
c. What are its most promising opportunities?
d. What are the most significant threats facing the company?
e. Based on your analysis, do you think that this company will be successful in the future? Why or why not?

11. Select a company in which you have an interest, or that has been previously assigned by your instructor, and whose stock is publicly traded in a U.S. equity market. Address the following requirements:

a. Using the Securities and Exchange Commission's EDGAR search website, access, download, and save your company's most recent annual report (Form 10-K). For detailed instructions on how to access a company's 10-K, please refer to the discussion of EDGAR in the Net Gains section of this chapter.
b. Find the 10-K report section entitled "Management's Discussion and Analysis of Financial Condition and Results of Operations" (MD&A) and answer the following questions:

i. What factors has the company identified as being critical to its *current* success? What are its current internal and external business opportunities?
ii. What expectations does management have for the *future*? What potential opportunities, threats, and risks has the company identified for the future?
iii. Does the MD&A refer to any externally prepared economic data to support its discussion of current and future market environments? If so, describe the data and how they contribute to the MD&A.

12. Find a mission statement for a company whose stock is publicly traded in any global equity market. Some companies will provide a link to their mission statement on their home page. Other companies will provide their mission statement in a section on the website entitled About Us, Corporate Information, or Investor Relations. Some companies will not list their mission statement, so you may have to select a different company. Once you have found a company's mission statement, address the following requirements:

a. Evaluate the quality of the mission statement using the characteristics of a "good" mission statement outlined in the chapter.

b. Using information that you find either on the company's website or from some other market source (annual report, analyst reviews, or the like) identify several specific goals that the company has set to accomplish its mission. Frame your answers using Exhibits 1.7 and 1.8 as a guide.

13. Access a website for a company in which you have an interest, or that your instructor has previously assigned, and address the following requirements:

a. List and describe the various types of information provided to stakeholders on the website (for example, financial statements, product descriptions, and the like.).

b. Discuss how the information provided addresses the needs of each of the seven stakeholder classes discussed in the chapter.

c. Does the information provided appear to favor any particular stakeholder(s)? If so, which one(s)? Discuss why you think this may be the case?

d. What recommendations would you make to the company to improve the "informativeness" of its website?

BestSellers Bookstore

Bob Gilmartin decided to leave his job as a manager at a well-known corporate hotel chain to open BestSellers Bookstore in the heart of Toronto's business district. Many businesspeople worked in the area, and his plan relied on selling a high volume of "new release" books such as novels, biographies, and contemporary business books. After about six months of fairly successful business, he determined that there was also considerable demand for books by local authors. By selling the works of local authors, Bob hoped to create a "community feel"—an atmosphere where local residents could gather for book discussions and other social events. Bob envisioned a bookstore frequented by businesspeople during the day and local residents in the evenings.

To grow the business, he would need more cash. However, Maple Leaf Bank was unwilling to lend money to such a new enterprise. Fortunately, Bob's parents agreed to lend him $30,000, to be repaid over three years, to help expand the business. After two years, the business was exceeding its goals and most of the debt was repaid. Despite the success, Bob knew that the business faced some problems.

Inventory records on the computer system did not always accurately reflect the books in stock. Of the six employees hired to work on the night shift, one was fired for stealing and two quit within one month of being hired. One major supplier was facing bankruptcy. To confront these problems, Bob scheduled a meeting with store employees to develop a better business plan for BestSellers.

Questions

1. What is the business strategy for BestSellers Bookstore?
2. Who are the stakeholders in BestSellers Bookstore?
3. What information does Bob need to develop his business plan?
4. Prepare a mission statement that would help BestSellers to execute its strategy.
5. What is the role of your discipline (major) in resolving the various issues that Bob faces? Is there business information that your discipline does *not* provide that would be useful in managing this business?

Business Planning Application

Using Strategy in Business Planning

This chapter explored business strategy fundamentals. A good way to truly learn these concepts and to develop an appreciation for the importance of *managerial accounting information* is to actually write a strategic plan for a start-up business. The strategic plan for a start-up enterprise is commonly known as a **business plan**. This is a formal written document (usually twenty-five pages or more in length) that defines a business idea, provides a thorough description of the actions and resources needed for successfully executing the idea, and forecasts targeted financial results.

Assignment

Formulate and develop an initial idea or concept proposal (usually two to three pages in length) for a new, start-up company. The goal of the concept proposal is to show potential investors and/or lenders that you have an exciting and feasible business idea. These proposals typically address the market opportunities and stakeholder relationships discussed earlier in this chapter.

The concept proposal must include a well-defined mission statement and a clear description of business strategy. As discussed in this chapter, the company's mission statement should address the interests of owners, customers, and employees. Your description should identify existing competition and explain why customers will demand products and/or services from your company. The proposal also should include an explanation of how you will manage the business, specifically how you will deliver your product and/or service to customers.

In the upcoming chapters, you will learn how to develop and integrate this concept proposal into a complete business plan that will demonstrate to investors that your start-up business is more than just a "good idea": *one that can deliver on its promises*. Investors will be naturally skeptical about an idea that has not already been pursued in the market. Therefore, a clear and convincing business strategy is the heart and soul of a high quality business plan.

Image Credits

Fig. 1.1: Copyright © Depositphotos/Rawpixel.

Exhibit 1.6a: Evil Genius Beer Company Logo, http://www.evilgeniusbeer.com/.

Exhibit 1.6b: Brewers Association, "The Rise of Craft Brewing Graph" https://www.brewersassociation.org/statistics/number-of-breweries/.

Exhibit 1.8b: Copyright © Mr. Tickle (CC by 3.0) at https://commons.wikimedia.org/wiki/File%3AStarbucks_at_the_Forbidden_City.jpg.

Fig. 1.2: Copyright © BrokenSphere (CC by 3.0) at https://commons.wikimedia.org/wiki/File%3ASports_Authority_DC_exterior.JPG.

Chapter 2

1. Identify forces affecting business.

2. Define the elements of the customer value imperative.

3. Explain the value chain and its components.

4. Explain the importance of evaluating company performance.

The Business Value Chain

Success in business at the dawn of the twenty-first century depends on a firm's ability to manage change. Companies today confront many new challenges including technology innovations, global competition, and increased demand for timely, relevant decision-making information. According to the National Science Foundation, the U.S. aerospace industry exemplifies the changing global marketplace.

Collectively, market forces compel businesses to develop adaptive and innovative organizational structures that promote more efficient business processes and closer stakeholder relationships. These changes in the business environment affect all managers, not just executive-level decision-makers. Many routine, often labor-intensive business tasks are now performed by technology. In an age when preparing and distributing data occurs at little or no cost, managers are expected to possess the knowledge, skills, and abilities that allow them to offer insights that contribute to business success.

Chapter 1 discussed the way in which strategic planning helps a company meet the expectations of its customers, investors, and other stakeholders. As we learned, this process forces managers to evaluate both their current and future business operations. However, such an analysis depends on a keen awareness of what market forces potentially can affect a business. Therefore, this chapter discusses several major business forces that are shaping today's marketplace and their effects on companies and business professionals. This discussion highlights the important roles that business planning and information play in managing change in the twenty-first century. Understanding those roles will allow you to distinguish between the usefulness of data and information for decision-making, and it will give you an appreciation for the analytical abilities needed to transform one into the other.

Structural Forces

The past few decades have witnessed the emergence of the information age. Economies are shifting from industrial age manufacturing to service-based, technology-focused companies. Economic data indicate that manufacturing has experienced a considerable decline in its contribution to the U.S. economy when measured as a component of gross domestic product (GDP). GDP is the total market value of all goods and services produced in a country in a given year. Exhibit 2.1 reveals that the manufacturing sector's share declined to only 12.1 percent of total U.S. GDP in 2014. Conversely, the

service sectors (finance, insurance, and real estate) now account for 20.0 percent
of U.S. GDP.

Exhibit 2.1

Decline of the Manufacturing Industry According to the GDP

	1950	1960	1970	1980	1990	2000	2010	2014
Private industries	**88.0**	**85.4**	**83.2**	**85.7**	**85.5**	**87.1**	**85.7**	**86.9**
Agriculture, forestry, fishing, and hunting	6.6	3.7	2.5	2.2	1.6	1.0	1.1	1.2
Mining	2.6	1.9	1.4	3.2	1.5	1.1	2.2	2.6
Utilities	1.6	2.2	2.0	2.1	2.4	1.8	1.8	1.6
Construction	4.3	4.3	4.6	4.6	4.1	4.5	3.6	3.8
Manufacturing	26.8	25.4	22.9	20.5	17.3	15.1	12.2	12.1
Wholesale trade	6.2	6.4	6.3	6.5	5.8	6.1	5.8	6.0
Retail trade	8.7	7.6	7.7	7.0	6.7	6.8	5.8	5.8
Transportation and warehousing	5.6	4.3	3.7	3.6	2.9	3.0	2.8	2.9
Information	3.2	3.5	3.8	4.2	4.5	4.6	4.9	4.8
Finance, insurance, and real estate	11.2	13.7	14.2	15.7	17.5	19.4	19.7	20.0
Professional and business services	3.5	4.2	4.9	6.1	8.8	10.8	11.6	11.9
Educational services, health care, and social assistance	2.0	2.6	3.8	4.7	6.3	6.6	8.3	8.2
Arts, entertainment, recreation, accommodation, and food services	3.0	2.7	2.8	2.9	3.4	3.8	3.6	3.8
Government	**12.0**	**14.6**	**16.8**	**14.3**	**14.5**	**12.9**	**14.3**	**13.1**
Statistical Discrepancy	**2.7**	**2.9**	**2.6**	**2.4**	**2.7**	**2.5**	**2.3**	**2.2**
Total Gross Domestic Product	**100.0**	**100.0**	**100.0**	**100.0**	**100.0**	**100.0**	**100.0**	**100.0**

During the industrial age, which lasted almost two hundred years, leading
businesses depended heavily on *physical capital* such as production facilities and
factories to support their manufacturing activities. Recently, however, new technologies have dramatically altered the allocations of human and physical capital
that firms use to pursue their business strategies. Increasingly, businesses rely on
resources that only people can provide: knowledge and innovation. In fact, some of
today's best-known companies rely primarily on human rather than physical capital
to deliver their products and services. For example, Exhibit 2.2 shows the asset
section of the balance sheet for International Business Machines Corporation (IBM)
for the years ended December 31, 1950 and 2015. In 1950, IBM was a manufacturing firm that invested 60.9 percent of its assets in its production facilities (physical

capital) to produce business equipment. Notice, however, that by the year 2015, only 9.7 percent of the firm's asset base was invested in physical resources (plants, machines, and equipment). The largest shares of IBM's assets in 2015 were receivables (25.8 percent) and investments and intangibles (51.8 percent). This change in the balance sheet over sixty-five years reflects how significantly the company has transformed its business from manufacturing to the delivery of a mix of information technology infrastructure, data analytics, and consulting services.

Three factors drive much of the change in today's business world: innovation in *technology*, *globalization* of the economic markets, and the growing importance of *creating customer value*.

Technological Innovation

Recent developments in technology have significantly automated many of the business functions that were once performed by managers and employees. These new technologies have improved the quality, speed, and effectiveness of manufacturing and distribution processes. Firms that produce and deliver physical goods often rely on automated technologies in their core or primary business processes. For example, many complex production processes such as the manufacturing of semiconductor chips, as well as distribution activities like inventory management, now are fully automated. This has resulted in higher quality products, lower costs, and faster production and delivery of goods.

Some manufacturers have the flexibility to rely upon technology to design and manufacture golf club shafts and ski poles. To ensure quality and minimize waste, an automated production process prepares and rolls composite materials into tubes for use as golf club shafts or ski poles. The assembly line can be designed to run without interruption and can produce 15,000 shafts per day (or about one shaft

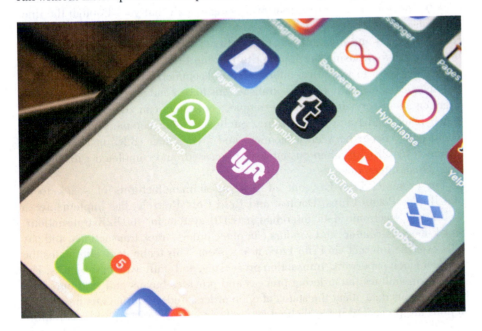

Figure 2.1
New technologies have improved customer service in many businesses. For example, companies like Lyft and Uber have developed on-demand ridesharing applications that have revolutionized the transportation industry.

Exhibit 2.2

IBM Balance Sheet Data

INTERNATIONAL BUSINESS MACHINES CORPORATION

Balance Sheet Data

	December 31, 1950		December 31, 2015	
Assets		% of total		% of total
Current assets:				
Cash and cash equivalents	$15,691,585	5.2%	$7,686,000,000	7.0%
Marketable securities	13,008,908	4.3%	508,000,000	0.5%
Receivables	25,273,835	8.4%	28,554,000,000	25.8%
Inventories	14,701,701	4.9%	1,551,000,000	1.4%
Prepaid expenses and other current assets*	–	0.0%	4,205,000,000	3.8%
Total current assets	$68,676,029	22.9%	$42,504,000,000	38.5%
Plant, rental machines and other property--net	182,704,558	60.9%	10,727,000,000	9.7%
Investments and intangible assets	48,572,004	16.2%	57,264,000,000	51.8%
Total assets	$299,952,591	100.0%	$110,495,000,000	100.0%

* Not reported separately in 1950.

every six seconds) for use as golf clubs or ski poles. A fully computerized machine tests the flexibility and strength of every single shaft that goes through the line. Technology allows such firms to maximize the number of units produced, while controlling costs and standardizing the quality of each golf club shaft and ski pole.

Many firms are using the Internet to provide their stakeholders with timely, worldwide access to a wealth of information and commercial opportunities. Today's technologies allow many business transactions to be conducted twenty-four hours a day on a self-service basis. For example, consumers can shop, bid on auction items, bank, and trade stock online. Such electronic commerce transactions, whether they occur between a business and a consumer (B2C) or between two businesses (B2B), are often customized, processed, and completed with little, if any, human interaction.

For example, Frito-Lay, one of the largest manufacturers of snack foods like Ruffles Potato Chips, Doritos, and Rold Gold Pretzels, has implemented a Web-based electronic data interchange (EDI) system for its B2B transactions. Snack-food distributors and vendors can place orders, track transactions, and pay bills over the Internet via Frito-Lay's new system. This technology eliminates the need for much paperwork, transaction processing, and staffing for call centers. The system streamlines the ordering process and provides buyers and suppliers with instantaneous data about the status of open orders. Today, routine business transactions are processed using technology; only special orders or problems require

Management Accounting: A Business Planning Approach

Cisco's Virtual Close

In many companies, the finance and accounting department often takes weeks to record and report business transactions. In fact, many firms take as many as fourteen days at the end of each fiscal period to close their books. Because of this lag, business executives and stakeholders may make important decisions without having the most current data about their firm's performance.

Cisco Systems, the world's largest provider of network servers and routers, decided it needed more timely information to run its business. So, the company set up a program to accelerate its bookkeeping and financial reporting system. The finance group set goals to generate financial statements within one day of transactions, cut the cost of the finance function in half, and transform the way they supported the company's decision-makers. The company far exceeded their expectations. They have achieved the "virtual close," meaning that they can close their books within *hours* and produce consolidated financial statements on the first workday following the end of *any* reporting period. As an added plus, all managers now have real-time access to all company data.

To achieve this virtual close, Cisco did everything it could to reduce the number of transactions that employees had to physically monitor. It consolidated responsibilities, which cut down errors and improved productivity. It developed Internet-based applications to report and reconcile numbers that further reduced mistakes and processing time. For example, when employees return from business trips, their travel expenses are posted to the company's system through the Internet directly from their credit card accounts.

These changes have saved time and allow employees to focus on managing the business. The virtual close allows Cisco to focus on things that generate value within the company. Executives and managers can now analyze the performance of the business at any time. Stakeholders no longer need to wait weeks for periodic reports.

This "real-time accounting" exemplifies the changes that companies are making (or will be expected to make) as technology replaces traditional transaction processing and reporting activities used by most companies. Today's firms require fewer "number crunchers." Instead, they increasingly demand accounting and finance trained individuals who can use their analytical abilities and insights to create information that is useful in business decision-making.

Source: *Harvard Business Review* April 2001, Volume 79, Issue 4; p. 22.

manager attention. Frito-Lay, its distributors, and retailers all benefit through quicker ordering and delivery times, greater accuracy of inventory records, and faster payments and refunds.

Likewise, many companies that deal directly with consumers have used Internet-based technology to replace human interaction for common transactions. For instance, airlines now rely on technology to conduct B2C commerce. In the past, passengers had to contact a travel agent and order a paper ticket for a flight. Today, American and most other airlines provide complete schedule information and electronic ticket booking through their websites. Passengers can access these sites at any time of day to make their travel plans. The airlines use e-mail to confirm purchases of electronic tickets, and notify passengers of schedule changes. This development has made the process of buying airline tickets much easier for the consumer and has eliminated the need for staffing to issue tickets and process transactions.

The Global Economy

Dealing with international suppliers, partners, and markets is now more common than ever for both large and small companies. This trend is frequently referred to as the globalization of markets. Worldwide economic growth, the increase in cross-border free trade agreements, and technology improvements have jointly facilitated the expansion of global business. Firms can now more easily enter customer markets across the world. Likewise, buyers have greater access to suppliers around the globe. Not surprisingly, this increased economic activity has increased competition.

The globalization of economies has certainly affected businesses, but it also allows individual consumers access to a wider range of products and services. For example, the *Train à Grande Vitesse* (TGV) is a high-speed train line that travels at speeds over 180 miles per hour and services much of France and Western Europe. In the past, access to information about a French rail system was quite complicated and time consuming. Today, through an English-version website, any English-speaking visitor can explore schedules and routes, check journey times, and book tickets with a credit card. You can even arrange to have tickets sent directly to your smartphone or picked up at a designated train station in France. That is all it takes to engage in your first global business transaction!

Businesses today can attract *financial capital* from a variety of global financial markets. It has become routine for multinational firms to issue stock and bond securities in different markets across the world. In fact, over the past decade, the number of non-U.S. firms that offer their company's securities in U.S. capital markets has soared. The true extent of globalization is reflected in the trillions of dollars of stock transactions that take place across borders each year.

The Information Value Chain

Technological advances, global forces, and the resulting heightened competition have dramatically increased the demand for timely and relevant information to support decision making. These developments have made company stakeholders more sensitive to what type of data or information they need and how much they are willing to pay to get it. Simple transaction or summary data is growing less valuable daily. Data includes facts, figures, and numbers that are readily available and that quickly change. Raw data usually are of little use. However, when human analysis converts data into a form that managers can use to make business decisions, information has been created. Companies are willing to pay highly for analyses that provide useful information for decision making. Twenty years ago, investment managers subscribed to fee-based services that provided them with market data such as securities prices, volumes, and trends, which they used as a basis for their trading decisions. Today, this information is available at little or no cost on the Internet at a variety of sites including Google Finance. However, investors continue to seek out and handsomely compensate financial advisors that deliver useful information in the form of investment strategies. This growing difference in value between data and information has significant implications for the long-term career prospects of the business professional.

Management Accounting: A Business Planning Approach

Exhibit 2.3

The Information Value Chain

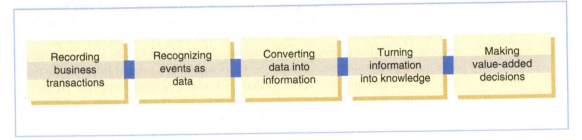

In today's market, regardless of functional specialization (whether it be accounting, finance, marketing, human resources, or something else), all managers are expected to satisfy the interests of their company's stakeholders. To do so, they must develop and apply insight about business operations, stakeholder expectations, and other market forces. Business professionals are expected to have an appreciation for how decisions will affect overall business performance. The American Institute of Certified Public Accountants (AICPA), a national professional organization for public accountants, recently developed the information value chain shown in Exhibit 2.3, which further highlights the difference in value between *data* and *information*. At each of the five stages in the chain, additional value is assigned to the activity.

Business Beacon

Accounting Professionals Need Business Insight

Companies today look to their accountants, financial managers, and consultants to provide advice about the company's performance. These financial professionals must understand and provide insight into the business—always keeping in mind the company's strategy and goals.

With this in mind, the American Institute of Certified Public Accountants (AICPA) and the Institute of Management Accountants (IMA) recently have redefined the skills expected of accounting and finance professionals. These core competencies include:

- **Adaptive Problem Solving and Critical Thinking.** Managers should be able to integrate data and knowledge to provide insights that yield quality advice for business decision-making.

- **Broad Business Sense.** Managers must understand how a business functions and quickly interpret the impact of market events such as changing customer needs, competitor actions, supplier expectations, and new governmental regulation.

- **Communication, Teamwork, and Leadership.** Managers are expected to be able to deliver and exchange information in both written and oral form. These abilities must be supported by interpersonal skills that allow diverse colleagues to work together. Such skills influence, inspire, and motivate others to cooperate and achieve results.

Source: http://www.cpavision.org/ and http://www.imanet.org/

Recording business transactions entails identifying and capturing a company's business activity. Increasingly, this process is automated by computerized and Web-based technologies. Consequently, the AICPA estimates that this first-stage activity is valued at only about $10 per hour in today's marketplace. In the next phase, captured transactions are processed and converted into basic report formats that provide the data used by business analysts. Analysts transform report data into information by applying their own unique skills and abilities in the third stage. When information from a variety of sources is combined, this yields the knowledge needed to make sound business decisions. In contrast to the first data-recording stage, the AICPA reports that the market is willing to pay over $1,000 per hour for accounting and consulting services that help business owners create knowledge to make good decisions. To achieve such salary levels, business professionals must think carefully about developing the skills and insights required to deliver services at the higher end of the information value chain.

In an age where you can instantaneously download complete, customized analyses from the Internet at little or no cost, managers must think seriously about the value of the services they provide to their companies. Specifically, managers must demonstrate how their *insights* add value to their firm. That so many organizations have been downsizing and restructuring provides strong evidence that many jobs will be eliminated and replaced by technology. If a company can find low- or no-cost data resources, why would it pay an employee or consultant to accumulate this same data? The answer is simple: It would not! Accounting and finance professionals must *provide insight or face extinction.* So what is insight? Insight is the application and integration of one's analytical abilities, technical skills, experience, and intuition to interpret data and address opportunities and problems that businesses face. Firms need people who can provide the *insight* needed to convert free or low-cost *data* into valuable *information.* Firms openly acknowledge their need for individuals who can transform *data* into the *information* that is so critical to decision-making.

The traditional accounting or bookkeeping equation (Assets = Liabilities + Equity) has historically provided an efficient and effective means to capture, process, and report the common business transactions of an industrial age economy. However, this time-tested fundamental relation, while still very relevant, may not be enough to meet the information needs of today's highly automated, knowledge-based economy. The recent move by accounting standard setters to give more weight to market values on the balance sheet and lessen their reliance on a historical cost perspective is one example of this shift. Managers now are expected to use their analytical abilities and insights to assess value, not just to report transaction costs as was the case in the past. Managers may need to supplement the traditional bookkeeping equation with a **new accounting equation**:

$$Data + Insight = Information™$$

When the relationship between data and information is expressed in this linear form, business professionals are forced to reconsider the work they do and its contribution. Although the terms *data* and *information* often are used interchangeably, the contexts in which the two terms are used can be, and frequently are, very different. The new accounting equation seeks to capture and highlight this difference. As previously noted, *data* generally refers to periodically changing facts and figures generated by bookkeeping and other types of computer systems. *Information,* on the other hand, exists only after a person has studied the data and applied *insight* to make a connection between the data and their impact on the company. Managers use their insight when they read, evaluate, and interpret computer-generated report data to determine the profitability of the products and services that their company sells. This information helps the company achieve its business strategy. The new accounting equation clearly illustrates why data preparers are less valued in today's market. Information has value only when it is relevant to decision making. The information value chain in Exhibit 2.3 clearly illustrates this point.

Creating Value for the Customer

In the past, markets were more limited than they are today, and dominant suppliers were usually able to dictate price and selection to customers. Now technology and global competition have increased product offerings and services. Where customers used to choose from products that were available locally, they now look farther afield and have more from which to choose. The selection leads them to expect quality, customization, and high levels of service. In the past, these product and service attributes were available only at a high price. Today, improved access to information and increased offerings from global suppliers have both benefited the consumer. When the consumer can choose, companies must fight for customers. Therefore, the consumer has become much more powerful in this faster-paced, more global business climate.

Learning Objective 2
Define the elements of the customer value imperative.

The Customer Value Imperative

Since customers today are more demanding than ever, businesses now generally embrace a philosophy called the **customer value imperative**. This attitude drives a company to create value for its customers by delivering a product or service that meets three key consumer expectations:

1. *Lower transaction costs.* Customers today expect lower prices, and many businesses deliver them by automating commercial transactions to achieve considerable cost savings. Today's technologies provide information to *both* the customer and company and often create savings that reduce product costs. For example, most travelers now book rental car reservations over the Internet directly from companies like Alamo and Hertz. Eliminating travel agents, paperwork, and other inefficiencies from the order process has reduced costs to the consumer.
2. *Greater customization.* Heightened competition, greater variety, and new technologies also allow customers the flexibility to tailor products and services

to their own unique needs. For example, athletic retailers like New Balance and Nike now permit customers to design and customize their apparel to their tastes and specifications through online tools.

3. *Improved service.* Technology also allows companies to meet growing customer information demands before, during, and after transactions. For example, shipping companies like Federal Express and Mayflower Van Lines allow customers to track deliveries as these carriers transport goods for them.

As Exhibit 1.2 in the last chapter indicated, customer expectations are critical success factors that must be addressed if a company's strategy is to succeed and its vision to materialize. The *customer value imperative* dramatically affects the way business organizations operate. Companies that do not focus on customer satisfaction are not likely to remain competitive or profitable.

C&F Enterprises, Inc.: Creating Value for Its Customers

With a sound business idea and adequate financing, Keith and Dale were feeling pleased with the state of their new lawn services venture. They were particularly happy at having negotiated several commercial maintenance contracts before actually starting the business, as this provided them with some much-needed cash flow to fund several unexpected operating expenses. Frances Chan, C&F's recently hired bookkeeper, was very concerned about some unexpected advertising costs, as she had never worked for a start-up business, nor did she have any experience in the lawn maintenance industry. She decided to approach Keith and Dale to get a better idea of how they intended to run their business.

Keith shared with Frances the results of the preliminary market study that seemed to suggest that the area needed another full-service landscaping company. Frances was somewhat skeptical of the rather superficial approach used to conduct this study (a search of the Internet). Dale responded to these concerns by citing the recently negotiated contracts as evidence of market demand.

Frances then asked the two entrepreneurs exactly what lawn maintenance services they would offer. Keith and Dale stated that as a full-service provider they intended to offer mowing, trimming, weed control, tree and shrub care, aeration, mulching, and any other lawn service requested by a customer or typically offered by their competition. They believed that offering a wide range of services was absolutely critical to establishing a presence in the market. To Frances's request for information on their pricing policies, Keith revealed that C&F would match their competitors' prices, at least in the short run.

Next, Frances asked if she should expect any more large advertising bills. Dale indicated that the unexpected marketing costs were associated with a full-page local magazine and online new site advertisement that would run for two years. Keith noted that future promotional efforts would also include to small

How Federal Express Creates Value for Customers

Federal Express is one of the world's largest shipping and delivery companies. The company employs over 200,000 people and delivers nearly 5 million shipments each day. Federal Express has built its business around global service and customer expectations.

Businesses rely on FedEx to deliver packages and letters overnight to anywhere in the United States and around the world. FedEx relies on technology to track packages and communicate with customers. Customers have access to a wide range of information about their shipments. For example, a customer can use the company's website to print out a mailing label, arrange package pickups, confirm the status of a delivery, and handle billing.

In addition to handling letters and documents, the company has expanded it business to handle special timely deliveries—such as live animals, food products, and human tissue for medical operations. The Smithsonian Institution's National Zoological Park relied on FedEx to deliver two pandas from China to Washington, D.C. Ford Motor Company uses the service to provide around-the-clock, critical-parts support for its commercial truck customers.

FedEx has grown its business to become a premier, well-recognized provider of global delivery through commitment to customer needs, integration of technology, and a long-standing record of quality performance.

Source: www.fedex.com

classified ads in local newspapers and distribution of flyers in the neighborhoods where they would be working.

Frances remembered hearing that C&F would rely on students and farm workers as a primary source of labor; she had also reviewed several rental agreements prior to issuing checks for truck and equipment deposits. However, she was curious about exactly how the lawn services would be delivered to the customer. Keith indicated that all new service orders would be taken over the phone. Since both he and Dale would be training and supervising work teams in the field almost every day, they would rely on an answering machine to take orders and messages. They would return the messages during the same evening or the next day. Initially, two lawn service teams would be fielded each day to meet customer requests. Staffing and equipment needs would be determined the day prior to each engagement. Any workers or special tools needed would be picked up early on the morning of the service to be delivered. Either Keith or Dale would inspect all work prior to leaving the work site and billing the client. Whenever possible, Keith and Dale hoped to include the client in their final inspection. If this was not practicable, they planned to use post-service "comment cards" attached to the bills to solicit feedback on their work. Although not completely satisfied with what she considered a "too casual" approach to business, Frances wished Keith and Dale luck on their new venture.

The Business Value Chain

Learning Objective 3
Explain the value chain and its components.

Managing even the simplest business properly is a complex proposition because companies must address so many issues when executing their business strategy. Just look at Keith and Dale's start-up venture. To date, these two budding entrepreneurs conducted a market analysis; identified a product and service offering; initiated a preliminary marketing effort; and acquired financial, human, and physical capital; and they have not yet even begun to operate at expected capacity.

As Exhibit 1.2 reveals, internal processes play a major role in company attempts to attain their vision. The set of the interrelated tasks or processes by which companies achieve their business strategy is known as the **value chain**. Consistent with the customer value imperative, the value chain starts with understanding what customers want and ends with customer satisfaction. The intervening internal business processes focus on the business operations needed to make the customer value imperative a reality. Therefore, it is essential for managers to think about how each individual process will help satisfy the customer.

For any company, the value chain can be described in terms of the five core business processes illustrated in Exhibit 2.4. The sections that follow describe each of the value chain activities and provide examples of the information each requires. Exhibit 2.5 specifically links the value chain to C&F's operations.

Figure 2.2
A critical link in Amazon's value chain is its distribution process. Prodcuts are housed in distribution centers across the United States for quick and reliable delivery.

Management Accounting: A Business Planning Approach

Market Analysis

As we learned in Chapter 1, the first step in strategic planning is a critical review of stakeholder relationships to evaluate potential external opportunities. A market analysis provides important information to managers as it identifies customers' preferences and needs, as well as identifying what existing businesses are doing to meet customer demand. This information is crucial to deciding which markets to enter because satisfying customer needs is fundamental to business strategy, revenue generation, and ultimately, profitability. For any start-up business, a market analysis requires a study of economic and market data to determine if potential customers indeed exist. In C&F's case, Keith and Dale relied on the telephone book and Internet resources to validate their belief that changing demographic and market conditions had increased demand for local lawn service businesses. For existing firms, a company's sales and marketing function interacts most closely with customers and generally has the best insights into what the company's customers value.

Chapter 1 described the strategic planning process and introduced the *business plan*, a formal output of this planning process. One of the primary goals of the business plan is to translate information from the marketplace into a foundation for developing, scheduling, and managing business operations. To that end, the market analysis section of the business plan should convince stakeholders, particularly potential investors and lenders, that sufficient demand exists for an enterprise's products or services.

Product Development and Design

Once a firm has identified a market opportunity, it must decide how to develop and design a product or service to meet customer needs. The product development and design process is a critical value chain activity. Keith and Dale adopted a simple, but practical approach to deciding what lawn services to offer their customers: They decided to offer the same services as their competition and to price them similarly.

During this stage, managers need information to help them evaluate whether they can actually create a successful product or service at a cost that is consistent

Exhibit 2.4
Business Value Chain

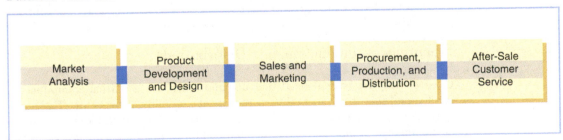

Exhibit 2.5
C&F Enterprises' Value Chain

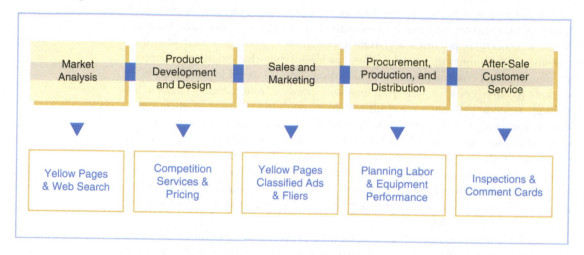

with a company's profit target. For example, when an automobile manufacturer develops a new product, market researchers work closely with customers to identify what automotive features they expect and how much they are willing to pay. While market studies can generate many good ideas, the burden is on the automotive design team to develop a vehicle that not only meets customer demand but also can realistically be manufactured.

Sales and Marketing

Once a company develops its product or service, the sales and marketing function begins promoting the product and securing sales commitments. Getting product and service information out to the customer is crucial to a company's marketing efforts. Even if a firm correctly identifies a market opportunity and develops a solution, without customer awareness and commitment to buy, the best ideas will not translate into sales, revenues, and financial success. Keith and Dale obviously believe that the local magazine and online news site are the most efficient and effective sales and marketing vehicles for their business. They appear to recognize that continual promotion is necessary and have planned for periodic low-cost classified advertising as well as for mailer distribution.

Procurement, Production, and Distribution

Once a company is convinced that demand exists for a particular product or service and that it can meet this market need profitably, it faces the challenges of producing and delivering a quality offering in a timely manner. The delivery of the finished product or service depends on three stages: *procurement, production,* and *distribution*. **Procurement**, also referred to as purchasing, is the use of

Management Accounting: A Business Planning Approach

financial capital to acquire the human and/or physical capital required to deliver a particular product or service. For manufacturers and retailers, this involves purchasing raw materials and finished goods for resale, respectively. Procurement is also important for service firms like accounting, law, and health care providers, since these firms need the appropriate people and supplies to deliver the services requested by their clients. In C&F's case, Keith and Dale's labor and equipment commitments represent the procurement or purchasing phase of C&F's value chain.

Production is the process of converting human and physical capital into a finished product or service. In a traditional manufacturing setting, production is the central process in the firm's value chain. For example, a bakery would have little to sell if it could not convert raw materials like flours, eggs, and milk into breads, pastries, and other delights in a timely, safe, and appealing manner. Professional service and consulting firms rely on employees to produce finished products such as legal documents or financial reports. In other cases, hotels or restaurants must be prepared to offer a specific vacation or culinary experience at a desired time and place. When Keith and Dale actually deliver a particular lawn service (that is, mowing, weeding, or fertilizing), they are engaging in the production phase of their business.

The remaining component of this fourth link in the value chain is *distribution*. Distribution refers to how the company physically delivers its product or service to its customers: how it brings the goods to market. Companies must develop reliable plans to bring the customer and the product or service together. In cases such as retail operations or restaurants, customers come to a business location to acquire the good or partake of the service. These sales are referred to as point-of-sale transactions. Alternatively, firms may deliver the goods or services to the customer. Some businesses perform the distribution task themselves. For example, a food delivery service or a furniture manufacturer often uses its own employees and vehicles to deliver its products directly to the customer. C&F Enterprises, Inc. also uses its own resources to provide services to its customers. Many firms rely on third-party carriers like Federal Express or UPS to distribute products to customers.

After-Sale Customer Service

The relationship with the customer does not end once the product or service has been delivered. In fact, one of the major roles of the sales and marketing function in most businesses is customer retention. Companies rely on customers' repeat business to provide the foundation for long-term sales growth and to enhance the company's reputation. Failure to retain customers can actually impair the company's reputation and reduces the likelihood of meeting annual or quarterly sales targets. Firms commonly provide after-sale service through Web-based resources, warranties, product updates, and technical support hotlines. Keith and Dale hope to solidify their business relationship with their clients by conducting post-service inspections with their customers during which any observed "deficiencies" can be addressed. The comment cards also might provide useful data for identifying customer concerns that might jeopardize a customer relationship. Operational excellence in after-sale customer service activities reduces the possibility that customers will replace the firm with a competitor in the future.

Managing the Value Chain

When developing a business plan, managers face seven primary questions related to managing the value chain:

1. What products or services do customers want and what price are they willing to pay?
2. What processes are necessary to support customer requirements?
3. What sales and marketing strategy is needed to promote the products or services?
4. How will the inputs be procured or acquired?
5. What production processes are central to creating the products or services?
6. How will the products or services be delivered to customers?
7. What follow-up support do customers need?

Once these core process issues are addressed, a company will be well on its way to meeting the customer value imperative and, hopefully, generating profits. As was shown in Exhibit 1.2 in the last chapter, the company's information systems

Figure 2.3
Apple must consider nonfinancial performance measures such as time to market, new offering adoption rates, unit sales, and the number of product defects when introducing new products and services to consumers.

Management Accounting: A Business Planning Approach

Dimension	Examples of Measures
Financial Results	Sales and profitability
	Cash flow from operations
	Dividends paid
	Debt levels
Customer Satisfaction	Market share
	Average transaction size
	Satisfaction survey ratings
	Number of new customers
	Number of product returns
Internal Business Processes	Percentage of on-time deliveries
	Time to market for new products
	Number of product defects
	Number of accidents
	Production downtime
Learning and Growth	Employee turnover
	Employee satisfaction ratings
	Number of training courses completed
	Employee credentials

Exhibit 2.6
Sample Balanced Scorecard
Measures

must be able to provide managers with performance indicators, both *financial* and *nonfinancial,* so that they can evaluate the organization's progress toward its goals.

The Balanced Scorecard: A Performance Evaluation Tool

In Chapter 1 we described how the balanced scorecard communicates an organization's strategy through a series of causal links. The balanced scorecard is particularly powerful because it relies on *both* financial and nonfinancial measures to communicate to managers how specific business processes drive results. Using both kinds of measures can give a company a more complete picture of its progress toward meeting its strategies and goals. Exhibit 2.6 lists several common indicators that companies use to measure performance along each of the four balanced scorecard dimensions discussed in Chapter 1. A more complete discussion of the balanced scorecard's usefulness as a performance measurement framework is provided in Chapter 9, together with its application to C&F Enterprises.

Evaluating Financial Performance

Company managers frequently evaluate the financial performance of their company against three standards: the previous actual performance of their company, the company's budgeted performance, and the performance of the company's peer group. Two of the most common financial measures used to evaluate performance are sales and profitability. The next chapter will discuss in greater detail how managers use financial reporting systems to gain insight into a company's operations. Recently, however, financial performance measurement systems, including financial statements, note disclosures, and the numerous ratios and statistics derived from them, have been criticized as being less relevant to managerial decision-making, given their historical focus and aggregation level. Therefore, managers increasingly are relying on nonfinancial indicators to evaluate operating performance.

Evaluating Nonfinancial Performance

A performance measurement system should provide managers with feedback on how well the company's value chain processes are functioning. Such a system allows managers to make decisions about the company's operations and determine whether any adjustments are needed for the company to reach its strategic goals.

Unlike common financial performance measures that are derived from rigidly structured financial statement formats and standards, nonfinancial performance measures often are tailored to the unique operations of a company. Nonfinancial performance measures used by one company may not be appropriate for another because the strategic goals of each are different. Therefore, managers must have a thorough understanding of the company's goals and business process to design nonfinancial measures that will assist them in evaluating the company's progress toward its goals.

To be useful in the strategic planning and evaluation process, nonfinancial performance measurement systems need to report on at least five dimensions:

1. Input information. Examples include raw material usage reports and product cost reports.
2. Information on the process that creates customer value. Examples include customer turnover, employee training, and processing costs.
3. Efficiency or productivity information. An example is customer account processing time.
4. Output or results information. Examples include customer sales data, production reports, and market share.
5. Product or service quality assessment information. Examples include the number of defects and market share data.

Customer Satisfaction. There are many ways to evaluate customer satisfaction. Market share is a popular measure that shows what percentage of the market's total sales of a particular product or service belongs to a company. This nonfinancial measure helps a company gauge its success relative to competitors. For example, Coca-Cola routinely measures and monitors its share of the soft drink market. Changes in market share point to successes or to opportunities to improve sales. Another way that companies measure customer satisfaction is by surveying customers. This feedback provides meaningful benchmarks to compare performance over time or against other firms. Similarly, the number of new customers that a company attracts provides insight into how customers perceive their product or service. In contrast, customer product returns suggest consumer dissatisfaction. Measures such as these can provide insight into changes in financial performance measures.

Internal Business Processes. Companies also measure the key value chain activities that drive customer satisfaction. Many firms count the percentage of on-time deliveries to make sure that promises to customers are fulfilled. Airlines, for example, frequently monitor the percentage of on-time departures and arrivals to assess service quality. Other companies are interested in the time it takes to bring new products to market. Software developers and movie producers routinely rely on new products for revenue; therefore, they must measure the time it takes to bring a product from the idea stage to the store shelf or the cinema screen—the "time-to-market." Companies also monitor the number of defects in the production process to unmask quality problems. Poor quality can damage a company's reputation and actually increase costs due to repair or replacement. Workplace accidents also can be costly, both to employees and to the company; therefore, businesses increasingly monitor safety records in their attempt to minimize on-the-job mishaps.

Learning and Growth. A company's success ultimately depends on its people. The recruiting, training, and hiring of new employees can be very expensive. Employee turnover, the number employees leaving the company as a percentage of total employees, is a common nonfinancial measure. As turnover increases, operating costs generally rise because new employees require training and need time to learn about the business's unique operations. Companies often survey employees to identify complaints and address satisfaction issues. In addition to managing work force turnover, many companies invest in employee development and education. To evaluate the extent of employee learning, companies can track the number of training courses completed by its workers or the number of specialized certifications they have obtained. Collectively these employee-related nonfinancial measures provide insight into whether a company is staffed adequately to support its business processes, satisfy customers, and deliver financial results.

Clearly, the balanced scorecard is a useful tool for evaluating the success of a business. All managers need a basic understanding of both the financial and nonfinancial performance issues addressed by the balanced scorecard and their relationship to business operations. Chapter 1 discussed the major role that financial projections play in the strategic planning process. Although this chapter acknowledges the usefulness of financial data in evaluating business process performance, it devotes more attention to nonfinancial measures. The next chapter explores in more detail how financial data can be used to evaluate performance and gain insight into the effectiveness of business processes.

Summary

This chapter introduced you to the forces affecting businesses. Technological innovation, the rise of the global economy, and increased demand for information in recent decades have heightened the importance of creating value for customers. These changes require businesses to accurately recognize what elements of their products or services customer value. Companies then must develop and manage processes, known as the value chain, to execute strategy and meet customer needs.

New technologies and globalization of economies have also *directly* affected individual managers. In today's marketplace, data about customer preferences and business processes are readily available at little or no cost. Technology, not people, are employed to process data and prepare reports. Managers are expected to develop the insight needed to use these data to manage the value chain and evaluate business performance. Business professionals must be able to analyze and communicate how business processes will effectively deliver products and services that meet customers' expectations. Managers must be prepared to adapt their insight to changes in the business marketplace.

A solid foundation in understanding the fundamentals of business processes and their effect on financial performance prepares managers to meet these new challenges. In the next chapter, we will examine how financial performance data are used to understand and evaluate business activities.

Net Gains

Market Analysis Resources on the Web

The following websites are indicative of the many data resources available to help managers gain an understanding of their potential customer markets:

- **U.S. Census Bureau http://www.census. gov/** The U.S. Census Bureau's County Business Patterns is an annual series that lists regional economic data by industry. The series is useful for studying the economic activity of small areas and analyzing economic changes over time. Businesses can use the data for analyzing market potential, measuring the effectiveness of sales and advertising programs, setting sales goals, and developing budgets.

- **Strategy and Business http://www.strategy-business.com/** *Strategy and Business* is both an online and hardcopy business journal that provides managers with insight on contemporary business topics. The journal includes case studies, interviews with executives, and reports on matters related to integrating strategy and performance measurement.

Summary of Learning Objectives

1. **Identify forces affecting business.** Companies today face many new challenges resulting from recent innovations in technology, heightened global competition, and increased customer quality expectations. These forces drive businesses to develop adaptive organizational structures, promote closer stakeholder relationships, restructure core business processes, and foster more responsive work environments.

2. **Define the elements of the customer value imperative.** The customer value imperative is an attitude or philosophy that drives a company to create value for its customers by delivering a product or service that meets three key consumer expectations: lower transaction costs, greater customization, and improved service. These customer expectations are critical success factors that must be addressed if a company's strategy is to succeed and its vision to materialize.

3. **Explain the value chain and its components.** The value chain describes how a business meets customers' demands. It is composed of five core business processes. (1) Market analysis identifies the preferences and needs of customers. (2) Product development and design involve the creation of the demanded product or service. (3) Sales and marketing are responsible for promoting the product and securing sales. (4) Procurement, production, and distribution encompass the manufacture and delivery of the product. (5) After-sale customer service includes any assistance given to the customer after the product or service has been delivered.

4. **Explain the importance of evaluating company performance.** For effective planning to take place, managers must monitor progress toward the established goals and objectives. To do this, they must evaluate financial *and* nonfinancial performance.

Glossary of Terms

Customer value imperative An attitude or philosophy that drives a company to create value for its customers by delivering a product or service that meets three main consumer expectations: lower transaction cost, greater customization, and improved service.

Distribution The value chain activity in which a business physically delivers its product or service to its customers.

Globalization of markets A growing trend by both large and small businesses to conduct commerce with international suppliers, partners, and markets.

Market analysis The value chain activity in which a business identifies customer preferences and needs, as well as identifying what existing firms are doing to meet market demand for a specific product or service.

Market share The percentage of the total sales of a particular product or service that is delivered by a single company, as compared to its competition.

New accounting equation A linear relationship between data and information that emphasizes the need for insight to transform one into the other. This equation illustrates why data preparers appear to be increasingly less valued in today's market.

Procurement The use of financial capital to acquire the human and/or physical capital required to deliver a particular product or service. Also referred to as *purchasing*.

Production The process of converting human and physical capital into a finished product or service.

Value chain The set of interrelated tasks or processes by which companies achieve their business strategy: market analysis; product development and design; sales and marketing; procurement, production, and distribution; and after-sale customer service.

Chapter Review Questions

1. What three factors are changing the way business is conducted today?
2. What effect has technology recently had on basic business *operations* (for example, manufacturing, distribution, etc.)?
3. How have technologies like the Internet affected the *information* provided to company stakeholders?
4. What do B2C and B2B mean?
5. What factors have contributed to the recent globalization of markets?
6. Describe the difference in value between data and information caused by recent developments in technology.
7. Define the *new accounting equation* and discuss its implications for what services managers will be expected to deliver in the twenty-first century.
8. Define the *information value chain* and discuss its implications on the activities business professionals should focus on.
9. What is meant by the *customer value imperative*?
10. How are consumers better served by the customer value imperative?
11. What are the five core business processes usually found in the business value chain?
12. Define procurement, production, and distribution in the context of value chain activities.
13. What three standards do company managers frequently use to evaluate financial performance?
14. Upon what five dimensions must nonfinancial performance measurement systems report?

Exercises and Problems

1. Discuss how technology and the global economy have affected each of the following businesses. Be specific.
   a. Fast-food restaurant chain
   b. Professional sports team
   c. Clothing store
   d. Automobile manufacturer
   e. Filmmaking company

2. Access the websites of both the American Institute of Certified Public Accountants (www.aicpa.org) and the Institute of Management Accountants (www.imanet.org) and address the following requirements:
   a. What skills or core competencies does each organization list as critical for financial professionals?
   b. How do these skills or core competencies differ for each organization? What do these differences or similarities suggest about what your future employer may expect of you?
   c. Are these skills or core competencies different from what you expected would be required of a business major? If so, how? If not, why not?
   d. Have you considered these new skills or core competencies in the selection of your major? In the selection of courses within your major?

3. Classify each of the following as either data or information. Explain your answer.
   a. Financial statements of a publicly traded company
   b. Consultant's report on the adequacy of a company's computer systems
   c. Accountants' opinion on the reasonableness of a tax strategy
   d. A company's general ledger
   e. Census report on population growth and income
   f. Manufacturer's monthly product defect report
   g. Monthly bank statement
   h. Investment advisor portfolio analysis

4. Describe the customer value imperative as it relates to each of the following businesses today. Address all three consumer expectations of the customer value imperative.
   a. Pizza parlor
   b. Movie theater
   c. Grocery store
   d. Hardware store
   e. Home construction company

5. Pick a company that you have done business with over the Internet and answer the following questions:
   a. What is the company's name and how did you find it?
   b. What does the company sell and what did you buy?
   c. Why did you choose to do business over the Internet?

     d. What do you perceive to be the advantages and disadvantages of executing your transaction over the Internet?

     e. How does your Internet business experience in this instance relate to the customer value imperative?

6. Identify three companies that sell a similar product or service. Rate your perception of each competitor's product or service on a scale of 1 (low) to 5 (high). Ask three classmates or friends to also rate their perceptions of these companies' products or services. Use this data to answer the following questions:

     a. What was the average rating assigned to each company by your classmates?

     b. Was their average higher or lower than yours?

     c. Why do you believe your classmates hold these perceptions about the three companies? Provide specific reasons or examples.

     d. What guidance would you give to the lowest-rated firm if it would like to raise customers' perceptions of its product or service?

7. Exhibit 2.4 identifies five core business processes in the value chain. Select the value chain activity to which each of the following items would best belong:

     a. Consultant's report on industry competition

     b. New product testing by an electronics manufacturer

     c. Customer complaint reports

     d. Freight carrier contracts for shipment of products to customers

     e. Employee hiring

     f. Billboard advertising for company services

8. Exhibit 2.4 identifies five major sets of value chain activities. Select the value chain activity to which each of the following items would best belong:

     a. Results of a customer satisfaction survey

     b. Advertising flyers and coupons distributed in the local newspaper

     c. A factory assembly line

     d. Contracts with suppliers to deliver raw materials

     e. Development and testing of new computer games by a software developer

     f. Packaging of orders for Internet customers by an online bookseller

9. Exhibit 2.6 illustrates five core business processes and related value chain activities for C&F Enterprises. Develop a similar diagram for a bakery and answer the following questions:

     a. Identify one major business activity for each of the five core business processes.

     b. How does your diagram differ from that of C&F Enterprises? Why?

     c. In your opinion, which activities are most important for the bakery? Why?

10. Exhibit 2.6 illustrates five core business process and related value chain activities for C&F Enterprises. Develop a similar diagram for a hotel and answer the following questions:

     a. Identify one major business activity for each of the five core business processes.

     b. How does your diagram differ from that of C&F Enterprises? Why?

     c. In your opinion, which activities are most important for the hotel? Why?

11. Describe the value chain for each of the following companies in terms of the five core business processes illustrated in Exhibit 2.4.
    a. Coffee shop
    b. Miniature golf course
    c. Ice cream parlor
    d. Sporting goods store
    e. Custom jewelry manufacturer
12. For each of the following measures, identify the balanced scorecard dimension (financial, customer satisfaction, internal business process, or learning and growth) to which it best belongs.
    a. Employee satisfaction ratings
    b. Sales of new products
    c. Percentage of employees with college degrees
    d. Production defect rates
    e. Number of workplace accidents
    f. Number of new contracts signed by the company sales force
13. For each of the following measures, identify the balanced scorecard dimension (financial, customer satisfaction, internal business process, or learning and growth) to which it best belongs.
    a. Market share
    b. Product profitability rankings
    c. Time-to-market for new products
    d. Number of new products released in the last year
    e. Number of employee resignations
    f. Hours of training completed by new employees
14. For each of the following businesses, identify one measure for each of the four balanced scorecard dimensions. Explain how your choices measure performance.
    a. Donut shop
    b. Amusement park
    c. Grocery store
    d. Hardware store
    e. Bicycle manufacturer
15. Visit one of the following types of businesses near your home or school: landscaper, supermarket, convenience store, theater, music store, fast-food restaurant, or dance club. Collect enough information during your visit to answer each of the following questions:
    a. How have recent developments in technology affected the way business is conducted today? Be specific.
    b. Did you notice any aspects of the business that suggest the business has been affected by the globalization of markets? If so, what? If not, why not? Be specific.
    c. What evidence did you find that the business embraces the customer value imperative? Specifically address transaction cost, customization, and service levels.

16. Your instructor may invite a local business owner to class (or you should visit with a business owner or manager near your home or school). Collect enough information during your visit to answer each of the following questions:
    a. What evidence (either direct or indirect) did you find that suggests the company conducted a *market analysis* to identify customer needs and existing competitor responses to these needs? Be specific.
    b. What evidence (either direct or indirect) did you find that suggests the company considered the needs of customers in the *development and design* of their products and/or services? Did you find any indication that the company considered the cost of producing a product or delivering a service in the development and design stage? Be specific.
    c. What evidence (either direct or indirect) did you find that the company has promoted customer awareness of its product or service through *sales and marketing*? Be specific.
    d. What does the company's website reveal about its *procurement, production, and distribution* processes? Specifically, what resources does the company use to create a product or service? How does the company convert these resources to a final product or service? Finally, how does the company deliver its product or service to its customers? Be specific.
    e. Does the company appear to support *after-sale customer service*? What evidence on its website indicates what the company does to retain its customers? Be specific.
    f. Based on your responses to questions (a) through (e), develop a value chain diagram similar to one the presented in Exhibit 2.6.

17. Search the Internet for a website for a company in which you have an interest (or that was previously assigned by your instructor). Review the company's website thoroughly (including the annual report, if available) making sure it is sufficient to evaluate its business value chain. Address each of the following questions and provide address links to support your answer in class:
    a. What evidence (either direct or indirect) did you find that suggests the company conducted a *market analysis* to identify customer needs and existing competitor responses to these needs? Be specific.
    b. What evidence (either direct or indirect) did you find that suggests the company considered the needs of customers in the *development and design* of its products and/or services? Did you find any indication that the company considered the cost of producing a product or delivering a service in the development and design stage? Be specific.
    c. What evidence (either direct or indirect) did you find that the company has promoted customer awareness of its product or service through *sales and marketing*? Be specific.
    d. What does the company's website reveal about its *procurement, production, and distribution* processes? Specifically, what resources does the company use to create a product or service? How does the company convert these resources to a final product or service? Finally, how does the company deliver its product or service to its customers? Be specific.
    e. Does the company appear to support *after-sale customer service*? What does the website indicate the company does to retain its customers? Be specific.

18. Review the annual report for a company in whose operating performance you have an interest or that was previously assigned by your instructor. Address each of the following questions and be sure to collect sufficient information to support your answer in class:

a. List all of the *financial* performance measures and ratios provided in the body of the annual report (excluding those contained in the set of audited financial statements and related notes). For purposes of this exercise, financial measures are those indicators derived from information provided in the balance sheet, income statement, statement of cash flows, and related note disclosures. Classify each of these financial measures according to whether it compares the company's performance to (1) previous company performance, (2) the company's expected or budgeted performance, or (3) the company's peer group.

b. List all of the *nonfinancial* performance measures provided in the body of the annual report. For each of these measures, indicate which of the following five dimensions is assessed by the measure:

  i. Input information
  ii. Process information
  iii. Efficiency or productivity information
  iv. Output or results information
  v. Product or service quality information

Group Consulting Exercise

The purposes of this group exercise are to (1) encourage you to begin working in groups on a simulated consulting engagement, (2) provide you an opportunity to apply what you have learned about strategy, the value chain, and business processes in a real-world setting, and (3) stimulate your thinking about business processes that may relate to the enterprise you will be starting shortly in the Business Planning simulation.

Schedule a convenient meeting time (approximately sixty minutes) for your group, during which *your entire team* will visit a local or on-campus business. Your consulting team has been assigned the task of gathering information (not just data) about a potential new client for which your firm hopes to provide future professional services. Your instructor will tell you what type of business establishment you will be visiting.

Prior to visiting your potential future "client," familiarize yourselves with the business process concepts outlined in this chapter. Then, visit the business and observe its operations for about thirty minutes.

Required

Consider the following questions, summarize your responses in a brief memo, and be prepared to discuss your team responses in class during the next class period:

1. What do you think the company's business strategy is?
2. What structural forces affect the way it conducts business?
3. How does the company create value for its customers? What kind of products or services does the company sell? Do all products and services require the same set of business processes or are they different? Why?
4. Do you have any ideas as to what your client's value chain might look like? Refer to the value chain shown in Exhibit 2.6 as an example.
5. Does your client produce or manufacture any of its products?
6. Develop a list of financial and nonfinancial measures that might help the company to measure its performance.
7. What types of costs are specific to your client? Which are related to manufacturing, merchandising, and/or service?

Conducting a Market Analysis

As discussed in this chapter, today's business environment is defined by change. To support strategy, a company's business plan must include a thorough business analysis of current and potential customers as well as industry competitors. A thorough market analysis consists of both customer and competitor analyses.

Assignment

Carefully define the market for your company and evaluate your customers and competition according to the following guidelines.

Customer Analysis

A complete customer analysis documents and analyzes the demographics, spending habits, preferences, and size of the target customer base. Once business owners adequately identify a target customer base, the biggest challenge they face is deciding which goods and services to deliver and which *not* to deliver. In other words, what competitive strategy will the business adopt? Which segment(s) of the market will the business pursue? The issues surrounding the customer analysis should address four fundamental questions, which you should discuss with your team in regard to your business venture:

1. What do customers value? Is it price, convenience, quality, or some combination?
2. What markets do we want to enter? Identify a specific list of products and services.
3. What customer segments will we serve? What are their demographics?
4. What is the market size in terms of sales volume in dollars and units? You may be able to estimate this by multiplying monthly demand by individual spending trends.

Your final business plan must address these questions. Business owners typically rely on surveys and credible, publicly available data to address these issues. You can find a wealth of information to help you in the library and on the Internet. However, remember that "you get what you pay for." While free, Web-based resources can often provide you with timely, aggregate industry and market data, it is the subscription, fee-based resources housed in the library that you will find most useful.

Every business must define its market and determine whether consumer demand will be strong enough to support operations. If the potential market opportunity is worth pursuing, the business then must determine how to deliver the product or service. For example, there might be a demand for a new restaurant in town, but it is important for investors to think about how they can marshal the expertise and financial resources required to actually start the business.

Competitor Analysis

Starting a business means entering a competition. Like any competition, it is important to know the strengths and weaknesses of your opponents and how well you compare. Answer the following questions relating to your business:

1. Who are the five nearest direct competitors? A search of the local web sites often can yield this information.

2. Who are the indirect competitors? Are there other products and services that could potentially compete for your customers? For example, a movie theater competes not only with other cinemas, but also with local entertainment alternatives such as sports teams, dance clubs, and concert halls.

3. What are the competitors' strengths and weaknesses? Existing competitors in the marketplace have an established reputation. What can you do to promote awareness and the credibility of your offering?

4. How does the competition's product or service differ from yours? Understanding what the customer values and delivering a product or service to meet those demands is the first step toward profitability. Pricing is an important factor in your overall competitiveness. Get a feel for the pricing strategy that your competitors are using. It is essential to determine whether your prices are in line with competitors in your market area and whether they are consistent with industry averages.

5. What is the economic growth rate in the area? Are similar businesses opening or closing? Do the businesses seem to be popular? A visit to a competitor's business location can yield a considerable amount of insight.

Image Credits

Chapter 3

LEARNING OBJECTIVES

1. Review the purpose of financial statements and their form.

2. Describe the use of pro forma financial statements.

3. Discuss and illustrate the use of financial ratio analysis.

4. Demonstrate the use of financial ratios in evaluating business strategy.

Evaluating Financial Performance

Financial statements provide a wealth of information that customers, creditors, investors, managers, employees, regulators, and other stakeholders use to assess a firm's past and future performance. The four reports that comprise a set of financial statements—the balance sheet, the income statement, the statement of cash flows, and the statement of owners' equity—summarize the economic transactions affecting a business. However, the quantity of financial information that is available today at little or no cost can be overwhelming or even intimidating. Evaluating a firm's business operations is often complicated by the complexity of the accounting policies on which financial statements are based. Therefore, financial statement users frequently use ratio analysis to manage this information overload and to capture the big picture of firm performance. This chapter will review financial statement fundamentals, introduce pro forma reporting, and discuss how ratio analysis can provide useful insights into a firm's business operations.

Financial Statement Basics

Before exploring the insights into operations that financial analysis provides, it will be helpful to review the basic financial statements and ratios that are traditionally used to measure a company's financial performance. Throughout this chapter, the financial statements of C&F Enterprises, Inc. are used to facilitate our understanding of financial analysis. This example will demonstrate how a fundamental set of measures can be used to evaluate the business performance of any firm.

The Balance Sheet

The balance sheet shows a firm's financial position (assets, liabilities, and owners' equity) at the end of its fiscal year or a shorter reporting period. This financial report is built on the fundamental accounting equation:

$$\text{Assets} = \text{Liabilities} + \text{Owners' Equity}$$

Any increase or decrease on one side of the equation must be offset by an equal increase or decrease on the other side, prompting the name *balance* sheet. This report

Learning Objective 1
Review the purpose of
financial statements and
their form.

also has been called the statement of financial position because it describes a company's financial status *on a particular date.*

Assets represent economic resources controlled by a company. They are reported in the balance sheet in the order of their liquidity—that is, when they are expected to be converted to cash. Current assets consist of cash and other resources like accounts receivable and inventory that are expected to be converted into cash within one year or the normal operating cycle of the firm, whichever is longer. These assets are listed first in the balance sheet so that financial statement users can quickly determine if a business will have sufficient cash to meet its obligations in the near future. Fixed assets—sometimes referred to as property, plant, and equipment—are those resources acquired for longer-term use in the business, such as land, facilities, vehicles, and machinery. Firms also frequently rely on intangible assets like goodwill, copyrights, and patents to accomplish their business strategy. These asset resources are unique in that they have no physical substance. Since fixed and intangible assets are not expected to be converted to cash in the short run, they are less liquid than current assets and are reported after them. Classifying assets by liquidity provides financial statement users with insights into how a business intends to use its assets.

Liabilities and owners' equity reflect claims on a firm's assets by its creditors and investors, respectively. Current liabilities are those debts and obligations

---

Business Beacon

Financial Information on the Internet

The Internet provides access to dozens of financial information websites. These sites contain complete financial statement data as well as financial summaries, ratios, and operating analyses. The very existence of these no-cost information libraries further confirms that today's business professionals will be rewarded, not for preparing such financial reports, but rather for the analysis and insight they develop from these data.

If downloading raw financial data is the goal, the Securities and Exchange Commission (SEC) provides access to the regulatory filings of all of its registrants at http://www.sec.gov/edgar.shtml.

EDGAR: A Database of Information about Public Companies (http://www.sec.gov/edgar/searchedgar/company search.html). The U.S. Securities and Exchange Commission's

EDGAR website hosts a database of various required filings of publicly owned companies. One of the most detailed reports about a company is known as the Annual Report or Form 10-K. To access a company's Form 10-K, log on to the link listed above and type (in the box labeled Company Name) the name of a company in which you are interested. Select Find Companies. A new screen will appear—click on the 10-digit CIK (Central Index Key) number that appears to the left of the name of your selected company. A chronological list of recent filings will appear in a new screen. Scroll down until you find the most recently filed 10-K report. Click on HTML or TEXT to read the 10-K in the format you prefer. This resource will be useful to learn about different companies and to complete many assignments in this text.

Figure 3.1
Investors rely on financial
statements to evaluate a
company's performance.
Creditors use such data
to determine whether a
business can repay its debts
while potential owners use it
to assess a firm's prospects.

that must be repaid using current assets (generally within one year), while long-term liabilities are those for which payment is due after one year. Owners' equity represents the owners' contributed capital to the business plus all undistributed earnings. The firm's earnings that have not yet been distributed to owners are called retained earnings. Therefore, owners' equity is the remaining interest in a firm after liabilities are deducted from assets. Owners' equity thus serves as the balancing factor on the balance sheet. Large businesses often have many owners who acquired their ownership by buying stock in the company. These owners are called shareholders or stockholders and their ownership interest is commonly called shareholders' or stockholders' equity.

As Exhibit 3.1 illustrates, C&F Enterprises' balance sheet at the end of its first year of operations is typical for that of a start-up business. Its $18,958 asset size is modest and reflects the service nature of the business, which relies on people rather than property and equipment to meet its customers' needs. The company appears very liquid with $16,558 in current assets (cash, accounts receivable, supplies, and prepaid advertising). The rather significant prepaid advertising amount reflects a multiyear contract executed during the year (discussed in Chapter 2). The limited investment in fixed assets of $3,000 confirms Keith and Dale's intention to rent rather than purchase landscaping equipment during the first few years of the company's operations. C&F has yet to acquire any intangible assets, which is consistent with the start-up nature of its business. C&F's current liabilities total only $1,000, suggesting that Keith and Dale are paying their bills in a timely manner. Company operations appear to have been financed primarily with a long-term liability or note payable ($2,000) and common stock ($12,000). Keith and Dale's ownership interests total $15,958; the retained earnings amount suggests that C&F earned profits of $3,958 in its first year of operations and did not distribute any of these earnings to the owners.

Figure 3.2
Small business owners around the world must keep accurate and current financial records. Banks use a borrower's financial statements to ensure the borrower's compliance with loan agreements.

Exhibit 3.1
C&F Enterprises'
Balance Sheet

C&F Enterprises, Inc.
Balance Sheet
December 31, 20X1

Assets		
Current Assets:		
Cash		$ 5,958
Accounts Receivable		5,500
Supplies		300
Prepaid Advertising		4,800
Total Current Assets		$16,558
Fixed Assets:		
Equipment	$3,000	
Less Accumulated Depreciation	(600)	
Equipment (net)		2,400
Total Assets		$18,958

Liabilities and Owners' Equity		
Current Accounts Payable		$ 1,000
Long-Term Note Payable		2,000
Common Stock		12,000
Retained Earnings		3,958
Total Liabilities and Owners' Equity		$18,958

The Statement of Changes in Owners' Equity

The statement of changes in owners' equity is a primary financial statement that details transactions that affect the balance sheet equity accounts during a financial reporting period. This statement specifically describes changes to the common or preferred stock accounts and retained earnings. In the case of C&F Enterprises, Inc., Exhibit 3.2 reveals that owners' equity increased by $15,958 due to the $12,000 in common stock financing and the $3,958 in net income earned and recognized during the fiscal year.

The Income Statement

The income statement (or profit and loss statement or "P&L") is a primary financial statement that lists the firm's revenues, expenses, and net income or loss for the year or for a shorter reporting period. Revenues usually are income generated from product or service sales, but other sources of income (rent, investments, interest) also frequently are found in the revenue section of the income statement. Occasionally, customers return products that they buy. Firms must deduct these returns or allowances from their sales revenues to yield net sales revenue. Expenses are the costs incurred by a company to produce revenue. Deducting the cost of goods sold (or services delivered) from sales revenue yields gross profit (or gross margin). Firms also incur a variety of other costs that relate to the normal functioning of the business. These are called operating expenses. Gross profit minus operating expenses equals net income (or loss). Net income (or loss) is intended to measure how the business has performed for its stakeholders during the reporting period.

Exhibit 3.3 indicates that Keith and Dale's new business generated $74,800 in revenues during its first year in operation. To provide these landscaping services, C&F incurred $58,300 in expenses associated with salaries, equipment rentals, and supplies, yielding a gross profit of $16,500. Operating expenses like advertising and bookkeeping, which are not directly related to delivery of landscaping services, approximated $12,500. Surprisingly, C&F's first year of operations yielded net income of $3,958.

C&F Enterprises, Inc.
Statement of Changes in Owners' Equity
For the Year Ended December 31, 20X1

Beginning Contributed Capital	$ —
Common Stock Issued During the Year	12,000
Ending Contributed Capital	$12,000
Beginning Retained Earnings	$ —
Net Income for the Year	3,958
Ending Retained Earnings	$ 3,958
Total Owners' Equity	$15,958

Exhibit 3.2
C&F Enterprises' Statement of Changes in Owners' Equity

The Statement of Cash Flows

The **statement of cash flows** is a primary financial statement that identifies company transactions that generate and consume cash. In summarizing these transactions, the statement explains how the cash balance reported on the balance sheet changed during the financial reporting period. Therefore, the statement of cash flows provides important information about the operating, investing, and financing cash flows of the business.

Cash Flows from (Used by) Operating Activities. Cash flows from operating activities are those directly associated with the acquisition and sale of a company's products and services—that is, the firm's primary business activity. Net income differs from cash flows from operating activities because the income statement is prepared using accrual accounting. Accrual accounting recognizes revenues and expenses when they are earned or incurred, not when they are collected or paid. In other words, the income statement ignores the timing of cash flows. Often, there can be a considerable difference in the timing of economic events and their related cash flows.

A company's operating cash flows can be reported on the statement of cash flows in one of two ways: the direct method or the indirect method. The direct

Exhibit 3.3	**C&F Enterprises, Inc.**	
C&F Enterprises'	**Income Statement**	
Income Statement	**For the Year Ended December 31, 20X1**	

Service Revenue		$74,800
Cost of Services Sold:		
Salaries and Wages	$43,000	
Rentals	11,000	
Supplies	3,000	
Fuel	700	
Depreciation	600	
Total Cost of Services Sold		58,300
Gross Profit		$16,500
Operating Expenses:		
Advertising		$ 4,800
Bookkeeping Services		2,500
Interest		200
Taxes		2,042
Other		3,000
Net Income		$ 3,958

Management Accounting: A Business Planning Approach

method shows how a company's operations have generated and consumed cash. When using the direct method, companies generally report each of the following six major categories of operating cash flows: cash received from customers; cash paid to suppliers; and cash paid for salaries, other operating expenses, interest, and taxes. Although the direct method is the more difficult of the two methods to prepare, it is considered to be more informative than the indirect method.

The indirect method of preparation is simply a reconciliation of net income to operating cash flows. Net income is adjusted for all noncash revenues and expenses that the accrual process requires be recorded. For example, depreciation and amortization expenses are noncash expenses that must be added back to net income when computing operating cash flows. Changes in current assets and liabilities also affect the indirect method reconciliation.

Cash Flows from (Used by) Investing Activities. Investing activities include cash flows related to the purchase and sale of a company's noncurrent (fixed or intangible) assets. For example, when a company uses its cash to buy equipment to support its operations for a period greater than one fiscal year, this cash flow is an *investment* in the future of the business. If a company sells a long-term asset like a building that it no longer needs, the cash proceeds from the sale are considered investment cash inflows.

Cash Flows from (Used by) Financing Activities. When companies raise or retire capital from creditors or shareholders (that is, liabilities and/or contributed capital) or pay cash dividends to shareholders, they engage in financing activities. The receipt of cash from a bank loan is a financing cash inflow, as is cash received from the issuance of stock to shareholders. Conversely, cash dividend payments to shareholders are financing cash outflows.

Although the statement of cash flows is not normally used in ratio analysis, its categorization of economic activities into operating, investing, and financing activities develops useful insights about a firm's uses and sources of cash and often explains how revenues and expenses differ from cash receipts and disbursements.

According to Exhibit 3.4, the operating activities of C&F Enterprises, Inc. consumed $5,042 during its first year of operations. This differs from the net income of $3,958 reported in the income statement for a number of reasons related to accrual accounting. Net income includes $5,500 of service revenues not yet collected (accounts receivable), but does not reflect $5,100 in expenses for which cash disbursements have been made ($300 for supplies and $4,800 for prepaid advertising). In addition, net income has been reduced by $1,600 of expenses for which cash has not been disbursed ($600 of depreciation and $1,000 of accounts payable). C&F's statement of cash flows also reveals that Keith and Dale used $3,000 to purchase equipment during the year (investing activity) and initially funded their business with $14,000 received from common stock issuance and bank borrowings (financing activities).

Exhibit 3.4
C&F Enterprises' Statement
of Cash Flows

C&F Enterprises, Inc.
Statement of Cash Flows
For the Year Ended December 31, 20X1

Cash from (Used by) Operating Activities:	
Cash Received from Customers	$69,300
Cash Paid for Salaries and Wages	(43,000)
Cash Paid for Other Operating Expenses	(25,800)
Cash Paid to Suppliers	(3,300)
Cash Paid for Taxes	(2,042)
Cash Paid for Interest	$ (200)
Cash Flow Used by Operating Activities	$ (5,042)
Cash from (Used by) Investing Activities:	
Cash Paid for Equipment	$ (3,000)
Cash from Financing Activities:	
Cash Provided by Issuing Stock	$12,000
Cash Provided by Long-Term Note Payable	2,000
Cash Flow Provided by Financing Activities	$14,000
Increase in Cash During Year	$ 5,958
Cash Balance at Beginning of Year	—
Cash Balance at End of Year	$ 5,958

Projected or Pro Forma Financial Statements

Financial statement projections help managers transform business strategy into shareholder value. These projections of the firm's future operations are frequently referred to as **pro forma financial statements**. These "as if" financial reports are based on a number of assumptions regarding future revenues, expenses, investment activities, financing arrangements, and other operating issues. These assumptions generally are outlined in a company's strategic or business plan. Established businesses possess a history of operating data that provide a useful start when preparing such pro forma balance sheets, income statements, and statements of cash flows. Start-up companies, on the other hand, usually rely on published statistics (discussed in the next section) when developing financial statement projections about future operations.

Pro forma financial statements usually are prepared using electronic spreadsheets or computerized mathematical models that facilitate the use of what-if analysis. Today, many such tools are available at no cost on the Internet. By simply changing a variable in many of these tools, projections are instantly revised, providing managers with a variety of planning *data*. However, managers must then apply their *insight* to transform this data into information that can be used in monitoring the implementation of a business plan. Chapters 7 and 8 will show you how to prepare and analyze pro forma financial statements.

The pro forma balance sheet lists the assets needed by the firm to generate specified revenue and net income levels. The pro forma income statement provides managers with insight about the potential profitability of the business. Managers have two options when creating this projection. They can either develop a sales forecast and work to net income from sales (the top-down approach), or they can set a profit figure and compute the necessary sales level to achieve a desired level of net income (bottom-up approach). In either approach, managers must estimate the expenses that will be incurred in meeting revenue projections. The pro forma statement of cash flows is particularly valuable in outlining the sources and uses of the company's cash, one of the most critical assets owned by a business. All pro forma projections should be compared with either past operating reports or data from legitimate external sources to validate the appropriateness of the pro forma statements and the underlying assumptions. It also is useful to evaluate these projections using ratio analysis.

Ratio Analysis

Managers frequently rely on a technique called **ratio analysis** to analyze company financial statements. Ratio analysis is a process in which ratios computed from accounting data are compared and analyzed to develop insights about a firm's performance and business risks. Using ratios generated by computers or Web-based applications, managers attempt to explain relationships between financial statement elements and the business operations that created them. While not a substitute for a detailed and thorough review of a company's complete set of financial statements and note disclosures, this technique does provide a useful "first look" at a company's vital signs. Ratio analysis is most commonly used to assess a company's *financial* health. However, astute managers also rely on such tools to identify *operational* problems in a company's business processes.

As one can imagine, the number of ratios that can be created is limited only by managers' creativity and their need for information to address a particular issue. In fact, financial accounting texts frequently cite as few as ten and as many as twenty ratios as key to understanding profitability and business strategy. This section describes ten ratios that *business owners* commonly use to monitor their company's financial details. The ratios are grouped into four categories: liquidity, leverage, activity or operating, and profitability and performance. Each ratio will be illustrated using financial information from C&F Enterprises, Inc.'s first year of business operations. Given the start-up nature of Keith and Dale's business, the company's ratios will be compared to industry averages for similar-sized landscaping businesses provided by Dun & Bradstreet in their publication entitled *Industry Norms and Key Business Ratios*. All of C&F's ratios and the comparable industry averages are shown in Exhibit 3.5.

Learning Objective 3
Discuss and illustrate the use of financial ratio analysis.

Pro Forma Financial Statement Abuse

Unfortunately, the term *pro forma* recently has been associated with a financial reporting abuse practiced by an increasing number of companies. Managers of firms whose stock is traded on public exchanges often suffer tremendous pressure to generate increased earnings to support higher values for their owners' shares. When "real earnings" like revenues and net income fail to meet market expectations, some managers attempt to steer analysts and investors away from their actual earnings to other numbers. Many companies often exclude some ordinary expenses, as defined by generally accepted accounting principles (GAAP), from the numbers they feed to investors and analysts. These companies use terms like "operating or core earnings" and "pro forma or as if earnings" to distort investor perceptions of their companies' value. These earnings amounts generally are *higher* than net income because certain expenses are considered "special" and are excluded from net income.

According to FactSet and the Wall Street Journal, the S&P 500 companies increased earnings by 0.4 percent more per share in 2015, based on so-called pro forma figures, results provided by companies that exclude certain items such as restructuring charges or stock-based compensation. The "same" results reported under GAAP show per share profit declines of 12.7 percent. Overall, the reported earnings were 25 percent lower than the pro forma figures.

Companies sometimes will also look past charges that result from big swings in the value of their assets. Chesapeake Energy, for example, reported a full-year 2015 loss of $14.9 billion under GAAP. However, after adjusting for items "typically excluded by securities analysts in their earnings estimates," it lost just $329 million. The major item Chesapeake and many other energy companies left out of their 2015 pro forma results were charges related to the steep decline in energy prices—one of the primary drivers of their profitability! Overall S&P 500 earnings under GAAP came to $787 billion in 2015—that is $256 billion less than the pro forma estimate of $1.04 trillion.

Companies that emphasize "pro forma" earnings argue that they are simply trying to help investors better understand their businesses by breaking out unusual or unimportant items from their GAAP financial statements. However, "operating earnings" and the other "pro forma" terms are not GAAP measures, nor are there any standards for their reporting. One thing is clear: "pro forma" earnings that intentionally misrepresent a firm's financial condition and performance to deceive financial statement users constitute *financial statement fraud.*

Source: *Wall Street Journal*, "Companies Pollute Earnings Reports, Leaving P/E Ratios Hard to Calculate" by Jonathan Weil. Copyright 2001 by Dow Jones & Co., Inc. and "S&P Results Far Worse Than Advertised," Wall Street Journal, February 24, 2016. http://www.wsj.com/articles/sp500earningsfarworsethanadvertised 1456344483. Reproduced with permission of Dow Jones & Co., Inc.

Figure 3.3
Many major airlines have experienced financial difficulties brought on by uncertain weather, fluctuating fuel prices, ever-present threat of terror, and competition. Financially challenged businesses like airlines use ratio analysis to evaluate whether their operating plans are responding to these business threats. Creditors also use financial ratios to evaluate the solvency of some airlines, many of which have operated on the brink of bankruptcy.

Liquidity Ratios

Liquidity ratios provide insight into whether a business has sufficient assets, either in cash or easily convertible to cash, to pay maturing obligations as they come due. The primary measures of liquidity are the *current ratio* and the *quick ratio*.

Ratio	C&F	Industry Average
Current Ratio	16.56	4.40
Quick Ratio	11.46	2.80
Financial Leverage	1.19	1.80
Debt to Equity	0.19	16.00
Accounts Receivable Turnover	13.60	8.93
Asset Turnover	3.95	1.35
Net Profit Margin	5.29%	6.70%
Return on Assets	20.88%	10.10%
Return on Equity	24.80%	20.20%

Exhibit 3.5
Financial Ratios for C&F Enterprises

Current Ratio. The current ratio, sometimes called the working capital ratio, measures the firm's ability to pay current liabilities from current assets. Many financial analysts believe that a current ratio of 2 : 1 represents a comfortable liquidity cushion for a small business. In general, the higher the current ratio, the stronger the financial position and liquidity. However, a very high current ratio may suggest inefficient use of company assets if cash balances are not earning a return or if the firm is not collecting its receivables or is overinvested in inventory.

$$\frac{\text{Current Assets}}{\text{Current Liabilities}} = \frac{\$16,558}{\$1,000} = 16.56$$

In C&F's case, we see a very strong current ratio driven by relatively high cash and receivable balances. Their prepaid advertising also increases the current ratio. In fact, the company's current ratio greatly exceeds the lawn service industry average of 4.40. It appears that Keith and Dale have not yet fully employed the cash raised by their borrowing and common stock issuance, thus contributing to the abnormally high ratio. The unusual size of this ratio calls attention to areas that may need improvement, in this case better utilization of cash balances. Keith and Dale might consider using surplus cash balances to purchase additional equipment, thereby reducing future equipment rental expenses. Alternatively, they may choose to maintain high liquidity levels until they more fully understand the seasonal cash requirements of their new business venture.

Quick Ratio. The quick ratio, also called the acid test ratio, is a more conservative measure of a company's liquidity because it eliminates inventory and prepaid expenses from the numerator. These eliminations are made because inventory is considered to be the least liquid current asset and also the most likely to be overvalued, and prepaid expenses such as rent, advertising, and insurance cannot easily be converted to cash. In general, a quick ratio of 1: 1 is considered satisfactory. A ratio of less than 1: 1 suggests that the company may be overly dependent on inventory and future sales to satisfy short-term debt.

$$\frac{\text{Current Assets} - \text{Inventory} - \text{Prepaid Expenses}}{\text{Current Liabilities}} = \frac{\$11,458}{\$1,000} = 11.46$$

As with its current ratio, C&F's quick ratio again is very high; it greatly exceeds the industry average of 2.8. C&F's quick ratio is lower than its current ratio because it excludes the limited level of inventory (supplies of only $300) and the prepaid advertising of $4,800. As the company's business grows, inventory levels are likely to increase, forcing the quick ratio down to levels more in line with industry norms. C&F's quick ratio helps Keith and Dale see how the most liquid assets (cash and receivables) compare to current payables.

Management Accounting: A Business Planning Approach

Leverage Ratios

Several ratios compare the amount of financing supplied by owners to that supplied by creditors. These ratios are known as leverage ratios. They assess the extent to which managers rely on debt capital rather than stock or retained earnings to finance operating and investing activities. Total equity includes all liabilities as well as owners' equity (stock and retained earnings); thus it equals total assets. High financial leverage ratios indicate that a firm relies on creditors to provide a large percentage of its financing, generally suggesting a higher risk of default than if owners had larger personal investments (higher owners' equity).

Financial Leverage Ratio. The financial leverage ratio reports the proportion of a firm's assets that owners control relative to the amount of the owners' investment in the company. The "lever" in financial leverage refers to the impact of using creditor funds to run a business. Highly "levered" or "leveraged" companies rely on debt or "outside" financing more than owner financing.

$$\frac{\text{Total Assets}}{\text{Owners' Equity}} = \frac{\$18,958}{\$15,958} = 1.19$$

C&F's financial leverage ratio is quite low, reflecting the recent start of its business operations. As with many small service ventures, the owners provide most of the initial start-up funds, or financial capital. As the business matures and establishes a strong performance record, creditors will increasingly become willing to extend the company funds to finance its operations. The industry average of 1.80 for this type of established business shown in Exhibit 3.5 reflects this willingness. C&F has a very low risk of default at the end of its first fiscal year because the low financial leverage ratio of 1.19 indicates that owners now control almost all of the firm's assets.

Debt to Equity Ratio. The debt to equity ratio is a leverage ratio that also expresses the relationship between the capital contributions of creditors and owners. This ratio simply compares what the firm "owes" to creditors with what the owners have invested. The higher the proportion of the debt, the greater the risk of default, since less protection is afforded creditors if the business should fail. When the firm's debt to equity ratio exceeds 1.00, the creditors' interest is greater than that of the owners, suggesting that the business may be undercapitalized (that is, overextended as to debt). Firms must be careful to balance the mix between debt and equity.

$$\frac{\text{Total Debt}}{\text{Owners' Equity}} = \frac{\$3,000}{\$15,958} = 0.19$$

In C&F's case, the debt to equity ratio is significantly lower than the industry average of 16.00, again confirming the start-up nature of the company's operations.

Exhibit 3.6

The Consequences of
Using Leverage

C&F Enterprises, Inc.
***Pro Forma* Income Statement**
For the Year Ended December 31, 20X1

	20X1 Actual Results	Double Operating Income Scenario	Reduced Operating Income Scenario
Operating Income	$6,200	$12,400	$3,100
Interest Expense	(200)	(200)	(200)
Income Before Taxes	$6,000	$12,200	$2,900
Tax Expense	(2,042)	(4,152)	(987)
Net Income	$3,958	$ 8,048	$1,913
Return on Equity	24.80%	50.43%	11.99%

Is Debt a Bad Thing? Using debt increases a company's risk. Debt often is considered a disadvantage and risky because it commits a firm to fixed financial obligations that it must meet if it is to continue its operations. Therefore, leverage ratios frequently are used to measure the degree of financial risk assumed by a company. However, when used successfully, debt (increased financial leverage) can be advantageous, actually increasing shareholder returns.

Consider, for example, the effects of increased financial leverage on C&F's performance. C&F's lender has provided a $2,000, 10 percent loan to partially finance C&F's first year of operations. The company's current total statutory tax rate (both federal and state together) is 34.03 percent (tax expense of $2,042 divided by income before taxes of $6,000). Operating income (sales revenue less all expenses except for interest and taxes) is $6,200.

As previously noted, C&F reported net income of $3,958 for its first year, which yielded a return on equity of approximately 25 percent for its owners. Look at C&F Enterprises' pro forma income statement shown in Exhibit 3.6 to see what happens if C&F successfully uses debt to grow revenues and doubles operating income.

Net income as well as the return on equity to owners will more than double. This illustrates the *advantage* of financial leverage. However, if C&F is not able to use the borrowed funds to increase earnings and earnings actually decline by half, financial leverage has disastrous effects on return on equity, reducing it by almost 13 percentage points from the 20x1 results. Consequently, when considering a firm's mix of debt and equity financing, managers must trade off the potential benefits and risks of financial leverage.

Activity or Operating Ratios

Managers also use ratios to monitor how effectively the business uses its resources. Monitoring activity ratios can contribute to efficient resource utilization, which in turn can reduce the need to borrow additional funds.

Accounts Receivable Turnover Ratio. The accounts receivable turnover ratio reports how frequently (on average) accounts receivable are collected during the year. This ratio measures both the quality of receivables as well as the efficiency of the firm's collection and credit policies. A high receivables turnover ratio is generally considered good because a company is rapidly converting customer receivables to cash.

$$\frac{\text{Net Sales Revenue}}{\text{Accounts Receivable}} = \frac{\$74,800}{\$5,500} = 13.60$$

C&F is quickly converting sales to cash and its high accounts receivable turnover ratio exceeds the industry average of 8.93. In fact, the company collects all of its receivables 13.6 times per year, an average of every 26.8 days (365 business days divided by the accounts receivables turnover ratio of 13.6). The high turnover ratio and quick collection period (within 30 days) provides evidence of the firm's solid overall financial flexibility and strong position to pay bills.

Inventory Turnover Ratio. The inventory turnover ratio measures the efficiency with which a firm manages and sells its inventory. It also can be used to evaluate the liquidity of a firm's inventory. Given that C&F operates in a service industry that does not produce or sell specific inventory products, one would not expect the inventory turnover ratio to be an appropriate measure. In fact, C&F's balance sheet does not report any inventory held for resale at all. However, for firms with retail inventory, the ratio is computed with cost of goods sold in the numerator. For example, assume that a retailing firm sells inventory costing $61,800 during its fiscal year. If its year-end balance sheet reports $6,500 in inventory, then its inventory turnover ratio would be 9.51. In other words, that company sells all of its inventory 9.5 times per year, an average of every 38.4 days (365 business days divided by the inventory turnover ratio of 9.5). Generally, a high inventory turnover ratio signals good inventory management since the faster inventory is sold, the less capital is tied up in inventory. Conversely, low turnover can suggest that a firm is carrying too much inventory or holding obsolete, slow-moving, or otherwise inferior goods.

$$\text{Inventory Turnover Ratio} = \frac{\text{Cost of Goods Sold}}{\text{Inventory}} = \frac{\$61,800}{\$6,500} = 9.51$$

C&F's lack of such a ratio highlights an important point about ratio analysis: *All ratios may not apply to all firms.* Business professionals must carefully analyze each company's operations to determine the appropriateness of a particular ratio. Frequently, unusual or abnormal ratios may signal that a particular measure should not be used in an analysis. For example, had C&F's net sales of $74,800 been mindlessly divided by its supplies of $300, one might have mistakenly concluded that the inventory turnover ratio was 249 times. Such a number is clearly irrelevant to C&F's analysis as it suggests that the company's inventory is being sold out almost on a daily basis. This ratio is not meaningful, since C&F is a service business.

Asset Turnover Ratio. The asset turnover ratio is a general measure of a firm's ability to generate revenues from its assets. Generally, the higher this ratio becomes, the smaller the investment required to generate sales and the more profitable the firm will be. Overinvestment in assets or sluggish sales are common explanations for low asset turnover ratios.

$$\frac{\text{Net Sales Revenue}}{\text{Total Assets}} = \frac{\$74,800}{\$18,958} = 3.95$$

The asset turnover ratio is very important in C&F's case given that its inventory turnover ratio is meaningless. Asset turnover indicates how many dollars of sales are being generated for each dollar invested in assets, an important indicator, particularly for a start-up business. During its first year of operation, C&F generated almost $4 in revenue for each dollar invested in assets. This is far superior to the industry average of 1.35 and may reflect Keith and Dale's cost consciousness in their new business venture.

Profitability and Performance Ratios

Three indicators commonly are used to evaluate how efficiently a firm is being managed and how successful its operations are: net profit margin ratio, return on assets or investment, and return on equity.

Net Profit Margin Ratio. The net profit margin ratio measures the firm's ability to translate sales dollars into profits after considering all revenues and expenses. A reasonable net profit margin varies from industry to industry. To evaluate this ratio properly, managers must consider the firm's asset value, its inventory and receivable turnover ratios, and its total capitalization (debt and owners' equity). However, one thing is indisputable: An excessively low net profit margin is a sign of a perilous future.

$$\frac{\text{Net Income}}{\text{Net Sales Revenue}} = \frac{\$3,958}{\$74,800} = 5.29\%$$

C&F's net profit margin of 5.29 percent is slightly lower than the industry's average of 6.7 percent. Although Keith and Dale should be concerned about this disparity, the result may simply reflect excess expenses unique to a start-up company's first year of operations.

Return on Assets. Return on assets (ROA), which is sometimes called return on investment, and return on equity are two ratios that measure the firm's overall efficiency in managing its assets and in generating return to shareholders.

Management Accounting: A Business Planning Approach

Naturally, higher results are better for each of these ratios. Moreover, if the return on equity is excessively low, this suggests that the owners' capital might be better used elsewhere. The return on assets or investment ratio frequently is used to measure performance in a firm's operating divisions.

$$\frac{\text{Net Income}}{\text{Total Assets}} = \frac{\$3,958}{\$18,958} = 20.88\%$$

C&F's ROA is more than double the industry average of 10.10 percent, indicating that the company is generating twice as much profit from every asset dollar as its industry peers generate. This result is consistent with C&F's higher asset turnover ratio and lower profit margin ratio, apparently confirming Keith and Dale's reliance on rented (higher expenses than industry peers) rather than purchased equipment (lower total assets than industry peers) during the first year of operations.

Return on Equity. Return on equity (ROE) shows profitability relative to each dollar invested by owners or stockholders. It measures the firm's ability to manage its assets to create net earnings. Since investors are interested in how much money their investments will yield, it serves as a universal metric that can be used to evaluate all businesses.

$$\frac{\text{Net Income}}{\text{Owners' Equity}} = \frac{\$3,958}{\$15,958} = 24.80\%$$

C&F's ROE exceeds that of the industry by 4.60 percent further confirming the above-average performance of the company during its first year of operations.

Summary of Financial Measures

Now that you can appreciate how ratio analysis is used to evaluate liquidity, leverage, operations, and performance, we will illustrate how managers can easily evaluate a company's business strategy by exploring the interrelationships among several of the ratios we have examined. The DuPont system can be used to evaluate how well a firm has executed its business strategy, as measured by the overall return generated for its owners. The DuPont Company, a well-known global manufacturer of chemicals, plastics, and other products, has used this technique to evaluate its performance since 1919. This tool provides managers with insight into how company decisions and activities, as measured by *several* financial ratios, interact to produce a return to shareholders (that is, ROE).

This analytical tool is particularly powerful because it allows a company's overall business strategy to be subdivided into *just three key ratios* that directly affect a manager's area of responsibility: profit margin, asset utilization (turnover), and financial leverage. This is illustrated in Exhibit 3.7.

Learning Objective 4
Demonstrate the use of financial ratios in evaluating business strategy.

Figure 3.4
Figure 3.4
Retailers like WalMart rely on key ratios to monitor the success of their operations. Turnover ratios for accounts receivable and inventory provide useful information on cash collections and inventory sales. The DuPont system ratios can also help a company evaluate how well it is achieving its business strategy as measured by the return it generates for its owners.

Using this system, managers can evaluate changes in the firm's performance (measured by return on equity) and determine whether they reflect improvement or deterioration (or some combination) in underlying business processes. The power of this tool lies in its ability to focus attention on specific areas of the company that affect performance. Exhibit 3.8 focuses on the ratios that we have already computed for C&F Enterprises that are important for this technique.

Exhibit 3.8 reveals that C&F outperformed its industry peers during its first year of operations. The DuPont system highlights those factors that caused this positive performance. Net profit margin, asset turnover, and financial leverage all affect ROE. Although trailing its industry slightly in both net profit margin and financial leverage, C&F's high asset turnover (almost three times the industry average) propelled its ROE to an above-industry return of 24.80 percent. In fact, C&F's asset turnover and net profit margin interact to produce an ROA for the company (20.88 percent) that is over double the industry average. Since these ratios represent observations of the firm's condition at a single point in time, only by examining trends in these ratios over time can managers detect shifts that might warrant further scrutiny and action.

Exhibit 3.7
The DuPont System

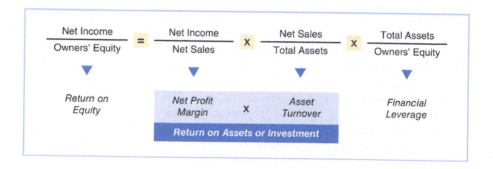

Management Accounting: A Business Planning Approach

Ratio	C&F	Industry Average
Return on Equity	24.80%	20.20%
Net Profit Margin	5.29%	6.70%
Asset Turnover	3.95	1.35
Financial Leverage	1.19	1.80

Exhibit 3.8
Using the DuPont System to
Evaluate C&F Enterprises

Other Financial Performance Measures

In addition to the fundamental ratios that we have reviewed so far in this chapter, companies use measures that incorporate some element of stock price to assess progress toward their goals. Most companies use earnings per share (net income divided by the number of shares of stock held by owners) to evaluate performance. Many firms also use the price-earnings ratio (stock price divided by earnings per share). Still others measure performance as the change in the market price of a company's stock over a specified period of time. Recently, some companies have adopted economic value added (EVA) analysis to measure the value created for stockholders during a reporting period. A common way to describe EVA is that it represents a company's profits after deducting the costs of raising capital. Whatever the measure, all of these techniques have one goal: to unmask the basic relationships hidden in the financial statements.

The Balanced Scorecard: Financial Performance Measures

Companies use many of the financial ratios discussed in this chapter to evaluate performance in the financial dimension of the balanced scorecard. Exactly which measures a firm relies upon depends on the industry in which it competes. Exhibit 3.9 describes several of the financial indicators more commonly used in ten well-known industries.

Return on assets and equity, operating income, earnings per share, stock price, and cash flow appear to be industry favorites. In addition to these, companies select other measures of financial performance that best reflect the unique nature of their industry and business processes. The next chapter will explore the links between these financial performance measures and the business processes that cause them.

Industry	Performance Measures
Automobile, Chemical, Computer, Pharmaceutical	Return on equity, return on assets, earnings per share, economic value added, stock price.
Banking	Operating income, capital ratio, income to expense ratio after loan losses.
Engineering and Construction	Return on capital, cash flow, project profitability, sales backlog.
Insurance	Return on capital, gross premiums written, value added per employee, assets managed.
Real estate	Operating income, return on investment, market value.

Exhibit 3.9
Balanced Scorecard
Financial Measures

Summary

This chapter reviewed the role of traditional financial statements and ratios in measuring and evaluating a company's operating performance. The primary financial statements used by stakeholders to assess a company's historical and prospective performance are the balance sheet, income statement, statement of cash flows, and statement of owners' or stockholders' equity. Since technology has made such financial information available to the market at little or no, business professionals are no longer rewarded for simply preparing such reports. Instead, managers now are expected to apply their analytical skills using such tools as ratio analysis to explain company operations in terms of liquidity, leverage, activity or operations, and profitability. The DuPont system of financial analysis was introduced as a powerful technique that focuses managers on underlying business processes when evaluating changes in company performance.

Summary of Learning Objectives

1. **Review the purpose of financial statements and their form.** Financial statements provide stakeholders with a wealth of information that can be used to assess a firm's performance. The balance sheet, built on the fundamental accounting equation, shows a firm's financial position at the end of a reporting period. The statement of changes in owners' equity describes changes in the equity accounts during a fiscal period. The income statement lists the firm's revenues, expenses, and net income for the reporting period. Finally, the statement of cash flows summarizes the increases and decreases in a firm's cash balance.

2. **Describe the use of pro forma financial statements.** Pro forma financial statements are used by managers to project a firm's future operations and financial position. Managers must use their insight to transform this data into information that can be used to monitor the implementation of a business plan.

3. **Discuss and illustrate the use of financial ratio analysis.** Managers use ratios to explain the relationships between financial statement elements. This gives an indication as to a company's financial health. Liquidity ratios indicate whether a business has enough assets to pay maturing obligations. Leverage ratios assess the extent to which a firm relies on debt capital rather than equity to finance operating and investing activities. Operating ratios monitor how effectively the business utilizes its resources. Profitability ratios are used to evaluate the overall success of a firm's operations.

4. **Demonstrate the use of financial ratios in evaluating business strategy.** The DuPont system uses ratios to evaluate how well a firm has executed its business strategy as measured by the overall return generated for its owners. Managers are expected to evaluate changes in a firm's performance and determine whether they reflect improvement or deterioration in the underlying business processes.

Management Accounting: A Business Planning Approach

Glossary of Terms

Accounts receivable turnover ratio An activity or operating ratio that reports how frequently collections from customers are received during the year.

Assets The economic resources controlled by a company used to pursue strategy.

Asset turnover ratio An activity or operating ratio that measures a firm's ability to generate revenues from its assets.

Balance sheet A primary financial statement that details a firm's financial position (assets, liabilities, and owners' equity) at the end of a reporting period.

Current assets Assets such as cash, accounts receivable, inventory, and prepaid expenses that can be converted to cash within one year or the normal operating cycle of the firm, whichever is longer.

Current liabilities Debts and obligations of a firm that must be repaid using current assets (generally within one year).

Current ratio (or working capital ratio) A measure of the firm's solvency which indicates its ability to pay current liabilities from current assets.

Debt to equity ratio A leverage ratio that compares what the firm owes to creditors with what has been invested by the owners.

DuPont system A financial analysis tool that uses several financial ratios to provide insight into how firm decisions and activities interact to produce a return to shareholders.

Earnings per share A financial performance measure computed by dividing net income by the number of shares of stock held by owners.

Economic value added (EVA) A financial performance measure intended to assess the value created for stockholders during a reporting period. Many view this measure as a company's profits after deducting the costs of raising financial capital.

Expenses Costs incurred by a company to produce revenues that are reported on the income statement.

Financial leverage ratio A leverage ratio that reports the proportion of a firm's assets that managers control relative to the amount of the owners' investment in a company.

Financial statements Financial reports that summarize the economic transactions affecting a business. Four primary statements comprise a set of financial statements: the balance sheet, the statement of changes in owners' equity, the income statement, and the statement of cash flows.

Financing activities Company activities related to the issuance or retirement of debt or equity, as well as the payment of dividends to shareholders.

Fixed assets Economic resources acquired for longer-term business use such as land, buildings, vehicles, and equipment.

Gross profit (also known as *gross margin*) The income statement amount that results when cost of goods or services sold is deducted from sales revenue.

Income statement The primary financial statement that lists the firm's revenues, expenses, and net income or loss for a reporting period.

Intangible assets Economic resources that have no physical substance such as goodwill, copyrights, and patents.

Inventory turnover ratio An activity or operating ratio that measures the efficiency of a firm's efforts to manage and sell its inventory.

Investing activities Company activities related to the purchase and sale of noncurrent (fixed or intangible) assets.

Leverage ratios Financial ratios that evaluate the extent to which firms rely on debt rather than owners' equity to finance operating and investing activities.

Liabilities Claims on a firm's assets by creditors.

Liquidity ratios Financial ratios that provide insight into whether a business has sufficient assets, either in cash or easily convertible to cash, to pay maturing obligations as they come due.

Long-term liabilities Debts and obligations of a firm for which payment is due after one year.

Net income (loss) The key income statement amount equal to total revenues minus total expenses.

Net profit margin ratio A profitability and performance ratio that measures a company's ability to transform sales dollars into profits after considering all revenues and expenses.

Net sales revenue Revenues from sales recorded by a firm less the amount of products returned by customers.

Operating activities Activities of a business that are directly associated with the acquisition and sale of a company's products and services.

Owners' equity Claims on a firm's assets by its owners. Generally, this represents the owners' capital contributions to the business plus undistributed earnings.

Pro forma financial statements Financial statement projections of the firm's future operations based on a number of assumptions regarding future revenues, expenses, investment activity, financing arrangements, and operating activities.

Quick ratio (or acid test ratio) A conservative measure of liquidity, which demonstrates a firm's ability to pay current liabilities from current assets excluding inventory and prepaid expenses.

Ratio analysis A process in which ratios computed from accounting data are compared and analyzed to develop insights about the performance and business risks of a firm.

Retained earnings The firm's earnings that have not yet been distributed to owners.

Return on assets A profitability and performance ratio that measures the firm's ability to manage its assets to create net income.

Return on equity A profitability and performance ratio that measures the firm's ability to generate a return to shareholders.

Revenues Income generated from product or service sales, or other sources such as rent, investments, or interest that is reported on the income statement.

Statement of cash flows A primary financial statement that summarizes a firm's cash inflows and outflows for a period by operating, investing, and financing activities.

Statement of changes in owners' equity A primary financial statement that details transactions affecting the balance sheet equity accounts during a financial reporting period.

Management Accounting: A Business Planning Approach

Chapter Review Questions

1. List the four main reports that make up a complete set of financial statements and describe the information contained in each.
2. To whom are financial statements useful and why?
3. Describe the fundamental accounting equation and its relationship to the balance sheet.
4. List and describe three classes or types of assets contained in the balance sheet.
5. How do current liabilities differ from long-term liabilities?
6. What is meant by *owners' equity*?
7. Define the four primary income statement items: *revenues, expenses, gross profit,* and *net income.*
8. What types of cash flows are classified as *operating activities* in a statement of cash flows?
9. What types of cash flows are classified as *investing activities* in a statement of cash flows?
10. What types of cash flows are classified as *financing activities* in a statement of cash flows?
11. Define *pro forma financial statements* and describe how they differ from a company's typical end-of-fiscal-period financial statements.
12. What are two possible options for preparing the pro forma income statement? How do they differ from each other?
13. What is meant by *ratio analysis*?
14. List and describe two ratios commonly used to assess whether a business has sufficient assets to pay obligations as they mature. How should a manager interpret the relative value of each ratio?
15. List and describe two ratios commonly used to evaluate the extent to which companies rely on debt rather than on owners' equity to finance operating and investing activities. How should a manager interpret the relative value of each ratio?
16. List and describe three ratios commonly used to monitor how effectively businesses use their resources. How should a manager interpret the relative value of each ratio?
17. List and describe three ratios commonly used to evaluate the success of company operations. How should a manager interpret the relative value of each ratio?
18. Is debt a "bad thing"? Discuss both the potential benefits and disadvantages of using debt to finance a company's operations.
19. Describe how the DuPont system of financial analysis can be used to evaluate business strategy execution.
20. What four ratios does the DuPont system rely upon to evaluate business strategy? Describe how the four relate to each other and how each provides insight into a firm's business processes.

Exercises and Problems

1. In which financial statement can each of the following data be found? Why would each of these items be of interest to a stakeholder?
   a. Inventory
   b. Cash collected from customers
   c. Stock issued to owners
   d. Depreciation expense on equipment
   e. Income taxes paid
   f. Salary expense
   g. Dividends declared and paid
   h. Loan from bank

2. In which balance sheet category (assets, liabilities, or owners' equity) would each of the following items belong?
   a. Prepaid advertising
   b. Cash
   c. Accounts receivable
   d. Accounts payable
   e. Retained earnings
   f. Common stock
   g. Inventory

3. In which section (operating, investing, or financing) of the statement of cash flows would each of the following items appear?
   a. Cash paid for interest
   b. Cash collected from issuing common stock
   c. Cash collected from customers
   d. Cash paid for equipment
   e. Cash paid for salaries and wages

4. This chapter discusses four categories of financial ratios (liquidity, leverage, activity, and profitability). Identify the category to which each of the following ratios belongs:
   a. Return on assets
   b. Inventory turnover ratio
   c. Current ratio
   d. Return on equity
   e. Debt to equity ratio

5. This chapter discusses four categories of financial ratios (liquidity, leverage, activity, and profitability). Identify the category to which each of the following ratios belongs:
   a. Quick ratio
   b. Financial leverage ratio
   c. Asset turnover ratio
   d. Net profit margin ratio
   e. Accounts receivable turnover ratio

6. For each of the following businesses, identify at least three performance measures for the balanced scorecard's financial dimension. Explain how your choices best reflect the unique nature of each company.
   a. Sports bar
   b. Miniature golf course
   c. Bakery
   d. Computer electronics store
   e. Backpack manufacturer

7. Speedy Delivery Company started its business on January 1, 20X1. The company's balance sheet and income statement at the end of its first year of operations follow.

Speedy Delivery Balance Sheet
December 31, 20X1

Assets

Cash		$36,088
Accounts Receivable		1,500
Supplies		300
Prepaid Advertising		2,000
Equipment	$ 5,000	
Less Accumulated Depreciation	(600)	
Equipment (net)		4,400
Total Assets		$44,288

Liabilities and Owners' Equity

Accounts Payable	$ 5,400
Long-Term Note Payable	3,000
Common Stock	25,000
Retained Earnings	10,888
Total Liabilities and Owners' Equity	$44,288

Speedy Delivery Income Statement
For the Year Ended December 31, 20X1

Service Revenue		$67,000
Cost of Services Sold:		
Salaries and Wages	$25,000	
Rentals	12,000	
Supplies	1,200	
Fuel	500	
Depreciation	600	
Total Cost of Services Sold		39,300
Gross Profit		$27,700
Operating Expenses:		
Advertising		$3,000
Bookkeeping Services		2,000
Interest		200
Taxes		5,612
Other		6,000
Net Income		$10,888

Based on the financial statements provided, compute the following ratios:

a. Return on equity
b. Return on assets
c. Financial leverage
d. Net profit margin ratio
e. Asset turnover ratio
f. Accounts receivable turnover
g. Current ratio

8. Chesterbrook Donuts provided the following data from its financial statements for 20X1 and 20X2:

Chesterbrook Donuts

On December 31	20X1	20X2
Inventory	$5,000	$3,000
Current assets	12,000	8,000
Total assets	45,000	40,000
Current liabilities	1,500	1,000
Total liabilities	22,000	19,000
Total owners' equity	23,000	21,000
For the year ended December 31	**20X1**	**20X2**
Sales revenue	$50,000	$49,000
Net income	2,500	2,000

Compute the following ratios for 20X1 and 20X2. For each ratio, indicate whether it has increased or decreased and whether the change is favorable or unfavorable.

a. Asset turnover
b. Financial leverage
c. Return on assets
d. Return on equity
e. Net profit margin
f. Current ratio
g. Quick ratio

9. We-Frame-It Shops provided the following data from its financial statements for 20X1 and 20X2:

We-Frame-It Shops

On December 31	20X1	20X2
Accounts receivable	$5,500	$3,500
Inventory	8,000	8,000
Current assets	16,000	14,000
Total assets	26,000	24,000
Current liabilities	9,000	10,000
Total liabilities	17,000	14,000
Total owners' equity	9,000	10,000
For the year ended December 31		
Sales revenue	$32,000	$41,000
Cost of goods sold	18,000	23,000
Net income	(1,000)	2,000

Compute the following ratios for 20X1 and 20X2. For each ratio, indicate whether it has increased or decreased and whether change is favorable or unfavorable.

a. Current ratio
b. Asset turnover
c. Inventory turnover ratio
d. Financial leverage

e. Return on assets
f. Return on equity
g. Net profit margin

10. Big Red Enterprises and True Blue Company compete in the same industry. Each company's financial results for the most recent year are presented below.

On December 31, 20X1	Big Red	True Blue
Total assets	$100,000	$80,000
Total liabilities	80,000	30,000
Total owners' equity	20,000	50,000
For the year ended December 31, 20X1		
Sales revenue	$120,000	$100,000
Net income	12,000	11,000

a. For each company, compute the following ratios:
   i. Return on equity
   ii. Financial leverage
   iii. Return on assets
   iv. Asset turnover
   v. Net profit margin

b. Based on your findings, in which company would you rather invest? Why?

11. Atlantic Company and Pacific, Inc. compete in the same industry. Each company's financial results for the most recent year are presented below.

On December 31, 20X1	Atlantic	Pacific
Total assets	$50,000	$45,000
Total liabilities	10,000	40,000
Total owners' equity	40,000	5,000
For the year ended December 31, 20X1		
Sales revenue	$25,000	$35,000
Net income	10,000	12,000

a. For each company, compute the following ratios:
   i. Return on equity
   ii. Financial leverage
   iii. Return on assets
   iv. Asset turnover
   v. Net profit margin

b. Based on your findings, in which company would you rather invest? Why?

12. Assume that Iverson Company reported $20,000 in net income in its most recent year. Some of its financial ratios for that year are as follows:

Return on equity	33.33%
Financial leverage	1.333
Return on assets	25.00%
Asset turnover	0.625
Net profit margin	40.00%

Based on the data provided, compute the following financial statement amounts:
a. Total assets
b. Total liabilities
c. Total owners' equity
d. Net sales revenue

13. Assume that Churchill Company reported $40,000 in net income in its most recent year. Some of its financial ratios for that year are as follows:

Return on equity	50.00%
Financial leverage	1.250
Return on assets	40.00%
Asset turnover	1.000
Net profit margin	40.00%

Based on the data provided, compute the following financial statement amounts:
a. Total assets
b. Total liabilities
c. Total owners' equity
d. Net sales revenue

14. Select a public company (one whose stock is actively traded on any major exchange) in which you are interested, or which your instructor has previously assigned. Do not pick a bank, insurance company, brokerage firm, any type of financial services entity, or a firm that operates in a regulated industry. It is very important that the company you select reports accounts receivable, inventory, and debt on its balance sheet. Once you have selected a company that meets these criteria, perform the following:
a. Using the Securities and Exchange Commission's EDGAR website, access, download, and save your company's most recent Annual Report (Form 10-K). For detailed instructions on how to access a company's 10-K, please see the Business Beacon early in this chapter. Click on the filing and then search the 10-K for the balance sheet and income statement. Once you have found them, print them out, as you will be required to attach these to your assignment.
b. Enter the balance sheet and income statement information into Excel and compute the following ratios: current ratio, quick ratio, financial leverage ratio, debt to equity ratio, accounts receivable turnover, inventory turnover,

asset turnover, net profit margin ratio, return on assets, and return on equity. Depending on the industry of the company that you select, several of these ratios may not be appropriate. If you find this to be the case, be prepared to thoroughly explain why the ratio is not appropriate for your company.

    c. Prepare a summary report that lists all of the required ratios (including detailed explanations for any ratio not considered appropriate for the company analyzed). Attach the company's balance sheet and income statement.

15. Select a public company (one whose stock is actively traded on any major exchange) in which you are interested, or which your instructor has previously assigned. Do not pick a bank, insurance company, brokerage firm, any type of financial services entity, or a firm that operates in a regulated industry. It is necessary that the company you select reports accounts receivable, inventory, and debt on its balance sheet. Once you have selected a company that meets these criteria, perform the following:

    a. Download the following ratios for your company from a business information website: current ratio, quick ratio, financial leverage ratio, debt to equity ratio, accounts receivable turnover, inventory turnover, asset turnover, net profit margin ratio, return on assets, and return on equity. You may have to consult multiple websites to find all of these ratios. Depending on the company or websites that you select, several of these ratios may not be available. If you find this to be the case, be prepared to thoroughly explain why the ratio is not appropriate for your company or why you believe it not to be available. Once you have located the ratios, print them out, as you will be required to attach these to your assignment.

    b. Prepare a summary report that lists all of the required ratios and the related Web source(s). Include detailed explanations for any ratio that could not be found, (i.e., why it is not appropriate for the company or why it is not available on the Web). Attach the website documentation used to prepare your summary report.

16. Perform Exercises 14 and 15 above. List all of the ratios that you computed in Exercise 14 together with each of the ratios collected on the Web in Exercise 15. Are each of the ratios the same? For each ratio that is not the same, explain why those obtained from the Web differ from your calculations. What conclusions can you draw about the "quality" of your information vis-à-vis what is available on the Web?

17. Select a public company (one whose stock is actively traded on any major exchange) in which you are interested or which your instructor has previously assigned. Using the four DuPont system ratios for the last two fiscal years, briefly describe the operating performance of your company. You may either compute the ratios yourself from data that you download from EDGAR, or you can use ratios that you find on the Web. However, do one or the other, not both, and make sure that your ratios reflect the same fiscal period. This analysis should not simply restate the ratios that you have calculated or found on the Web. Instead, you must develop conclusions about the company's operations. Were they favorable, unfavorable, or other? How do they compare between years? How do the DuPont ratios interact to affect shareholder returns? Why and how did you arrive at your conclusion? Be insightful, not descriptive.

Transaction Processing Review

Business professionals must have a basic understanding of how economic events are captured, processed, and converted into financial statement data if they are to properly transform such data into useful information for decision-making. The purpose of this mini-case is to review the fundamentals of transaction processing.

Transaction Processing Example

To review these principles, consider the following data from Deluxe Printing. Assume that Deluxe Printing started the fiscal period with the following account balances:

Deluxe Printing	
Account	**Beginning Balance**
Cash	$9,000
Accounts Receivable	12,000
Prepaid Rent	7,500
Supplies	400
Computers	35,000
Accumulated Depreciation, Computers	6,000
Accounts Payable	12,500
Common Stock	12,000

During the year, Deluxe recognized $75,000 of revenue and collected $50,000 of cash from accounts receivable. Other information from the accounting period included the following:

Deluxe Printing	
	Amount
Cash paid for rent in advance	$5,500
Rent expense from the income statement	4,800
Cash paid for supplies	850
Supplies expense from the income statement	900
Depreciation expense from the income statement	3,500
Operating expense incurred on account	38,000
Cash paid to settle accounts payable	30,000
Cash invested by owners for common stock	5,000
Cash distributions to owners for dividends	700

These data can be used to construct financial statements for the end of the year. The best method is to use a spreadsheet with columns for all balance sheet and income statement items.

The first step is to determine the opening balance of retained earnings. To do so, the beginning account balances should be entered into the appropriate columns. Retained earnings represents the missing balance necessary to keep the traditional accounting equation in balance. In this case, the beginning balance would be $33,400. Next, each transaction should be entered into the spreadsheet. Doing so completes the spreadsheet shown in Exhibit 3.10. The ending balances represent the totals that would appear on the financial statements. It is important to note that the total assets ($98,000) equal the total liabilities and owners' equity at the end of the period.

You can use the same technique to analyze a start-up enterprise. Set the beginning balances at zero and construct the pro forma financial statements by creating a similar worksheet and adding economic events as they are expected to occur.

Required

Using the following information provided by Frances Chan, C&F's bookkeeper, prove the accuracy of C&F's 20×1 financial statements reported in this chapter. Prepare a worksheet that generates each of C&F's financial statements (Exhibits 3.1 through 3.4 in this chapter). Use the worksheet format illustrated in Exhibit 3.10 and tailor it to C&F's landscaping business.

During the year, C&F recognized $74,800 of revenue. Of that amount, $46,000 was immediately collected in cash upon performance of services and $23,300 was subsequently collected from accounts receivable. Other information from the accounting period included the following:

C&F Enterprises, Inc.

	Amount
Cash received from issuance of common stock	$12,000
Cash received from long-term bank note	2,000
Cash paid for equipment purchase on January 1 (five-year life)	3,000
Cash paid for advertising on January 1 (two-year contract)	9,600
Cash paid for wages during the year	43,000
Cash paid for bookkeeping services	2,500
Cash paid for supplies during the year ($300 not used)	3,300
Cash paid for equipment rental during the year	11,000
Cash paid for fuel during the year	700
Cash paid for note interest on December 31	200
Cash paid for taxes	2,042
Expenses incurred but not paid during the year	3,000
Cash paid on unpaid accounts payable	2,000
Depreciation expense or equipment	600

Exhibit 3.10

Transaction Processing for Deluxe Printing

	Balance Sheet							Liabilities	Owner's Equity		Income Statement			Statement of Cash Flows	
	Assets						=						Net		
Event	Cash	A/R	Prepaid Rent	Supplies	Computers	Accumulated Depreciation		A/P	Common Stock	Retained Earnings	Revenue –	Expenses =	Income	Amount	Activity
Beginning Balances	$ 9,000	$ 12,000	$ 7,500	$ 400	$35,000	$(6,000)		$ 12,500	$12,000	$ 33,400					
Revenue on account		$ 75,000								$ 75,000	$75,000		$ 75,000		
Cash collections	$ 50,000	$(50,000)												$ 50,000	Operating
Cash paid for rent	$ (5,500)		$ 5,500											$ (5,500)	Operating
Rent expense			$(4,800)							$ (4,800)		$ 4,800	$ (4,800)		
Cash paid for supplies	$ (850)			$ 850										$ (850)	Operating
Supplies expense				$(900)						$ (900)		$ 900	$ (900)		
Depreciation expense						$(3,500)				$ (3,500)		$ 3,500	$ (3,500)		
Expenses on account								$ 38,000		$(38,000)		$38,000	$(38,000)		
Cash paid for A/P	$(30,000)							$(30,000)						$(30,000)	Operating
Cash from owners	$ 5,000								$5,000					$ 5,000	Financing
Cash paid to owners	$ (700)									$ (700)				$ (700)	Financing
Totals	$ 26,950	$ 37,000	$ 8,200	$ 350	$35,000	$(9,500)		$ 20,500	$17,000	$ 60,500	$75,000	$47,200	$ 27,800	$ 17,950	

Total assets $98,000

Total liabilities and owners' equity $98,000

Researching Financial Performance

Most business plans seem to be good ideas, at first glance. However, investors are most interested in the expected financial performance of the start-up enterprise. A detailed financial plan helps potential investors and lenders assess the relative risk of the proposed operation. After all, financial statements are the universal measure by which all businesses can be evaluated.

Pro Forma Financial Information for the Start-Up Business

Since a start-up enterprise, by its nature, does not have a history, investors expect pro forma financial statements to be supported by an industry comparison. A quality business plan should include the following data (with all assumptions clearly documented and justified).

- Three years of projected income statements, balance sheets, and statements of cash flows.
- A monthly operating plan for the first year of business.
- A description of the initial equity or debt capital needed and a plan to finance the growth of the business.
- A schedule of all financial ratios relevant to the business and industry.
- A comparison to industry averages and an explanation of any unusual or significant differences.

These data allow readers to assess the profitability of the firm, the expected level of financial capital required, and whether there will be adequate cash flow. These judgments are critical; unless investors feel comfortable with the answers, they will be unwilling to provide financing for the enterprise. Pro forma financial statements are subject to debate, but those that lack credibility are unlikely to receive even slight consideration.

Library Research

To aid in the development of pro forma financial statements, analysts compare them with those of similar businesses in the same industry whenever possible. Several organizations publish industry operating statistics and ratios, and many of these may be found in your library in hard copy or online:

- *Risk Management Associates* (formerly Robert Morris Associates) publishes its *Annual Statement Studies.*
- *Dun & Bradstreet, Inc.* annually publishes *Industry Norms and Key Business Ratios.*

In addition to industry comparisons, financial managers analyze firm ratios over time.

- *Almanac of Business and Industrial Financial Ratios* provides balance sheets, income statements and ratios, for businesses of different sizes across industries.
- The *Standard & Poor's* industry surveys are published throughout the year. Each survey provides current financial data and discussion of industry trends.

(continued)

Assignment

The guides we have listed should provide the basis for assessing whether the pro forma financial statements included in your business plan are reasonable. Visit your college or university library and complete the following tasks:

1. Identify which of the above or similar reference resources are available in your library.
2. In each of these reference resources (or for as many as possible), find the industry statistics (financial statements and ratios) that most closely match the business that you propose to start.

Make copies of this data so that you can refer to it later when preparing, evaluating, and defending your formal business plan.

Image Credits

Chapter 4

1. Define value drivers and explain their usefulness in understanding business processes.

2. Identify the resources necessary to support the value chain.

3. Define business risk and describe the uncertainties affecting value creation.

4. Discuss how companies identify and manage business risk.

Business Processes and Risks

Company managers need to understand the link between business processes and financial results. To do so, they must understand the variety of risks that can influence the success of their operating activities. In the first two chapters, we discussed business strategy, market forces, and how organizations implement business processes to create value for their stakeholders. Chapter 3 explored the use of financial statements to evaluate company performance. In this chapter, we explore how business processes influence a company's financial results and how business risk affects those same processes. We then discuss strategies that companies use to manage business risks. The Business Planning Application at the end of this chapter will help you to complete the risk assessment portion of a business plan.

Linking Business Processes and Financial Results

In the previous chapter, we discussed the common financial ratios that investors use to compare companies. Since financial statements measure the outcomes of a firm's business activities, they provide a logical starting point for thinking about business processes. However, to fully understand the outcomes presented in balance sheets and income statements, it is necessary to understand how a firm's many business processes affect what is reported in these statements. Such insight is critical in analyzing past performance and developing realistic plans and projections of future operating performance.

As introduced in Chapter 1, the balanced scorecard communicates a company's strategy through a series of causal linkages. We saw how employee training can improve business processes that in turn influence customer satisfaction and ultimately affect financial performance. In Chapters 2 and 3, we reviewed a variety of financial and nonfinancial performance measures that companies use to assess progress along each of the balanced scorecard's four dimensions. Exhibit 4.1 illustrates again how business processes impact outcomes. It motivates managers to ask tough questions about how they are conducting their business: what is the organization's strategy, how do mission and strategy distinguish the business from its competition, what must the company specifically do to succeed, and how will the firm measure its performance? Simply put, how will the company manage the causal linkages between its people and its operating results? The shaded area in Exhibit 4.1 highlights the focus of our discussion in this chapter: the link between business processes and financial results.

Learning Objective 1
Define value drivers and
explain their usefulness
in understanding business
processes.

As discussed in Chapter 2, the business processes that make up a company's value chain include a wide variety of activities. How well these activities are carried out ultimately determines the worth of the company to its owners. Therefore, these activities are often referred to as **value drivers**. The next sections explore the primary value drivers that affect the results reported in balance sheets and income statements.

Balance Sheet Value Drivers

Every decision that managers make affects the company's balance sheet in some way. For example, managers routinely make choices about the amount and type of assets that the business needs. In the short term, managers must decide how to use current assets like cash, receivables, and inventories to meet daily, weekly, and monthly customer demands. Over the long run, companies choose how and when to acquire, maintain, or dispose of property, plant, and equipment and how to utilize intangible assets, such as trademarks, copyrights, and patents. To acquire assets, firms make choices about the mix, types, and amounts of liabilities and owners' equity. Liability decisions often involve the selection and management of the types, amounts, and timing of short-term credit and long-term debt. Owners' equity is the source of financing that generates funds by issuing stock to investors and reinvesting company profits.

In Chapter 3, you analyzed C&F Enterprises, Inc.'s balance sheet at the end of its first year of operations. Exhibit 4.2 annotates C&F's year-end balances by showing the business process value drivers that affect the reported financial position. Accounts receivable is driven by Keith and Dale's collection efforts. Their willingness to extend credit for their services and the likelihood of collection

Figure 4.1
**Managers routinely
make choices that affect
their company's financial
statements. For example,
decisions affecting assets like
the purchase of real estate or
the use of equipment will have
an impact on a company's
balance sheet.**

Exhibit 4.1
Linking Strategy to Results

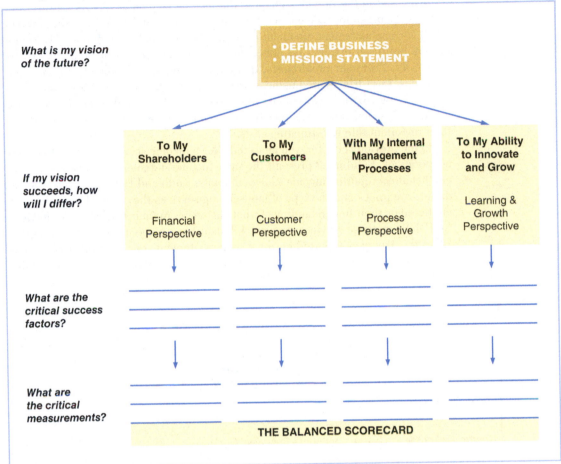

depends on the creditworthiness of their customers. Prepaid advertising is driven by their marketing decision to enter into a multiyear, Internet advertising contract. Limiting the purchase of equipment drives down the reported fixed asset amounts on C&F's balance sheet.

Other basic business processes affect liabilities and owners' equity. Current liabilities reflect the willingness of suppliers to extend credit to C&F and the company's commitment to pay its bills on time. Keith and Dale also must decide how much to borrow and when to repay loans. Although C&F's equity financing comes primarily from Keith and Dale's investments, retained earnings is driven by C&F's net income. C&F's value drivers and their link to the balance sheet focus Keith and Dale on the operating, investing, and financing activities of their business. The factors that drive company profitability are discussed in the next section.

Income Statement Value Drivers

As discussed in the previous chapter, the income statement reports a firm's revenues, expenses, and net income for a given period. Two types of value drivers affect income statement amounts: revenue drivers and cost drivers. Revenue drivers are those factors that affect the quantity and prices of products or services sold. Customer preferences, quantity discounts, and promotions are some examples. Cost drivers are business process factors that drive expense totals. For example, ingredients, equipment, and entrée complexity influence the cost of a restaurant's menu items. Chapter 6 will explore cost drivers in more detail and their important role in estimating costs.

In the previous chapter, you analyzed C&F's income statement for its first year of operations. Exhibit 4.3 presents the same income statement with the value drivers that affect reported income statement totals. Keith and Dale's primary revenue drivers are prices and the type of landscaping services they offer. These offerings are based on their understanding of what customers in their market value and how C&F delivers those services. Exhibit 4.3 also shows some of the cost drivers that affect the expenses reported on the income statement. For example, cost of services sold includes five major categories of expenses: salaries and wages, rentals,

Exhibit 4.2

The Value Drivers That Influence C&F Enterprises' Balance Sheet

Value Drivers	C&F Enterprises, Inc. Balance Sheet December 31, 20X1		
	Assets		
	Cash		$ 5,958
Customers' credit worthiness ⟶	Accounts Receivable		5,500
	Supplies		300
Marketing choices ⟶	Prepaid Advertising		4,800
Machine purchases and usage ⟶	Equipment	$3,000	
	Less Accumulated Depreciation	(600)	
	Equipment (net)		2,400
	Total Assets		$18,958
	Liabilities and Owners' Equity		
Suppliers' terms ⟶	Accounts Payable		$1,000
Loan management ⟶	Long-Term Note Payable		2,000
	Common Stock		12,000
Profitability and dividend policy ⟶	Retained Earnings		3,958
	Total Liabilities and Owners' Equity		$18,958

Management Accounting: A Business Planning Approach

supplies, fuel, and depreciation. Salaries and wages depend on Keith and Dale's hiring and staffing decisions about the number of workers and their experience. Keith and Dale decided to rent most of their physical capital (landscaping equipment). This decision *drives* rental expense, depreciation on owned equipment, and fuel costs.

C&F must employ reliable people, use quality equipment, and operate efficiently to minimize unnecessary costs, such as overtime pay, wasted fuel, and repairs. C&F also incurs administrative costs each period. Keith and Dale's decision to use certain marketing tools drive advertising costs. The relative financial complexity of their business, as represented by the number of transactions, drives fees charged by the bookkeeper for accounting services. Finally, their decision to borrow money results in interest expense. Collectively, these examples demonstrate the complexity of running a business and highlight the importance of understanding how business processes affect income statement results.

Exhibit 4.3
Value Drivers That Influence C&F Enterprises' Income Statement

	C&F Enterprises, Inc. Income Statement For the Year Ended December 31, 20X1		
Value Drivers			
Service Offerings ⟶	Service Revenue		$74,800
	Cost of Services Sold:		
Hiring and staffing ⟶	Salaries and Wages	$43,000	
Equipment leasing ⟶	Rentals	11,000	
Purchasing ⟶	Supplies	3,000	
Equipment age ⟶	Fuel	700	
and usage ⟶	Depreciation	600	
	Total Cost of Services Sold		58,300
	Gross Profit		$16,500
	Operating Expenses:		
Marketing decisions ⟶	Advertising		4,800
Financial complexity ⟶	Bookkeeping Services		2,500
Borrowing ⟶	Interest		200
	Taxes		2,042
	Other		3,000
	Net Income		$ 3,958

Converting Resources into Results

Learning Objective 2
Identify the resources
necessary to support the
value chain.

As introduced in Chapter 2 and shown again in Exhibit 4.4, the value chain is the interrelated set of five basic business processes necessary to execute business strategy. If firms effectively manage these business processes, they will satisfy their customers, owners, and other stakeholders.

Exhibit 4.5 shows the role of the value chain in converting resources into financial results. As introduced in Chapter 1 and depicted at the bottom of Exhibit 4.5, companies need three fundamental resources to create value for stakeholders: human, physical, and financial capital. Companies rely on people, or human capital, to manage the business and to utilize physical capital such as machines, buildings, and information technology. Finally, companies require financial capital to pay workers, purchase inventories, acquire fixed assets, and cover operating expenses. Limited or insufficient amounts of any of these resources can jeopardize the success of business processes and the company's ability to create value for its stakeholders.

The following questions can be used to determine what resources are needed to support the value chain:

- What skills and experience do employees need to manage business processes?

- What equipment and technology are needed to run basic business processes?

- How much financial capital do operating, investing, and financing activities require?

To answer these difficult questions, organizations need managers who possess a thorough understanding of business processes, who know how processes drive

Exhibit 4.4
Business Value Chain

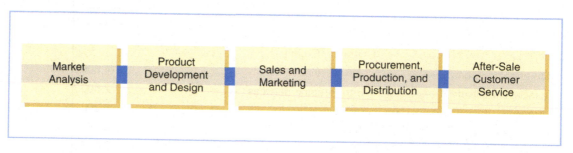

Management Accounting: A Business Planning Approach

Figure 4.2
Companies require human, physical, and financial capital to convert resources into financial results. In this case, a candy manufacturer used financial capital to acquire both the human capital (employees) and physical capital (equipment and ingredients).

financial outcomes, and who recognize the risks that underlie business activities. When executing strategy, managers take risks in running business processes as they convert financial, human, and physical capital resources into financial results. The next section discusses how companies identify, assess, and manage business risks.

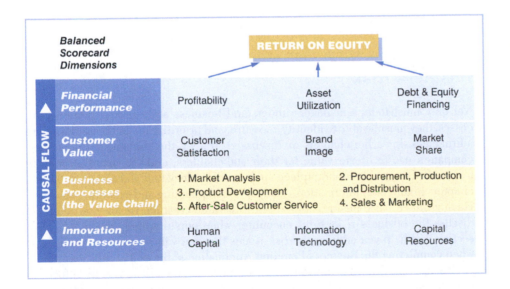

Exhibit 4.5
Converting Resources into Results

Managing Risk to Drive Value

Many companies still don't realize that how they approach risk management can create and sustain or destroy shareholder value. Ernst & Young's (EY) Global Enterprise Risk Management practice has devised a four-step approach to risk management.

Step 1—Figure out what shareholders value about your company. EY suggests talking with equity analysts, institutional investors, and other members of the investment community to understand what their shareholders desire. For example, do they value a long-term increase in their investment's value, or current dividend payouts? Then you can identify the business processes that contribute to this perceived value and break them down to ones that create value and can be used to measure performance.

Step 2—Identify the risks around the key shareholder-value drivers. You'll need to assess all forms of risk that affect the business. Capital markets specialists can help with industry-specific risks, and analysts can help with intangible parameters such as quality of management, people competency, and brand strength and reputation. You also need to do some internal risk assessment.

Step 3—Determine how you are going to handle the risks. This means you need to figure out what shareholders would consider acceptable, such as avoiding the risk; managing, insuring, or hedging it; or implementing a combination of treatments.

Step 4—Tell shareholders what you're going to do about the risks. EY emphasizes that the long-term growth of your company depends on keeping your shareholders informed about your risk management program. This is especially important right now, given the state of the markets and the economy.

Source: Kathy Williams, "Four Steps to Managing Risks," *Strategic Finance*, Institute of Management Accountants, May 2001. Copyright IMA; reprinted with permission from the Institute of Management Accountants, Montvale, New Jersey, www.imanet.org.

Business Risk

Learning Objective 3
Define business risk and describe the uncertainties affecting value creation.

Not only must today's managers understand business strategy and related processes, they must be able to identify, measure, and prioritize the business risks that a firm faces. In earlier chapters we discussed strategy, the fundamental processes company's use to create value for their stakeholders, and the major structural forces affecting today's marketplace such as technology and globalization. These chapters highlighted information's critical role in planning and executing strategy. Having linked basic business processes with value creation, we are now ready to discuss the business risks firms encounter when pursuing their strategies. This section will help you address the risk issues that you will be required to discuss when completing the Business Planning Application at the end of this chapter.

Business risk is the threat that an event or action will adversely affect an organization's ability to achieve its business objectives and execute its strategies successfully. As we have seen, a firm creates value by interacting with its stakeholders and environment. During this value creation process, managers take risks as they attempt to convert financial, human, and physical resources into the goods and services their customers demand. However, value creation is not guaranteed. In fact, the complex set of stakeholder relationships and process interactions that characterize business create many uncertainties that companies attempt to manage.

Recently, the Economist Intelligence Unit, a global think tank and consulting group, developed a practical framework for identifying and discussing business risk. Its business-risk model summarizes many of the key underlying variables that create business risk and affect firm value. Three broad categories of risk are identified:

- **Environmental risk** is the risk that external forces can affect a company's ability to achieve its objectives or threaten its existence.

- **Process risk** is the risk that the processes within a company do not perform efficiently or effectively in meeting business objectives or do not protect the physical, financial, intellectual, or information assets they use or consume; included here are information-processing and information-technology risks.

- **Information for decision-making risk** is the risk that information used to support strategic, operational, and financial decisions is not relevant or reliable or could be misused.

This multicategory approach to business-risk identification provides a rich template for strategic and operational decision making. The approach attempts to capture all significant business risks that could materially affect achievement of an organization's goals. Exhibit 4.6 provides specific examples of such risks from each of the three categories.

Business Risks Facing a Start-up Enterprise

Budding entrepreneurs have their own unique subset of risks to manage as they attempt to create stakeholder value. Research studies indicate that the failure rate for new businesses can be as high as 80 percent during the first five years of operations. Keith and Dale assume a variety of risks as they begin the process of converting their financial (invested cash), human (student and migrant workers), and physical (equipment) capital into services valued by their customers.

Environmental Risks. Environmental risks challenge C&F Enterprises, Inc. in three major areas: competition, catastrophe, and regulation. The threat of *competition* is a major risk for C&F. As you may recall from Chapter 1, Keith and Dale restricted their preliminary market analysis to a search of the telephone book and Internet resources. In fact, Frances Chan, C&F's bookkeeper, expressed some concern over this rather "superficial approach" in Chapter 2. If Keith and Dale have overestimated their market's need and/or willingness to pay for landscaping services, their new venture could be off to a shaky start.

Exhibit 4.6
Identifying Risk

Business Risk Classes	Examples of Business Risk
Environmental Risk Risks from *outside* the organization. These risks can be natural, economic, political, and social. Although external to the firm and often beyond the direct control of managers, these risks can and do impact both strategy and the related business processes.	• *Natural risks* include the possibility of fire, floods, hurricanes, tornadoes, etc. • Uncertainties associated with commodity prices, employment rates and wages, inflation, and interest rates are examples of *economic risks*. • *Political risks* can be both national (e.g., potential enactment of restrictive legislation) and international (e.g., the likelihood of regional conflict or war). • *Social risks* can include such issues as diversity, as well as age and gender discrimination.
Process Risk Risks *within* the organization (operating, empowerment, technology, integrity, and financial) that can be prevented, detected, corrected, and managed through effective systems of control.	• *Operating risk* involves the possibility that the value chain will not function as planned. • *Empowerment risk* relates to the likelihood that human resources are not employed optimally. • Common *technology risks* include those associated with unauthorized data and system access, integrity, and availability. • *Integrity risk* (risk of illegal acts and fraud committed by employees) is another type of process risk. • *Financial risks* are uncertainties associated with commodity prices, liquidity, and creditworthiness.
Information for Decision-Making Risk Risks that arise from the use of poor-quality information for operating, financial, or strategic decision making within the business, and providing misleading information to stakeholders both within and outside the organization.	• The lack of solid *operational information* to measure performance and evaluate contractual and regulatory commitments creates huge business risks for companies. • Uncertainties raised by poor budgeting, improper accounting and *financial reporting*, and inaccurate tax and regulatory filings can negatively affect stakeholder relationships. • Failure to plan and accurately project future performance and resource allocations can lead to significant *strategic* blunders.

Management Accounting: A Business Planning Approach

Figure 4.3
In creating value for themselves, entrepreneurs often adopt their own, unique method of managing business risk. Elon Musk, for example, takes an assertive approach that includes targeted lobbying, agile business strategies, DIY solutions to issues, and personal financial infusions.

The risk of *natural catastrophe* will continually plague this new venture. Since C&F delivers services that are directly affected by weather, any unexpected or unusual weather conditions will undoubtedly influence the company's ability to deliver on its business strategy. For example, a drought may result in the imposition of watering restrictions by local water authorities. Such regulation means that lawns and other landscaping will require substantially less servicing due to slow or no growth. Watering restrictions also may curtail fertilizing and weed-control services, both of which generally require subsequent watering for effective treatment. Excessive rains and flooding, on the other hand, may be equally problematic. Weekly client servicing may not be possible due to excessive rain days that make service delivery impractical. Unseasonable rains also can wash away weed-control applications, and as a result C&F may have to reapply treatments at no cost to their customers, which will drive down company profits.

Finally, Keith and Dale must be sensitive to certain *legal* and *regulatory* uncertainties that their new company faces. Government municipalities like cities, towns, townships, and counties, frequently require licenses for entities conducting business in their jurisdiction. Therefore, C&F must take care to apply for the appropriate operating permits in all the areas in which it operates. In addition, the company must closely monitor its use of non–U.S. citizen migrant farmworkers to ensure that it complies with appropriate federal and/or state immigration and labor laws. As if this were not enough, Keith and Dale must carefully research the type of fertilizers and pesticides they employ. The last thing they need as they begin their venture is "bad press" or even a lawsuit over the use of toxic, illegal chemicals in their landscaping business.

Process Risks. Process risks are among the biggest challenges that start-up businesses face. A new business must create awareness among customers and attract market share. More importantly, once a product or service attracts customers, the

Figure 4.4

Managing integrity risk improperly can dramatically affect a company's business processes. In Volkswagen's case, a perceived lack of integrity has significantly impaired both the market value of the company and its future business prospects.

business must be able to effectively manage processes and "deliver the goods." C&F's major operating risk is an unexpected flaw in its value chain that prevents it from delivering on its mission statement of "providing timely, responsive, and high quality services" to all of its customers. Given the service nature of their business, personnel quality, training, and supervision will be particularly critical. Keith and Dale must be vigilant in monitoring both cost and quality of services delivered as they commence operations, or there may be no future.

Managing empowerment risk is particularly critical in using human resources effectively. This is the risk that a company's personnel will have insufficient authority, responsibility, training, or incentive to execute the value chain process. As owner-managers, Keith and Dale appear to have sufficient authority and incentives (they are empowered) to make the tough decisions that they undoubtedly will face during the start-up phase. Particularly important is that these two entrepreneurs communicate frequently and openly about all aspects of the business. They also must recognize that their original assumptions, expectations, and plans for C&F may have to change as unexpected risks manifest themselves.

Information processing or technology risk is the risk that a company does not completely, accurately, and promptly capture, process, and record all the *data* needed to monitor its economic transactions and related performance. As with most small businesses, Keith and Dale are initially relying on their bookkeeper, Frances Chan, to provide them with this data.

Companies assume integrity risk when they ignore value chain process controls that can minimize fraud or illegal acts or that can create a positive reputation for the company. This risk does not initially appear to be much of a problem for C&F given Keith and Dale's planned involvement in and control of daily operations. The separation of operating activities (Keith and Dale) from reporting (Frances Chan) also seems to mitigate the risk of manager or employee fraud, unauthorized transactions, or other illegal acts. However, a major integrity risk often overlooked by many start-up companies is *reputation risk,* the failure to deliver on its commitments to customers and other stakeholders. Nothing can shut down a new company quicker than its customers losing confidence in its ability to deliver on promises or its creditors' loss of faith in its ability to repay its outstanding bills.

Financial risks are the uncertainties businesses face in managing commodity price changes, cash flows, collection of receivables, and repayment of debts. Keith and Dale must carefully manage *price, liquidity,* and *credit* risk if they are to succeed. As you will recall from Chapter 1, C&F initially plans to require its customers to provide the materials like the seed, fertilizer, and weed-killer used in their maintenance services. As long as their competition permits this, Keith and Dale have a terrific idea because it protects C&F from price increases (*price risk*) for these items. However, if increased competition forces their company (rather than the customer) to bear these costs and prices rise, then C&F's performance may be adversely affected if it cannot pass such increases on to its customers. Also critical is Keith and Dale's ability to collect cash from customers for services performed on a timely basis. Managing cash collections (customer *credit* or *default* risk) as well as costs for labor, rent, fuel, and other expenses is critical if the company is to maintain sufficient cash to pay its bills—in other words, to manage *liquidity risk*. After all, insufficient liquidity, the inability to pay bills, is what forces companies to fail.

Information for Decision-Making Risk. This risk occurs when an organization fails to develop the information that it needs (from its information processing system) to efficiently and effectively manage its value chain, honor its stakeholder reporting responsibilities, or implement and monitor its business strategy. As you will recall from Chapter 1, Frances Chan was hired with the assistance of a local accounting and business advisory services firm to set up C&F's accounting information system. Keith and Dale's challenge in the future will be to evaluate whether Frances is providing them with the information they need to make decisions and satisfy stakeholder information requests.

Assessing and Managing Business Risk

With a basic familiarity of business risk and its various subsets firmly established, we now explore how organizations analyze and manage the uncertainties they face.

Business Risk Assessment

Through a process of risk assessment, firms evaluate how identified risks may affect strategy. While specific techniques vary across firms, most risk assessment programs accomplish three important tasks:

1. Identify the risks that might affect the success of the firm's business strategy.

2. Determine why, how, and where the risks originate (outside the firm or within the business processes).

3. Measure the severity, likelihood, and financial impact of the risk.

This simple three-step approach helps managers develop a common framework for assessing and managing risk. Addressing the following questions to senior managers often can provide significant insight into whether a firm is adequately identifying and evaluating its business risk:

- Have you identified the external factors that currently affect your organization, and have you prioritized your response to the key factors? Are all your business entities included in your risk scenarios, including concessionaires, partnerships, associations, volunteer groups, and contractors/agents? In other words, have you assessed *environmental risk*?

Learning Objective 4
Discuss how companies identify and manage business risk.

- Do you know the firm's growth rate for sales? Are different parts growing at different rates, and do you understand why? In other words, have you assessed *operating process* risk?

- Are your employees encouraged to be alert for changes in key environmental factors that might affect your organization? How do you encourage your staff to think "outside the box"? In other words, have you assessed *empowerment process* risk?

- What information do you rely on when making major decisions or formulating major projects? Does the information include perspectives from other stakeholders? In other words, have you assessed *information for decision-making risk*?

Consistent risk assessment addresses critical questions that must be answered if a business is to develop appropriate risk-coping strategies. As we saw in a previous section, Keith and Dale addressed similar questions as they prepared to get C&F's operations up and running.

Business Risk Management

Managing risk means making sound decisions about strategy and the business processes used to accomplish it. Therefore, managing business risk is actually managing the organization: planning, organizing, directing, and controlling firm resources and systems to achieve objectives. Each firm establishes strategies to manage risk based on its own level of tolerance for uncertainty, given the potential rewards of a particular outcome.

Risk management strategies generally fall into one of four broad categories:

1. Avoidance is the conscious choice not to proceed with the activity that creates risk. In C&F's case, Keith and Dale have decided not to provide their customers with the materials they use in their maintenance services (e.g., seed, fertilizer, weedkiller). This policy frees C&F from a variety of inventory management risks including incorrect orders and obsolescence; it also frees up cash flow that would be needed to fund material purchases.

2. Transference involves reducing exposure to a risk by transferring it to unrelated third parties (for example, buying insurance and hedging with financial instruments). For those clients whose lawns may be ravaged by insects or pests, Keith and Dale have decided to recommend another company to provide the required pest control services. At this stage of their business, the two entrepreneurs are simply unwilling to assume the variety of environmental and health risks associated with mixing and spraying toxic chemicals.

3. **Mitigation** means reducing the likelihood or economic consequence of risk by controlling the processes that cause it (for example, locating company facilities in widely dispersed geographic locations reduces the impact of the occurrence of a single risk event on a company). Keith and Dale are very concerned about employee safety on their job sites. Since their service relies on a variety of high-powered cutting machines, they plan to deliver an employee safety training program twice each year, preferably during periods of low service demand, to mitigate the possibility of work-related accidents.

4. **Acceptance** means tolerating a risk because the potential rewards exceed the consequences of the risks when they are properly controlled. As previously discussed, Keith and Dale have assumed a variety of environmental, process, and information risks as they begin to deliver services to their customers.

Summary

This chapter discussed the importance of understanding how business processes drive financial statement results. To successfully execute strategy, managers must convert financial, human, and physical capital into the goods and services their customers demand. This chapter also introduced business risk and its numerous subsets and described some of the techniques managers use to assess and manage risk. To effectively manage profitability, a major strategic objective for most companies, managers must understand how value chain activities affect costs. The next two chapters introduce the principles of cost measurement and cost behavior. These chapters provide concrete examples of how cost management can improve business performance. The calculations behind cost management are important because they help managers develop insight into how business processes affect financial performance.

Summary of Learning Objectives

1. **Define value drivers and explain their usefulness in understanding business processes.** To interpret past results and take the appropriate actions to achieve desired outcomes, managers need to understand how specific business activities drive results on the financial statements. These factors that affect financial statement results are referred to as value drivers. By understanding how processes drive financial results, managers can focus on executing the company's operating, investing and financing activities.

2. **Identify the resources necessary to support the value chain.** Companies require three primary resources to enable the value chain: human, physical, and financial capital. Firms must be sure to have people with the right experience, skills, and collective morale, supported by the appropriate equipment, technologies, and financial capital, to be able to implement the value chain activities necessary to execute strategy. Successful firms use the value chain to transform resources into results.

3. **Define business risk and describe the uncertainties affecting value creation.** Business risk is the threat that an event or action will adversely affect a firm's ability to achieve its business objectives and execute its strategies successfully. This risk stems from the complex and dynamic interactions a firm has with its environment. The complex set of stakeholder relationships and process interactions that characterize business create many uncertainties that managers attempt to control or mitigate. The business risk model highlights the relationships among different types of risks.

4. **Discuss how companies identify and manage business risk.** A successful risk management program will (1) identify the risks that might affect the success of the firm's business strategy; (2) determine why, how, and where business risks originate (outside the firm or within the business processes); and

(3) measure the severity, likelihood, and financial impact of the risk. Managing business risk is actually managing the organization: planning, organizing, directing, and controlling firm resources and systems to achieve objectives.

Glossary of Terms

Acceptance A risk management strategy in which an organization tolerates a risk because its potential rewards exceed the possible negative consequences when they are properly controlled.

Avoidance A risk management strategy in which an organization makes a conscious choice not to proceed with an activity that creates risk.

Business risk The threat that an event or action will adversely affect an organization's ability to achieve its business objectives and execute its strategies successfully.

Cost drivers Business process factors or activities that determine expense totals on the income statement.

Empowerment risk The risk that company personnel will have insufficient authority, responsibility, training, or incentive to execute the value chain process.

Environmental risk The risk that external forces can affect a company's ability to achieve its objectives or threaten its existence.

Financial risks The uncertainties businesses face in managing commodity price changes, cash flows, collection of receivables, and repayment of debts.

Information for decision-making risk The risk that information used to support strategic, operational, and financial decisions is not relevant or reliable or could be misused.

Information processing or technology risk The risk that a company will not completely, accurately, and promptly capture, process, and record all the data needed to monitor its economic transactions and related performance.

Integrity risk The risk that employee or manager fraud, illegal acts, or a breakdown of the value chain will negatively affect a company's performance or its reputation.

Mitigation A risk management strategy in which an organization reduces the likelihood of economic consequences of risk by controlling the processes that cause it.

Operating risk An unexpected flaw in the value chain that prevents a company from functioning as planned.

Outsourcing A practice in which companies contract with firms outside the organization to perform services.

Process risk The risk that the processes within a company do not perform efficiently or effectively in meeting business objectives or do not protect the physical, financial, intellectual, or information assets they use or consume.

Revenue drivers Customer-related factors that affect the quantity and prices of products or services sold and determine total sales on the income statement.

Transference A risk management strategy in which an organization reduces its exposure to a specific risk by transferring it to an unrelated third party.

Value drivers The business process factors, or activities, that affect the data presented on financial statements.

Chapter Review Questions

1. What are value drivers?
2. Identify three balance sheet value drivers and describe how a related business process affects a specific balance sheet account.
3. What are revenue drivers?
4. What are cost drivers?
5. Identify three income statement value drivers and describe how a related business process affects a specific income statement account.
6. Identify three fundamental capabilities or resources that are needed by the value chain.
7. What is business risk?
8. Why do managers of companies assume business risk?
9. Describe the business risk model and its three main risk categories.
10. Define environmental risk and provide specific examples of how this type of risk affects business strategy.
11. Define process risk and list the five risk categories that the business risk model classifies as a subset of this risk.
12. Define information for decision-making risk and provide specific examples of how this type of risk affects business operations, financial reporting, and strategy.
13. Define operating risk and provide specific examples of how this type of risk affects the value chain process.
14. Define empowerment risk and provide specific examples of how this type of risk affects the value chain process.
15. Define information processing or technology risk and provide specific examples of how this type of risk affects the value chain process.
16. Define integrity risk and provide specific examples of how this type of risk affects the value chain process.
17. Define financial risk and provide specific examples of how this type of risk affects the value chain process.
18. What three important tasks do most risk assessment programs accomplish?
19. List and describe four common risk management strategies.

Exercises and Problems

1. Identify the business activities or processes that affect each of the following balance sheet accounts. Relate each process to a specific business decision that managers make.
   a. Accounts receivable
   b. Inventory
   c. Prepaid expenses
   d. Building
   e. Short-term notes payable
   f. Common stock
   g. Retained earnings

2. Identify the business activities or processes that affect the following income statement accounts. Relate each process to a specific business decision that managers make.
   a. Sales
   b. Cost of goods sold
   c. Salaries and wages
   d. Utilities
   e. Insurance expense
   f. Depreciation
   g. Income taxes

3. Speedy Delivery Company started its business on January 1, 20X1. The company's balance sheet at the end of its first year of operations is presented below.

Speedy Delivery		
Balance Sheet		
December 31, 20X1		
Assets		
Cash		$36,088
Accounts Receivable		1,500
Supplies		300
Prepaid Advertising		2,000
Equipment	$5,000	
Less Accumulated Depreciation	(600)	
Equipment (net)		4,400
Total Assets		$44,288
Liabilities and Owners' Equity		
Accounts Payable		$ 5,400
Long-Term Note Payable		3,000
Common Stock		25,000
Retained Earnings		10,888
Total Liabilities and Owners' Equity		$44,288

Match each of the following balance sheet value drivers with the balance sheet account(s) that it most likely affects:
a. Customer creditworthiness
b. Loan management
c. Profitability and dividend policy
d. Machine purchases
e. Financing terms obtained from suppliers
f. Purchasing policies

4. Speedy Delivery Company started its business on January 1, 20X1. The company's income statement at the end of its first year of operations is presented below.

Speedy Delivery Income Statement For the Year Ended December 31, 20X1		
Service Revenue		$67,000
Cost of Services Sold:		
Salaries and Wages	$25,000	
Rentals	12,000	
Supplies	1,200	
Fuel	500	
Depreciation	600	
Total Cost of Services Sold		39,300
Gross Profit		$27,700
Operating Expenses:		
Advertising		$ 3,000
Bookkeeping Services		2,000
Interest		200
Taxes		5,612
Other		6,000
Net Income		$10,888

Match each of the following income statement value drivers with the income statement account(s) that it most likely affects:
a. Service offerings
b. Price of services
c. Marketing decisions
d. Loan financing
e. Equipment age and usage
f. Purchasing efficiency
g. Employee experience

5. This chapter discusses three broad categories of business risks: *environmental, process,* and *information for decision-making.* Classify each of the following items according to the general risk category in which it best belongs.
a. Earthquakes and natural disasters
b. Poor production quality
c. Employee turnover
d. Failure to generate monthly product sales reports
e. Introduction of new products by competitors
f. Major customer's failure to pay its invoices

6. This chapter discusses three broad categories of business risks: *environmental, process,* and *information for decision-making.* Classify each of the following items according to the general risk category in which it best belongs.
   a. Ineffective sales staff
   b. Failure to update the strategic plan
   c. Lawsuits arising from flawed products
   d. Frequent equipment and machinery breakdowns
   e. Inability to obtain loans from local banks
   f. Major flood that destroys inventory and equipment
7. This chapter discusses three broad categories of business risks: *environmental, process,* and *information for decision-making.* Classify each of the following risks facing a local restaurant according to the general risk category in which it best belongs.
   a. Employee theft of food products
   b. Improper financial reporting
   c. Inadequate employee training
   d. New municipal laws prohibiting smoking in dining establishments
   e. Lowering of prices by competing dining establishments
   f. Regional economic recession
8. For each of the following businesses, list a significant *environmental risk* that it must manage.
   a. Fast-food restaurant
   b. Skateboard park
   c. Flower shop
   d. Automobile manufacturer
9. For each of the following businesses, list a significant *process risk* that it must manage.
   a. Fast-food restaurant
   b. Skateboard park
   c. Flower shop
   d. Automobile manufacturer
10. For each of the following businesses, list significant *information for decision-making risk* that it must manage.
   a. Fast-food restaurant
   b. Skateboard park
   c. Flower shop
   d. Automobile manufacturer
11. Select a public company (one whose stock is actively traded on any major exchange) in which you are interested or which your instructor has previously assigned. Do not pick a bank, insurance company, brokerage firm, any type of financial services entity, or a firm that operates in a regulated industry. It is very important that the company you select reports accounts receivable, inventory, and current liabilities on its balance sheet. Once a company has been selected that meets these criteria, perform the following:
   a. Download the company's balance sheet and income statement from the Securities and Exchange Commission's EDGAR data site: http://www.sec.gov/edgar.shtml. Select "Search for a company's filings." Then select

"Companies and Other Filers." Simply enter the company's name and then select "Find Companies." Select the company from the generated list. Once a listing of filings has been provided, select the *most current* 10-K filing. Note that the 10-K filing could be listed simply as 10-K, or 10-K could be followed by other letters and numbers, for example, 10KT405. Click on the filing and then search the 10-K filing for the balance sheet and income statement. Once you have found them, print them out, as you will be required to attach these to your assignment.

b. Identify the accounts with the three largest values in each section of the balance sheet: assets, liabilities, and owners' (or stockholders') equity (for a total of nine accounts). Compute the percentage by which each of the accounts has increased or decreased over the past year?

c. For each account identified in part (b) of this question, identify a business process that drives the values reported on the balance sheet. What factors are likely to have contributed to changes in these balances?

d. Identify the company's primary source of revenue (i.e., products or services) and its four largest expenses on the income statement. Has each of these expenses increased or decreased over the past year?

e. For sales revenue and each expense item identified in part (d) of this question, identify a business process that drives the values reported on the income statement. What factors are likely to have contributed to these totals for the period?

f. Based on your analysis, what are the company's most important business processes?

g. What type of insight and information would a manager or consultant need to be able to make suggestions to improve the business processes you selected in response to part (f)?

12. Assume that some friends have come to you with a preliminary business idea to open Scoops Ice Cream Shoppe as a summer business in a popular beach area. Scoops will feature family entertainment on a regular basis and make-your-own sundae stations. The prospective owners realize that while this clever marketing concept may differentiate Scoops from the existing competition, they need a business plan before moving forward with the idea.

a. What are the primary value chain activities that Scoops Ice Cream Shoppe will need to engage in?

b. What are the major accounts that are likely to appear on its balance sheet and income statement?

c. For each account that you identified in part (b), list at least one major business decision and describe how it will affect the totals that ultimately appear on the financial statements.

13. Select a public company (one whose stock is actively traded on any major exchange) in which you are interested or which your instructor has previously assigned. Do not pick a bank, insurance company, brokerage firm, any type of financial services entity, or a firm that operates in a regulated industry. Once you have selected a company, perform the following:

a. Visit the Securities and Exchange Commission's EDGAR data site (http://www.sec.gov/edgar.shtml), and select "Search for the company's filings."

Then, select "Companies and Other Filers." Enter the company's name and then select "Find Companies." Select the company from the generated list. Once you have the listing of filings, select the most current S-1 or S-3 filing in text form. These are regulatory forms that a company must file prior to issuing securities in the capital markets. Carefully search the document for the section that discusses risk factors. Print out **only** the sections of the S-1 or S-3 related to risk, as the entire filing can often be quite lengthy.

b. Review the "risk factors" section of the registration statement. Make a list of the risk factors that the company has identified.

c. Classify these risk factors as environmental, process, or information for decision-making risks using the business risk model criteria provided in this chapter.

d. Next, classify each process risk as operating, empowerment, information processing, integrity, or financial risk.

e. Discuss how each of these risks potentially will impact the business strategy of the company that you selected.

f. What strategy might the company use to manage each of these risks?

g. Of the major risk classes and categories listed in the business risk model (environmental, operating, empowerment, information processing/technology, integrity, financial, and information for decision-making risk), which are *not* disclosed as risks—identified in steps (c) and (d) above—by the company you selected? Why do you think this might be the case?

h. Discuss how each of the risks listed in the registration statement potentially affects the investment of an investor who decides to purchase the securities described in the S-1 or S-3.

i. What strategy might a potential investor use to manage his or her investment risk in the securities that the company intends to issue?

14. Recent alumni of your institution are considering opening a tanning and nail styling salon in an empty storefront near campus. Perfections Tanning & Nails will target students at your school as well as local residents. You have reviewed the business plan and noticed that it lacks a risk assessment section. The owners have asked for your input in developing this section.

a. Make a list of the company's most important risk factors and classify them as environmental, process, or information for decision-making risks using the business risk model criteria provided in this chapter.

b. Classify each process risk as operating, empowerment, information processing, integrity, or financial risk.

c. Discuss how each of these risks potentially will impact the business strategy of Perfections Tanning & Nails.

d. List the strategy the company might use to manage each of these risks?

e. If this company implements its business plan, list the information that would be useful in assessing its success in managing each of these risks?

15. Local investors have decided to open the Hat Tricks Sports Bar & Grill in an existing restaurant building near campus. These investors feel that Hat Tricks will fill a void in the market and meet the demand of the many sports enthusiasts near campus. You have reviewed the business plan and noticed

that it lacks a risk assessment section. The investors have asked for your input in developing this section.

a. Make a list of the company's most important risk factors and classify them as environmental, process, or information for decision-making risks using the business risk model criteria provided in this chapter.

b. Classify each process risk as operating, empowerment, information processing, integrity, or financial risk.

c. Discuss how each of these risks potentially will impact the business strategy of Hat Tricks Sports Bar & Grill.

d. List the strategy the company might use to manage each of these risks?

e. If this company implements its business plan, list the information that would be useful in assessing its success in managing each of these risks?

Keystone Academy (Part 1)

Keystone Academy, a private college preparatory school serving grades 9 through 12, has hired your consulting firm to help analyze the academy's costs. Recently, the school's revenues failed to cover its costs, forcing it to fund the excess expenditures with endowment monies. Some faculty believe that this situation may be due to the academy's newly adopted practice of giving each new student his or her own laptop computer at no charge. Not wishing to dip into the endowment again in the future, the academy needs your expert advice.

Required

Your manager on this engagement has decided that you should begin by analyzing the academy's value chain activities. Your manager noted that since expenses are driven by process, identifying each cost driver is critical to analyzing and lowering costs. For each item listed below, identify specifically what activities, decisions, and factors make the cost increase or decrease. For example, wages and fringe benefits for the academy's administrative staff (item 1 below) are affected by employees' education level and experience, the use of technology, and the percentage of full-time employees, among other factors.

1. Wages and fringe benefits for the academy's administrative staff.
2. Academic materials (e.g., books and laptop computers) provided to students by the academy at no charge.
3. Wages and fringe benefits for the academy's full-time faculty.
4. Repairs to student laptop computers. The school recently hired a full-time repair technician. Repairs that are beyond the technician's abilities are outsourced to a local computer repair shop.
5. Fee charged by a local public accounting firm to audit the academy's financial records.
6. Wages for the school's part-time athletic coaches (baseball, football, basketball, tennis, and soccer). These coaches are hired on a temporary basis. The number of hours they work is dictated by the number of students participating in each sport (at Keystone every student must participate

in at least one of the five sports). On average, each coach is used about 10 hours per week during the full academic year.

7. Depreciation on the academy's recently completed performing arts pavilion.
8. Rent for the buses the academy uses to transport its students to and from school.
9. Electricity to operate the academy's facilities. The local utility's charge is composed of a fixed monthly minimum charge plus a charge per kilowatt-hour of electricity used.

Risk Assessment and Management Strategies

Because a business plan is based on the company's expectations and assumptions, it is important to disclose to its readers the risks that could affect the plan's success. At first, this may seem counterintuitive to an individual who is promoting a new business idea. However, such disclosure demonstrates the thoroughness with which the plan has been developed. Every business plan must list the most critical risks and management's strategies for handling these uncertainties. The business risk model presented in this chapter provides a framework for discussing risks.

Assignment

Evaluate the *most relevant* business risks facing your start-up business using the following guidelines.

Business Risk Analysis

Environmental Risks

- What characteristics best describe the start-up enterprise's business environment?
- What are the important economic factors that will affect your product or service (i.e., trade area growth, industry health, economic trends, taxes, rising energy prices, etc.)?
- What are the important legal/regulatory factors that affect your market?
- Are there any other environmental factors that will affect your market over which you have no control?

Process Risks

- What are your most important business processes (that is, your value chain)? Why?
- What are the important factors that will affect your ability to deliver your product or service successfully?
- What controls, policies, and procedures can you put in place to manage each of these risks?

Information for Decision-Making Risks

- What specific types of information will your business need to manage strategic, operating, and financial decisions?
- Specifically, how and how often will you collect and analyze the most important types of information?
- What are the potential hazards that your business may face if information is not properly collected, processed, and utilized?

Image Credits

Fig. 4.1: Copyright © Depositphotos/pressmaster.

Exhibit 4.1: Adapted from: R.S. Kaplan and D.P. Norton, "Putting the Balanced Scorecard to Work," Harvard Business Review. Copyright © 1993.

Exhibit 4.4: Adapted from: Institute of Management Accountants, www.imanet. org.

Fig. 4.2: Copyright © Depositphotos/lucidwaters.

Fig. 4.3: Copyright © kris krüg (CC by 2.0) at https://www.flickr.com/photos/kk/50083704/.

Fig. 4.4: Copyright © Depositphotos/ifeelstock.

Chapter 5

LEARNING OBJECTIVES

1. Describe the primary types of cost behaviors.

2. Define the relevant range and a firm's total cost function.

3. Describe cost-volume-profit (CVP) analysis and explain its usefulness.

4. Demonstrate the use of breakeven analysis.

5. Identify strategies that companies use to lower their breakeven points.

Planning Profitable Operations

As discussed in Chapter 4, businesses create value for their customers by designing efficient and effective business processes. To create value for investors, managers must generate profits. This chapter introduces the concept of profit planning and presents the fundamental tools and techniques needed to transform sales price and cost *data* into the *insights* necessary to build a profit plan. These techniques help managers plan and monitor business operations, allocate scarce resources, and manage expenses. This chapter specifically identifies the relationship between business processes and a firm's cost structure. Future chapters will demonstrate how these tools can be applied to profit-plan development and performance evaluation.

Managers in all businesses need to plan effectively so that they will have the necessary human, physical, and financial capital to execute strategy. As managers convert these resources into financial results, they are particularly interested in the cost of their business operations. To create value for investors, managers must generate profits. As discussed in Chapter 3, profits occur when firms generate enough revenue to cover operating costs. The traditional income statement classifies costs by type or purpose, like cost of sales or operating expenses, to inform users about the business function that generates each major expense. However, to effectively plan business operations, managers also need to understand cost behavior—specifically, how costs react to changes in business activity. Understanding cost behavior allows managers to forecast future profits and evaluate the results expected from their decisions. The next sections present the fundamental tools managers need to develop credible profit projections.

C&F Enterprises, Inc.: Reacting to an Unforeseen Environmental Shock

Keith and Dale were in a state of shock. They had just learned that a national lawn care franchising operation, Tru-Lawn Care (TLC), had just opened for business in their market area and was offering the same full-service menu that C&F had just introduced to the marketplace. Keith and Dale were particularly concerned by the aggressive marketing and pricing strategies that TLC had recently initiated. In fact, the phone had been ringing off the hook with customer questions about whether C&F planned to match

TLC's lower prices. Keith attempted to address these pricing queries by emphasizing the specialized customer focus that a smaller firm like C&F could provide. However, the customers were not easily swayed and demanded to know about price!

Despite a profitable first year, Keith and Dale were worried that blindly matching TLC's price reductions would wipe out the meager gains they had scratched out in their first year of business. In a panic and recognizing that they might have to take some quick and dramatic action with respect to their operating costs, they asked their bookkeeper, Frances Chan, to give them whatever cost data she had gathered. Several days passed and Frances showed up with the following report that summarized costs for the first year of operations. She indicated that it was the best she could do on such short notice.

Costs	Fixed	Variable	Total
Salaries and wages	$ 9,500	$33,500	$43,000
Rentals	—	11,000	11,000
Supplies	—	3,000	3,000
Fuel	—	700	700
Depreciation	600	—	600
Advertising	4,800	—	4,800
Bookkeeping	2,500	—	2,500
Interest	200	—	200
Taxes	—	2,042	2,042
Other	1,500	1,500	3,000
Total Costs	$19,100	$51,742	$70,842

Understanding Cost Behavior

In Chapter 4, we learned that cost drivers are business process factors that cause expenses to increase or decrease. Understanding how processes cause costs to change over different levels of business activity is critical to forecasting profitability. This issue will be explored more fully in Chapter 6. Regardless of how costs are incurred, they generally can be classified into one of three behavior categories: variable, fixed, or mixed costs. Each type of cost is defined as follows:

- **Variable costs.** These costs change in *direct* proportion to some level of business activity. When the activity is sales, the sales can be measured in either dollars or units sold. For retailers the most common variable costs are those associated with purchasing each unit of the product that they sell. Another common example is the commissions paid to salespeople; commissions are commonly paid as a defined percentage of sales dollars. In C&F's case, Frances Chan has identified employee wages, equipment rentals, supplies, fuel, and taxes as variable costs: costs whose amounts are associated with the operating activities of the business.

Exhibit 5.1
Cost Behavior Concepts

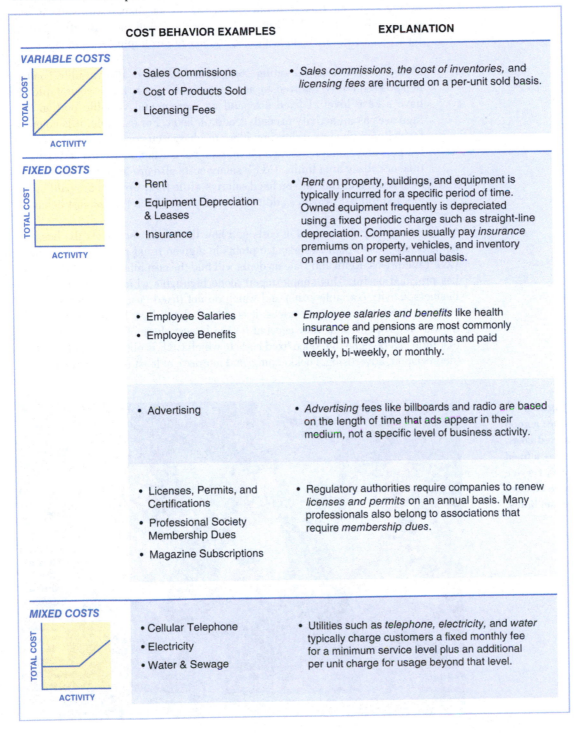

	COST BEHAVIOR EXAMPLES	EXPLANATION
VARIABLE COSTS	• Sales Commissions • Cost of Products Sold • Licensing Fees	• *Sales commissions, the cost of inventories,* and *licensing fees* are incurred on a per-unit sold basis.
FIXED COSTS	• Rent • Equipment Depreciation & Leases • Insurance	• *Rent* on property, buildings, and equipment is typically incurred for a specific period of time. Owned equipment frequently is depreciated using a fixed periodic charge such as straight-line depreciation. Companies usually pay *insurance* premiums on property, vehicles, and inventory on an annual or semi-annual basis.
	• Employee Salaries • Employee Benefits	• *Employee salaries and benefits* like health insurance and pensions are most commonly defined in fixed annual amounts and paid weekly, bi-weekly, or monthly.
	• Advertising	• *Advertising* fees like billboards and radio are based on the length of time that ads appear in their medium, not a specific level of business activity.
	• Licenses, Permits, and Certifications • Professional Society Membership Dues • Magazine Subscriptions	• Regulatory authorities require companies to renew *licenses and permits* on an annual basis. Many professionals also belong to associations that require *membership dues*.
MIXED COSTS	• Cellular Telephone • Electricity • Water & Sewage	• Utilities such as *telephone, electricity,* and *water* typically charge customers a fixed monthly fee for a minimum service level plus an additional per unit charge for usage beyond that level.

- **Fixed costs.** These costs remain the same across different activity levels. Examples include certain rents, insurance, and salaries that are incurred during a specific time interval. Such costs do not change with sales or any other activity. For C&F Enterprises, Inc., the Internet advertising fees, bookkeeping charges, and interest expense are examples of fixed costs.

- **Mixed costs.** Some operating costs have *both* fixed and variable components. Frequently referred to as semivariable costs, these costs typically have a base level of fixed cost and an incremental variable portion that increases as an activity exceeds a certain level. For example, it is common for cellular phone service providers to charge customers a fixed monthly fee plus additional costs on a per-minute basis when usage exceeds certain time or calling area limits. C&F's salary costs also are mixed in behavior, as both Keith and Dale are on fixed salaries while their workers are paid by the job. Exhibit 5.1 provides additional examples of each type of cost behavior.

Understanding these types of costs and how their *behavior* affects the business helps companies to plan and manage profits in a given fiscal period. In the case of C&F Enterprises, Keith and Dale no doubt will find the cost information that Frances has provided useful. This simple report alone highlights which costs change with business activity (variable costs) and which do not (fixed costs). To address recent customer pressures to reduce prices, it is clear that Keith and Dale must focus on the variable expenses, as they account for the largest share of costs. It is also true that little can be done to reduce fixed costs to which C&F is obligated or "locked in" (depreciation, advertising, bookkeeping, and interest), at least in the short term.

Figure 5.1
Mobile phones are a good example of mixed costs. Generally, users pay a fixed monthly fee for basic service and additional variable charges for usage above preset limits.

Management Accounting: A Business Planning Approach

Relevant Range

When analyzing cost behavior, another important assumption to consider is the relevant range. The term *relevant range* is used to describe the levels of activity at which assumptions about cost behavior (variable, fixed, or mixed) remain valid. The concept of relevant range is particularly important for businesses that begin to operate at activity levels never before encountered. As illustrated in Exhibit 5.2, a cost that is fixed at a certain dollar amount within a *relevant range* may increase in a "step" fashion to higher amounts at different activity levels, which represent new relevant ranges. Variable cost assumptions also remain constant within relevant ranges; over wider ranges of activity, they may actually be nonlinear. For example, businesses may benefit from discounted prices when they purchase large volumes of products or services. When this occurs, the variable cost assumptions for purchased products change based on the activity level experienced by or planned for the business.

In C&F's case, Frances Chan's classification of fixed and variable costs only holds at certain activity levels. For example, Frances charges a fixed rate of $2,500 per year for her bookkeeping services—the going rate for businesses like C&F with less than $125,000 in sales. However, for businesses with more than $125,000 in sales, she typically charges $5,500 per year. Therefore, C&F's bookkeeping costs currently are fixed within a *relevant range* of sales between zero and $125,000. However, Keith and Dale realize that if future sales exceed $125,000, their bookkeeping costs will rise to a new fixed level that reflects the increasing complexity of their growing business. This "step" increase for fixed bookkeeping costs is illustrated in Exhibit 5.2.

Supplies represent one of C&F's major variable costs. Keith and Dale currently buy their supplies at retail prices from a local garden shop. The variable cost per unit assumed for various supply purchases will remain the same only within a *relevant*

Learning Objective 2
Define the relevant range and a firm's total cost function.

Figure 5.2
When a business, such as a construction company, expands its operating levels to address new commercial opportunities, it may be necessary to acquire new equipment through either purchase or leasing arrangements. When this occurs, managers must determine how these asset additions affect the relevant range assumptions about fixed and variable costs.

Exhibit 5.2
Relevant Range for Fixed
and Variable Costs

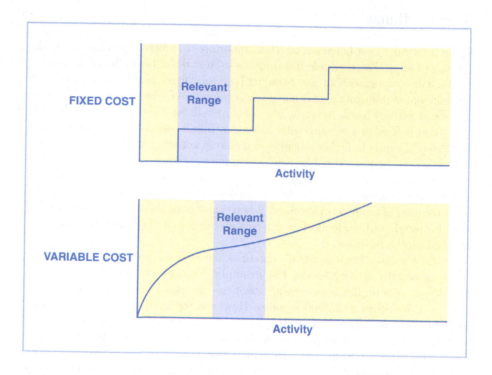

range that reflects the activity level of current operations. If C&F's operations were to grow significantly, it might be possible for Keith and Dale to buy supplies in bulk at a substantially lower cost per unit. If they realized such growth, and made bulk supply purchases, Keith and Dale would need to reconsider their variable cost assumptions for supplies since new activity levels will cause the *relevant range* for C&F to change. As can be seen in Exhibit 5.2, variable cost assumptions can change when a company enters a new *relevant range* of business activity.

Large businesses face similar relevant range issues when forecasting costs. For example, newly hired sales personnel may work for a fixed salary during the training phase of their employment and then move to commission (which is variable) or to a mixed compensation basis (part commission, part fixed salary) in the future. In this case, it is important for managers to recognize the activity ranges across which assumptions about salary cost behavior hold. Clearly, an awareness of relevant range assumptions is essential to computing and evaluating a firm's total costs at various levels of business activity.

Computing Total Costs

The total cost that a business incurs in a period equals the sum of its fixed, variable, and mixed costs. Since mixed costs can be broken down into fixed and variable costs, we can simplify our analysis with the following equation:

Total Costs = Total Fixed Costs + Total Variable Costs

Management Accounting: A Business Planning Approach

This mathematical formula represents the firm's total cost function. As we will see in the next section, this formula can be used to project profits at various levels of sales.

Cost-Volume-Profit (CVP) Analysis

The fundamental technique that managers use to analyze the relationships between revenues, expenses, and profits at different sales levels is commonly known as cost-volume-profit (CVP) analysis. Since total sales must exceed total costs to earn a profit, CVP analysis provides a structured way to analyze sales prices and costs. To conduct CVP analysis, managers need the following data:

Learning Objective 3
Describe cost-volume-profit (CVP) analysis and explain its usefulness.

1. Sales price per unit sold or service delivered
2. Sales volume (total number of units sold or services delivered)
3. Variable cost per unit of product or service
4. Total fixed costs

Managers frequently create a "special" income statement that considers cost behavior, allowing them to see the relationships underlying CVP analysis. This special income statement highlights the differences between variable and fixed expenses and shows the *contribution margin*. While managers rely on this report to monitor internal operations, it is not a substitute for the GAAP income statement described in Chapter 3 that is used by investors, lenders, and regulators. Exhibit 5.3 illustrates the contribution margin income statement.

Contribution margin is the amount by which total sales revenue exceeds total variable costs. If a company cannot sell its product or service for an amount greater than its variable cost, it is impossible to generate a profit. Contribution margin analysis also can show how much *each* unit sold (after variable costs are considered) *contributes* to covering fixed costs and, ultimately, to generating profits. Contribution margin per unit can be calculated as follows:

Contribution Margin per Unit = Sales Price per Unit − Variable Cost per Unit

Assume that a retail business sells a product for $12 that has a variable unit cost of $8. As illustrated in Exhibit 5.4, the contribution margin per unit sold is

Contribution Margin Income Statement
For the Year Ended December 31, 20X1

Sales
− Variable costs
Contribution margin
− Fixed costs
Net income

Exhibit 5.3
Contribution Margin Income Statement

Exhibit 5.4
Contribution Margin

	Per Unit	×	Units Sold	=	Total
Sales	$12	×	100	=	$1,200
– Variable costs	8	×	100	=	800
Contribution margin	$ 4	×	100	=	$ 400

$4 (selling price of $12 less variable cost per unit of $8). Since total contribution margin equals the contribution margin per unit multiplied by the number of units sold, total contribution margin would be $400 if the retailer sold 100 units ($4 per unit times 100 units sold).

C&F's contribution margin can be computed easily from the information Frances provided. With total revenues of $74,800 and variable costs of $51,742, the company's contribution margin is $23,058.

Contribution margin also is commonly expressed on a percentage basis. Known as the **contribution margin ratio (or percentage)**, this percentage represents the amount earned by a company (before fixed costs) on every dollar of sales. The contribution margin ratio or percentage can be computed as follows:

$$\text{Contribution Margin Ratio} = \text{Contribution Margin per Unit} \div \text{Sales Price per Unit}$$

or

$$\text{Contribution Margin Ratio} = \text{Total Contribution Margin} \div \text{Total Sales}$$

As shown in Exhibit 5.5, using the data from the preceding example, the retailer's contribution margin percentage is 33.33 percent ($4 contribution margin per unit divided by $12 sales price per unit). For every dollar of sales, the company earns 33.33 cents that it can apply toward covering fixed costs.

Managers use this important ratio to quickly determine the contribution margin (in total dollars) of a given level of sales, thereby comparing the relative profitability of different products and services. In this example, if the retail store sold $100,000 of its product, the managers would have $33,333 (33.33 percent multiplied by $100,000 in sales) to apply toward covering fixed costs. In C&F's case, the contribution margin is $23,058 (revenues of $74,800 less variable costs of $51,742). The company's contribution margin percentage is 30.83 percent

Exhibit 5.5
Contribution Margin Ratio

	Per Unit	Percent
Sales	$12	100.00%
– Variable costs	8	66.67%
Contribution margin	$ 4	33.33%

($23,058 in contribution margin divided by total revenues of $74,800). The company has earned $23,058 that it can apply to covering its $19,100 in fixed costs.

If total contribution margin exceeds fixed costs then the company earns a profit. This relationship is expressed in the following equation:

Net Income = Total Contribution Margin – Total Fixed Costs

Since total contribution margin also equals total sales less total variable costs, we could expand the equation in the following form:

Net Income = (Total Sales – Total Variable Costs) – Total Fixed Costs

Since total cost equals the sum of total fixed and variable costs, we can simplify the equation in the following logical form:

Net Income = Total Sales – Total Costs

These relationships provide the foundations for tools that managers use to develop profit plans.

CVP Assumptions

CVP analysis is based on three important assumptions:

1. CVP analysis assumes that total revenue behaves in a *linear* fashion. This means that the unit price of a product or service does not change as its sales volume changes within the relevant range. For example, some companies do not offer the same prices to all customers, choosing instead to offer discounts to customers who buy large quantities of a product. Take the case of Home Depot, which sells building materials like lumber and piping to construction contractors at discounted prices. Managers must factor such discounts and similar pricing arrangements into CVP analysis.

2. CVP analysis also assumes that total expenses behave in a linear manner over the relevant range. This implies that total fixed expenses remain *constant* as activity changes and that a *unit's variable cost* remains unchanged as activity varies. Consequently, if a firm's sales activity changes dramatically (either increasing or decreasing), the reasonableness of cost classifications as variable, fixed, or mixed must be reviewed. For example, a company may pay a delivery service a fee per shipment. As shipping volume increases, the vendor may reduce the delivery fee to retain a high-volume customer. In such cases, managers must reconsider CVP analysis based on these new cost assumptions.

3. For firms that deliver multiple products or services, CVP analysis assumes that the sales mix (the relative percentage of each of the products or services that make up a company's total sales) remains constant over the relevant range. For example, restaurants sell food and beverages. Beverages typically provide a higher contribution margin than food. If the ratio of food to beverages

Contribution Margin Analysis "Contributes" to Marketing

Supermarkets use "frequent shopper" clubs, coupons, and other promotional discounts to attract customers. Technology at the checkout lane allows the stores to collect incredible amounts of data about their customers' buying habits. Computer scanners use product bar codes to track the quantity, dollar value, and product mix of customers' purchases.

Major supermarket chains rely on their accountants to analyze these data to assess the profitability of various marketing programs. Accounting professionals frequently work with the marketing team to determine which coupons are most profitable and whether the marketing programs are achieving their desired effects. They calculate contribution margins before and after promotions to evaluate whether a marketing program's benefits outweigh its costs. For example, a store may promote a product by distributing coupons via various outlets (for example, newspapers, mailings, and the Internet). By analyzing coupon redemption rates, product contribution margins (in total or per unit), average sales per customer (existing and new), and sales mix, managers can evaluate whether the promotion is generating enough sales to warrant the price discounts.

By relying on the input provided by their accounting advisors, the marketing team can better decide how and where to advertise in the future. It is important to remember that, to provide such valuable guidance, managers must thoroughly understand the supermarket's strategy, customer preferences, and the effects of marketing programs on financial performance. Contribution margin analysis is critical to those assessments.

Source: "Business Intelligence: How Accountants Bring Value to the Marketing Function," *Strategic Finance*, Institute of Management Accountants, May 2002.

changes, it will affect the profits of the restaurant. A greater percentage of food relative to beverages will mean lower margins, and vice versa. Consequently, managers must carefully consider the effect of sales mix on CVP analysis.

Despite these assumptions, CVP analysis provides a useful way to think about profit planning. The next section discusses breakeven analysis, a common technique used to determine how much a company needs to sell to cover costs and meet profit targets.

C&F Enterprises, Inc.: Developing an Appreciation for Information

As Keith and Dale stared at the numbers, one fact was becoming crystal clear. They had not done a very thorough job of planning their business. Sure they had earned a profit, but it was probably due more to a good market and a little luck than to their financial expertise. They would not make this mistake again!

Although the numbers that Frances provided did highlight variable costs as an area deserving of attention, Keith and Dale still had questions. Since their new competitor was initially targeting residential customers more aggressively

Figure 5.3
Companies are increasingly using innovative technologies and business analytics to monitor consumer purchasing behavior and to accumulate product cost data. For instance, grocery stores track past purchases, predict future shopping lists, and manage contribution margins.

than commercial, Keith and Dale were seriously considering scaling back their residential business and focusing on commercial lawn services. They suspected that this was where they made the most money, but they were not absolutely sure. They asked Frances if she could provide them with cost information just for the commercial part of their business. Frances informed them that the fixed costs would remain unchanged from the previous totals that she gave them because they were unrelated to any specific business activity. However, she did provide the following variable cost data for last year's operations:

Commercial Services

	Variable Costs
Revenue	$53,500
Costs	
Wages	$23,961
Rentals	7,868
Supplies	2,146
Fuel	501
Taxes	1,461
Other	1,071
	$37,008
Contribution margin	$16,492

Frances also noted that these revenues and costs were generated from 214 commercial lawn care service calls.

Performing Breakeven Analysis

Learning Objective 4
Demonstrate the use of
breakeven analysis.

Breakeven analysis is a basic tool that managers use to determine the level of sales needed for their company to earn a profit. The **breakeven point** represents either the level of sales in dollars or units at which the company's profits are equal to zero (that is, total sales equal total costs). Breakeven analysis allows managers to quickly see how changing sales prices or costs affect profitability.

Computing the breakeven point for a product or service requires four basic steps:

1. Determine the total expenses that the business likely will incur in delivering a product or service.

2. Classify these expenses as either fixed or variable costs. Mixed costs must be separated into their fixed and variable components.

3. Calculate both the contribution margin ratio and the contribution margin per unit.

4. Compute the breakeven point in sales dollars using the following formula:

Breakeven Point (in Dollars) = Total Fixed Costs ÷ Contribution Margin Ratio

Alternatively, calculate the breakeven point in units using the following formula:

Breakeven Point (in Units) = Total Fixed Costs ÷ Contribution Margin per Unit

It is important to remember that to compute the breakeven point (zero profit level), total contribution margin must equal total fixed costs. When total contribution margin equals total fixed costs, profit or net income equals zero. Therefore, the company "breaks even." Exhibit 5.6 reviews and summarizes the profit-planning formulas discussed to this point in this chapter.

Exhibit 5.6
Profit-Planning Formulas

Net Income	=	Total Contribution Margin – Total Fixed Costs
Contribution Margin per Unit	=	Sales Price per Unit – Variable Cost per Unit
Contribution Margin Ratio	=	$\dfrac{\text{Contribution Margin per Unit}}{\text{Sales Price per Unit}}$
Breakeven Point (in Dollars)	=	$\dfrac{\text{Total Fixed Costs}}{\text{Contribution Margin Ratio}}$
Breakeven Point (in Units)	=	$\dfrac{\text{Total Fixed Costs}}{\text{Contribution Margin per Unit}}$

Computing the Breakeven Point

Assume that the simple retail company described in Exhibit 5.4 had fixed monthly costs for rent, insurance, and salaries equal to $10,000 per month. Exhibit 5.4 assumed that the company generated $1,200 in product sales. However, the amount of sales that a company needs to break even is not always known. To break even (that is, earn no profit) each month, the company must generate a total contribution margin of $10,000 to cover its monthly fixed costs (see Exhibit 5.7). In the exhibit, s and v represent total sales and total variable costs, respectively, at the breakeven point.

To calculate the breakeven point in total sales dollars, divide total fixed costs by the contribution margin ratio. Dividing total fixed costs of $10,000 by the contribution margin ratio (33.33 percent) yields the breakeven point in total sales dollars, $30,000 in Exhibit 5.8. Total sales of $30,000 yield a total contribution margin of $10,000 since total variable costs equal $20,000 (66.67 percent of total sales). As Exhibit 5.8 illustrates, this contribution margin is just enough to cover fixed costs; it generates neither a profit nor a loss.

Sometimes managers prefer to think about the breakeven point in terms of *units* sold. In Exhibit 5.9, q represents units sold at the breakeven point. To calculate q, divide total sales ($30,000), variable costs ($20,000), or contribution margin ($10,000), by their respective per-unit amounts ($12, $8, or $4). This yields a breakeven point in units of 2,500 for the store.

The breakeven point shows managers just how difficult it may be to earn a profit. Sales levels below 2,500 units per month will result in a loss. In the example above, the first 2,500 units sold result in zero profit. Each additional unit sold contributes $4 to profit. As shown in Exhibit 5.10, if the store sells 2,501 units, net income will be $4.

As we learned earlier, Keith and Dale are considering restricting their business in the coming year to commercial customers. Therefore, they need a contribution margin ratio for their commercial operations. Using last year's numbers, they found C&F's commercial contribution margin ratio to be 30.83 percent ($16,492 in contribution margin divided by total commercial revenues of $53,500). Using this ratio, their breakeven point in sales dollars is $61,953. This is computed by dividing C&F's total fixed costs of $19,100 by the contribution margin ratio for the commercial line of business (30.83 percent). Keith and Dale thought this sounded doable, since it only represented a 15.8 percent increase in commercial sales, and after all, they were eliminating the residential service line.

However, to check themselves, Keith and Dale wanted to know how many actual service calls $61,953 in sales represented. So, they computed the breakeven point in units. To do so, they needed the contribution margin per unit. They found this by dividing the total commercial contribution margin of $16,492 by the number of service calls that generated this margin, 214. As illustrated in Exhibit 5.11, this yielded a contribution margin per unit of $77.07.

After dividing total fixed costs of $19,100 by the contribution margin per unit of $77.07, they found the breakeven point in service calls to be 248. Keith and Dale agreed, this sales level didn't sound impossible.

Exhibit 5.7
Breakeven Analysis

	Total	Percent
Sales	*s*	100.00%
– Variable costs	*v*	66.67%
Contribution margin	$10,000	33.33%
– Fixed costs	10,000	
Net income	$ —	

Note: Net income is set to zero at the breakeven point.

Exhibit 5.8
Breakeven Point (Dollars)

	Total	Percent
Sales	**$30,000**	100.00%
– Variable costs	**20,000**	66.67%
Contribution margin	$10,000	33.33%
– Fixed costs	10,000	
Net income	$ —	

Note: Net income is set to zero at the breakeven point.

Exhibit 5.9
Breakeven Point (Units)

	Per Unit	×	Quantity	=	Total
Sales	$12	×	*q*	=	$30,000
– Variable costs	8	×	*q*	=	20,000
Contribution margin	$ 4	×	*q*	=	10,000
– Fixed costs					10,000
Net income					$ —

Note: Net income is set to zero at the breakeven point.

Exhibit 5.10
CVP Analysis

	Per Unit	×	Quantity	=	Total
Sales	$12	×	2,501	=	$30,012
– Variable costs	8	×	2,501	=	20,008
Contribution margin	$ 4	×	2,501	=	$10,004
– Fixed costs					10,000
Net income					$ 4

Exhibit 5.11
C&F Commercial Services
Contribution Margin
Analysis

	Total	Percent
Revenues	$53,500	100.00%
– Variable costs	37,008	69.17%
Contribution margin	$16,492	30.83%
Unit sales	÷ 214	
Contribution margin per unit	$ 77.07	

Meeting Profit Targets

Breakeven analysis tools also can be modified to help managers determine what sales volume is needed to meet profit targets. To find a specific sales level needed to yield a certain targeted profit level, we first calculate the *target contribution margin* by adding desired profit to total fixed costs.

Target Contribution Margin = Target Net Income + Total Fixed Costs

When calculating the breakeven point, target net income was assumed to be zero. However, companies generally aim to create profits. Assume that the retailer described in Exhibit 5.7 now desires $12,000 in net income (profit). As seen in Exhibit 5.12, the company needs a total contribution margin of $22,000 to cover its total monthly fixed costs of $10,000 and yield its target profit of $12,000. Similar to the breakeven calculations in Exhibit 5.7, s and v represent total sales and total variable costs, respectively, at the target net income level.

To calculate the sales dollars needed to earn the targeted net income of $12,000, divide *target contribution margin* (total fixed costs plus target net income) by the contribution margin ratio. As Exhibit 5.13 illustrates, dividing the *target contribution margin* of $22,000 by the contribution margin ratio of 33.33 percent indicates that $66,000 in sales is needed to earn a $12,000 profit. Total sales of $66,000 yield a total contribution margin of $22,000 since total variable costs (v in Exhibit 5.12) are $44,000 (66.67 percent of total sales). This contribution margin is just enough to cover fixed costs and generate a profit of $12,000.

In Exhibit 5.14, q represents the number of units that the company needs to sell to achieve the desired net income. To calculate q, divide total sales ($66,000), variable costs ($44,000), or contribution margin ($22,000), by their respective per-unit amounts ($12, $8, or $4). This yields a required number of units sold of 5,500 for the store to attain its targeted profit level.

Keith and Dale also were curious about how much in commercial sales they would need to generate the same amount of net income that they earned last year. To calculate the dollar level in sales, they added their prior year's fixed costs of $19,100 to their first year's net income of $3,958 and divided this sum (their *target contribution margin* of $23,058) by the contribution margin ratio for the commercial line of business, which was 30.83 percent (see Exhibit 5.11). This resulted in required commercial sales dollars of $74,791. Similarly, they

	Total	Percent
Sales	s	100.00%
− Variable costs	v	66.67%
Contribution margin	$22,000	33.33%
− Fixed costs	10,000	
Net income	$12,000	

Exhibit 5.12
Target Contribution Margin

Hitting a Home Run on the Income Statement

Professional and minor league sports are very popular in the United States. Major league teams generate enormous revenues from lucrative television contracts, stadium advertising, and premium ticket prices. The major sports franchises operate with limited variable costs per customer like ticket printing, promotional gifts, and concession items, and heavy fixed costs such as players' salaries and stadium maintenance charges.

However, at the minor league level, the pay scale is much smaller and television contracts are rare. Nonetheless, the pressure to break even is equally demanding. For example, the St. Paul Saints are a minor league baseball team in the AA-level Northern League. The team estimated that it needed to sell 2,500 tickets per game to break even. Fortunately, the team's success on the field attracted crowds of over 5,000 fans in its first season. The team's attendance routinely ranks it in the top 10 percent of all minor-league baseball teams in the United States.

This popularity has also attracted many advertising sponsors. More than eighty corporate sponsors post ads on the outfield fences and promote group sales for company events. Advertising revenue has allowed the Saints to spend more than the average minor league team on creative promotions and game-day entertainment. Now in its tenth season, the team estimates that advertising and ticket sales each account for 40 percent of total revenue, with the remaining 20 percent of revenues generated by concessions (that is, food and souvenirs). The company needs to understand what its fans value and how to continue to generate enough revenue from ticket sales, advertising revenue, and concessions to cover the costs of running the team. CVP analysis helps managers to balance sales mix and cost structure while attempting to meet fan expectations.

Source: "Saints Alive!," by Susan Greco, *Inc Magazine*, August 1, 2001, p. 44.

computed the target sales level in units by dividing the same *target contribution margin* of $23,058 by the commercial contribution margin per unit of $77.07 (see Exhibit 5.11). This indicated that 300 commercial lawn service calls would be needed to maintain the same level of profits as last year. This meant that Keith and Dale would have to increase commercial service by over 40 percent (from 214 to 300 service calls) from the prior year assuming they ceased residential services and wanted to maintain the prior year's level of profitability.

Exhibit 5.13
Target Contribution Margin
(Dollars)

	Total	Percent
Sales	**$66,000**	100.00%
− Variable costs	**44,000**	66.67%
Contribution margin	$22,000	33.33%
− Fixed costs	10,000	
Net income	$12,000	

Exhibit 5.14
Target Contribution
Margin (Units)

	Per Unit	×	Units Sold	=	Total
Sales	$12	×	*q*	=	$66,000
− Variable costs	8	×	*q*	=	44,000
Contribution margin	$ 4	×	*q*	=	$22,000
− Fixed costs					10,000
Net income					$12,000

Safety Margin

When companies operate above the breakeven point (earn a profit), managers often want to know how far they are beyond the breakeven point (in terms of sales dollars or units sold). Managers use the term **safety margin** to describe the extent to which the firm's expected level of sales exceeds the breakeven point. The safety margin can be expressed in terms of either sales dollars or units sold.

In the case of the retailer described in Exhibits 5.7 and 5.9, the breakeven point was $30,000 in sales dollars, or 2,500 units sold. To earn the target profit of $12,000 per month illustrated in Exhibit 5.12, the company needs $66,000 (or 5,500 units) in sales. In this case, the safety margin in dollars would be $36,000 ($66,000 in target sales minus $30,000 in breakeven point sales). Expressed in terms of units sold, the safety margin is 3,000 units (5,500 units in target sales minus 2,500 units in breakeven point sales). Exhibit 5.15 illustrates these safety margin calculations.

Pricing Strategies

Choosing the right price for a product or service can affect both the level of sales and profits. Depending on the degree of competition in their markets, companies adopt different pricing strategies. Several of the more popular pricing strategies are:

- *Premium pricing.* Some firms price goods and services higher than competitors. Higher prices often are justified by higher quality or the image associated with the product. Rolls Royce, for example, sells fewer cars than other manufacturers, but at a much higher price. Their cars are perceived to be luxurious and command high prices from customers. Similarly, some clothing makers like Polo and Tommy Hilfiger establish prestigious brands and successfully charge higher prices than competitors for similar garments.

Exhibit 5.15
Safety Margin

	Units	Dollars
Expected sales	5,500	$66,000
− Breakeven sales	2,500	30,000
Safety margin	3,000	$36,000

- *Cost leadership.* Some firms price their products or services below the competition. These companies rely on high volume and target "value" shoppers. However, if a company prices its product too low, it may attract many customers, yet fail to generate profits. Some retailers like Wal-Mart rely on cost leadership to attract customers and develop a brand reputation. However, many failed to set prices high enough to offset costs.

- *Cost-based pricing.* Some businesses set their prices at some fixed percentage above costs. These firms must carefully control costs to ensure that their prices do not exceed market expectations and that their bids remain competitive. Construction firms and defense contractors rely on this pricing strategy to cover costs and ensure profits.

Companies must price their products and services appropriately to attract a sufficient number of customers to generate enough revenue to cover costs. A quality business plan must document the competitive nature of the business and justify the use of a particular pricing strategy.

Lowering the Breakeven Point

Learning Objective 5
Identify strategies that companies use to lower their breakeven points.

The breakeven point is where companies start to earn a profit. Obviously, companies are eager to reach this sales level as quickly as possible. Companies usually seek to lower the breakeven point, often by using one of the following three strategies:

1. *Decrease variable costs.* Decreasing variable costs increases contribution margin per unit. Companies can decrease variable costs by producing more efficiently or by using less expensive resources. They must be careful, however,

Management Accounting: A Business Planning Approach

not to sacrifice quality. Defects and returns go hand in hand with dissatisfied customers, higher warranty costs, and repairs and replacements. Similarly, reducing sales commissions can demotivate the sales force. Managers must carefully consider the business effects of reducing variable costs.

2. *Decrease fixed costs.* Decreasing fixed costs lowers the breakeven point by reducing the total amount of contribution margin necessary to break even. Companies frequently seek to eliminate or reduce fixed commitments. Many companies, for example, rely on external suppliers to perform administrative tasks such as payroll processing and technology support. As noted in Chapter 4, this is referred to as *outsourcing* of services. These outside vendors help companies minimize fixed costs by delivering services on an as-needed basis rather than requiring a company to employ and support a full-time staff to handle these business activities. Similarly, companies can reduce fixed costs by monitoring and "shopping" services such as insurance and utilities. As with variable costs, managers must be careful not to simply select the least expensive alternative: The quality and reliability of these services often can affect business performance.

3. *Increase sales prices.* In addition to managing costs, companies may elect to raise or lower sales prices. Raising sales prices will increase contribution margin per unit, but it may decrease quantities sold. Managers must evaluate market competition and customer loyalty before raising sales prices.

Each of these strategies requires considerable insight into customer satisfaction and business processes. To make the business decisions necessary to achieve profitability goals, managers must have a thorough understanding of cost-volume-profit relationships.

Multiproduct Breakeven Analysis

The CVP discussion in this chapter has assumed that the retailer sells only one product. However, most companies sell more than one product or service. Therefore, managers must understand how changes in a firm's sales mix can affect profitability. Sales mix is the relative proportion or percentage of total sales that each product or service represents. For example, a company might increase its total sales, but if the mix is weighted toward products with lower contribution margins, profits will decline.

In the single-product CVP example in this chapter, the retailer had one product (Product A), monthly fixed expenses totaled $10,000, and unit variable expenses were $8. Assume that the company decided to offer a second product (Product B) to its customers. Product B sells for $20 per unit, has unit variable costs of $12, and entails no additional fixed costs. Product B accounts for 25 percent of sales. These facts are summarized in Exhibit 5.16.

To compute the breakeven point in a multiproduct setting, we must calculate the weighted average contribution margin of the products based on the sales mix (75 percent for A and 25 percent for B). By weighting each product's contribution

Exhibit 5.16
Multiproduct Example

	Product A	Product B
Selling price per unit	$12	$20
− Variable cost per unit	8	12
Contribution margin per unit	$ 4	$ 8
Sales mix	75%	25%

Exhibit 5.17
Multiproduct Average
Contribution Margin

	Contribution Margin		Percentage of Sales		
Product A	$4	×	75%	=	$3
Product B	$8	×	25%	=	2
Weighted average contribution margin per unit					$5

Exhibit 5.18
Multiproduct Breakeven
Point (Total Units)

	Per Unit	×	Quantity	=	Total
Contribution margin	$5	×	2,000	=	$10,000
− Fixed costs					10,000
Net income					$ 0

Exhibit 5.19
C&F Data by Product Line

	Commercial	**Residential**	**Other**
Percentage of revenues (A)	71.52%	19.49%	8.99%
Contribution margin per unit (B)	$77.07	$ 9.25	$13.87
Contribution margin weightings (A × B)	55.12 +	1.80 +	1.25
Weighted average contribution margin per unit	$ 58.17		

margin by its percentage of sales, we create (for analysis purposes) "average product" data. This procedure is shown in Exhibit 5.17, which shows the resulting weighted average contribution margin per unit of $5. Managers can then use these "average product" data to compute the breakeven point.

As shown in Exhibit 5.18, dividing the required contribution margin at breakeven ($10,000) by the weighted average contribution margin per unit ($5) results in 2,000 units required at the breakeven point.

Finally, to determine the number of units of *each product* to be sold at the breakeven point, we multiply the total breakeven quantity by each product's respective percentage of sales. For example, Product A will account for 75 percent of sales, or 1,500 of the 2,000 units sold at the breakeven point. Likewise, Product B will account for 25 percent of sales, or the remaining 500 units sold at the breakeven point.

The commercial sales increases needed by C&F to achieve last year's profit levels were daunting. So, Keith and Dale decided to see what the numbers looked like if they continued to run all three lines of business (commercial, residential, and other services [i.e., snow removal]). Frances was able to finally get them the sales mix and contribution margin unit data by service line. This is shown in Exhibit 5.19.

Using this data, Keith and Dale computed a weighted average contribution margin per unit of $58.17. They then divided this into the target contribution margin of $23,058 (fixed costs of $19,100 and prior-year net income of $3,958) to find the targeted sales level in units. The result was 397 total unit sales. When multiplied by the sales mix percentages, this yielded the following required unit sales by service line: 284 commercial service calls, 78 residential service calls, and 36 snow removal calls. Although the required commercial service sales were still quite high, this analysis seemed to confirm that commercial lawn service was the business to be in with its high unit contribution margins.

Summary

This chapter discussed the importance of cost behavior and breakeven analysis. To successfully manage business processes, managers must understand how business decisions affect profits. This chapter introduced several formulas that managers use to forecast net income at various levels of business activity. These calculations are essential because they allow companies to manage the business processes that drive financial performance. The next chapter illustrates how these fundamental concepts and tools are applied in a forecasting context.

Summary of Learning Objectives

1. **Describe the primary types of cost behaviors.** Costs can be classified as variable, fixed, or mixed. Variable costs change in direct proportion to some level of activity, such as sales. Fixed costs remain constant across different levels of activity. Mixed costs have some base level of fixed costs and some incremental variable portion as activity exceeds a certain level.

2. **Define the relevant range and a firm's total cost function.** Relevant range describes the levels of activity or sales volume where assumptions about the fixed or variable nature of costs hold. A firm's total cost function is an equation that expresses total cost as the sum of total fixed costs and total variable costs. Mixed costs are disaggregated into fixed and variable components for this formula.

Net Gains

Breakeven Analysis Resources on the Web

Many breakeven analysis calculators and downloadable resources (that is, spreadsheets) are now available for little or no cost on the Internet. These high-quality resources demonstrate the declining value assigned in the marketplace to computational tasks. These tools free up valuable manager time for data analysis and the creation of information that is useful for decision-making.

Conducting a search for the terms *breakeven analysis*, *CVP*, or *cost-volume-profit* with any of the major search engines will yield countless interactive profit-planning tools. We strongly encourage you to try a search to gain an appreciation for the vast amount of resources that are available. Your search will likely yield some very useful tools!

3. **Describe cost-volume-profit (CVP) analysis and explain its usefulness.** CVP analysis is a fundamental tool that managers use to analyze the relationships between revenues, expenses, and profits at different levels of sales. As part of this analysis, a contribution margin income statement frequently is used to highlight the differences between variable and fixed expenses. Total contribution margin is the excess of sales revenues over variable costs and represents the amount available to cover fixed expenses.

4. **Demonstrate the use of breakeven analysis.** Breakeven analysis allows managers to clearly determine the level of sales that a firm needs to earn a profit. This tool allows managers to quickly see how changing sales prices or costs can affect profitability.

5. **Identify strategies that companies use to lower their breakeven points.** Companies seeking to lower their breakeven point may choose to do so in one of several ways. They can either decrease fixed or variable costs or they can increase sales price. Since both of these approaches potentially can affect business processes and ultimately customer satisfaction, managers must carefully evaluate their impact prior to implementation.

Glossary of Terms

Breakeven analysis A basic tool that managers use to determine the level of sales needed for their company to earn a profit.

Breakeven point The level of sales in either dollars or units at which profits equal zero or at which total sales equal total costs.

Contribution margin The amount by which total sales revenue exceeds total variable costs.

Contribution margin ratio (or percentage) The amount earned by a company (before fixed costs) on every dollar of sales; calculated by dividing contribution margin per unit (or dollars) by sales price per unit (or total sales dollars).

Cost-volume-profit (CVP) analysis A fundamental profit-planning technique used to analyze the relationships between revenues, expenses, and profits at different levels of sales.

Fixed costs Costs that remain unchanged across different activity levels.

Mixed costs Costs that have both fixed and variable cost components.

Relevant range The level of activity at which assumptions about the fixed or variable behavior of costs remain valid.

Safety margin The extent to which the expected level of sales exceeds the breakeven point.

Sales mix The relative proportion or percentage of total sales attributable to each product or service sold by a company.

Total cost function A mathematical formula that expresses total cost as the sum of total fixed costs and total variable costs.

Variable costs Costs that change in direct proportion to a specific type of activity.

Chapter Review Questions

1. What is CVP analysis?
2. What are the three primary types of cost behavior and how do they differ?
3. Give an example of a variable cost.
4. Give an example of a fixed cost.
5. Give an example of a mixed cost.
6. What is the contribution margin?
7. What is the difference between the contribution margin expressed in dollars and the contribution margin ratio?
8. What four pieces of data do managers need to conduct CVP analysis?
9. What three assumptions underlie CVP analysis?
10. What is meant by sales mix?
11. What is the breakeven point?
12. How do you compute the breakeven point in dollars?
13. How do you compute the breakeven point in units?
14. What is safety margin?
15. When is weighted average contribution margin used?
16. What are three strategies that a firm can pursue to lower its breakeven point and what are the obstacles to pursuing each of these strategies?

Exercises and Problems

1. Assume you have been asked to analyze the cost behavior of a movie theater chain as part of a consulting engagement. Classify the following costs as fixed, variable, or mixed.
   a. Building depreciation
   b. Employee wages
   c. Ticket printing costs
   d. Manager salaries
   e. Utilities
   f. Food and beverage costs
   g. Grounds maintenance
   h. Movie licensing fees
2. Assume you have been asked to analyze cost behavior for a local daily newspaper publisher as part of a consulting engagement. Classify the following costs as fixed, variable, or mixed.
   a. Janitorial services
   b. Paper and ink costs
   c. Advertising
   d. Equipment depreciation
   e. Repair and maintenance
   f. Delivery driver salaries

g. Sales force commissions

h. News wire annual subscription fees

3. Fill in the missing components for each of the following profit-planning formulas:

   a. Contribution Margin Ratio (%) = _____ ÷ Unit Sales Price

   b. Net Income = _____ − Total Fixed Costs

   c. _____ = Total Fixed Costs ÷ Contribution Margin Ratio (%)

   d. Contribution Margin per Unit = Unit Sales Price − _____

   e. Breakeven Point (in Units) = Total Fixed Costs ÷ _____

   f. Total Contribution Margin = _____ × Sales Volume (in Units)

   g. Total Sales = _____ × Sales Volume (in Units)

   h. Total Costs = Total Fixed Costs + _____

4. Local investors are considering opening a pizza shop near campus. The shop will offer pizza, pasta dishes, sandwiches, and soft drinks at affordable prices to college students. While the investors are confident that there will be sufficient customer demand for this business, they are unsure of what costs they will incur.

   a. Identify ten specific costs (for example, rent and wages) that the pizza shop will incur.

   b. Classify each cost that you identified in part (a) as variable, fixed, or mixed and justify your classification.

5. Durango Company sells its product for $48. Its variable cost per unit is $40.

   a. If fixed costs total $8,000, how many units must the company sell to break even? What are total sales in dollars at the breakeven point?

   b. If fixed costs total $12,000, how many units does the company need to sell to break even? What are total sales in dollars at the breakeven point?

   c. If fixed costs total $20,000, how many units must the company sell to break even? What are total sales in dollars at the breakeven point?

6. Albuquerque Company sells one product with a variable cost per unit of $10. Fixed costs each year are $50,000.

   a. If sales price per unit is $12, how many units must the company sell to break even? What are total sales in dollars at the breakeven point?

   b. If sales price per unit is $20 and the company sells 6,500 units in a year, compute the company's net income.

   c. If sales price per unit is $20 and the company sells 9,000 units in a year, compute the company's net income.

7. Mardi Gras Company sells three different products:

Product	Unit Sales Price	Unit Variable Cost
Masks	$ 5.00	$3.00
Costumes	18.00	9.00
Noisemakers	1.50	0.50

   a. Compute the contribution margin per unit (in dollars) of each product.

   b. Compute the contribution margin ratio of each product.

8. Big Circus Toy Company needs assistance computing its breakeven point. Compute the missing values in the figure below:

	Per Unit	×	Quantity	=	Total	Percent
Sales	$20	×	(f)	=	(c)	100.00%
– Variable costs	12	×	(f)	=	(d)	(g)
Contribution margin	(b)	×	(f)	=	(e)	(h)
– Fixed costs					$15,000	
Net income					(a)	

a. Net income
b. Contribution margin per unit
c. Total sales
d. Total variable costs
e. Total contribution margin

f. Quantity sold
g. Variable costs as a percentage of sales
h. Contribution margin ratio

9. The Ice City Blades are a minor league ice hockey franchise. Their arena has 5,000 seats, all of which sell for $11 per ticket per game. The team plays 40 home games and expects to average 70 percent attendance at each game. Variable costs related to ticket printing, promotions, and mailings are estimated to be $1 per ticket. Fixed costs including player salaries and operating expenses total $1.2 million for the season.
a. What are the expected total sales in dollars and units (tickets)?
b. What would total sales be if the team sold every ticket to every game?
c. What is the team's projected net income at its planned sales level?
d. What is the team's breakeven point in terms of total tickets sold?
e. How many tickets per game on average does the team need to sell to break even?
f. Compute the team's safety margin in sales dollars and units (tickets).

10. Heart & Soul Vintage Vinyl Record Emporium provided the following information:

Average selling price per record:	$15
Average variable cost per record:	$10
Monthly fixed costs:	$10,000

Compute the following:
a. What is Heart & Soul's contribution margin per unit in dollars?
b. What is Heart & Soul's contribution ratio?
c. How many records must Heart & Soul sell to break even?
d. How many records must Heart & Soul sell to earn $5,000 per month?
e. What is Heart & Soul's net income for the month if it sells 1,500 records?
f. What is Heart & Soul's net income for the month if it sells 3,500 records?
g. Are your responses to parts (e) and (f) consistent with your calculation of Heart & Soul's breakeven point? Why?

11. Clayre's Candies sells cotton candy swirls at local sporting events. The company sells cotton candy for $4 per swirl. Cotton candy costs 80 cents per swirl in materials (i.e., ingredients and packaging). Equipment and vendor carrying

boards cost $12,000 per year to rent. The company pays its vendors 20 cents per swirl sold rather than an hourly wage. Based on this information, answer the following questions:

a. What is the contribution margin per unit?
b. How many swirls must the company sell to break even?
c. How many swirls must the company sell to earn $27,000?
d. What is the company's safety margin if it sells $50,000 of cotton candy?
e. Prepare a contribution margin income statement, assuming that the company sold 30,000 swirls last year.

12. Hutchinson's Bakery provided the following income statement for 20X1:

Hutchinson's Bakery	
Income Statement	
For the Year Ended December 31, 20X1	
Sales	$100,000
– Cost of goods sold	48,000
Gross margin	$ 52,000
– Sales and marketing expense	20,000
– Utilities expense	11,000
Net income	$ 21,000

Cost of goods sold is a variable expense. Sales and marketing is 20 percent variable and 80 percent fixed. Utilities expense is 10 percent variable and 90 percent fixed. Prepare a contribution margin income statement for Hutchinson's Bakery.

13. MicroTechnologies Company sells two products: X and Y. The selling price, variable cost, and sales mix for the products are presented in the table below.

Product	Unit Sales Price	Unit Variable Cost	Percentage of Sales
X	$20	$15	70%
Y	$10	$ 4	30%

Based on the data in the table above:

a. Compute the contribution margin per unit for each product.
b. Compute the weighted average contribution margin.
c. How would your results differ if Product X accounted for 80 percent of sales and Product Y accounted for the remaining 20 percent?
d. If total fixed costs are $78,000, what are the company's breakeven quantities (for each product) if it continues to sell both products in the same sales mix (80/20)?

14. For each of the actions listed, describe its effect on a firm's breakeven point (increase, decrease, no effect):

a. Lowering fixed costs
b. Increasing variable costs
c. Purchasing supplies on credit
d. Raising sales price
e. Lowering sales price

Keystone Academy (Part 2)

In Chapter 4's Mini-Case, you were introduced to Keystone Academy, a private college preparatory school serving grades 9 through 12. You were asked to identify activities and related cost drivers for nine separate costs. The school principal is now interested in how each cost behaves. For each item listed, specify whether the costs associated with each activity are fixed, variable, or mixed.

Required

1. Wages and fringe benefits for the academy's administrative staff.
2. Academic materials (e.g., books and laptop computers) provided to students by the academy at no charge.
3. Wages and fringe benefits for the academy's full-time faculty.
4. Repairs to student laptop computers. The school recently hired a full-time repair technician. Repairs that are beyond the technician's abilities are outsourced to a local computer repair shop.
5. Fee charged by a local public accounting firm to audit the academy's financial records.
6. Wages for the school's part-time athletic coaches (baseball, football, basketball, tennis, and soccer). These coaches are hired on a temporary basis. The number of hours they work is dictated by the number of students participating in each sport (at Keystone every student must participate in one of these five sports). On average, each coach is used about 10 hours per week during the full academic year.
7. Depreciation on the academy's recently completed performing arts pavilion.
8. Rent for the buses the academy uses to transport its students to and from school.
9. Electricity to operate the academy's facilities. The local utility's charge is composed of a fixed monthly charge plus another fixed charge per kilowatt-hour of electricity used.

Casino Express Bus Lines (Client Review for a Business Consulting Firm)

Casino Express Bus Lines provides transportation from several regional locations to Casino City. Casino Express operates 365 days a year and offers several convenient daily departure and return times to each of its five metropolitan stations. Each bus holds up to 100 passengers per trip. The company's strategy is to offer comfortable, moderately priced transportation to this popular gaming destination.

A round-trip ticket costs each passenger $28 from any location. Based on seasonal demand, the company is committed to offering 7,300 total round-trips next year. The company's president estimates that each round-trip has $1,000 in costs related to fuel, vehicle rental fees, inspections, driver salaries, highway tolls, and miscellaneous regulatory fees. Casino Express incurs the following costs per passenger ($10 total): soft drinks and snacks ($1), casino meal-discount vouchers ($4), and slot machine coins ($5). The bus line also incurs $200,000 each year for administration and marketing fixed costs.

Background Questions

a. What is the contribution margin per passenger?

b. Describe the cost structure of this company. Are they more heavily committed to fixed or variable costs?

c. What is the breakeven point for Casino Express? How many passengers per roundtrip are required to break even? How many passengers per round-trip are needed to earn $900,000 each year?

Breakeven Analysis and Financial Forecasting

Investors and creditors frequently use breakeven analysis to quickly screen business plans by evaluating a firm's cost structure and the sales volume needed to generate profits. All business plans are expected to include a breakeven analysis. A detailed financial forecast will supplement this basic analysis to help investors decide whether or not to provide funding for a start-up enterprise. Create your own using the following guidelines.

Assignment

Identifying Costs

The first step in breakeven analysis is to identify and properly classify all of the costs that your business is likely to incur. For your start-up enterprise, you should do the following:

- Visit a local business owner in a similar business. Some businesses will be reluctant to share information to potential competitors. Be sure to inform the business owner (or manager) that you are conducting research for an academic project.
- Observe operations at a busy time and identify key business operations.
- Develop a list of all costs that the business incurs on a regular basis.
- Classify each cost as variable, fixed, or mixed. Develop one to two paragraphs about each set of costs, explaining the behavior and purpose of each cost.
- For each of your expected costs, estimate variable cost per unit and total fixed costs. For mixed costs, be sure to identify the variable and fixed components.

These data and the related discussion will allow people who read your business plan to see the research behind your calculations. Thorough research enhances the credibility of your analysis.

Preliminary Breakeven Analysis

The next component of your breakeven analysis is to determine contribution margin. To do so, you must estimate the selling price of your product or service. After estimating your selling price, complete the following calculations:

1. What is the contribution margin per unit of your product or service? (If you plan to sell multiple products, you must compute the weighted average contribution margin.)
2. What is the contribution margin ratio?
3. What are total fixed costs?
4. What is sales volume in *dollars* at the breakeven point?
5. What is sales volume in *units* at the breakeven point?
6. What sales volume in *dollars* is required to have $10,000 in net income? $50,000 in net income? $100,000 in net income?
7. What sales volume in *units* is required to have $10,000 in net income? $50,000 in net income? $100,000 in net income?

In addition to your calculations, prepare a one-page discussion describing your results. This preliminary breakeven analysis provides the basis for assessing the reasonableness of your business idea. Keep copies of this analysis so that you can refer to it later when preparing, evaluating, and defending your formal business plan.

Image Credits

Chapter 6

1. Demonstrate the importance of sales forecasting.

2. Describe the role of cost drivers in estimating costs.

3. Demonstrate the use of graphical and statistical forecasting techniques.

4. Demonstrate the use of cost estimates in cost-volume-profit (CVP) analysis.

5. Discuss qualitative factors that affect costs.

Forecasting Tools and Techniques

The profit-planning tools introduced in Chapter 5 can depend on a variety of assumptions and estimates. This chapter builds on that discussion and illustrates how managers use statistical techniques to forecast. Forecasting supplies data that can be used in breakeven analysis and provides the foundation for developing credible and meaningful budgets and business plan projections. The chapter concludes with a brief discussion of qualitative factors that managers must also consider when making business decisions. In coming chapters, we will apply these tools to budget development and performance evaluation.

Sales Forecasting

Sales revenue is the primary source of a firm's cash flow. Companies must accurately forecast customer demand to determine whether they can sell enough of their products or services to cover costs. Therefore, forecasting sales is particularly critical—it is the cornerstone of the budgeting process. For an established business, sales projections often are based on past performance. For startup enterprises, managers must carefully consider expected customer demand, competition, market size, economic conditions, and other trends. As you may recall from Chapter 1, even Keith and Dale, two inexperienced entrepreneurs, did some market analysis before incorporating C&F Enterprises.

Forecasting sales requires a thorough appreciation of the unique market forces that have the potential to affect a company's business. For example, managers must consider the seasonality of demand when estimating sales revenues and planning resource utilization. It is highly unlikely that customer sales will occur evenly throughout most companies' fiscal years. In C&F's case, landscaping, mowing, and other yard-related services will be in heavy demand from early spring through late fall, with snow removal being the primary revenue generator in the winter. It is important to recognize that assumptions will be necessary when estimating future sales. Therefore, the reliability of the sales forecast depends on the quality and reasonableness of each assumption and estimate.

As discussed in Chapter 1, successful companies periodically evaluate both current and future operations as part of their strategic planning. This process can provide significant information on market opportunities, information that is critical for predicting

Learning Objective 1
Demonstrate the importance
of sales forecasting.

sales. Strategic planning provides "answers" to such questions as, how large is the product or service market and how much will revenues grow? Chapter 1 also highlighted the important role that economic data plays in strategic planning. This same data often provides significant insights into customer demand and competition, key determinants of the sales forecast. Two useful sources of demographic data are the U.S. Census (www.census.gov) and the local chamber of commerce. Data on market competition can be found by using Internet searches for market sources or by contacting local business and trade associations. Product or service demand can be evaluated through surveys, as well as through industry and trade publications. Refer back to Exhibits 1.6 and 1.7 in Chapter 1 for examples of useful publication data. All of these resources contribute to the creation of a credible sales forecast.

As you will recall from Chapter 3, C&F Enterprises, Inc. managed to return a thin profit in its first year of operations despite Keith and Dale's inadequate planning techniques. Chapter 5 introduced an aggressive new competitor into C&F's market, which motivated Keith and Dale to seek information that would allow them to better manage costs. Developing accurate sales forecasts will also help C&F better manage the business risks associated with this recent threat to its future profitability.

When Keith and Dale initially planned their business, they relied heavily on the existence of several prenegotiated commercial lawn maintenance contracts to generate revenue. Although they also intended to service residential customers, they did little to forecast this source of revenues beyond Internet searches. Exhibit 6.1 illustrates what C&F's quarterly sales projection for residential customers might have looked like for 20x1, had Keith and Dale prepared it.

Figure 6.1
To achieve their business objectives, companies must accurately forecast customer demand for their products and services. For example, a toy retailer's failure to successfully forecast and plan for its holiday season sales would negatively impact its business results.

Management Accounting: A Business Planning Approach

C&F Enterprises, Inc. Projected Residential Service Revenue For Fiscal Year 20×1	Q1	Q2	Q3	Q4
Number of residential customers (A)	15	20	21	23
Average quarterly demand per customer (B)	0	10	12	2
Estimated total customer demand (A × B)	0	200	252	46
Average $ price per customer (C)	$30	$30	$30	$30
Estimated total residential revenues (A × B × C)	$0	$6,000	$7,560	$1,380
				$14,940

The forecast is based on a calendar fiscal year with the first quarter (Q1) representing the months of January through March. Keith and Dale could have "surveyed" potential customers by mailing flyers and following up on any responses they received. In the illustration, out of the hundreds of flyers distributed, 15 residential families committed to use C&F for lawn care service at the outset. Next, Keith and Dale would need to consider potential growth in demand resulting from customer referrals once the quality of their services became evident to the market. In this case, new customers are projected to increase rapidly in the second quarter and then more gradually in subsequent quarters. Next, the amount of services demanded each quarter must be estimated. The forecast should reflect the seasonal nature of lawn care services (minimal during the winter months and high in the spring and summer). In this case, the majority of residential services are expected to occur between April and September with the greatest demand in third quarter (Q3). An average quarterly demand of 12 indicates that a customer will require a weekly lawn cutting for each month in the quarter (4 weeks times 3 months). Total quarterly customer demand is easily computed by multiplying the estimated number of residential customers by the expected average quarterly demand per customer. Finally, Keith and Dale must decide what they think the average revenue generated per customer will be, given that residential lawns are of all sizes and shapes and are located on all types of terrain. In this illustration, they assume an average price of $30 per lawn cutting. The forecasted revenue of $14,940 assumes that Keith and Dale will not have any customer collection problems and provides them with additional information that they can use to manage their profitability.

Forecasting Costs

Chapter 5 discussed the importance of understanding cost behavior. It also described how managers use that insight in profit planning. The examples provided in that chapter were based on *known* fixed and variable costs. However, as

Learning Objective 2
Describe the role of cost
drivers in estimating costs.

Brewery Goes Flat Due to Faulty Sales Forecasting

Guild Hall, a microbrewery, opened in a one-time Rolls Royce showroom by a husband and wife in suburban Philadelphia. The brewery closed after just four months. The owners invested $1.9 million for the purchase and rehab of the venue. It turned out that $1.9 million was insufficient for the capital investment and construction delays that pushed the opening out nearly six months.

On top of the budget overruns and despite the past brewing experience of one of the owners, the beer quality was quite poor. The problem stemmed from the incorrect calibration of the brewery's fermentation tanks. A scale alongside the tank's sight-glass (which shows the level of liquid inside) had been improperly placed and was off by five-eighths of a barrel. The brewers compensated by adding too much liquid to his recipes, diluting flavor and appearance of the beer. Online sites criticized the new venture.

After several wasted batches of beer, the team improved the quality, but it was too late to attract enough customers. The original business plan projected sales of between $25,000 and $30,000 a week. Guild Hall never met the required weekly amounts to break even.

Sadly, the fledging restaurant and brewery met a quick demise. The case is one of many where accurate budgeting, realistic sales forecasting, and successful execution of a business plan are so critical for the launch of a new business.

Sources: http://articles.philly.com/2015-11-06/news/68047030_1_brewpub-jenkintown-breweries

http://www.philly.com/philly/blogs/the-insider/Guild-Hall-Brewing-Co-announces-closing.html#dqf5j2fYGVOXlqwh.99

we also saw in that chapter, some costs have both fixed and variable components (mixed costs). In addition, we learned that relevant ranges of cost behavior are important in analyzing costs and profits, but that identifying these ranges is not always an easy process. Consequently, managers often must estimate fixed and variable cost amounts. **Cost estimation** is the process of determining the relative fixed and variable components of expected total costs at various activity levels. The first step in estimating these costs is identifying those factors or activities that make them go up or down: the cost drivers.

Identifying Cost Drivers Across Industries

To effectively estimate costs, managers must understand which activities *drive* costs. As discussed in detail in Chapter 4, cost drivers are the business process factors that determine the expenses ultimately incurred by a company. Cost estimation allows managers to approximate the fixed and variable components of each cost total since the exact behavior of all costs cannot always be observed.

Cost drivers and cost structure differ across industries because of dissimilarities in business processes. Companies in different industries do business in different ways. Therefore, factors that affect costs in one industry may not in another. Exhibit 6.2 illustrates how a major cost and its cost drivers differ in seven different types of organizations in the manufacturing, retail, and service sectors.

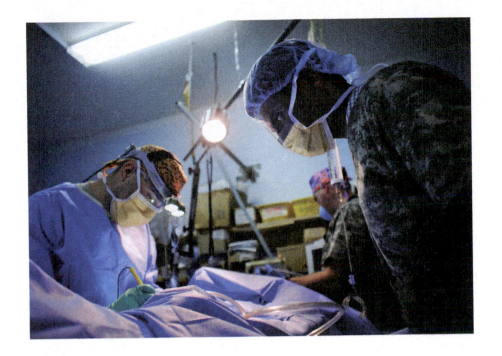

Figure 6.2
Environmental factors beyond a company's control can often affect costs. For example, rising medical costs are causing major increases in employee and retiree health insurance premiums. Consequently, qualitative considerations can lead to higher costs that may translate into higher sales prices, reduced profits, or both.

Hospitals. Hospitals deliver a wide array of services to a diverse set of patients. Surgeries account for a large percentage of a hospital's costs, and the cost of a particular procedure often varies with its complexity and risk. Heart surgery, for example, is more complicated, risky, and expensive and than an appendectomy. Hospital managers closely examine surgical procedures and their costs to identify cost drivers. Generally, surgery costs are a function of staffing requirements (that is, the number of nurses and specialists), procedure type (for example, heart surgery or cosmetic surgery), and patient condition (for example, age and health status). Understanding the relationships between procedures and their costs allows a hospital to prepare realistic forecasts of resource requirements, which ultimately can promote quality patient care.

Pizza Delivery Services. The cost of vehicle fuel is a major cost for a pizza delivery service (for example, Domino's, Pizza Hut, Papa John's). The amount of fuel consumed depends on a vehicle's age, condition, type, and usage (that is, the number of miles driven). Delivery services must ensure that vehicles are maintained and that drivers operate their vehicles in a responsible manner. These companies rely on formal employee education programs to instruct drivers on how to plan routes, drive safely, and care for their vehicles. These factors not only affect costs but also promote employee safety, vehicle longevity, and timely deliveries.

Lawn Mower Manufacturers. Production costs account for the majority of costs in manufacturing businesses. If a lawn mower manufacturer such as John Deere sacrifices the quality of its mowers, it will incur repair and replacement costs as required under warranties. Warranty costs typically depend on the quality of production process (that is, the number of defects) and product complexity (that is,

Exhibit 6.2
Differences in Cost Drivers
Across Business Sectors

Organization	Cost	Possible Cost Drivers
Hospital	Surgeries	Staffing requirements Procedure type Patient condition
Pizza delivery service	Vehicle fuel	Vehicle age Vehicle type Miles driven
Lawn mower manufacturer	Product warranties	Number of defects Number of parts
Retailer	Store rent	Property size Property age Location
College or university	Repairs to student computers	Instructional methods Computer usage Computer age
Accounting, consulting, law firm	Salaries	Experience Education Certifications
Airline	Flight cost	Distance Aircraft age Aircraft type Number of passengers

the number of parts). In addition to warranty repair costs, faulty products may jeopardize customer safety and impair the manufacturer's reputation. They may even lead to unexpected litigation and/or liability costs. Dissatisfied customers also may be less likely to buy the firm's products in the future, further impacting profitability. Therefore, manufacturers are very attentive to the factors that drive warranty costs, continually seeking ways to monitor and improve design and production.

Retailers. Rent is a major cost for most retail businesses (for example, candy stores or electronics shops). A property's location, size, and age all influence the amount of rent paid. For example, the rent for a storefront in a popular new urban mall is likely to be significantly higher than one in a rural setting. Retailers take great care in selecting locations that attract customers in quantities sufficient to generate sales that will cover this major fixed cost as well as other operating costs. Not only do the age and condition of a store affect repair and remodeling costs, but poor appearance may tarnish a company's image and reputation and discourage people from shopping there. Understanding the factors that affect rent helps managers select locations that are consistent with a company's strategic goals and profit expectations.

Colleges and Universities. Student activities drive the costs at colleges and universities. If the educational institution provides technology (for example, tablets or laptop computers) to students, administrators must consider those factors that may drive up repair costs. For example, instructional methods that use computers in the classroom, or rely on online courses affect computer usage; increased usage generally escalates the need for repairs. Similarly, the type, quality, and age of the computers impact the likelihood of repair. If a program administrator chooses inferior student machines, initial savings on the purchase may be offset by repair and replacement costs in the future. More importantly, computer breakdowns resulting from the choice of an inferior machine may hamper student learning, the institution's primary strategic goal.

Accounting, Consulting, and Law Firms. Professional service firms rely on highly educated individuals to meet their clients' needs. They must identify people who possess the proper abilities, skills, and backgrounds. Since these firms rely on their human capital to execute strategy, their primary cost is salary. Salaries for these professionals are a function of education (that is, degrees and quality of the educational institution), experience, and certifications (for example, CPAs or licensed attorneys). Since labor markets for professionals are highly competitive, quality individuals command premium compensation. Therefore, it is important for these firms not only to recruit and retain quality employees but also to recognize the effect of these decisions on costs.

Airlines. Airlines focus much of their attention on the cost of the numerous flights they provide. Several factors affect flight costs. Routes and distances (domestic versus trans-Atlantic flights, for example) together with plane type (for example, prop or jet) affect fuel usage. The need for on-board supplies (to provide for meals versus snacks) also impacts costs. The number of passengers aboard and their ticket type also can affect those costs. Full flights and first-class tickets generate more revenue for the airline but also require additional costly services (meals, ticketing, and baggage handling). Finally, the condition and type of aircraft in the fleet will affect maintenance and repair costs. Airlines must carefully evaluate how these cost drivers affect profitability when scheduling flights.

The above examples illustrate the importance of understanding one's business when evaluating costs and their drivers. As we have seen, many factors drive costs. The following sections introduce methods that managers can use to identify drivers and forecast *both* sales and costs.

Forecasting Techniques

In the past, managers have relied on sales and cost estimates based on such simple techniques as historical averages and opinion surveys. These methods still may be useful, particularly for very small or start-up businesses like C&F Enterprises, Inc., where the owner or manager can easily review the accounting records to analyze costs. However, today's technology allows anyone with a personal computer equipped with a standard software package to use powerful and sophisticated statistical techniques in business forecasting. This section demonstrates how three common analytical tools (scatter plot, correlation, and regression) found in Microsoft Excel can be used to identify revenue and cost drivers and generate meaningful forecasts.

Learning Objective 3
Demonstrate the use of graphical and statistical forecasting techniques.

Exhibit 6.3
Revenue Driver Data

	Sales Dollars	Advertising Dollars	Retail Outlets	Website Visits
District 1	1,000,000	33,000	27	30,000
District 2	1,140,000	35,000	29	31,000
District 3	1,340,000	40,000	34	35,000
District 4	980,000	43,500	25	27,000
District 5	1,035,000	26,000	26	35,000
District 6	1,540,000	38,000	31	43,000
District 7	870,000	39,000	29	25,000
District 8	800,000	27,500	28	26,000
District 9	830,000	30,000	36	28,000

Identifying Revenue Drivers

Assume that a large retail business has nine regional districts across the United States and that each district operates multiple outlets and manages its own website. Company managers disagree as to what the company's primary revenue driver is. Some believe that sales revenue is a function of how much money each district spends on advertising. Others believe that the number of retail outlets drives sales. Still other managers suspect that the number of visits on each district's website is the primary driver of sales since the company has recently adopted a very popular Internet-based sales strategy. To test these competing theories, the company president asked each district to collect data for the most recent year about each of these possible revenue drivers. Exhibit 6.3 shows total sales and related data for each district.

The Scatter-Plot Method

Data graphed across two dimensions is known as a **scatter plot**. Scatter plots show managers the general relationship between results and a selected activity (that

Exhibit 6.4
Advertising Expenditures

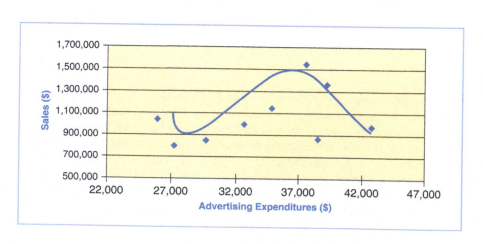

Management Accounting: A Business Planning Approach

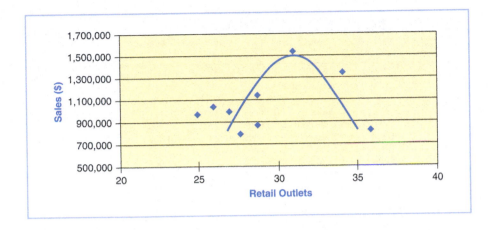

Exhibit 6.5
Retail Outlets

is, the revenue or cost driver). Activity is measured along the horizontal (x) axis. Dollar values (that is, total sales or total costs) are measured on the vertical (or y) axis. Managers look for linear (that is, straight-line) relationships between the activity driver on the x-axis and the variable on the y-axis. A linear relationship indicates that revenues or costs will increase or decrease in some *direct* proportion to activity-level changes. This relationship gives managers confidence that they have identified a driver that accurately predicts revenues or costs.

To create scatter plots using the data in Exhibit 6.3, we label the y-axis as total sales and plot its suspected revenue drivers along the x-axis. The scatter plot in Exhibit 6.4 is based on the idea that total sales are a function of advertising expenditures. The data plots yield an S-shaped pattern and do not reflect a linear relationship between sales and advertising costs.

In Exhibit 6.5, total sales data (y-axis) is plotted against the number of retail outlets (x-axis). The data yield a parabolic form (or "inverted-U" pattern) and once again fail to reveal a linear relationship between sales and retail outlets.

Exhibit 6.6 plots total sales (y-axis) against the number of website visits (x-axis). The scatter plot suggests that a linear relationship may exist between these variables. That is, increases or decreases in the number of website visits appear to be directly related to corresponding changes in total sales.

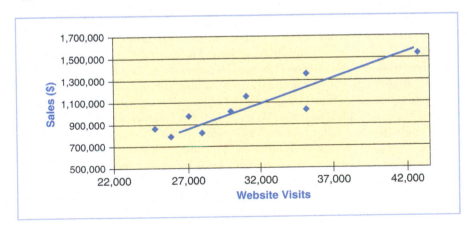

Exhibit 6.6
Website Visits

Chapter 6

Exhibit 6.7
Revenue Driver Data in
Excel Format

		Sales	Advertising Dollars	Retail Outlets	Website Visits
District 1		$1,000,000	$ 33,000	27	30,000
District 2		$1,140,000	$ 35,000	29	31,000
District 3		$1,340,000	$ 40,000	34	35,000
District 4		$ 980,000	$ 43,500	25	27,000
District 5		$1,035,000	$ 26,000	26	35,000
District 6		$1,540,000	$ 38,000	31	43,000
District 7		$ 870,000	$ 39,000	29	25,000
District 8		$ 800,000	$ 27,500	28	26,000
District 9		$ 830,000	$ 30,000	36	28,000

From a review of the scatter plots in Exhibits 6.4 through 6.6 it appears that the number of website visits is the best predictor of a district's sales. It displays a more linear relationship with sales than either advertising expenditures or the number of retail outlets. These results are consistent with the argument that technology is driving sales. However, the company president was not satisfied with the rudimentary graphs and wanted managers to conduct a statistical analysis to support this conclusion.

Correlation Analysis

Correlation analysis is a common statistical technique used to assess and measure the degree of relationship between variables. Correlation expresses the extent to which changes in one variable are associated with changes in another. Correlations range from 1.0 to 1.0. A correlation of 1.0 (referred to as perfect correlation) indicates that variables change together in an *identical* manner. Correlations approaching 1.0 are known as high correlations. For example, car insurance premiums and the number of speeding tickets are often highly correlated. Drivers with a greater number of traffic violations often pay higher rates. A correlation of 1.0 is known as a perfect inverse correlation and suggests that variable changes move in opposite directions. For example, insurance premium rates and driver age variables are likely to be inversely related as younger drivers often pay higher rates than older drivers with similar driving records.

A correlation of 0.0 indicates that no statistical relationship exists between the changes in the variables. Correlations close to 0.0 are known as low correlations. For example, the first letter of a student's name is likely to have no relationship with the letter grade that student receives in a college course.

Correlation analysis can easily be performed using Microsoft Excel. We will use the sales data from Exhibit 6.3 as an example. Carefully enter the data from Exhibit 6.3 into an Excel worksheet in Columns B through F and Rows 2 through 12, as shown in Exhibit 6.7.

Management Accounting: A Business Planning Approach

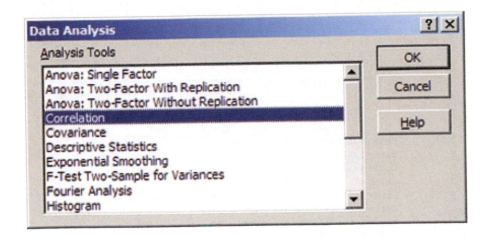

Next, select Data Analysis from the menu. If this item does not appear in your Tools menu, please refer to the Help menu and search under correlation to find out how to install this feature. After selecting Data Analysis, the pop-up menu illustrated in Exhibit 6.8 will appear. From that menu, select Correlation (the fourth item) and click OK.

Next the Correlation box will appear. Fill in the requested data as illustrated in Exhibit 6.9. Under Input, for Input Range type $C$3:$F$12 in the box. This represents the data from Exhibits 6.3 and 6.7 for sales and its three possible revenue drivers (advertising dollars, retail outlets, and website visits) that will be analyzed using correlation analysis. Be sure that Columns is selected for Grouped By and that the Labels in First Row box is checked. Under Output options, for Output Range, type $B$16 in the box. Click OK.

Your results should look like the screen shown in Exhibit 6.10, with the correlation results displayed in cells B16 through F20.

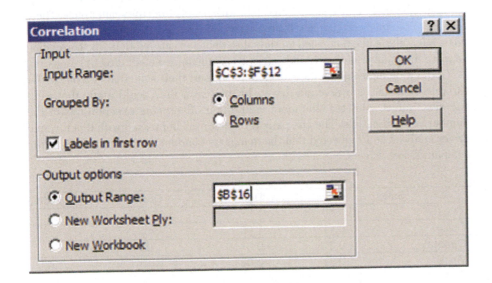

Exhibit 6.9
Selecting Data for
Correlation Analysis

Exhibit 6.10
Correlation Analysis Results

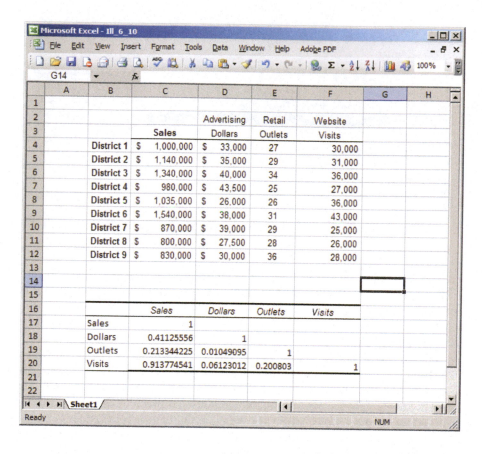

Exhibit 6.11
Correlation Table for
Revenue Drivers

Exhibit 6.11 shows the correlation table (data rounded to two decimals) extracted from the Excel worksheet. This table displays the correlations between all of the possible pairings of the variables from Exhibit 6.3. The highest correlation (.91) is between sales and website visits, consistent with results from the scatter plots. There appears to be some correlation (.41) between advertising expenditures (dollars) and sales, but nothing like that noted for the sales-website visits relation. The correlation between the number of outlets and sales (.21) is the lowest of all three relations.

Correlation analysis allows managers to support their selection of a particular variable or factor as a revenue driver. In this case, they could argue that website visits affect sales revenue more than either advertising expenditures or the number of retail outlets. The company president was impressed with this revenue driver analysis and requested that the managers conduct a similar analysis of the company's cost drivers.

	Sales	Dollars	Outlets	Visits
Sales	1.00			
Dollars	0.41	1.00		
Outlets	0.21	0.01	1.00	
Visits	0.91	0.06	0.20	1.00

	Total Costs	Units Sold	Number of Employees	Retail Sq. Ft.
District 1	$513,466	910	85	14,500
District 2	$646,518	11,920	92	14,800
District 3	$723,678	14,560	103	14,500
District 4	$817,610	17,300	78	16,000
District 5	$709,812	13,450	80	17,000
District 6	$766,528	16,500	84	14,800
District 7	$778,954	16,840	91	12,800
District 8	$800,986	18,010	108	17,000
District 9	$725,573	13,980	81	14,350

Exhibit 6.12
Sales and Cost Data

Identifying Cost Drivers

Just as they disagree about revenue drivers, the managers hold competing ideas about the company's primary cost driver. A few believe that total cost depends on units sold. Others believe that the number of employees in a district drives total costs. A third set of managers contends that retail space (measured in square feet) is the primary cost driver. To test these competing theories, each district provided data from the most recent year for total costs and these possible cost drivers. Exhibit 6.12 shows total sales and related data for each district.

Using Correlation Analysis to Identify Cost Drivers. The data in Exhibit 6.12 can be charted in scatter plots, with total costs set as the *y*-axis. The scatter plot in Exhibit 6.13 illustrates total costs (*y*-axis) and units sold (*x*-axis). The data appear along an upward sloping diagonal and seem to suggest a linear relationship between total costs and units sold.

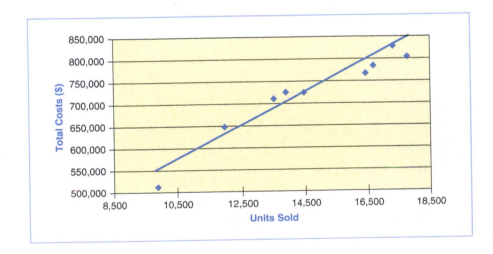

Exhibit 6.13
Units Sold

Exhibit 6.14
Number of Employees

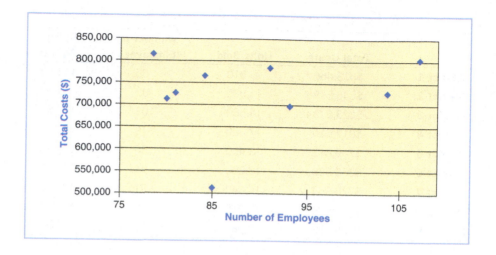

Exhibit 6.14 plots total cost data (y-axis) against the number of employees per district (x-axis). The data are scattered across the graph and do not appear to reflect any relationship between these variables.

Exhibit 6.15 plots total costs (y-axis) against the retail square feet per district (x-axis). These data also fail to disclose any relationship between the two variables.

A review of the scatter plots in Exhibits 6.13 through 6.15 suggests that units sold is a better predictor of a district's total costs than either number of employees or retail square feet. This result makes sense since a retailer's major cost is usually its cost of goods sold. Also, the company's heavy reliance on technology reduces the likelihood that retail space (physical capital) or employee costs (human capital) are driving costs.

We can perform correlation analysis on these cost drivers, just as we did with revenue drivers. To do so in Excel, use a format identical to that shown in Exhibit 6.12 and create a spreadsheet for total costs and the related data. Follow the same steps outlined in Exhibits 6.7 through 6.10 earlier in this chapter. Your spreadsheet will yield a correlation table similar to one presented in Exhibit 6.16.

Exhibit 6.15
Retail Square Feet

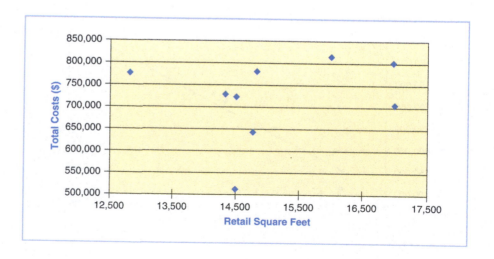

	Total Costs	Units Sold	Employees	Sq. Ft.
Total costs	1.00			
Units sold	0.96	1.00		
Employees	0.13	0.25	1.00	
Sq. ft.	0.21	0.17	0.04	1.00

Exhibit 6.16
Correlation Table for
Cost Drivers

This table displays the correlations between all of the possible pairings of the variables from Exhibit 6.12. The highest correlation is between total costs and units sold (0.96), which appears to confirm the findings from the scatter-plot analysis. The correlations of total cost with the number of employees (0.13) and retail square feet (.21) are both quite low. These results are consistent with a retailer who relies on a Web-based sales strategy.

Correlation analysis allows the company to support its selection of units sold as the primary cost driver. Using statistical techniques to analyze data allows managers to make much more credible arguments about revenue and cost behavior, two key inputs of the company's business plan.

Regression Analysis

Once a company identifies its cost driver, it can use statistical tools to more accurately define the relationship between the driver and its cost. This relationship then can be used to specify the fixed and variable components of a cost and to predict costs across levels of business activity. These data also provide the required inputs for performing cost-volume-profit or breakeven analyses, topics that we discussed in Chapter 5. Cost-behavior patterns can easily be estimated by a technique called regression analysis using statistical tools that are part of common computer software packages. Regression analysis determines the best-fitting line among a set of data points (similar to that in Exhibits 6.6 and 6.13), yielding an equation that can be used to estimate costs.

A popular form of regression analysis is a technique known as ordinary least squares (OLS) regression. OLS measures the squared distances of each data point from a "best-fitting" straight line. This "fitted" regression line expresses total cost as a function of both fixed and variable costs. Similar to the total cost equation described in Chapter 5, the regression line equation is expressed as follows:

$$Y = a + bX$$

Y is known as a dependent variable because its data values rely or "depend" on (are a function of) other variables. When estimating costs, Y represents total costs. The a in the equation represents the point where the regression (or total cost) line crosses the y-axis. This point is called the intercept and represents fixed costs in the total cost equation. X is called an independent variable. An independent variable drives (or affects) the dependent variable in the regression equation. When using regression analysis to estimate costs, X represents the cost driver. The b in the equation, the coefficient of the independent variable X, is an

"Reel" Life Regression

What makes a movie a hit? The Economist studied that by analyzing the budgets and performance of more than 2,000 films over a two decade period. Using data from The Numbers, a website that collects data on film releases, and Rotten Tomatoes, an aggregator of critics' and punters' reviews, the study found the strongest predictor of box office receipts was a film's budget. In North American theaters, a movie would generate an average of 80 cents for every dollar a studio promised to spend on it.

The more a studio commits to producing a film, the more it is likely to spend on advertising it and determines how widely a film is shown. All other things being equal, sequels earn $35 million more than nonsequels at the box office. Franchise films increasingly depend on superhero characters. A superhero film with a budget of $200 million will earn $58 million more than its nonsuperhero film competitor. Films that receive an "R" (restricted) certificate typically earn $16 million less in cinemas, as children cannot attend, limiting the viewer pool.

Movie stars do not make as big of a difference, as expected. Each $1 earned by a leading actor's previous, nonsequel films in the past five years adds 2 cents to their current one's takings. Each extra percentage point in critic scores on Rotten Tomatoes was worth far less than positive audience reviews. Audience reviews were most highly associated with box office revenue increases. The wisdom of crowds matters more these days: the same increase in positive audience reviews on Rotten Tomatoes is associated with an $1.2 million increase in box office revenues.

Taken together, these factors explain about 60 percent of the variation in box office sales. Adding an estimate of marketing costs increased the predictive accuracy by another 20 percentage points. That leaves about one fifth due to factors not explained by the model.

The advice from The Economist: Maximize the chance of box-office success by: (1) creating a child-friendly superhero film with franchise (sequel) potential; (2) budgets of $85 million are most profitable; (3) summer movie releases earn an average of $15 million more than other seasons, and (4) cast two lead actors with a respectable ticket history, who are thus not too expensive. With reasonable reviews from critics and audiences alike, a film in this model would earn about $125 million at the American box office. However, do not expect an Oscar—such a film would have just a 1 in 500 chance of winning Best Picture.

Sources: "Silverscreen playbook: How to make a hit film" The Economist, February 27, 2016.

http://www.economist.com/node/21693594/print 1/3

Figure 6.3
Companies increasingly use technology (physical capital) to automate business processes and reduce labor costs (human capital). For example, the automobile industry relies heavily on robotics to manufacture its products.
Source: © Luis Castaneda Inc./Getty Images

Exhibit 6.17
Cost Driver Data in
Excel Format

		Y	X		
		Total Costs	**Units Sold**		
	District 1	$ 513,466	9,901		
	District 2	$ 646,518	11,920		
	District 3	$ 723,678	14,560		
	District 4	$ 817,610	17,300		
	District 5	$ 709,812	13,450		
	District 6	$ 766,528	16,500		
	District 7	$ 778,954	16,840		
	District 8	$ 800,986	18,010		
	District 9	$ 725,573	13,980		

estimate of the variable cost per activity unit. Multiplied together, bX yields an estimate of total variable cost. Putting each of these variables together yields the total cost equation:

$$\text{Total Costs} = \text{Total Fixed Costs} + \text{Total Variable Costs}$$

or

$$Y = a + bX$$

This technique is particularly effective for companies needing to disaggregate mixed costs for CVP or breakeven analysis. The next section describes how to use Microsoft Excel to estimate costs.

Estimating Costs Using Regression Analysis in Microsoft Excel. Regression analysis can be performed using Microsoft Excel. When we performed correlation analysis earlier in this chapter, we identified units sold as the cost driver for total costs. Therefore, we will use only the total cost and units sold cost data from Exhibit 6.12 in our OLS regression. In a new Excel worksheet, carefully enter the data from Exhibit 6.12 into Columns B and C and Rows 2 through 12, as shown in Exhibit 6.17. Total costs in Column C will be the Y (dependent) variable and units sold in Column D will be the X (independent) variable in the regression equation.

Next, in Excel select Data Analysis from the Tools menu. After selecting Data Analysis, the pop-up menu illustrated in Exhibit 6.18 will appear. From that menu, scroll down and select Regression and click OK.

Next the Regression box will appear. Fill in the requested data as illustrated in Exhibit 6.19. Under Input, for Input Y Range, type $C$3:$C$12 in the box.

Chapter 6   181

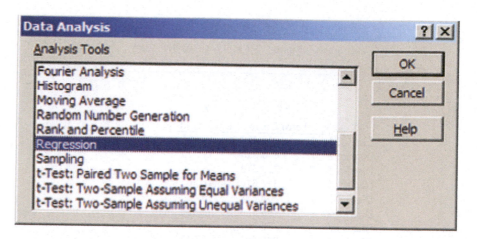

For Input X Range, type $D$3:$D$12 in the box. Be sure that the Labels box is checked. Under Output options, be sure that the New Worksheet Ply box is selected. Click OK.

Your results will appear in a *new* worksheet (in the same Excel file) titled "Sheet1" as shown in Exhibit 6.20. To make the results easy to read, under the Format menu select Column and choose Autofit Selection. Your results should appear identical to the spreadsheet in Exhibit 6.20.

Exhibit 6.19
Selecting Data for
Regression Analysis

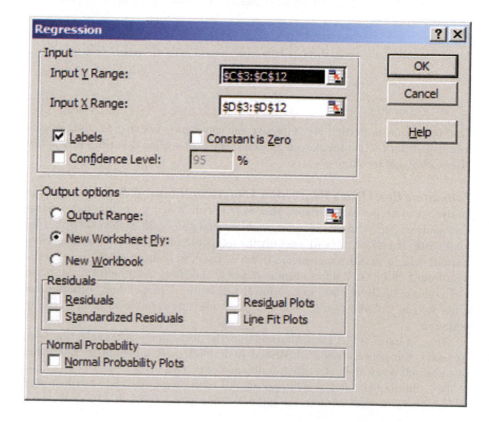

Exhibit 6.20
Regression Analysis Results

Interpreting Regression Analysis Results

There are three primary data points that we will use from this output. First, under Regression Statistics, the second row is called R Square (R^2) and lists a value in Cell B5 of 0.917 (rounded). R^2 is sometimes called the **coefficient of determination**. It tells how well the regression line fits the data and shows the extent to which the variation in the independent variable (units sold) explains the variation in the dependent variable (total cost). The maximum possible value for R^2 is 1.00. A high R^2 (closer to 1) tells us that the independent variable (in this case unit sold) is a good predictor of the changes in the dependent variable (total cost). In this case, the R^2 of 0.917 suggests that managers can predict total costs using the single variable units sold with a high degree of confidence.

We also can use the regression output appearing in cells A16 to A18 and B16 to B18 in Exhibit 6.20 to derive the total cost equation. These data are excerpted and presented in Exhibit 6.21.

	Coefficients
Intercept	232537.1994
Units Sold	33.14401149

Exhibit 6.21
Select Regression Output Data

Exhibit 6.22
Estimating Total Costs

Units sold	10,000
× Variable cost per unit	$ 33.14
Total variable costs	$ 331,400
+ Total fixed costs	$ 232,537
Total costs	**$563,937**

As discussed earlier, the intercept represents fixed costs. The coefficient of the X variable (units sold) represents variable costs per unit. Using these data to formulate the total cost equation yields the following result:

$$\text{Total Costs} = \$232,537 + \$33.14X$$

Fixed costs total $232,537, and variable costs per unit sold are $33.14. Managers can use this equation to predict costs at various levels of business activity. For example, if a retailer sold 10,000 units, we would estimate that total costs would be $563,937, as shown in Exhibit 6.22.

Predicting costs is critical to business planning. Once managers can predict costs, they have the data necessary to run a breakeven analysis.

Once a company can estimate its costs, it can use the total cost equation to perform breakeven and CVP analysis. Exhibit 6.23 illustrates how to use regression analysis output and sales price per unit data to compute the total unit sales needed to break even. In the case of our retailer, assume that the average selling price of its products is $60.00, and that its fixed and variable costs are as estimated in Exhibit 6.21 (fixed costs of $232,537 and variable costs per unit of $33.14).

To calculate the required breakeven sales unit level, divide total sales ($519,442), variable costs ($286,905), or total contribution margin ($232,537), by their respective per-unit amounts ($60.00, $33.14, or $26.86). This yields a breakeven point in units of 8,657 for the company. As discussed in Chapter 5, managers use breakeven and CVP analysis to develop profit plans. Consequently, the cost forecast is an integral component of breakeven and CVP analysis.

Data Limitations

Despite the relative ease of using sophisticated cost-estimation models, several issues can undermine the credibility or usefulness of our statistical output. First, managers must recognize that predictions based on the past—on historical data—may not accurately forecast future performance if business conditions change. Environmental risks, like inflation, new competitors, or supply changes all affect costs.

Exhibit 6.23
Using Cost Estimates in
Breakeven Analysis

	Per Unit	×	Quantity	=	Total
Sales	$60.00	×	**8,657**	=	$519,442
– Variable costs	33.14	×	**8,657**	=	286,905
Contribution margin	$26.86	×	**8,657**	=	232,537
– Fixed costs					232,537
Net income					$ —

Figure 6.4
Cost controllability is an issue that affects restaurant operations. Managers and chefs can control food costs through menu selections that drive the ingredients needed for specific entrees. However, some menu items may remain fixed to meet customer expectations. Managers have much less control over such entrees, and are forced to incur market prices, whatever they may be.

As noted in Chapter 5, managers must identify the relevant range in which cost-behavior assumptions remain valid. Therefore, some observations may not be reliable and, in some cases, may not even be available (for example, start-up enterprises lack historical data).

Finally, managers must determine if extreme or unusual data points are biasing results. For example, if a company encounters an employee strike, its cost data are not likely to reflect normal operations. It is critical that managers recognize this and adjust for data limitations that might invalidate statistical analyses. More sophisticated statistical techniques are available to handle such complex data issues.

Qualitative Cost Considerations

Learning Objective 5
Discuss qualitative factors that affect costs.

The statistical techniques discussed in this chapter yield results based solely on quantitative (numerically focused) data. However, past financial patterns do not always dictate future results. Therefore, managers must supplement their quantitative analyses by considering qualitative factors as well. Several such factors were introduced in Chapter 2 as structural forces that affect business. In this section, we examine how the environment, industry structure, technology, and business strategy specifically affect costs. We also discuss managers' ability to control costs.

Environmental Factors

As noted in Chapter 4, environmental risks can affect business decisions. Changes in market forces (for example, the economy, competition, and regulation) influence both the manner and extent to which managers rely on cost data. For example, if the government mandates an increase in the minimum wage, assumptions about employee labor costs founded on historically based quantitative analyses will no longer be valid. Similarly, inflation may increase the cost of resource inputs that companies use to deliver goods and services. Clearly, environmental risk factors can influence cost and must be considered when developing business plans.

Industry Structure

Another major qualitative factor affecting costs is the operating structure of the industry in which a firm operates or is required to operate. Since business processes drive profitability, the manner in which an industry conducts business directly impacts costs. In manufacturing, for example, production quantity, direct labor hours, and machine hours are common activities that drive costs. Material and labor costs incurred in creating a product are usually considered variable costs. Fixed manufacturing costs relate to the production capacity and include equipment depreciation, property taxes, and the plant manager's salary. Other costs, such as utilities and equipment maintenance, are usually mixed costs that must be disaggregated into their fixed and variable components for business planning.

Merchandising firms (that is, retailers) buy goods wholesale and then resell them. For retailers, the activity that drives costs is usually sales volume, and the total cost of merchandise (that is, inventory) is a variable cost. Most labor costs are considered fixed since merchandising firms require at least a minimum number of personnel to conduct daily operations. Store facility costs, such as rent, depreciation, insurance, and property taxes also are considered fixed costs.

In some industries, however, the activity that drives costs may not be obvious. For example, in the airline industry, the cost driver could be one of at least three activities: air miles flown, passengers flown, or passenger miles flown (transportation of a passenger for one mile). Fuel costs may be variable for air miles traveled, but they may not be variable for passenger miles flown. Airport landing fees, on the other hand, are fixed costs for a particular number of aircraft arrivals, regardless of miles flown or passengers transported. In the case of the airline industry, managers will find the use of both quantitative and qualitative analyses critical in forecasting and managing costs.

Technology Considerations

As discussed in Chapter 2, technological innovation is a major structural force affecting business. For manufacturers, automation and the increased reliance on robotics and other computer-integrated manufacturing systems continue to reduce reliance on human labor. Consequently, work forces no longer can be adjusted quickly to respond to changes in economic conditions. Instead, companies are investing heavily in computerization (a fixed cost) and staffing their work forces with highly skilled operators of sophisticated production equipment—individuals who are not likely to be laid off even in an economic downturn. Consequently, labor at technology-intensive firms increasingly is considered a fixed cost.

Similarly, many companies are using technology to sell products and services via the Internet. The World Wide Web has helped companies streamline processes, eliminate costs, and improve customer service. Many companies rely on secure Internet sites to manage transactions with customers, suppliers, employees, and investors. For example, customers and suppliers can place orders and check the status of those order through company websites. Technology eliminates paper costs, processing, and call center staffing. Likewise, employees now routinely use the Web to process expense reports, register for company benefits programs, and take care of other personnel matters. Indeed, many companies allow investors to use the Internet to download or view financial reports and manage direct investment accounts. Technology has dramatically changed how business is conducted and has considerable effects on the scale and scope of a company's costs.

Learning and Cost Behavior

Any discussion of cost behavior would not be complete without recognizing that learning affects cost behavior. In many businesses, efficiency increases with experience. As cumulative outputs from these business processes increase, the average labor time required and costs per unit usually decline. This phenomenon is often referred to as the learning curve. As employees become more familiar with or adept at executing a particular process, their experience creates efficiencies that reduce costs. Therefore, many companies invest heavily in training and professional development to expedite learning and improve business processes. They believe that learning and development reduce costs.

Business Strategy

A firm's strategy also affects cost. Managers must be aware of which business commitments are most important to the company. For example, a business may choose to dedicate time and resources to a particular product line or subset of customers. While such strategic decisions are likely based on detailed analysis of the firm's operating environment, managers must consider how such initiatives will affect future sales and costs. Making sales or cost decisions without considering this broader context may ultimately jeopardize strategy execution.

Cost Controllability

One final cost issue that managers must consider is cost controllability. Managers can control some costs on a regular basis. For example, the food and beverage manager at a hotel can select vendors, manage purchases on a weekly basis, and set procedures for stock usage. These costs are typically known as controllable costs because managers can exercise some degree of discretion over the extent to which (if at all) they are incurred. Alternatively, once a hotel has committed to rent or build at a specific location, it is almost impossible to change or renegotiate those costs in the short run. Recognizing which costs are controllable allows managers to determine how much flexibility they have to adapt to changing business conditions. Generally, costs that allow the user greater short-term flexibility are higher than those which require some long-term course of action (as in the case of leasing versus purchasing an asset). Qualitative issues require significant insight into business processes and how they affect costs. Managers must recognize that many qualitative factors can affect their cost estimates.

Summary

This chapter introduced tools that managers use to forecast revenues and costs when developing profit plans and budgets. These techniques require an operating history to supply the data needed to satisfy statistical modeling assumptions. Recent technology innovations now enable all managers to conduct sophisticated data analyses using common personal computer software. These vital statistical analyses can validate suspected relationships between revenues and costs and the activities that drive results. Start-up companies like C&F Enterprises, Inc., however, generally lack the operating history needed to use the statistical tools discussed in this chapter. Instead, they generally rely on industry averages to forecast revenues and costs. While both established and new companies may forecast revenues and costs differently, their forecasts are central to the budgeting process, which is the focus of the next chapter.

Net Gains

Forecasting Resources on the Web

The following websites provide tools and resources about business forecasting.

- **Forecasting Principles (http://morris.wharton.upenn.edu/forecast).** This site, which boasts the ability to provide "the accumulated wisdom of the ages about forecasting methods," offers many valuable resources including links to data sources for economic, demographic, and corporate statistics. The site also defines, discusses, and demonstrates popular forecasting techniques.

- **Bizstats.com (http://www.bizstats.com/).** Bizstats provides a wealth of business statistics and industry analyses. The site supplies statistics about business performance at national and industry levels. The site also presents up-to-date industry averages for balance sheets and income statements for companies of various sizes. The site includes an interactive benchmarking tool that allows companies to compare their financial performance to other firms in their industry at comparable sales levels.

- **Beyond Technology (http://www.beyondtechnology.com/profile_shellcheops.shtml).** Beyond Technology offers advanced instructions and guidance about how to use Excel in sales forecasting. The tips include formulas and examples for using Excel to conduct and solve routine problems as well as sophisticated forecasting analysis. The website includes a detailed example of how these tools were used to help well-known clients such as Shell Oil.

Summary of Learning Objectives

1. **Demonstrate the importance of sales forecasting.** Sales forecasting is the foundation of budgeting. Companies forecast customer demand and use this data to estimate sales revenue. Established companies often use historical trends to predict future sales. Start-up enterprises rely on surveys, industry data, and regional economic and demographic data to forecast revenues and costs.

2. **Describe the role of cost drivers in estimating costs.** Cost estimation requires that companies identify the factors that determine costs. These activities commonly are known as cost drivers. Cost drivers vary across industries and business processes. Managers must understand the relationships between business activities and related costs to determine the amount of fixed and variable costs that a company will incur.

3. **Demonstrate the use of graphical and statistical forecasting techniques.** Companies use graphical and statistical techniques to forecast revenues and costs. A common graphing technique is the scatter-plot method. The scatter plot is a graph with dollar revenue or cost volume plotted along the y-axis and business activity plotted along the x-axis. Scatter plots provide managers with a picture of the relationship between two variables. Today's technology allows managers to use statistical techniques, such as correlation and regression analysis, to formulate quantitative revenue and cost predictions.

4. **Demonstrate the use of cost estimates in cost-volume-profit (CVP) analysis.** Statistical techniques yield estimates for fixed and variable costs. These results can be incorporated in a firm's total cost equation, which in turn can be used in cost-volume-profit and breakeven analyses.

5. **Discuss qualitative factors that affect costs.** When making business decisions, managers must consider qualitative factors in addition to quantitative results. They must recognize environmental, industry, and other strategic factors that may impact cost estimation as well as the interpretation of quantitative data. The nature of costs varies across businesses, and past performance may not be indicative of future results. Further, companies must recognize how technological innovation and the learning curve increase efficiency and lower costs over time.

Glossary of Terms

Coefficient of determination A statistical variable (R^2) calculated in regression analysis that indicates how well a regression line fits the given data and shows the extent to which the variation in the independent variable explains the variation in the dependent variable.

Controllable cost A cost over which managers have some discretion or degree of control.

Correlation analysis A common statistical technique used to assess and measure the degree of relationship between variables.

Cost estimation The process of determining expected cost totals and their relative fixed and variable components at a given level of activity.

Dependent variable A data variable whose value is determined by other variables.

Independent variable A data variable that does not rely on other variables to determine its value, and that drives (or affects) the dependent value.

Learning curve The phenomenon of generating increased efficiency from increased experience.

Ordinary least squares (OLS) regression A popular form of regression analysis that measures the squared distances of each data point from a "best-fitting" straight line. This "fitted" regression line expresses total cost as a function of fixed and variable costs. The regression line in equation form is expressed as $Y = a + bX$.

R^2 See *coefficient of determination.*

Regression analysis A statistical tool used to identify the relationship between two factors, such as an activity driver and its revenue or cost, by determining the best-fitting line among a set of data points.

Scatter plot Two-dimensional graph showing the general relationship between two factors.

Chapter Review Questions

1. What is sales revenue forecasting?
2. What types of data are needed to forecast sales or revenues?
3. What is cost estimation?
4. What is the first step managers need to complete when estimating costs?
5. What is a scatter plot?
6. What is typically measured along the x-axis of a scatter plot?
7. What is typically measured along the y-axis of a scatter plot?
8. What is indicated by a linear relationship among data on a scatter plot?
9. What is correlation analysis?
10. What is meant by a high correlation?
11. Give an example of two variables that you would expect to be highly correlated.
12. What is meant by a correlation at or close to zero?
13. What is meant by an inverse correlation?
14. Give an example of two variables that you would expect to be inversely correlated.
15. What is regression analysis?
16. What is a dependent variable?
17. What is an independent variable?
18. What does the R^2 in a regression output represent?
19. Is a high or low R^2 preferred in cost estimation?
20. How does technology affect costs?

21. Identify several data limitations that can undermine the usefulness of statistical analysis.
22. Identify three environmental factors that affect business decisions related to costs.
23. Describe the nature of costs in manufacturing industries.
24. Describe the nature of costs in merchandising industries.
25. How does technological innovation generally affect a firm's costs?
26. Give an example of how technological innovation has changed a company's business processes.
27. What is meant by the learning curve?
28. What are controllable costs?

Exercises and Problems

1. Identify a major cost and two possible cost drivers for that cost for each of the businesses listed. For each business, also briefly discuss the major issues that should be considered in managing its major cost.
   a. Ski resort
   b. Bakery
   c. Computer manufacturer
   d. Taxi service
   e. Sporting goods store
   f. Sports bar
2. Identify a major cost and two possible cost drivers for that cost for each of the businesses listed. For each business, also briefly discuss the major issues that should be considered in managing its major cost.
   a. Tanning salon
   b. Ice cream shop
   c. Barber or hair salon
   d. Art gallery
   e. Microbrewery
   f. Wedding photography service
3. Durango Mountain Bike Company wants to open a bicycle repair shop in a suburb of a major metropolitan area. The industry association estimates that 20 percent of bicycles are repaired by similar service companies and that the average owner spends $100 per bicycle on maintenance each year. The census and local chamber of commerce data indicate that there are 10,000 bicycles in the county. Three other competitors exist within a twenty-five-mile radius of the proposed business location. Based on a consumer survey, the owners believe that they can capture 30 percent of the market in the first year of operation. Based on these data, address the following requirements:
   a. What is the potential number of bicycles likely to be commercially repaired?
   b. What is the total potential bicycle repair revenue available in the market?
   c. How much revenue can Durango Mountain Bike expect to generate?

4. Greco's Barber Shop estimates that it has 300 customers per fiscal quarter. Each customer uses the barbershop three times per quarter, except for Q3 when customers average four visits each. The average cost of a haircut is $12.
   a. Compute the estimated total customer demand (number of haircuts) for each quarter.
   b. Compute the estimated total revenues for each fiscal quarter.
5. The Happy Valley Hotel has 50 rooms to rent each night. It is open 365 days per year and estimates that it rents 80 percent of its rooms each night. The average cost of a room is $100.00.
   a. Compute the estimated total customer demand (number of room rentals) for each year.
   b. Compute the estimated total revenues for the fiscal year.
6. MegaProfits Company estimated its annual total cost function to be:

$$Y = \$150,000 + \$.57x$$

   Assuming that Y represents total cost and x equals the number of units sold, use this equation to answer the following questions:
   a. What is the firm's total fixed cost?
   b. What is the firm's variable cost per unit?
   c. Compute total costs if the firm sells 100,000 units.
   d. Compute total costs if the firm sells 200,000 units.
   e. If the firm's product sells for $1.00, how many units does the firm need to sell to break even?
   f. If the firm's product sells for $1.50, how many units does the firm need to sell to break even?
7. Morrison Hotel uses its banquet room to host parties, dinner dances, and business meetings. The hotel serves meals and provides a variety of services for each event. A local consultant analyzed recent cost data and estimated the total cost function per event to be as follows:

$$Y = \$1,000 + \$9.00x$$

   Assuming that Y represents total cost and x equals the number of guests, use this equation to answer the following questions:
   a. What is the firm's total fixed cost per event?
   b. What is the firm's variable cost per guest?
   c. Compute total costs if 50 guests attend the event.
   d. Compute total costs if 100 guests attend an event.
   e. If the hotel charges $25.00 per guest, how many guests must attend for the hotel to break even at each event?
   f. If the hotel charges $28.00 per guest, how many guests must attend for the hotel to break even at each event?
   g. If the hotel charges $28.00 per guest, would you advise this hotel to host events for 50 or fewer guests? Why or why not?
8. Sylvia Jackson, a colleague of yours, ran a regression analysis on some cost data for a local bakery, but she is unsure how to interpret the results. She has given you the following output from her Microsoft Excel spreadsheet.

Regression Statistics

Multiple R	0.956284779
R Square	0.914480578
Adjusted R Square	0.905928635
Standard Error	289.2759941
Observations	12

ANOVA

	df	SS	MS	F	Significance F
Regression	1	8948175.992	8948175.992	106.9325018	1.16817E-06
Residual	10	836806.0079	83680.60079		
Total	11	9784982			

	Coefficients	Standard Error	t Stat	P-value	Lower 95%
Intercept	968.650259	170.0100132	5.697607105	0.000198961	589.8442779
Units	1.413553607	0.136696508	10.34081727	1.16817E-06	1.108974755

Based on this output, answer the following questions (round all answers to two decimal places):

a. What is the firm's total fixed cost?
b. What is the firm's variable cost per unit?
c. What is the firm's total cost equation?
d. Based on the data provided, should the analyst have confidence in the estimated total cost equation? Why or why not?
e. Compute total costs if the firm sells 10,000 units.
f. Compute total costs if the firm sells 20,000 units.
g. If the firm's product sells for $2.00, how many units does the firm need to sell to break even?
h. If the firm's product sells for $2.00 and it sells 8,000 units, compute total profit?

9. Quickie Shop Convenience Stores operates convenience stores across the United States. The company is organized around eight regional districts. The company provided the following table with data on sales, advertising, and the number of retail outlets per district for the past year.

	Sales	Advertising Expenditures	Retail Outlets
District 1	$2,000,000	$120,000	54
District 2	$2,140,000	$141,000	58
District 3	$1,800,000	$132,000	68
District 4	$1,400,000	$ 91,500	50
District 5	$1,500,000	$ 92,000	52
District 6	$2,000,000	$125,000	55
District 7	$1,300,000	$ 87,000	51
District 8	$1,200,000	$ 90,000	52

The company president wants you to complete the following tasks (use Microsoft Excel, if available):

a. Create a scatter plot of sales and advertising expenditures.

b. Create a scatter plot of sales and the number of retail outlets.

c. On which scatter plot do the data appear to have a linear relationship?

d. What is the implication of this linear relationship?

e. Conduct a correlation analysis using all three variables?

f. Which pair of variables has the highest correlation?

g. Is your response to question (f) consistent with your response to question (c)?

h. What conclusion can you draw from your analysis?

10. School Spirit Company manufactures insignia items (sweatshirts, key chains, and coffee mugs) for university bookstores. The table below provides sales volume and total costs for each month of the past fiscal year.

	Total Costs	Units Sold
January	$ 98,000	11,200
February	$121,000	12,000
March	$151,000	17,500
April	$131,000	17,000
May	$125,000	16,000
June	$100,000	12,000
July	$154,000	17,000
August	$175,000	18,000
September	$ 82,000	9,000
October	$108,000	13,000
November	$114,000	13,500
December	$119,000	15,000

Enter these data into Microsoft Excel and address the following requirements:

a. Create a scatter plot of the data.

b. Using correlation analysis, what is the correlation between units sold and total costs per month?

c. Using regression analysis, determine the following:
   i. R^2
   ii. The company's estimated monthly fixed costs
   iii. The company's estimated variable costs per unit
   iv. The company's total cost equation

d. Based on your response to question (c), what amount of total costs would you predict at the following sales levels?
   i. 8,000 units
   ii. 12,500 units
   iii. 20,000 units

e. If the weighted average selling price of the firm's products is $15.00, how many units does it need to sell to break even?

f. If the weighted average selling price of the firm's products is $15.00, how many units does it need to sell to generate a profit of $10,000?

11. Safe and Sound Delivery Company delivers packages for retailers with online businesses. The company operates in nine regions across the United States. The company is interested in identifying its primary cost driver. Each region has calculated the number of packages, labor days, and miles driven in the past month, as presented in the table below.

Region	Total Costs	Number of Packages	Labor Days	Miles Driven
Atlantic	$1,540,398	29,703	261	43,500
Central	$1,939,553	35,760	276	44,400
Midwest	$2,171,034	43,680	318	43,800
Mountain	$2,452,830	52,300	234	48,000
North	$2,129,435	40,350	240	51,000
Northwest	$2,299,583	49,500	252	44,400
Pacific	$2,336,862	50,520	273	38,400
Southeast	$2,402,957	54,030	324	51,500
West	$2,176,720	41,940	243	43,050

Enter these data into Microsoft Excel and address the following requirements:

a. Create a scatter plot with total costs along the y-axis and number of packages along the x-axis.

b. Create a scatter plot with total costs along the y-axis and labor days along the x-axis.

c. Create a scatter plot with total costs along the y-axis and miles driven along the x-axis.

d. Based on your scatter plots, describe the relationships between total costs and each of the variables

e. Using correlation analysis, compute the correlation between each of the pairs of variables.

f. Based on the results of your correlation analysis in question (e), which variable would you conclude is the firm's primary cost driver?

g. Using regression analysis, determine the following:
   i. R^2
   ii. The company's estimated monthly fixed costs
   iii. The company's estimated variable costs per unit of the selected cost driver
   iv. The company's total cost equation

12. A manufacturing plant has implemented a new assembly process for circuit boards used in car dashboards. The company is concerned about product quality and has invested heavily in employee training. Management is eager to see the results of its training programs. The table lists each of its fourteen employees' experience with the new assembly process and the number of defects found in a recent production run.

Employee Name	Experience in Weeks	Number of Defects
Alb	6	27
Barrow	9	20
Casario	8	24
Durango	17	12
Escondido	9	22
Franklin	10	22
Hirsch	5	26
Isgro	2	39
Jak	11	20
Kaplan	1	45
Lamonica	8	19
Majesty	20	8
Zwanetz	5	17

Enter these data into Microsoft Excel and address the following requirements:
a. Create a scatter plot of the data.
b. Using correlation analysis, what is the correlation between weeks of experience and number of defects? What does this result indicate about the relationship between the two variables?
c. Do these data suggest that a learning curve exists for this company? Why or why not?

Top Flight Airlines

Top Flight Airlines provides private jet service to business executives in the Midwest region of the United States. Business has been more successful than the owners ever anticipated and Top Flight is eager to formulate a new business plan. The company's managers realize that reliable cost forecasts are critical to the company's future profitability. The company provided the following data about the number of passengers (i.e., seats occupied on a flight) and total costs for the past fiscal year.

Month	Passengers	Total Cost
January	891	$ 51,346.59
February	1,192	64,651.76
March	1,456	72,367.79
April	1,876	81,761.01
May	1,345	70,981.18
June	1,567	76,652.76
July	1,632	77,895.39
August	1,851	80,098.55
September	1,398	72,557.34
October	1,478	73,447.81
November	1,209	68,992.96
December	1,908	88,993.08
Total	**17,803**	**$879,746.22**

Required

Create a scatter plot of these data and run a regression analysis to answer the following questions:

a. Is the number of passengers per month a reliable indicator of total costs? Why or why not?

b. What is Top Flight's total cost equation?

c. Determine the expected costs if Top Flight flies 1,400, 1,500, and 2,000 passengers during a month.

d. Are these results consistent with what appears on your scatter plot?

e. If Top Flight sells tickets (seats) to passengers for $50 per one-way trip, what is the required level of sales (in dollars and passengers) to break even?

f. If Top Flight sells tickets (seats) to passengers for $50 per one-way trip, what is the required level of sales (in dollars and passengers) to generate $10,000 net income per month?

g. If Top Flight sells tickets (seats) to passengers for $50 per one-way trip, what is the required level of sales (in dollars and passengers) to generate $30,000 net income per month?

h. To triple profits from $10,000 to $30,000, does Top Flight need to triple the number of passengers carried per month? Why or why not?

i. Are each of the activity levels that you presented in response to questions (e), (f), and (g) feasible?

Sales Forecasting and Cost Estimation

Revenue and cost forecasts are key financial projections in a business plan. Startup enterprises lack historical data and therefore must rely on external sources to develop forecasts. A credible revenue and cost forecast based on sound and reasonable assumptions increases a business plan's likelihood of receiving funding. At the end of Chapter 5, you used estimates of sales and costs for a preliminary breakeven analysis. This Business Planning Application extends that analysis to provide the basis for the financial projections in your business plan.

Assignment

Creating a Sales Forecast

To create your sales forecast, you should visit with local business owners, survey customers, review industry association websites and trade journals, and contact the local chamber of commerce. Each of these resources will provide a wealth of data about the expected demand for your product or service in your local marketplace. Your sales forecast should clearly answer the following questions:

1. What is the size of your market place?
2. What are some important demographic features (e.g., age, income, and growth) of your market?
3. How many people in your market are likely to buy your product or service?
4. What is the average amount each customer spends per week, month, or year on your product or service?
5. What market share can you expect in your first year of operation?
6. Is your business seasonal for some reason? (Is it based on a school terms, summer or winter activities, or holidays?)
7. How much revenue can you expect in your first year of operation?

Remember that compiling a credible sales forecast is the first step in projecting profits.

Estimating Costs

To estimate costs, start-up companies consult with industry guides and other entrepreneurs. There are several subscription-based industry guides available in most libraries. These annual publications include *Standard & Poor's Industry Surveys, RMA Annual Statement Studies, Dunn & Bradstreet Industry Norms,* and the *Almanac of Business and Industrial Financial Ratios.* Online resources such as Bizstats.com also provide industry cost estimates. These resources typically present income data based on company sales volume. Your sales forecast will enable you to select the data that are most appropriate for your enterprise.

At the end of Chapter 5, you developed cost estimates by visiting local business owners. If possible, you should use correlation or regression analysis to analyze the data. Also, you should compare your estimates to the industry averages presented in the library and Web resources. Your cost forecast should clearly and convincingly answer the following questions:

8. What is the variable cost per unit as a percentage of sales in the industry?
9. What are fixed costs as a percentage of sales?
10. What are the different types of fixed costs that the company will incur?
11. Are your cost estimates as a percentage of sales consistent with industry averages?
12. Why do your estimates differ from the industry, if they do?

Considering each of these issues will allow to you develop a convincing budget for your business plan.

Image Credits

Chapter 7

LEARNING OBJECTIVES

1. Describe budgeting and its potential benefits.

2. Define the master budget and discuss its components.

3. Illustrate the development of the operating budget.

4. Demonstrate the creation of the cash flow and capital use budgets.

5. Discuss the preparation of pro forma financial statements.

Budgeting Fundamentals

As noted in Chapter 1, financial projections are an integral part of a company's strategic plan. The previous two chapters introduced the fundamentals of profit planning and business forecasting, respectively. This chapter shows how managers use these techniques in the formal budgeting process. This chapter also describes the advantages and limitations of the budgeting process. Knowing how to budget helps managers effectively plan and execute their company's business strategies. In coming chapters, we will explore how managers use budgets to make business decisions and evaluate company performance.

A budget is a financial plan for the future operations of a business. Budgets provide interested stakeholders with a numerical picture of the company's strategic plan that details how managers intend to allocate and use financial, physical, and human capital in the coming fiscal periods. Budgets typically include a detailed balance sheet, income statement, and statement of cash flows.

C&F Enterprises, Inc.: Realizing the Need for a Budget

Keith and Dale were confused and frustrated! They felt they had a good handle on the costs of their new business venture. They also were confident in their analysis of their local market's risks and opportunities, but they were struggling to put all of their sales projections and cost analyses together into a financial plan that would show them how C&F would perform in the coming year. The two entrepreneurs recognized that such a task was probably beyond the scope of services that their current bookkeeping service could provide. So, they turned to the local accounting and business advisory services firm that had helped them set up their initial information system.

Keith and Dale scheduled a meeting with the accountants to brief them on C&F's past operations and plans for the future. They updated them on last year's profitability, the entrance of new competition (Tru-Lawn Care) into the market, and their planned product offerings. Keith and Dale also provided the accountants copies of C&F's 20X1 financial statements, cost schedules, and CVP analyses to supplement their presentation. When their presentation was complete, Keith and Dale bluntly asked the accountants what they needed to do to turn all of their hard work into something they could use to guide the business. The accountants responded in unison: "You need a budget!"

Introduction to Budgeting

Learning Objective 1
Describe budgeting and its
potential benefits.

The primary objective of budgeting is to create a detailed plan that guides managers in the acquisition and use of an organization's resources as it pursues its business strategy. Most companies engage in at least an annual budgeting exercise in which managers attempt to forecast the firm's business prospects for the next fiscal year. Organizations also may prepare budgets for longer periods of time (that is, for five or ten years) depending on their needs. However, these longer-term financial plans generally are much less detailed than annual budgets because of the uncertainties associated with predicting economic outcomes far in advance. Typically, budgets result from multiple rounds of review, revision, and negotiation across multiple levels in the organization. When the plans and projected results are acceptable to senior management and the company's owners, the resulting budget is adopted to guide the next year's operations and serves as a basis for performance evaluation. This chapter describes the preparation of these pro forma financial statements and their supporting schedules.

Benefits of Budgeting

Budgeting can provide many benefits to a company. It is a high-profile activity that affects virtually all operating areas and support functions within the organization. Consequently, every manager in a firm is affected in some way by budgets. Given this pervasive influence, budgeting offers several important benefits.

Figure 7.1
Budgeting plays a major role in highway projects. Managers rely on budgeting techniques to plan, organize, and control construction efforts. The budget allows the various construction contractors to communicate with each other and coordinate their work, and it also sets performance goals to ensure that the job is completed according to plan.

Management Accounting: A Business Planning Approach

Exhibit 7.1
Benefits of Budgeting

Benefit	Example
Planning	Businesses often expand their product and service offerings. For example, a local restaurant may elect to start a delivery service. The new line of business may require additional equipment, employees, advertising, and supplies. Budgeting helps managers make the necessary plans to bring the new product or service to market.
Organization	Budgets help the company acquire the required resources. A company looking to upgrade its technology may use the budgeting process to coordinate spending across different areas of the business.
Control	Budgets help managers see if they are meeting expectations. If managers see that a product is not selling as expected, a new marketing strategy may be used to help stimulate sales.
Coordination	Some businesses have very different, but interrelated business processes. Purchasing and production managers often work together during the budgeting process to ensure that plans for ordering materials are reasonable and consistent with the organization's goals.
Communication	Company executives use budgets to set financial expectations for the coming fiscal period. Budgets help to align the actions of employees with the interests of investors.
Motivation	A common use of budgeting is to set targets and goals for employees. Salespeople, for example, are often rewarded based on total revenue and sales volume. Budgeted expectations set specific goals that the sales force seeks to achieve.

- **_Planning_**—Budgeting forces managers to think ahead and systematically anticipate the future. Budgets also are a method of formalizing ideas and forecasts about the company's future operations.

- **_Organization_**—Budgets help firms to allocate their human, financial, and physical capital in pursuit of their business strategy. Budgets often highlight scarce resources and help managers direct these resources to the most financially rewarding activities.

- **_Control_**—Budgets can provide managers with realistic performance benchmarks against which actual results can be compared and evaluated. Managers then can investigate operating results that differ from budget and adjust business processes to execute the company's business strategy.

- **_Coordination_**—Budgets help companies coordinate and align the activities of departments and units within the organization. Budgets also help managers throughout the company understand how their operating plans relate to those of other managers.

- *Communication*—Budgets are useful tools for informing managers about the company's goals, ideas, and achievements. Budgets communicate to managers how their plans affect the company as a whole and create an awareness of how each business process contributes to the company's overall success.

- *Motivation*—By setting goals and performance targets, budgets can motivate manager and employee performance. To properly motivate managers and employees, goals must be challenging but attainable—and properly rewarded.

Potential Barriers to Effective Budgeting

Although it is a critical tool for effective business decision-making, budgeting does have some limitations. Many managers and employees view budgeting negatively, frequently associating it with excessive pressure related to unrealistic goals, unreasonable restrictions, authoritarian decision-making, lack of control, and subjectivity. To maximize the benefits of budgeting, managers must recognize such perceptions and attempt to avoid or minimize them by considering the following potential limitations:

- *Failure to Reflect Reality*—Because of their many inherent assumptions, budgets can oversimplify the facts of a real-world situation. Budgets perceived as "unrealistic" are less likely to be effective planning and control tools.

- *Focus Only on Results*—Since budgets represent a financial plan, users frequently focus on whether a target number is achieved, rather than why a business met or failed to achieve its projected results. Overemphasizing reported results rather than their underlying causes can lead managers to take actions that may not be in the best interest of the company's other stakeholders.

- *Not "My" Budget*—Budgets often are developed by the firm's senior executives with little or no input from middle or lower managers. Successful budgeting demands the complete involvement and participation of all managers. Otherwise, budgets can undermine employee initiative by discouraging new developments and actions that are omitted from the budget.

- *Not an Exact Science*—Budgeting is a planning tool based on assumptions and judgment. Managers must recognize that most budgets will require revision and modification during the course of a company's fiscal year to reflect unanticipated changes in the operating environment.

With meaningful employee participation and attention to detail throughout the budgeting process, companies can avoid these potential pitfalls.

The initial information for the budgeting process comes from the firm's strategic plan, which outlines the organization's future goals, objectives, and related action plans. During the annual budgeting process, managers create more detailed implementation plans that are consistent with the broader context of the strategic plan.

The Master Budget

The term **master budget** frequently is assigned to the set of financial schedules that describe a company's operating plans for a specific future fiscal period. The master budget usually contains four separate budget schedules that address operations, cash flow, capital usage, and financial statement reporting. Each type of budget and its integrated data flows are illustrated in Exhibit 7.2 and described briefly in the following sections.

Operating Budgets. The **operating budget** details the expected financial outcomes arising from a firm's business processes. Operating budgets are based on managers' forecasts of sales and costs as well as assumptions about inventory purchases and operating cash flows. For example, to meet customer needs, retailers must purchase inventory and pay operating expenses (for example, salaries, rent, and utilities) on a timely basis. Since sales of goods and services create the revenues and costs appearing in the income statement, managers must carefully evaluate customer demand and the company's business processes when preparing operating budgets. Their assumptions about sales and related costs dramatically affect the cash flows and profits projected in a given fiscal period. The operating budget provides the basis for a firm's pro forma financial statements each fiscal period.

Cash Flow Budgets. As discussed in Chapter 3, cash inflows and outflows arise from operating, investing, and financing activities. The **cash flow budget**

Learning Objective 2
Define the master budget and discuss its components.

Exhibit 7.2
The Integrated Data Flows of the Master Budget

OPERATING BUDGET
(Start of the Budget Process)

Sales Budget
Operating Expense Budget
Inventory Purchases Budget

FINANCIAL STATEMENT BUDGET
(Final Output of the Budget Process)

Balance Sheet
Income Statement
Statement of Cash Flows

CAPITAL USE BUDGET

CASH FLOW BUDGET

Cash Receipts Schedule
Cash Payments Schedule

More than Budgeting: What Makes a CFO "the Best?"

Technology shifts, globalization (e.g., accounting standards, exchanges, foreign exchange rates, taxing authorities), and the increasing impact of intellectual/human capital, culture, and intangible assets all create market turmoil. Today's CFOs must possess a much broader skill set than in the past, a skill set that addresses three key dimensions: strategy, process, and performance measurement. To be value creators under challenging conditions, CFOs must clearly understand the plan (how the company intends to create value for its customers and differentiate itself in the market place). They also must be process experts so that they can oversee the creation and maintenance of the company's business model (i.e., value chain). Finally, comes the more traditional CFO role - CFOs must create key performance metrics (both financial and non-financial) to provide feedback on the business model, as well as to meet any budgeting and regulatory reporting requirements.

Now for the hard part - how can a rising financial professional acquire these skills? The smaller your organization, the less likely that strategy and process will play major roles in your responsibilities, but performance measurement will. Conversely, large company CFOs will find themselves delegating their performance measurement duties to controllers and chief accounting officers, while they focus on more strategic issues and related processes. Regardless of company size, however, strategy, process, and measurement will dominate the CFO skill set for the foreseeable future.

Source: N. P. Barsky and A.H. Catanach, Jr. "What Makes a CFO 'the Best?'" Strategic Finance, 2014.

summarizes a company's expected cash receipts and payments from these three activities during an operating period. Over the long run, it is essential that a firm generate positive cash flow to continue in business. The cash flow budget informs managers whether the business will generate surplus funds or require cash infusions during the planning period. It also provides the basis for preparing the pro forma statement of cash flows.

Capital Use Budgets. The capital use budget describes what investments (that is, cash disbursements) a firm intends to make in new plant facilities, equipment, products, locations, and other long-term operating activities. When a business wants to open a new store, managers must determine if the location will generate enough *cash flow* from its operations to justify an investment in the facility.

Similarly, before a company buys a new piece of equipment, its managers must evaluate whether the *cost savings* from using the new machine are enough to warrant its purchase. Capital use decisions also are frequently referred to as *capital expenditure* or *capital budgeting* decisions. As might be expected, companies base such decisions on a number of assumptions. First, the cash flows or cost savings generated by an investment usually are not readily observable, and they must be estimated. In addition, managers may not know exactly how long an investment will be productive or how its age will affect future cash flows or cost savings. These factors also demand assumptions.

Investment decisions also require managers to consider the time value of money. This concept suggests that it is better to receive a sum of money today, rather than in the future. If cash is received today, it can be invested, and by the end of the investment period, the amount of cash available will be greater than the original amount received. Therefore, the timing of an investment, as well as its useful life and related cash flows, have value implications that must be considered. Sophisticated capital budgeting techniques generally are used to address the time-value-of-money issues involved in capital use decisions. Although in-depth discussions of capital budgeting techniques usually are reserved for more advanced cost accounting and finance courses, several basic tools are introduced later in this chapter.

Finally, it should be noted that the investment assumptions made in the capital use budget can also affect the operating and cash flow budgets. For example, adding equipment not only results in a cash outflow but also increases depreciation expense, a line item on both the operating budget and pro forma income statement. The effects of capital budgeting decisions on other components of the master budget will be illustrated later in this chapter as C&F Enterprises, Inc. begins to develop its budgets.

Financial Statement Budgets. The master budget commonly includes the three primary financial statements—the balance sheet, the income statement, and the statement of cash flows—as pro forma projections, which are often referred to as financial statement budgets. Chapter 3 discussed the content and application of each of these financial statements. When used in a budgeting process, the financial statement budgets summarize the information contained in the operating, cash flow, and capital use budgets. Ratio analysis, also reviewed in Chapter 3, should be employed to assess the completeness and credibility of financial statement budgets. Start-up businesses typically provide their lenders and investors with three years of pro forma financial statement information. Established businesses sometimes use even longer planning time horizons.

Developing Budgets

As Exhibit 7.2 indicates, the master budget consists of four separate sets of financial projections: the operating budget, the cash flow budget, the capital use budget, and the pro forma financial statements. Since the U.S. economy increasingly is dominated by retail and service organizations rather than by manufacturing enterprises, this introductory text explores budgeting in the context of retail and services firms, leaving more advanced cost accounting courses to discuss the complexities of the manufacturing process. In this section, we will use C&F Enterprises, Inc. to illustrate how each of these budgets is prepared and relates to each other.

Learning Objective 3
Illustrate the development of the operating budget.

Operating Budgets

The budgeting process begins with the preparation of operating budgets. Because they provide the data required to address subsequent budgeting issues, these budgets are prepared first. Consistent with the customer focus discussed in Chapter 2, budgeting begins with a sales forecast that considers many of the issues discussed in Chapter 6. Managers in different departments of a company prepare operating budgets for their unique business units, often using pre-established criteria and formats that ultimately are integrated into the company's master budget. The number of operating budgets is a function of the business strategy a company pursues. Budgeting for inventory in a manufacturing company is much more complex than in a merchandising or retail operation. A manufacturer requires separate budgets to forecast raw materials, labor, and overhead, while a retail firm only needs to estimate the purchase of finished goods inventory for resale. Whether a manufacturer, retailer, or service provider, most businesses generally use three basic *operating budgets:* a sales or revenue budget, the operating expense budget, and the inventory purchases budget.

The Sales Budget

The sales budget is a company's revenue plan for a given fiscal period. Preparing the sales budget requires a thorough and accurate market analysis. In fact, as noted in Chapter 6, forecasting sales is so important that it is often considered the cornerstone of the budgeting process. Responsibility for estimating sales falls on the marketing department in most companies. Data from industry and trade journals, economic analyses, surveys, historical sales figures, and assessments of competition and other market forces usually supplements their estimates. Sales forecasts depend on a company's expectations for consumer demand, sales mix, and price.

As you will recall from Chapter 6, C&F developed a sales forecast for 20X2 for its residential customers. That schedule appears again in Exhibit 7.3. The forecast is based on a calendar fiscal year with the first quarter (Q1) representing the months of January through March. The forecast reflects the seasonal nature of lawn care services. In this case, the majority of residential services are expected to occur between April and September (Q2 and Q3) with the greatest demand in third quarter (Q3). The average quarterly demand of 12 assumes that a customer will require a weekly lawn cutting for each month in the quarter (4 weeks times 3 months). Assuming an average price of $30 for each lawn cutting, the forecasted revenue from this business line totals $14,940.

C&F also developed sales forecasts for its commercial customers and other lines of business (that is, snow removal and weed control). The breakeven analysis in Chapter 5 suggested that commercial business was C&F's most profitable line of business, so Keith and Dale decided to focus on growing this customer base. Since raising prices was not practical with the new national competitor now operating in town, they would have to find new clients. Keith and Dale were hoping that their "personal hometown touch" would draw customers away from the large national competitor.

Exhibit 7.3

C&F Enterprises, Inc. Projected Residential Services Revenue For Fiscal Year 20X2	Q1	Q2	Q3	Q4
Number of residential customers (A)	15	20	21	23
Average quarterly demand per customer (B)	—	10	12	2
Estimated total customer demand (A × B)	—	200	252	46
Average $ price per customer (C)	$30	$ 30	$ 30	$ 30
Estimated total residential revenues (A × B × C)	$—	$6,000	$7,560	$1,380
			$14,940	

Exhibit 7.4 shows a forecast for the commercial line that Keith and Dale thought they could achieve. Keith and Dale believed that if they worked hard to market and promote their services, they could attract even more commercial customers. In this case, new customers are projected to increase in the second and third quarters. The forecast also reflects the seasonal nature of lawn care services (minimal during the winter months and high in the spring and summer). In this case, most commercial services are expected to occur between April and September with the greatest demand in the third quarter (Q3). This illustration assumes an average price of $250 per lawn cutting, a price far exceeding that for the residential business ($30), resulting in forecasted revenue of $79,750 if Keith and Dale meet their commercial customer growth targets.

C&F's sales forecast is not complete until it includes the other services that they offer. Keith and Dale believe that weed and fertilization services will increase along with the growth in commercial customers. Snow removal is expected to remain a minor convenience service for residential lawn care customers, with revenues estimated to be unchanged from 20X1. The sales forecast for these "other" services appears in Exhibit 7.5. They are expected to contribute a total of $7,800 to C&F's 20X2 sales revenue.

Combining each of these forecasts for residential, commercial, and other services allows C&F to see how much potential revenue it will generate in 20X2. Exhibit 7.6 shows C&F's consolidated sales forecast.

Exhibit 7.4

C&F Enterprises, Inc. Projected Commercial Services Revenue For Fiscal Year 20X2	Q1	Q2	Q3	Q4
Number of commercial customers (A)	9	12	14	11
Average quarterly demand per customer (B)	1	10	12	2
Estimated total customer demand (A × B)	9	120	168	22
Average $ price per customer (C)	$ 250	$ 250	$ 250	$ 250
Estimated total commercial revenues (A × B × C)	$2,250	$30,000	$42,000	$5,500
			$79,750	

Exhibit 7.5

C&F Enterprises, Inc. Projected Other Services Revenue For Fiscal Year 20X2					
	Q1	Q2	Q3	Q4	Total
Snow removal	$1,030	—	—	$ 430	$1,460
Weed control and fertilization	900	1,240	2,100	2,100	6,340
Estimated total other revenues	$1,930	$1,240	$2,100	$2,530	$7,800

C&F expects to generate $102,490 of revenue in 20X2. Although a considerable increase from 20X1, Keith and Dale are confident in the assumptions underlying their forecasts and optimistic about their chances of achieving these targets. Generating accurate sales forecasts is critical for estimating the company's expenses, planning for inventory purchases, and managing other resource requirements, topics that will now be more fully explored.

Operating Expense Budget

The next step in developing the operating budget is to estimate expenses for the anticipated level of sales. The operating expense budget captures the primary expenses, both fixed and variable, that a company will incur while executing its business strategy. Such expenses might include salaries, supplies, utilities, depreciation, and rent. To accurately prepare this budget, managers must not only thoroughly understand their business, they also must be proficient in CVP analysis and be able to estimate costs at different sales levels.

As discussed in Chapters 5 and 6, Keith and Dale worked hard to estimate fixed and variable costs for their business. After carefully reviewing their 20X1 business records and some industry association data, they believe that they now understand what it will cost C&F to deliver its services. After careful analysis, the two entrepreneurs have identified ten costs of servicing and have separated each into its *fixed* and *variable* components.

Fixed Costs. Keith and Dale estimate that six of their operating costs have some fixed component. As for amounts, they expect fixed costs to be similar to 20X1's with only a few exceptions. These projected fixed operating costs are shown in Exhibit 7.7. First, Keith and Dale have agreed to accept the same salary ($9,500) as last year. Although they do not believe that a salary increase in the second year of operations is justified, they do favor receiving their first dividends if the business meets its profit targets. In addition, they have no current plans to acquire any equipment or borrow any more money, so depreciation and loan interest are expected to remain constant. However, both agree to reevaluate these investing and financing decisions once they have a better idea of the C&F's cash flow picture. Keith and Dale also do not expect any additional or unusual miscellaneous expenses, so they have budgeted other fixed costs at last year's actual total of $1,500.

Exhibit 7.6
Consolidated
Revenue Forecast

C&F Enterprises, Inc. Projected Revenues for Fiscal Year 20X2					
	Q1	Q2	Q3	Q4	Total
Residential	$ —	$ 6,000	$ 7,560	$1,380	$ 14,940
Commercial	2,250	30,000	42,000	5,500	79,750
Other	1,930	1,240	2,100	2,530	7,800
Total	$4,180	$37,240	$51,660	$9,410	$102,490

Two fixed costs, however, will increase: bookkeeping and advertising. C&F's bookkeeper informed Keith and Dale that the price of her services will rise by $500 in 20X2. The cost increase was prompted by C&F's numerous requests for planning data, which she considered beyond the scope of her traditional write-up services. Despite the price increase, Keith and Dale recognize the importance of accurate historical transaction data for managing their company. Therefore, their 20X2 budget shows $3,000 as the total expected bookkeeping fees.

C&F prepaid $9,600 for two years of Internet advertising (20X1 and 20X2) when they started the company. As a result, half, or $4,800, of this cost should be considered fixed advertising expense in the 20X2 operating expense budget. However, Keith and Dale also realize that they will have to significantly increase advertising to meet their new service growth goals. Therefore, they plan to enlist a local marketing firm to promote the business for one year with flyers and mailings for a fixed fee of $5,000. In total, the operating expense budget includes $9,800 for fixed advertising costs. Exhibit 7.7 summarizes all of the fixed operating costs that C&F expects to incur in 20X2.

Variable Costs. Keith and Dale carefully reanalyzed the 20X1 cost data that their bookkeeping service provided in Chapter 5. This time they decided to look at variable costs as a percentage of sales for each business line (residential, commercial, and other). After preparing the schedule shown in Exhibit 7.8 from their 20X1

Exhibit 7.7
Projected Fixed
Operating Costs

C&F Enterprises, Inc. Projected Fixed Costs For Fiscal Year 20X2	
Salaries	$ 9,500
Depreciation	600
Advertising	9,800
Bookkeeping	3,000
Interest	200
Other	1,500
Total	$24,600

Exhibit 7.8
20X1 Variable Cost Analysis

C&F Enterprises, Inc. Variable Costs as a Percentage of Sales For Fiscal Year 20X1			
	Residential	Commercial	Other
Wages	40.00%	44.79%	31.00%
Rentals	20.00%	14.70%	18.00%
Supplies	3.00%	4.01%	2.00%
Fuel	1.50%	0.94%	2.00%
Taxes	2.73%	2.73%	2.73%
Other	1.50%	2.00%	5.00%
Total	68.73%	69.17%	60.73%

* All percentages have been rounded to two decimals.

data, they noted dissimilarities in variable cost percentages across all three lines of business because of differences in how each service is delivered. Exhibit 7.8 indicates that commercial customers cost the greatest amount as percentage of sales (69.17 percent). This percentage is computed by dividing the total commercial variable costs for 20X1, $37,008 (provided by the bookkeeper in Chapter 5), by the total commercial revenues for 20X1, $53,500 (from Exhibit 5.11). Still, Keith and Dale are committed to developing this business line given the new competition entering their market and the CVP analysis they previously performed in Chapter 5. They consider the fact that commercial service costs exceed those for the residential line by less than 1 percent to be inconsequential given that the commercial segment generated over 70 percent of revenues in 20X1. Keith and Dale also decided to base their 20X2 variable cost estimates on the data in Exhibit 7.8.

Analyzing historical variable costs as a percentage of sales allows companies to estimate costs at various future sales levels. In the case of C&F Enterprises, multiplying each historical variable cost percentage expected in 20X2 (Exhibit 7.8) by the forecasted total revenue for 20X2 (Exhibit 7.6) for each business line yields an operating expense estimate for variable costs in 20X2. This is shown in Exhibit 7.9.

With fixed and variable cost data now computed, C&F can prepare a schedule of total anticipated 20X2 operating costs. Exhibit 7.10 aggregates the results of Exhibits 7.7 and 7.9 to show total expenses by category. C&F projects total operating costs of $94,771 for 20X2: $70,171 variable and $24,600 fixed.

Contribution Margin Versus the Traditional Income Statement

As discussed in Chapter 3, the income statement shows a company's sales and expenses for a fiscal period. When sales exceed expenses, the company has a profit for the period. Alternatively, when expenses exceed sales, the company has a loss for the period. Chapter 3 introduced the traditional income statement—one

Exhibit 7.9
20X2 Variable
Cost Projection

C&F Enterprises, Inc.
Projected Variable Costs
For Fiscal Year 20X2

	Residential	Commercial	Other	Total
Wages	$ 5,976	$35,717	$2,418	$44,111
Rentals	2,988	11,728	1,404	16,120
Supplies	448	3,199	156	3,803
Fuel	224	746	156	1,126
Taxes	408	2,177	213	2,798
Other	224	1,599	390	2,213
Total	$10,268	$55,166	$4,737	$70,171

* Data based on rounded percentages in Exhibit 7.8.

prepared in accordance with generally accepted accounting principles (GAAP). The traditional income statement shows expenses in terms of categories (for example, cost of goods sold and selling and administrative expenses). It allows financial statement users to easily compare companies across and within industries.

Chapter 5 introduced a second common form of income statement, known as the contribution margin income statement. The contribution margin income statement differs from the traditional GAAP income statement by categorizing costs in terms of behavior (that is, fixed or variable) rather than by purpose. In the contribution

Exhibit 7.10
Total 20X2 Cost Projections

C&F Enterprises, Inc.
Projected Fixed and Variable Costs
For Fiscal Year 20X2

	Fixed	Variable	Total
Salaries and wages	$ 9,500	$44,111	$53,611
Rentals	—	16,120	16,120
Supplies	—	3,803	3,803
Fuel	—	1,126	1,126
Depreciation	600	—	600
Advertising	9,800	—	9,800
Bookkeeping	3,000	—	3,000
Interest	200	—	200
Taxes	—	2,798	2,798
Other	1,500	2,213	3,713
Total	$24,600	$70,171	$94,771

margin income statement, variable costs are first deducted from sales to show contribution margin. Subtracting fixed costs from contribution margin yields net income. This presentation emphasizes cost-volume-profit (CVP) relationships discussed in Chapter 5, and allows managers to readily see how changes in sales or costs affect profits. Managers rely on this income statement format to quickly assess the feasibility of sales and cost forecasts.

If the contribution margin does not show a desired level of profitability, managers will typically look for ways to increase sales or cut certain costs. The effects of such decisions on profit are easy to see because costs are categorized by behavior in the contribution margin income statement. For example, the contribution margin income statement highlights which costs are fixed and not subject to immediate change. This distinction would not be apparent in the traditional income statement. Therefore, managers use the contribution margin format in the initial stages of the budgeting process.

Estimated Contribution Margin and Projected Net Income

Keith and Dale next computed the contribution margin in dollars for each quarter. While they were confident in the assumptions underlying the sales and cost forecasts, they wanted to see if their operating budgets projected a profit. The contribution margin income statement also provided a quick and clear way for

Exhibit 7.11

C&F Enterprises, Inc.						
Projected Quarterly Contribution Margin						
For Fiscal Year 20X2						
	Q1	Q2	Q3	Q4	Total	Percentage of Revenue
Residential						
Revenue	—	$ 6,000	$ 7,560	$1,380	$14,940	100.00%
Variable costs	—	4,124	5,196	948	10,268	68.73%
Contribution margin	—	$ 1,876	$ 2,364	$ 432	$ 4,672	31.27%
Commercial						
Revenue	$2,250	$30,000	$42,000	$5,500	$79,750	100.00%
Variable costs	1,556	20,752	29,053	3,805	55,166	69.17%
Contribution margin	$ 694	$ 9,248	$12,947	$1,695	$24,584	30.83%
Other						
Revenue	$1,930	$ 1,240	$ 2,100	$2,530	$ 7,800	100.00%
Variable costs	1,172	753	1,275	1,537	4,737	60.73%
Contribution margin	$ 758	$ 487	$ 825	$ 993	$ 3,063	39.27%

Management Accounting: A Business Planning Approach

them to recognize which costs were fixed and to consider any possible changes to the operating budgets across each of the three business lines. As illustrated in Exhibit 7.11, multiplying forecasted quarterly revenue from Exhibit 7.6 by the variable costs percentages from Exhibit 7.8 for each business line yields quarterly contribution margin by quarter and in total. For example, in the third quarter (Q3) of 20X2, the commercial line is expected to generate $42,000 in revenues and $12,947 in contribution margin. The total contribution margin for the commercial line in 20X2 is estimated to be $24,584.

Exhibit 7.12 combines the budgeted data for all three business lines and shows C&F's aggregate revenue, variable costs, and contribution margin for each quarter and for the 20X2 fiscal year in total. After deducting fixed costs of $24,600 (Exhibit 7.7), Keith and Dale saw that their revenue and cost forecasts resulted in a projected net income for the year of $7,719. This is nearly double what they had earned in 20X1 ($3,958).

Keith and Dale were satisfied with these projections and felt no changes to the sales operating expense budgets were necessary. They decided to proceed with the rest of the budgeting process.

Inventory Purchases Budget

After estimating sales, managers must determine what inventories of products and supplies they need to satisfy forecasted sales demand. This budget is called the inventory purchases budget. Budgeting inventory purchases is particularly critical for retailers. Companies must order and receive inventories in advance of customer demand. To meet sales demand, a firm must maintain both the right amount and the right mix of products to satisfy expected sales. Therefore, the total amount of inventory needed for a specific time period is the amount of budgeted sales for the period plus any required ending inventory needed to meet unanticipated future sales.

Although C&F Enterprises is a service business, its timely purchase of supplies is critical to the company's success. Without supplies (that is, gloves, trash bags, trimmer line, deicing chemicals, etc.), C&F could not successfully execute its business processes. Keith and Dale's preparation of C&F's supplies inventory budget is quite similar to what a retailer might do to acquire goods for resale to

Exhibit 7.12

C&F Enterprises, Inc. Projected Contribution Income Statement For Fiscal Year 20X2					
	Q1	Q2	Q3	Q4	Total
Total revenue	$ 4,180	$37,240	$51,660	$9,410	$102,490
Total variable costs	2,728	25,629	35,524	6,290	70,171
Total contribution margin	$ 1,452	$11,611	$16,136	$3,120	$ 32,319
Fixed costs					24,600
Net income					$ 7,719

Figure 7.2
Budgeting is used to allocate resources to the purchase, storage, and distribution of goods and services. Budgeting inventory purchases is critical for retailers, particularly those who sell their products over the Internet. Online retailers like Amazon must stock larger quantities, as well a greater variety of products, to meet customer expectations.

its customers. First, the company must forecast how much inventory it will use (or sell), as well as the ending inventory required at the end of each operating period (that is, month, quarter, or year).

Exhibit 7.13 shows the amount of supplies each business line is expected to use based on the 20X1 variable costs percentage presented in Exhibit 7.8. Multiplying the respective percentages (3.00 percent for residential jobs, 4.01 percent for commercial, and 2.00 percent for other) by the expected quarterly revenues shown in Exhibit 7.6 yields an estimate of the amount of supplies that will be used each quarter. Exhibit 7.13 indicates that C&F plans to use $3,803 of supplies in 20X2.

Using this data, Keith and Dale can develop a supplies inventory purchases budget. Exhibit 7.14 illustrates the general form used to prepare an inventory purchases budget. Companies first determine the amount of inventory required each period. The amount required equals the amount to be used (or sold) plus any desired ending inventory. Once the total required is computed, deducting the supplies or inventory on hand (that is, unsold inventory from the previous period) yields the purchases required.

After reviewing operating data from 20X1 and factoring in their own projections of inventory use, Keith and Dale estimated that each quarter's ending supplies inventory should be approximately 50 percent of the following quarter's estimated usage. Additionally, they budgeted for only $250 of supplies to remain at the end of 20X2, since the first quarter of 20X3 was expected to be very slow and there was no need to warehouse supplies for those months. According to Exhibit 7.15, C&F plans to use only $129 of supplies in the first quarter (Q1) and needs to purchase $533 of supplies to meet expected demand in the second quarter. Ordering inventories in advance is not unusual because shipments and deliveries

Management Accounting: A Business Planning Approach

Exhibit 7.13

						Percentage
	Q1	Q2	Q3	Q4	Total	of Revenue

C&F Enterprises, Inc.
Projected Supplies Expense Budget
For Fiscal Year 20X2

	Q1	Q2	Q3	Q4	Total	Percentage of Revenue
Residential						
Revenue (Exhibit 7.6)	$ —	$6,000	$7,560	$1,380	$14,940	$100.00%
Supplies Expense (A)	$ —	180	227	41	448	3.00%
Commercial						
Revenue (Exhibit 7.6)	2,250	30,000	42,000	5,500	79,750	100.00%
Supplies Expense (B)	90	1,203	1,684	221	3,199	4.01%
Other						
Revenue (Exhibit 7.6)	1,930	1,240	2,100	2,530	7,800	100.00%
Supplies Expense (C)	39	25	42	51	156	2.00%
Total Supplies Expense	$ 129	$1,408	$1,953	$ 313	$ 3,803	
(A + B + C)						

Note: Amounts shown in this exhibit are rounded up to the nearest dollar.

often can take a considerable amount of time. Advanced courses in production management and cost accounting often explore the tools and techniques needed to optimize inventory reorder points.

Once a company has quantified the revenues and expenses associated with executing its business strategy, it must determine whether sufficient cash flows exist to support business operations. The profits projected on the income statement do not mean that cash inflows will exceed cash outflows in any given fiscal period. As noted in Chapter 3, net income and operating cash flows usually differ because the accrual-basis GAAP income statement recognizes revenues and expenses when earned or incurred, not when collected or paid. These potential timing differences mean that managers must budget cash flows. Failure to accurately forecast and generate positive cash flow has been the downfall of many businesses.

Inventory used (or sold)
+ Desired ending inventory
Inventory required
− Inventory on-hand
− Required purchases

Exhibit 7.14
Computing Inventory
Purchase Requirements

Exhibit 7.15

C&F Enterprises, Inc. Projected Supplies Purchases Budget For Fiscal Year 20X2	Q1	Q2	Q3	Q4	Total
Supplies used (Exhibit 7.13)	$129	$1,408	$1,953	$313	$3,803
+ Desired ending inventory[a]	704	977	157	250	2,088
Supplies required	$833	$2,385	$2,110	$563	$5,891
– Supplies on-hand[b]	300	704	977	157	2,138
Required purchases	$533	$1,681	$1,133	$406	$3,753

[a] 50% of next quarter's usage; $250 at year end.

[b] $300 of supplies on hand in first quarter per the 12/31/X1 balance sheet.

* All numbers have been rounded.

The Cash Flow Budget

Cash is the most important asset that a business owns. A company must have enough cash to meet its obligations or it will fail. Creditors, employees, and lenders expect to be paid on time, and cash is the most widely accepted medium of exchange. Therefore, effective cash management is critical and the cash flow budget is a useful tool for monitoring cash position. As indicated by Exhibit 7.2, the cash flow budget is composed of two schedules: one for cash receipts and the other for cash payments.

Cash Receipts. The cash receipts schedule reflects the firm's expected cash inflows from customers as well as receipts from investing and/or financing activities. When a firm sells its goods and services on credit, the cash flow budget must

Exhibit 7.16

C&F Enterprises, Inc. Projected Cash Receipts For Fiscal Year 20X2	Q1	Q2	Q3	Q4	Total
Revenue (Exhibit 7.6)	$4,180	$37,240	$51,660	$ 9,410	$102,490
Cash Receipts					
Collection of 90% of current quarter's sales	$3,762	$33,516	$46,494	$ 8,469	$ 92,241
Collection of prior quarter's uncollected sales	5,500	418	3,724	5,166	14,808
Total	$9,262	$33,934	$50,218	$13,635	$107,049

account for the delay between when the sale occurs and when the sale proceeds are ultimately collected. Keith and Dale, for example, after reviewing their bank statements and invoices for 20X1 learned that 90 percent of their services are paid for during the quarter in which services are provided. The remaining 10 percent are collected in the following quarter. Also, they were fortunate not to have had any uncollectible accounts receivable from customers during 20X1, and they expect a similar record in 20X2. Given these assumptions, Keith and Dale prepared the schedule in Exhibit 7.16 to transform their accrual-based revenue forecast in Exhibit 7.6 into a projection of cash receipts.

First-quarter estimates of cash collections include 90 percent of the estimated revenues of $4,180 plus the $5,500 outstanding accounts receivable from December 31, 20X1 (see Exhibit 3.1). It should also be noted that $941, 10 percent of fourth-quarter projected revenues, will appear as accounts receivable on the December 31, 20X2, budgeted balance sheet.

Cash Payments. The cash payments schedule details the cash disbursements that the firm expects to make during a given fiscal period. This cash budget schedule records disbursements in the period they are expected to be paid, not in the period when the obligation is incurred. Cash disbursements vary with each particular business, but the following disbursement categories are common for retail or service companies: inventory purchases, salaries and wages, rent, taxes, loans, interest, selling expenses, and miscellaneous.

C&F's cash payments schedule consists of two parts: payments for supplies inventory purchases and payments for operating expenses. Payment for supplies inventory purchases is based on Exhibit 7.15's estimate of inventory purchases. Keith and Dale reviewed their payments to suppliers in 20X1 and found that they paid for 80 percent of inventory acquisitions in the quarter they were purchased, with the remaining 20 percent paid in the subsequent quarter. They expected this pattern to continue. Given these assumptions, they prepared the 20X2 inventory purchases payment schedule that appears in Exhibit 7.17.

Exhibit 7.17

C&F Enterprises, Inc. Projected Cash Payments for Purchases For Fiscal Year 20X2					
	Q1	Q2	Q3	Q4	Total
Purchases (Exhibit 7.15)	$ 533	$1,681	$1,133	$406	$3,753
Cash Payments					
Payment of 80% of current quarter's purchases	$ 426	$1,345	$ 906	$325	$3,002
Payment of prior quarter's unpaid purchases	1,000	107	336	227	1,669
Total	$1,426	$1,451	$1,242	$552	$4,671

First-quarter projected cash payments include 80 percent of the estimated inventory purchases of $533 plus payment of the $1,000 accounts payable listed on the December 31, 20X1, balance sheet (see Exhibit 3.1). Of the $406 of fourth-quarter purchases, 20 percent ($81) are expected to remain unpaid at year end and will appear as accounts payable on the December 31, 20X2, budgeted balance sheet.

Keith and Dale realized that preparing the cash payments schedule for their non-inventory-related operating expenses would be much easier. Except for depreciation (which is a noncash expense) and advertising (which was prepaid for two years in 20X1), they expect to pay fixed costs evenly throughout the year. Non-inventory-related variable costs generally will be paid in the period incurred. Given these assumptions, C&F's schedule of cash payments for non-inventory operating expenses appears in Exhibit 7.18.

Subtracting cash payments from cash receipts yields a firm's net operating cash inflow or outflow for the fiscal period. Net operating cash inflows result when cash receipts exceed cash payments for a particular period. Net operating cash outflows result when cash payments exceed cash receipts for a particular period. Net operating cash flows for C&F are presented in Exhibit 7.19.

Due to differences between cash and accrual accounting, C&F's forecasted net income of $7,719 is significantly less than projected operating cash flows of $16,809. Fortunately for C&F, they will have positive operating cash flow each fiscal quarter, reducing the likelihood that they will have to borrow additional funds to execute their business strategy.

Other Cash Flows. As discussed in Chapter 3, a company also can have cash inflows or outflows arising from investing or financing activities. These sets of activities fill out the remaining sections of the cash flow budget. Keith and Dale carefully discussed their 20X2 operating plans and decided that they might need an additional $10,000 in equipment to support their expanded service offerings. However, instead of borrowing to fund this acquisition, they decided to rent whatever they needed during 20X2 and use any surplus cash generated by the business to fund the equipment purchase at year end. Therefore, if any investing cash outflows occurred, they would be late in the fourth quarter of 20X2. Keith and Dale also agreed that if the business meets its budgeted goals, they would pay themselves their first dividend of $5,000 (financing cash outflow) at the end of the year. Exhibit 7.20 incorporates these assumptions into a schedule that shows the quarter-to-quarter expected changes in C&F's cash balances.

Exhibit 7.20 indicates that C&F will have a positive cash balance at the end of each quarter as well as at year end. Many companies reach this stage of the budgeting process and realize that they will not have a positive cash balance. If the cash budget shows a deficit cash balance, managers need to revise their budgets to reflect (1) cash receipts from additional financing, (2) business processes that consume less cash, and/or (3) improved cash collection and management procedures.

Management Accounting: A Business Planning Approach

Exhibit 7.18

C&F Enterprises, Inc. Projected Cash Payments for Operating Expenses For Fiscal Year 20X2	Q1	Q2	Q3	Q4	Total
Variable costs (Exhibit 7.12) less total supplies expense (Exhibit 7.13)	$2,600	$24,221	$33,571	$ 5,977	$66,369
Fixed costs excluding depreciation and prepaid advertising (Exhibit 7.10)	4,800	4,800	4,800	4,800	19,200
Total	$7,400	$29,021	$38,371	$10,777	$85,569

Note: Amounts rounded up to the nearest dollar.

Exhibit 7.19

C&F Enterprises, Inc. Projected Net Operating Cash Flows For Fiscal Year 20X2	Q1	Q2	Q3	Q4	Total
Cash receipts (Exhibit 7.16)	$9,262	$33,934	$50,218	$13,635	$107,049
Cash payments					
Inventory purchases (Exhibit 7.17)	1,426	1,451	1,242	552	4,671
Operating expenses (Exhibit 7.18)	7,400	29,021	38,371	10,777	85,569
Total cash payments	$8,826	$30,472	$39,613	$11,329	$ 90,240
Net operating cash inflow (outflow)	$ 436	$ 3,462	$10,605	$ 2,306	$ 16,809

Exhibit 7.20

C&F Enterprises, Inc. Total Projected Net Cash Flows For Fiscal Year 20X2	Q1	Q2	Q3	Q4	Total
Beginning cash balance	$5,958	$6,394	$ 9,856	$20,461	
Net operating cash flow (Exhibit 7.19)	436	3,462	10,605	2,306	16,809
Net investing cash flow	—	—	—	(10,000)	(10,000)
Net financing cash flow	—	—	—	(5,000)	(5,000)
Ending cash balance	$6,394	$9,856	$20,461	$7,767	

Figure 7.3
Net Present Value is a
capital budgeting technique
that many companies use
when deciding to purchase
equipment. For example,
major farming operations
often use this technique when
deciding whether to buy or
lease major equipment like a
harvester or combine.
This approach helps
managers buy or invest in
an asset whose present value
today exceeds its cost.

Capital Use Budget

The capital use budget is a company's plan for acquiring long-term physical resources (property, plant, and equipment) that it will use in executing the organization's strategy. However, before managers can prepare this budget, they must decide what investments they are going to make.

Evaluating Investment Opportunities. As noted earlier in this chapter, capital budgeting decisions can be complex and often involve a number of assumptions. Although companies use a wide variety of approaches to evaluate their capital investments, many of these often-simple techniques do not address critical assumptions related to cash flows or cost savings, nor do they consider the time value of money. The net present value (NPV) method, however, does not have these limitations, is widely used in industry, and can be easily performed using a hand-held calculator or Excel. This technique guides managers to choose investments whose present value exceeds their cost. The NPV approach consists of four steps:

1. First, estimate the *amount* of the net cash flows expected from the potential investment and the *time periods* in which they are likely to occur. Cash inflows are considered to be positive and cash outflows negative.

2. Next, using Excel or a hand-held calculator, discount the investment cash flows projected in step 1 to their present value—that is, their estimated value today after considering the time value of money. The discount rate used in this calculation should be the minimum return percentage that the company's

Management Accounting: A Business Planning Approach

senior managers expect to earn on the firm's investments: the **required rate of return**. In practice, the required rate of return is estimated by management after considering the cost of the debt and equity it issues to raise the funds to make investments.

3. Next, compute the investment's NPV by subtracting the actual cost of the investment from its estimated present value (computed in the preceding step).

4. Finally, evaluate the NPV. If the NPV is greater than or equal to zero, the investment should be made since it is expected to generate a return that exceeds or equals the required rate of return. However, if the investment's NPV is negative, it should be rejected because its estimated rate of return is less than the required rate of return.

The following example illustrates how managers use NPV to evaluate investment decisions. A business is considering the purchase of a new piece of equipment costing $30,000 to increase the efficiency of its operations. The equipment's estimated useful life is four years. After carefully evaluating how the equipment will be integrated into their business processes, operating managers expect that the equipment will provide annual cost savings of $10,000 during the first two years of its use and $7,500 for the final two years if its useful life. The company also anticipates a resale value of $2,000 for the equipment at the end of the four-year period. Senior management has established a 9 percent required rate of return for all capital expenditures. Should the company buy the equipment?

The cash flows *expected from* the new equipment purchase are summarized in Exhibit 7.21. The present value of these cash flows (cost savings and resale proceeds) can easily be computed using Microsoft Excel. In Excel under the Insert menu, select Function.

After selecting Function, the pop-up Insert Function menu illustrated in Exhibit 7.22 will appear. From that menu, select the category entitled Financial (the third item). Then select a function by scrolling down until you see NPV. Click on the NPV function and then again click OK.

Next the Function Arguments box will appear. Fill in the requested data as illustrated in Exhibit 7.23. Begin with the rate, which is the company's required rate of return. Then input the total annual cash flows expected from the new equipment listed in Exhibit 7.21. Remember that cash inflows (and savings) are positive numbers and cash outflows are negative. Click OK.

	Cost Savings	Sales Proceeds	Total
Year 1	$10,000	$ —	$10,000
Year 2	10,000	—	10,000
Year 3	7,500	—	7,500
Year 4	7,500	2,000	9,500
	$35,000	$2,000	$37,000

Exhibit 7.21
New Equipment Cash Flow Projections

Exhibit 7.22
Selecting the Net Present
Value Function in Excel

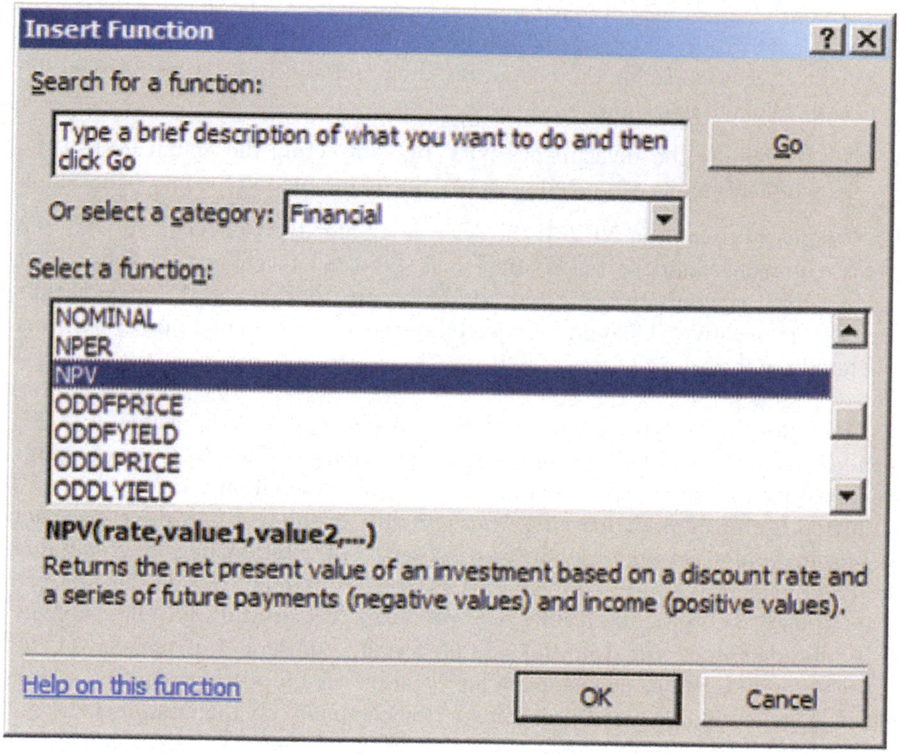

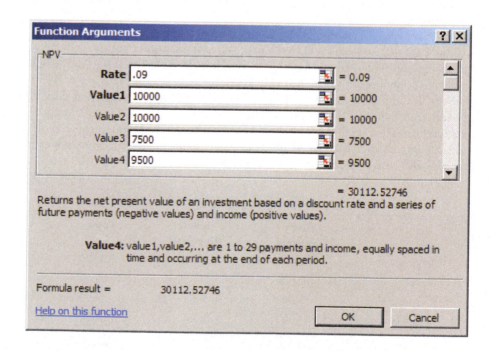

Exhibit 7.23
Entering Data for Excel's Net
Present Value Function

Management Accounting: A Business Planning Approach

If you enter the data from Exhibit 7.21 into cells A2 through D9, your results should look like the screen shown in Exhibit 7.24, with the present value of $30,112.53 displayed in cell D11. Note that the result also can be found at the bottom of the Function Argument box in Exhibit 7.23. If you click on the cell containing the present value result in Exhibit 7.24, the inputs to the present value calculation can be seen in the formula bar at the top of the Excel worksheet.

With the calculation of the present value of the new equipment's cash flows complete, the equipment's *net present value* can be computed. Since the equipment's cost is $30,000, its NPV would be $112.53, the present value of the expected cash flows (cost savings and salvage value) less the cost. The positive NPV suggests that the company should buy the equipment.

Preparing the Capital Use Budget. The capital use budget is important because it clearly outlines potential drains on a company's cash reserves. It also can provide input for the operating expense budget since capital asset acquisitions that occur will need to be depreciated, thus affecting budget estimates for noncash fixed depreciation expenses.

Keith and Dale believed they needed additional mowing equipment to support their projected landscaping activity next year. After several calls to local equipment leasing companies, they learned that they could rent the required lawn tractor for $3,500 a year. However, their accountants suggested that purchasing the

Exhibit 7.25
Capital Budgeting Worksheet
for Equipment Purchase

	A	B	C	D	E
1					
2	**Lawn Tractor Purchase Decision Analysis**				
3					
4		**Cost**	**Sales**		
5		**Savings**	**Proceeds**	**Total**	
6					
7	**Year 1**	$ 3,500.00	$ -	$ 3,500.00	
8	**Year 2**	3,500.00	-	3,500.00	
9	**Year 3**	3,500.00	500.00	4,000.00	
10		$ 10,500.00	$ 500.00	$ 11,000.00	
11					
12	**Present Value of Cash Flows**			$ 9,079.64	
13					
14	**Equipment Purchase Price**			$ 8,000.00	
15					
16	**Net Present Value**			$ 1,079.64	
17					

lawn tractor was also an option, but that they would have to run an NPV analysis to determine if a purchase was the right decision. The accountants learned that the mowing equipment under consideration cost $8,000 and had an expected life of about three years; they estimated its salvage value to be $500. They also assumed C&F's required rate of return to be 10 percent, equal to the interest rate it incurs on its note payable. The accountants put all of this information into an Excel spreadsheet to compute the equipment's NPV. Their calculations are illustrated in Exhibit 7.25.

Keith and Dale will save $3,500 in annual rental expenses if they buy the equipment. They also will receive $500 in cash flow when they dispose of the equipment at the end of its useful life. The present value of these future cash savings and inflows is $9,079.64 and the NPV is $1,079.64. Since the NPV is greater than zero, the accountants recommended that Keith and Dale buy the equipment for $8,000. In addition to the new mower, the two owners plan to purchase a new computer and laser printer for $2,000 at a local office supply store.

C&F's capital use budget is rather simple with only $10,000 in capital expenditures for equipment forecasted to occur late in the fourth quarter. The purchases include $8,000 for the new landscaping equipment and $2,000 for the new computer and laser printer. Since it is unlikely that C&F will actually begin using this new landscaping or office equipment until the spring of 20X3, due to the seasonality of the business, Keith and Dale have not budgeted any depreciation expense for these capital assets in 20X2. Exhibit 7.26 illustrates C&F's capital use budget for 20X2. Once the operating, cash flow, and capital use budgets are complete, the firm can create pro forma financial statements.

Exhibit 7.26

C&F Enterprises, Inc. Capital Use Budget For Fiscal Year 20X2					
	Q1	Q2	Q3	Q4	Total
Landscaping equipment	$ —	$ —	$ —	$ (8,000)	$(8,000)
Computer and printer	$ —	$ —	$ —	$ (2,000)	$(2,000)
Total	$ —	$ —	$ —	$(10,000)	

The last step in budgeting is developing the financial statement budgets. Financial statement budgets also are commonly known as pro forma financial statements. These financial statement budgets usually follow a format consistent with generally accepted accounting principles (GAAP) except that supporting note disclosures are omitted. Typically, companies prepare three pro forma financial statements: the budgeted balance sheet, the budgeted income statement, and the budgeted statement of cash flows.

An efficient way to create financial statements is to use an electronic worksheet similar to the one presented in Exhibit 7.27. Similar to the transaction worksheet presented in Exhibit 3.10, this worksheet uses the set of projected assumptions about C&F's 20X2 business activity to generate the financial statement budget. The fifteen line items presented in Exhibit 7.27 are drawn from the projections in the operating, capital use, and cash flow budgets. The basis for each line's amounts is described below.

Learning Objective 5
Discuss the preparation of pro forma financial statements.

Beginning Balances. Since C&F Enterprises, Inc. is budgeting its second year of operations, beginning balances are the December 31, 20X1 balance sheet totals as reported in Chapter 3. Income statement and cash flow items reflect only one operating period and therefore start with zero balances.

Revenue from Services and Cash Collections. These amounts reflect the data in Exhibits 7.6 and 7.16. During 20X2, C&F estimates it will generate $102,490 in revenue (Exhibit 7.6), of which $101,549 will be collected in 20X2. This leaves an accounts receivable balance of $941 (remember that Keith and Dale assume that they will collect 10 percent of fourth-quarter 20X2 revenues in the first quarter of 20X3. The second entry shows that $5,500 in accounts receivable outstanding at year end 20X1 was collected. The sum of the two cash collection entries of $101,549 and $5,500 equal the total cash receipts ($107,049) shown in Exhibit 7.16.

Cash Paid for Salaries and Wages and Bookkeeping. The amounts for salaries and wages ($53,611) and bookkeeping ($3,000) come from Exhibit 7.10 As discussed previously, these costs are assumed to be paid in full in the fiscal quarter in which they are incurred.

Cash Paid for Supplies. The amount paid for supplies ($4,671) is drawn from Exhibit 7.17. This amount exceeds the $3,803 of the projected supplies expense for two reasons. First, as discussed in the text following Exhibit 7.17, the payments include $1,000 of accounts payable outstanding at December 31, 20X1, while $81 of inventory purchases are estimated to remain unpaid at December 31, 20X2. The net effect of these two assumptions results in a decrease in accounts payable of $919, as shown. Second, it is necessary to reduce inventory by $50, as C&F will hold $250 of supplies inventory at December 31, 20X2 rather than the $300 of inventory it held to start the year.

Cash Paid for Rentals and Fuel. The amounts for rentals ($16,120) and fuel ($1,126) come from Exhibit 7.10. As discussed previously, these variable costs are paid in full in the fiscal quarter in which they are incurred.

Cash Paid for Advertising. As discussed in the text following Exhibit 7.7, advertising expense for 20X2 is projected to be $9,800. This amount includes $5,000 paid to a marketing firm, as well as the expiration of the $4,800 of prepaid advertising related to C&F's 20X2 newspaper and online advertising.

Cash Paid for Interest, Taxes, and Other Expenses. The amounts for interest ($200), taxes ($2,798) and other expenses ($3,713) are drawn from Exhibit 7.10. As discussed previously, these costs are paid in full in the period incurred.

Cash Paid for Equipment. The amount for equipment purchases ($10,000) comes from Exhibit 7.26. As discussed previously, C&F assumes it will pay for its new lawn tractor, computer, and printer in cash in 20X2.

Cash Paid for Dividends. The amount for dividends paid ($5,000) is drawn from Exhibit 7.20. As discussed previously, Keith and Dale assume that the company will have enough cash at year end 20X2 to pay its first dividend.

After recognizing all of the projections arising from the budgets, the "Balances, December 31" row provides the necessary data for the budgeted (pro forma) balance sheet and income statement. The far right column provides data for the budgeted statement of cash flows. The financial statement budget worksheet is useful to managers because it provides the data for the pro forma financial statements and reconciles various totals from the operating, cash flow, and capital use budgets.

Each of the final pro forma budgeted financial statements is presented in the following sections.

The Budgeted Balance Sheet

The totals in the balance sheet columns in Exhibit 7.27 provide the data for C&F's December 31, 20X2, budgeted balance sheet shown in Exhibit 7.28. Each balance sheet line item equals the amounts shown in Exhibit 7.27. As we can see, C&F expects to have $20,758 of assets at the end of 20X2. Note that the prepaid advertising asset appears with a zero balance since the two-year newspaper and online advertising contract expired at year end.

Exhibit 7.27
C&F Enterprises, Inc. 20X2 Financial Statement Budget Worksheet

Projections	Cash	A/R	Sup	PP Ad	Equip	A/D	=	A/P	N/P	C/S	R/E	Rev	− Exp	= N/I	Amount	Type
Beginning balances	$5,958	$5,500	$300	$4,800	$3,000	$(600)	=	$1,000	$2,000	$12,000	$3,958	$—	$—	$—	$—	
Revenue from services[a]	101,549	941									102,490	102,490			101,549	OCF
Cash collections (Exhibit 7.16)	5,500	(5,500)													5,500	OCF
Cash paid for:																
Salaries and wages (Exhibit 7.10)	(53,611)										(53,611)		(53,611)		(53,611)	OCF
Bookkeeping service (Exhibit 7.10)	(3,000)										(3,000)		(3,000)		(3,000)	OCF
Supplies[a]	(4,671)		(50)					(919)			(3,803)		(3,803)		(4,671)	OCF
Rentals (Exhibit 7.10)	(16,120)										(16,120)		(16,120)		(16,120)	OCF
Fuel (Exhibit 7.10)	(1,126)										(1,126)		(1,126)		(1,126)	OCF
Advertising[a]	(5,000)			(4,800)							(9,800)		(9,800)		(5,000)	OCF
Interest (Exhibit 7.10)	(200)										(200)		(200)		(200)	OCF
Taxes (Exhibit 7.10)	(2,798)										(2,798)		(2,798)		(2,798)	OCF
Other expenses (Exhibit 7.10)	(3,713)										(3,713)		(3,713)		(3,713)	OCF
Equipment (Exhibit 7.20)	(10,000)				10,000										(10,000)	ICF
Dividends (Exhibit 7.20)	(5,000)										(5,000)				(5,000)	FCF
Depreciation expense (Exhibit 7.10)						(600)					(600)		(600)			
Balances, December 31	$7,767	$941	$250	$—	$13,000	$(1,200)	=	$81	$2,000	$12,000	$6,677	$102,490	$(94,771)	$7,719		

Legend (as abbreviations appear from left to right):

A/R = Accounts Receivable   N/P = Notes Payable   OCF = Operating Cash Flow
PP Ad = Prepaid Advertising   A/P = Accounts Payable   ICF = Investing Cash Flow
Sup = Supplies Inventory   C/S = Common Stock   FCF = Financing Cash Flow
Equip = Equipment   R/E = Retained Earnings
A/D = Accumulated Depreciation   N/I = Net Income

[a] The basis for each of these items is explained in detail in the text preceding this exhibit.

Note: Numbers in parentheses in this exhibit represent decreases on the respective financial statements.

The Budgeted Income Statement

The revenue and expense columns in Exhibit 7.27 provide the data for C&F's budgeted income statement for the year ended December 31, 20X2, shown in Exhibit 7.29. C&F expects to sell $102,490 of services and generate net income of $7,719 in 20X2.

The Budgeted Statement of Cash Flows

The cash transactions listed in the cash flows column on the far right side of Exhibit 7.27 provide the data for C&F's budgeted statement of cash flows for the year ended December 31, 20X2. As discussed in Chapter 3, the statement of cash flows explains the change in a company's end-of-period cash balance in terms of its operating, investing, and financing activities. The pro forma statement of cash flows in Exhibit 7.30 shows that C&F plans to increase cash by $1,809 during the

Exhibit 7.28
Pro Forma Balance Sheet

C&F Enterprises, Inc.
Budgeted Balance Sheet
December 31, 20X2

Assets

Cash		$ 7,767
Accounts Receivable		941
Supplies		250
Prepaid Advertising		—
Equipment	$13,000	
Less Accumulated Depreciation		
Equipment (net)	(1,200)	11,800
Total Assets		$20,758

Liabilities and Owners' Equity

Current Accounts Payable		$ 81
Long-Term Note Payable		2,000
Common Stock		12,000
Retained Earnings		6,677
Total Liabilities and Owners' Equity		$20,758

Management Accounting: A Business Planning Approach

```
                 C&F Enterprises, Inc.
               Budgeted Income Statement
             For the Year Ended December 31, 20X2

Service Revenue                                        $102,490
Cost of Services Sold:
    Salaries and Wages              $53,611
    Rentals                          16,120
    Supplies                          3,803
    Fuel                              1,126
    Depreciation                        600
        Total Cost of Services Sold                      75,260
Gross Profit                                          $ 27,230
Operating Expenses:
    Advertising                                           9,800
    Bookkeeping Services                                  3,000
    Interest                                                200
    Taxes                                                 2,798
    Other                                                 3,713
Net Income                                            $  7,719
```

Exhibit 7.29
Pro Forma Income Statement

```
                 C&F Enterprises, Inc.
          Budgeted Statement of Cash Flows
           For the Year Ended December 31, 20X2

Cash from (Used by) Operating Activities:
    Cash Received from Customers                       $107,049
    Cash Paid for Salaries and Wages                   (53,611)
    Cash Paid for Other Operating Expenses             (28,959)
    Cash Paid to Suppliers                              (4,671)
    Cash Paid for Taxes                                 (2,798)
    Cash Paid for Interest                                (200)
Cash Flow From Operating Activities                   $ 16,809
Cash from (Used by) Investing Activities:
    Cash Paid for Equipment                            (10,000)

Cash (Used by) Financing Activities:
    Cash Dividends Paid to Owners                       (5,000)

Increase in Cash During Year                          $  1,809
Cash Balance at Beginning of Year                        5,958
Cash Balance at End of Year                           $  7,767
```

Exhibit 7.30
Pro Forma Statement of
Cash Flows

year. This increase comes from the $16,809 generated by operating activities less equipment purchases of $10,000 (investing activity) and the $5,000 dividend (a financing activity) that Keith and Dale plan to pay themselves.

Pro forma financial statements allow managers and other stakeholders to evaluate the viability of the company's financial plan for operating the business. To the extent that the pro forma financial statements do not meet stakeholder expectations, managers must modify their budgets. However, any such changes must accurately reflect the environmental conditions that the business can expect to encounter. In short, budget revisions should reflect economic reality.

The New Accounting Equation Revisited

Historically, students of the budgeting process have been asked to devote significant amounts of time and energy to the *design* and *creation* of manual or electronic master budgeting spreadsheets. However, technology and the Internet have greatly reduced the importance of such exercises since these common budgeting tools are now given away at no cost by a variety of business-education websites. Since budgeting tools no longer need to be created, more time can be devoted to developing the information content of the budgets. For example, how does the company:

- Evaluate its market and forecast sales?
- Determine the mix of cash versus credit sales?
- Estimate cash collections on receivables?
- Compute its inventory requirements?
- Develop its selling and administration expense estimates?
- Manage the variability in its cash forecasts?

The budgeting process presents an ideal forum for managers' to think about their personal contribution to the firm's success. In developing budgets, managers can show how their actions directly contribute to financial outcomes. Furthermore, the planning process provides managers with the opportunity to demonstrate and apply their insight.

As discussed in Chapter 2, the new accounting equation (Data + Insight = Information™) highlights the widening gap between computation and the delivery of relevant information to decision-makers: It underscores the role of insight in data transformation. Most college graduates possess the technical competency and integrity required to produce the *data* component of the *new* accounting equation. However, advances in technology diminish the likelihood that they will continue to be compensated for such routine data creation and processing activities.

The new accounting equation (Data + Insight = Information™) provides managers with a useful framework in which to view their current and future roles in creating value for their firm or clients. To succeed, managers must refine their analytical skills to provide *insight* into the context and relevance of financial data. This insight is essential if these professionals expect to participate in strategy formulation, risk assessment, and business decision-making. Professionals also bear the burden of convincingly demonstrating to clients and colleagues that their insights help the business create measurable value for customers, shareholders, and other stakeholders. Therefore, it is critical that financial professionals adopt personal strategies that focus on insight development to deliver what today's dynamic business marketplace requires—timely and relevant decision-making information. The budgeting process provides an ideal forum to demonstrate such insight.

Source: Reprinted by permission.

Management Accounting: A Business Planning Approach

Summary

Budgeting is the core of a company's business-planning process. It is the final step in translating company strategy into an action plan. Effectively allocating resources to support business processes is a critical step in determining a firm's success. The value of the budgeting process rests in the final product—a pro forma set of financial statements. These projected financial statements provide clear objectives that can motivate and direct managers; they also serve as benchmarks that can be used to evaluate actual performance. While strategies and processes can differ across firms, the pro forma financial statements provide a means to compare future operating plans across companies.

Summary of Learning Objectives

1. **Describe budgeting and its potential benefits.** The budget is a financial plan that guides the future operations of a business. The budgeting process usually entails several rounds of review, revision, and negotiation across the entire organization. Budgets can help companies plan and organize their operations, coordinate and control their business processes, communicate plans, and motivate employees. However, budgeting does have some limitations that managers must understand in order to use budgets effectively. For

Net Gains

Budgeting Resources on the Web

Today's technologies have inundated consumers with facts, numbers, and records in a variety of forms: reports, plans, Web- or computer-based interactive tools, and more. Only if someone is willing to pay for a pool of "statistics" does informational value exist. As noted in Chapter 2, the market now assigns a significant premium to the preparation of information as compared with the production of data. A cursory review of Internet business websites reveals numerous financial reports, tools, and plans. In the past, public dissemination of such products at little or no charge would not have been envisioned.

- **PlanWare (http://www.planware.org).** This website offers no-cost Excel-based tools for writing a business plan, making financial projections, business planning, and developing business strategies—software, shareware, freeware, white papers, samples, templates, and other useful features and resources.

- **Excellence in Financial Management (http://www.exinfm.com/free_spreadsheets.html).** Excellence in Financial Management provides a wealth of business-planning tools. This website provides free downloadable templates and guidance for the preparation of *pro forma* financial statements and various analyses.

example, budgets often oversimplify economic reality. They also can undermine managers' initiative by discouraging new developments. Finally, managers often focus on budget results rather than on the reasons for the results.

2. **Define the master budget and discuss its components.** The master budget is a set of financial reports that describe a company's operating plans for a specific future fiscal period. A master budget is usually composed of four separate budget schedules that address operations, cash flow, capital usage, and financial statement reporting. Operating budgets detail the expected financial outcomes arising from a firm's business processes. Cash flow budgets summarize a company's expected cash receipts and payments arising from operating, investing, and financing activities. Capital use budgets describe a firm's planned investment activities in new plant facilities, equipment, products, locations, and other long-term operating activities. Financial statement budgets summarize the data from all the other budgets into pro forma financial statements.

3. **Illustrate the development of the operating budget.** Preparation of the operating budget starts the budget process. The operating budget generally includes three distinct parts: the sales or revenue budget, the operating expense budget, and the inventory purchases budget. These forecasts define the resources needed to execute basic business processes to meet customer demand. The operating budgets give managers preliminary insight into the anticipated profitability of the firm.

4. **Demonstrate the creation of the cash flow and capital use budgets.** Cash flow is critical to a firm's success and survival. A company must have enough cash to meet its obligations or it will fail. The cash flow budget is a useful monitoring tool that details cash receipts and payments. The cash flow budget differs from the operating budget because of differences between cash and accrual accounting. Managers rely on cash flow budgets to ensure that employees, suppliers, and creditors are paid on a timely basis. The cash flow budget is the foundation for the pro forma statement of cash flows.

5. **Discuss the preparation of pro forma financial statements.** Pro forma financial statements or financial statement budgets are prepared using data from all the other budgets. Companies prepare balance sheets, income statements, and statements of cash flows using formats consistent with generally accepted accounting principles. These budgeted financial statements represent the end of the budgeting process and give users insight into the expected outcomes of the business.

Glossary of Terms

Budget A financial plan for the future operations of a business.

Capital use budget A financial plan that describes planned investments in new plant facilities, equipment, products, locations, and other long-term operating activities.

Management Accounting: A Business Planning Approach

Cash flow budget A summary of a company's expected cash receipts and payments resulting from operating, investing, and financing activities.

Cash payments schedule The schedule within the cash flow budget that details the cash disbursements the firm expects to make in a given fiscal period.

Cash receipts schedule The schedule within the cash flow budget that reflects the firm's expected cash inflows from customers as well as receipts from financing and/or investing activities.

Financial statement budgets Budget schedules that consolidate data from operating, cash flow, and capital use budgets into pro forma financial statements.

Inventory purchases budgets Schedules that estimate the timing and amount of inventory needed to satisfy forecasted sales demand.

Master budget A set of financial schedules that describe a company's operating plans for a specific future fiscal period.

Net present value (NPV) method A widely used capital budgeting technique that guides managers to choose investments whose present value exceeds their cost.

Operating budget A set of schedules that details the expected financial outcomes arising from a firm's business processes. This budget is generally composed of three parts: a sales or revenue budget, the operating expense budget, and the inventory purchases budget.

Operating expense budget A schedule that captures the primary expenses, both fixed and variable, that a company will incur while executing its business strategy.

Required rate of return The discount rate commonly used in calculating the present value of an investment. It is generally the minimum return percentage that a company's senior managers expect to earn on the firm's investments.

Sales budget A company's revenue plan for a given fiscal period.

Time value of money A concept that suggests that it is better to receive a sum of money today, rather than in the future. Cash received today can be invested, and by the end of investment period, the amount of cash available will be greater than the original amount received. Sophisticated capital budgeting techniques generally are used to address the time value of money issues found in capital use decisions.

Chapter Review Questions

1. What is a budget?
2. What are the primary benefits of budgeting?
3. Name at least three barriers to effective budgeting?
4. What can companies do to overcome common budgeting barriers?
5. What is a master budget?
6. What are the four primary components of a master budget?
7. What is an operating budget?
8. What is a cash flow budget?
9. What are the components of a cash flow budget?
10. What is a capital use budget?

11. What are financial statement budgets?
12. What is considered to be the starting point of the budgeting process?
13. What data are needed to construct a sales budget?
14. What data sources do managers rely on to create sales budgets?
15. What is an operating expense budget?
16. What is an inventory purchases budget?
17. Name the three primary categories of cash inflows and outflows.
18. Give three examples of cash inflows.
19. Give three examples of cash outflows.
20. What is meant by net operating cash inflow?
21. What is meant by net operating cash outflow?
22. Which component of the master budget is prepared last?

Exercises and Problems

1. Provide a specific example to show how each of the six budgeting benefits described in this chapter could help each of the following organizations.
   a. Supermarket
   b. Pizza shop
   c. College sorority
   d. Video store
2. Provide a specific example to show how each of the six budgeting benefits described in this chapter could help each of the following organizations.
   a. High school
   b. Movie theater
   c. Hardware store
   d. Sports bar and grill
3. A company president wants you to review the company's projected financial statements and their supporting budgets. This chapter discussed several types of budgets (sales budget, operating expense budget, inventory purchases budget, capital use budget, and cash flow budget) that are used to generate projected financial statements. From this set of five supporting budgets, match each of the following items to the budget in which it is most likely to appear:
   a. Equipment purchases
   b. Estimated customer demand per fiscal quarter
   c. Advertising expense
   d. Inventory purchases in each fiscal quarter
   e. Cash payments for inventories
   f. Depreciation expense
   g. Collections of prior-year accounts receivable
4. Visit a small local business and arrange to meet with the manager or owner. Ask this person the following questions about budgeting at his or her enterprise:
   a. How often does the company prepare a budget?
   b. What is the biggest challenge to budgeting?
   c. Who prepares the budget? Is it someone internal or external to the business?

d. What items appear in the operating budget?

e. How are budgets used throughout the year?

f. How are budgets used to evaluate performance?

Prepare a memo to your instructor summarizing your findings.

5. Shatz Fine Clothiers expects to make inventory purchases in the first quarter of 20X5 as follows:

January	$50,000
February	60,000
March	70,000

Historical data shows that the company pays for 70 percent of its purchases in the month of purchase and the remaining balance is paid in the month following the purchase. On January 1, 20X5, the company owed $20,000 for prior-year purchases.

a. Prepare a schedule of cash payments for January, February, and March.

b. What amount of accounts payable will be outstanding on March 31?

6. Major Drumstick Poultry Company expects to have the following sales in the first quarter of 20X5:

January	$70,000
February	80,000
March	90,000

Historical data shows that the company collects 80 percent of its sales in the month of the sale and the remaining balance is collected in the month following the sale. On January 1, 20X5, accounts receivable related to December sales totaled $10,000.

a. Compute total sales for December 20X4.

b. Prepare a schedule of cash receipts for January, February, and March.

c. What amount of accounts receivable will be outstanding on March 31?

7. Smith Company estimates that it will sell 1,000 units of its product in each of the first three fiscal quarters of the coming year. It expects to sell 1,500 units in the fourth quarter. Its product sells for $10 per unit. The company president expects 90 percent of sales to be collected in cash in the quarter when sold, and the remaining 10 percent will be collected in the following quarter. Accounts receivable totaling $3,000 was outstanding at the beginning of the year. Based on these data, complete the following requirements.

a. Prepare a sales forecast for the coming year.

b. Prepare a cash receipts schedule for the coming year.

c. What amount of receivables is expected to be outstanding at year end?

8. Seattle Brewing Company incurs the following fixed costs each quarter:

Advertising	$30,000
Rent	20,000
Salaries	80,000
Insurance	2,000
Depreciation	15,000

The company pays 80 percent of it cash expenses in the period incurred. The remaining 20 percent are paid in the following fiscal quarter. Accounts payable totaling $25,000 were outstanding at the beginning of the year. Using these data, complete the following requirements.

a. Prepare a quarterly fixed cost budget for the coming year.

b. Prepare a cash payments schedule for the coming year.

c. Compute the total accounts payable expected to be outstanding at year end.

9. Heart & Soul Music Store expects to sell 20,000 CDs in the first four months of business in 20X1. Each CD sells for $12 and costs $8. Management wants to prepare an operating budget for the first fiscal quarter (Q1). Q1 consists of January, February, and March. Monthly sales are projected to be as follows:

20X1	January	February	March	April
Expected sales (in units)	2,500	4,000	7,500	6,000

a. Prepare a monthly sales forecast in dollars for Q1 (January, February, and March).

b. Prepare a monthly contribution margin statement for Q1.

c. Assume that for Heart & Soul's operations, ending inventory is projected to be 80 percent of next month's sales. Assume the company started 20X1 with 2,000 CDs in its inventory. How many CDs does the company need to buy in each month of Q1?

d. What is the cost of inventory purchases for each month?

10. Eggs Cetera is new breakfast café. Based on a recent market analysis, the company expects the following quarterly demand (number of customers):

Q1	10,000
Q2	15,000
Q3	20,000
Q4	18,000

The typical customer spends $10 per meal at the restaurant. Management estimates that food accounts for 80 percent of each customer's bill. The other 20 percent comes from beverages. Food costs the café 75 percent of its selling price, while beverages cost only 20 percent of their selling price. Based on these data, prepare the following:

a. A quarterly sales forecast.

b. A quarterly contribution margin forecast.

11. Lincoln Cafe is considering buying a new oven that is expected to provide annual savings of $8,000 in the first year of its life, $7,500 in its second year of life, and $5,000 for the final two years of its useful life. It is expected to have a resale value of $2,000 at the end of the four-year period. Assume a 7 percent interest rate and that savings occur at year end.

a. Find the present value of the cost savings and resale proceeds of the oven.

b. If Lincoln Cafe could purchase the new oven for $26,000, should the company buy it?

Management Accounting: A Business Planning Approach

12. London Carpet Cleaning Service is considering buying new equipment that is expected to provide cost savings of $6,000 in the first year of its life and $4,000 for the final two years of its useful life. It is expected to have a resale value of $1,000 at the end of the three-year period. Assume an 8 percent interest rate and that savings occur at year end.
    a. Find the present value of the cost savings and resale proceeds of the equipment.
    b. If London Carpet Cleaning Service could buy the equipment for $10,000, should the company buy the new equipment?
13. Next Generation Computer Consulting is considering a new laser printer that is expected to provide cost savings of $1,000 in the first year of its life, $800 in its second year of life, and $500 for the final two years of its useful life. It is expected to have a resale value of $200 at the end of the four-year period. Assume a 9 percent interest rate and savings at year end.
    a. Find the present value of the cost savings and resale proceeds of the printer.
    b. If Next Generation could purchase it for $2,400, should the company buy the new printer?
    c. If the company assumed a 12 percent interest rate, recompute the present value of the cost savings and resale proceeds of the printer. Would your answer to question (b) change at the new interest rate?
14. Big Foot Shoe Company sells two kinds of boots: hiking and ski. Its hiking boots sell for $100 and cost $60 per pair. Its ski boots sell for $150 and cost $75 per pair. Big Foot also has provided the following data:
    - In 20X2, the company expects to sell 48,000 pairs of hiking boots and 23,000 pairs of ski boots. The company has 4,000 pairs of hiking boots and 2,000 pairs of ski boots on hand at the beginning of the year. They want to hold 10 percent of annual sales of each product in inventory for the following year.
    - They expect to collect 90 percent of sales in cash each year and the remaining 10 percent as credit sales. Eighty percent of credit sales are collected in the current year and 20 percent are collected in the following year. Accounts receivable at the beginning of the year was $9,000, all of which will be collected in 20X2.
    - Big Foot Shoe Company pays for 80 percent of its purchases in the current year and the remaining 20 percent in the next fiscal year. Accounts payable at the beginning of the year were $12,000, all of which will be paid in 20X2.
    - Cash on hand at the beginning of the year was $50,000.
    Based on these data, prepare the following:
    a. Sales forecast for 20X2.
    b. Estimated contribution margin for 20X2.
    c. Cash receipts schedule for 20X2.
    d. Cash payments schedule for 20X2.
    e. Current assets section of the balance sheet at December 31, 20X2.

Sweet 16 Donut Shop

Sweet 16 Donut Shop is located in a busy downtown commercial district of a major southwestern city. Sweet 16 is widely known for their sixteen varieties of fresh-baked donuts. Although Sweet 16 has been in business for many years, recent new competition from larger chains has prompted the owners to think more seriously about budgeting. They have hired you to prepare their 20X2 operating, cash flow, and financial statement budgets. To help you do so, they have provided the following information about the business.

Sweet 16 sells 45,000 donuts per fiscal quarter, except for Q4 when it sells 60,000 donuts. The donuts arrive each morning from a local baking distributor. Sweet 16's employees add toppings and bake the donuts. No donuts are held overnight (after all, who wants a day-old donut?). Sweet 16 typically collects cash for each sale. However, some local corporations order donuts in bulk and have thirty days to pay. Management estimates that 90 percent of sales are collected in the fiscal quarter of sale and the remaining 10 percent is collected in the following fiscal quarter.

The company pays its employees a total of $2,000 per quarter, plus 5 cents per donut sold. The donuts sell for 50 cents each and the ingredients cost 20 cents each. In addition, Sweet 16 incurs $1,000 of fixed operating costs each month (that is, rent, insurance, and advertising) of which $300 is depreciation (a non-cash expense). Sweet 16 pays its variable costs in the month incurred. It pays 80 percent of its fixed costs in the quarter incurred and the remaining amounts in the following quarter, except for wages which are paid 100 percent in the quarter incurred.

In addition, supplies inventory (napkins, boxes, and the like) cost 12 percent of quarterly sales. Sweet 16 would like to hold $2,000 of supplies at the end of each quarter of 20X2. Supplies inventory at year end 20X1 totaled $1,600. Supplies inventory is paid for in the quarter the supplies are received.

The balance sheet from the end of the prior year is presented below.

Sweet 16 Donut Shop Balance Sheet December 31, 20X1	
Assets	
Cash	$100,000
Accounts Receivable	1,000
Supplies Inventory	1,600
Equipment (net of $10,000 depreciation)	47,000
Total Assets	$149,600
Liabilities and Owners' Equity	
Accounts Payable	$ 1,100
Common Stock	80,000
Retained Earnings	68,500
Total Liabilities and Owners' Equity	$149,600

Required

Based on these data, prepare operating, cash flow, and financial statement budgets for Sweet 16 Donut Shop for 20X2. Compose a short paragraph to the owner, Art Vanderlei, about the nature of your work and any insights that you can draw from the results.

Budgeting Basics

Creating a Start-Up Budget

The first complete set of budgeted transactions for a start-up company's initial fiscal period is known as the start-up budget. This is an important part of the business plan because it tells investors how much financial capital is necessary to start the business. You may want to ask a local business owner about the types of expenses that they incurred when opening their operation. The start-up budget is a financial schedule that documents a complete list of expenditures (and reserve funds) that the founders consider necessary to begin operations. This section is critical because it gives potential investors and creditors a sense of the amount of money that will be needed to start operations. The business plan also will include a description of financing sources.

Businesses incur a considerable number of expenses prior to opening. Some of these expenditures appear on the income statement as expenses, while others are capitalized on the balance sheet as assets. Items should include, but are not limited, to:

- Legal costs, utility deposits, down payments, licenses/permits,
- Beginning inventories, cash, and other current assets
- Investments in equipment, facilities, and so forth

It is important for the business plan to completely reflect all costs that are necessary to support operations. The start-up budget should include enough cash to cover future expenditures until the business can rely on operations to pay bills. The local chamber of commerce and area business can give you some insight into the expected cost of each of these items.

Developing an Operating Budget

A budget can be created by following the steps set forth in this chapter. The critical first step is to create a credible sales forecast and operating budget.

The sales forecast should be based on the customer analysis section of the market analysis. The customer analysis should document the size of the customer base, customer preferences and income levels, and the expected level of demand. The sales forecast should show how sales will vary based on different ranges for:

- Product/service prices
- Expected quantities of sales (based on your market analysis)
- Sales mix assumptions

In other words, what effect do changes in prices, quantities, and mix have on the projected sales level? Entrepreneurs often have optimistic and ambitious sales expectations. It is important to demonstrate how lower levels of sales will affect the overall business plan. You should develop a monthly operating budget for the first year. The monthly budget will show investors if there is any seasonality in your business. For example, a campus pizza shop is likely to sell more during the school year.

The sales forecast is based on key assumptions about quantities, prices, and mix. It is essential to document and clearly explain each of these key assumptions. The thoroughness of these explanations enhances the overall credibility of the business plan. The sales forecast drives the operating budget. You can use industry resources or data to gain a perspective on the percentage of expenses and resources typically needed to support your expected sales level. These percentages can be used to create expense forecasts that drive your cash flow and financial statement budgets.

Assignment

You should provide pro forma balance sheets, income statements, and statements of cash flow for three years. Your budget should be accompanied by a text discussion that (1) explains and shows how you will finance the growth of the business and (2) documents any accounting assumptions (for example, depreciation). Such accompanying text explains to readers how the budget was developed and makes your business plan creditable.

Image Credits

Management Accounting: A Business Planning Approach

Chapter 8

Analyzing and Using Budgets

The previous chapter showed how managers use profit-planning and forecasting techniques to prepare budgets. This chapter focuses on how they actually use budgets to monitor and control business operations. The chapter extends our discussion of business planning by discussing how nonfinancial data can enhance a manager's understanding of financial results, thus improving decision making. It begins by discussing how managers evaluate the reasonableness or credibility of their budgets. The chapter then illustrates how flexible budgets can be used to accommodate changes in sales forecasts or cost projections. The chapter concludes by demonstrating how managers evaluate operating results that differ from budgeted expectations. Such insight is critical to effectively evaluate performance and plan for future periods.

In Chapter 7 you learned how to develop the master budget. C&F's budgeting process began with the sales budgets and ended with a set of pro forma financial statements (that is, the financial statement budget) for 20X2. Budgets were based on a broad set of assumptions that included estimates of sales volume, customer demand, average selling price, fixed and variable costs, and cash receipts and payments. Ultimately, the usefulness of the entire budget depends on its credibility, which depends on the validity of each underlying assumption. To assess a budget's credibility, managers must evaluate each underlying assumption and its impact on projected outcomes.

C&F Enterprises, Inc.: Realizing the Need for a Budget

Keith and Dale were quite pleased with themselves! After much hard work and technical assistance from their accounting advisors, they now had what appeared to be a comprehensive plan to guide their business operations in the coming year. They had budgets for virtually any aspect of their business, including sales, expenses, capital expenditures, and cash flows.

While admiring the clarity and detail of C&F's new budget for fiscal year 20X2, a cold chill came over Keith. Although he and Dale had carefully followed the budget preparation instructions provided by their accounting advisors, what if they had made a mistake? How would they know? After discussing this possibility with Dale, an even worse scenario occurred to both of them. Would all of their planning efforts be in vain if their budgetary assumptions and forecasts proved to be inaccurate! What then? Were their budgets still valid? Could they still be used? If so, how?

Keith and Dale rushed to call the accountants! After anxiously explaining their concerns to their financial advisors, they learned that several other budgeting tools could complement their new plan to more effectively monitor their 20X2 operations. The accountants invited Keith and Dale over to their offices the next day to review the reasonableness of their final budgets and to discuss how sensitivity analyses and flexible budgeting might be incorporated into C&F Enterprises' 20X2 profit plan.

Does the Budget Hold Water?

Learning Objective 1
Demonstrate how budget credibility can be assessed.

Managers frequently compare budgeted projections to past performance to determine the *reasonableness* of the business forecasts that they are making. Significant differences suggest assumptions or estimates that need revisiting before managers can use the budget to execute strategy. Examples of the budget reasonableness review for C&F Enterprises' 20X2 projected financial statements follow.

Comparing Balance Sheets
(Current Year Budget vs. Prior Year Actual)

Exhibit 8.1 compares C&F's 20X2 year-end projected balance sheet to its 20X1 year-end actual balance sheet. Changes in each balance sheet category are computed by subtracting the actual 20X1 results from the 20X2 projections. For example, cash at the end of 20X2 is budgeted to be $1,809 ($7,767 less $5,958) higher than at the end of 20X1. Conversely, year-end 20X2 accounts receivable are projected to decline by $4,559 from the beginning of the year, a decrease of 82.9 percent. Changes in percentage terms are computed by dividing the dollar amount of the change by the 20X1 year-end (base) amount for each financial statement category. For example, the $1,809 projected increase in cash represents a 30.4 percent increase in that account ($1,809 increase in cash divided by $5,958).

Each change provides a starting point for managers to evaluate the reasonableness of budget assumptions and calculations. While meeting with the accountants, Keith and Dale identified many significant differences between the 20X2 budgeted and 20X1 actual balance sheets. They decided to review the budget detail to assess each major change.

Each balance sheet difference found in Exhibit 8.1 can be explained by closely examining the budgets created in Chapter 7. The cash increase is driven primarily by the significant rise in sales and operating cash flow projected to occur in 20X2 (see Chapter 7, Exhibit 7.30). This increase would have been $15,000 higher if C&F had not planned to buy equipment ($10,000) and issue its first dividend ($5,000) at the end of 20X2. The decline in accounts receivable is attributed to

Management Accounting: A Business Planning Approach

Exhibit 8.1

C&F Enterprises, Inc.
Comparative Balance Sheets
December 31, 20X2 and 20X1

Assets	20X2 (Projected)	20X1 (Actual)	Change	Percentage Change
Cash	$ 7,767	$ 5,958	$ 1,809	30.4%
Accounts Receivable	941	5,500	(4,559)	(82.9%)
Supplies	250	300	(50)	(16.7%)
Prepaid Advertising	—	4,800	(4,800)	(100.0%)
Current Assets	$ 8,958	$16,558	$ (7,600)	(45.9%)
Equipment	$13,000	3,000	10,000	333.3%
Less Accumulated Depreciation	(1,200)	(600)	(600)	100.0%
Equipment (net)	$11,800	$2,400	$ 9,400	391.7%
Total Assets	$20,758	$18,958	$ 1,800	9.5%
Liabilities and Owners' Equity				
Current Accounts Payable	$ 81	$ 1,000	$ (919)	(91.9%)
Long-Term Note Payable	2,000	2,000	—	—
Common Stock	12,000	12,000	—	—
Retained Earnings	6,677	3,958	2,719	68.7%
Total Liabilities and Owners' Equity	$20,758	$18,958	$ 1,800	9.5%

enhanced collections of accounts due from customers. The $50 change (decrease) in supplies is based on C&F's goal of holding only $250 of supplies inventory at year end rather than $300 (as in the prior year). Prepaid advertising is expected to be zero at the end of 20X2 since the advertising contract expired during the year without renewal. The increase in equipment reflects Keith and Dale's decision to buy new equipment with C&F's projected cash flow surplus. The addition of a second year of depreciation ($600) on the equipment acquired in 20X1 causes accumulated depreciation to double in 20X2. Since 20X2 equipment purchases are assumed to occur at fiscal year end, C&F does not expect to take depreciation on the new equipment until it is placed in service in early 20X3. Collectively, these differences explain the changes in assets between 20X2 budgeted and 20X1 actual amounts.

On the financing side of the balance sheet (that is, liabilities and owners' equity), the first major change is the decrease in accounts payable. This decline results from the payment of the 20X1 outstanding year-end balance and the expectation of more timely payables settlement in 20X2. C&F did not expect to issue or redeem any of its long-term debt or common stock in 20X2. Finally, the change in retained earnings can be traced to income statement projections and the anticipated year-end dividend of $5,000. Income statement comparisons are discussed next.

Exhibit 8.2

	20X2 (Projected)	20X1 (Actual)	Change	Percentage Change
C&F Enterprises, Inc.				
Comparative Income Statements				
For the Years Ended December 31, 20X2 and 20X1				
Service Revenue	$102,490	$74,800	$27,690	37.0%
Cost of Services Sold:				
Salaries and Wages	53,611	43,000	10,611	24.7%
Rentals	16,120	11,000	5,120	46.5%
Supplies	3,803	3,000	803	26.8%
Fuel	1,126	700	426	60.9%
Depreciation	600	600	—	—
Total Cost of Services Sold	$ 75,260	$58,300	$16,960	29.1%
Gross Profit	$ 27,230	$16,500	$10,730	65.0%
Operating Expenses:				
Advertising	9,800	4,800	5,000	104.2%
Bookkeeping Services	3,000	2,500	500	20.0%
Interest	200	200	—	—
Taxes	2,798	2,042	756	37.0%
Other	3,713	3,000	713	23.8%
Net Income	$ 7,719	$ 3,958	$ 3,761	95.0%

Comparing Income Statements
(Current Year Budget vs. Prior Year Actual)

Exhibit 8.2 compares C&F's budgeted 20X2 and actual 20X1 income statements. As with the balance sheet comparison, account changes are calculated by subtracting actual 20X1 results from 20X2 projections. For example, service revenue is expected to be $27,690 ($102,490 less $74,800) higher in 20X2, a 37.0 percent increase ($27,690 divided by $74,800) from 20X1, a rise driven by the ambitious sales budget described in Exhibit 7.6.

Net income is projected to grow by $3,761 or 95.0 percent, a much faster rate than sales (37.0 percent) because Keith and Dale have budgeted only modest increases in total fixed costs (that is, bookkeeping and advertising). The percentage of variable costs to sales in 20X2 is assumed to be that actually incurred in 20X1. Therefore, any increases in variable costs in 20X2 are a function of increases in sales from the prior year. Meeting the 20X2 budget will require C&F to generate sales growth while controlling expenses.

Exhibit 8.3

C&F Enterprises, Inc.
Comparative Financial Ratios
20X2 Budgeted vs. 20X1 Actual Performance

Curent Ratio				Profit Margin Ratio			
20X2	$\dfrac{\text{Current Assets}}{\text{Current Liabilities}}$	$= \dfrac{\$\ 8{,}958}{\$\ 81}$	$= 110.24$	20X2	$\dfrac{\text{Net Income}}{\text{Net Sales Revenue}}$	$= \dfrac{\$\ 7{,}719}{\$102{,}490}$	$= 7.5\%$
20X1	$\dfrac{\text{Current Assets}}{\text{Current Liabilities}}$	$= \dfrac{\$\ 16{,}558}{\$\ 1{,}000}$	$= 16.56$	20X2	$\dfrac{\text{Net Income}}{\text{Net Sales Revenue}}$	$= \dfrac{\$\ 3{,}958}{\$\ 74{,}800}$	$= 5.3\%$
		Change	93.68			Change	2.2%

Financial Leverage				Return on Assets			
20X2	$\dfrac{\text{Total Assets}}{\text{Owners' Equity}}$	$= \dfrac{\$\ 20{,}758}{\$\ 18{,}677}$	$= 1.11$	20X2	$\dfrac{\text{Net Income}}{\text{Total Assets}}$	$= \dfrac{\$\ 7{,}719}{\$\ 20{,}758}$	$= 37.2\%$
20X1	$\dfrac{\text{Total Assets}}{\text{Owners' Equity}}$	$= \dfrac{\$\ 18{,}958}{\$\ 15{,}958}$	$= 1.19$	20X1	$\dfrac{\text{Net Income}}{\text{Total Assets}}$	$= \dfrac{\$\ 3{,}958}{\$\ 18{,}958}$	$= 20.9\%$
		Change	(0.08)			Change	16.3%

Asset Turnover				Return on Equity			
20X2	$\dfrac{\text{Net Sales Revenue}}{\text{Total Assets}}$	$= \dfrac{\$102{,}490}{\$\ 20{,}758}$	$= 4.94$	20X2	$\dfrac{\text{Net Income}}{\text{Owners' Equity}}$	$= \dfrac{\$\ 7{,}719}{\$\ 18{,}677}$	$= 41.3\%$
20X1	$\dfrac{\text{Net Sales Revenue}}{\text{Total Assets}}$	$= \dfrac{\$\ 74{,}800}{\$\ 18{,}958}$	$= 3.95$	20X1	$\dfrac{\text{Net Income}}{\text{Owners' Equity}}$	$= \dfrac{\$\ 3{,}958}{\$\ 15{,}958}$	$= 24.8\%$
		Change	0.99			Change	16.5%

Using Ratios to Evaluate the Reasonableness of a Budget

Since balance sheet and income statement changes are often related, ratio analysis is useful in assessing the credibility or reasonableness of budgeted financial statements. Ratios show the relative changes (on a percentage basis) in company performance and often signal problems in a company's budget assumptions. In fact, managers commonly use many of the financial ratios described in Chapter 3 to compare budgeted financial statements to actual past performance. Exhibit 8.3 illustrates a comparison of C&F's 20X2 budgeted and 20X1 actual results using six key financial ratios.

Current Ratio. The current ratio measures liquidity. By dividing current assets by current liabilities, this ratio shows the extent to which a firm has enough liquid assets to meet near-term liabilities. For C&F, the budgeted 20X2 current ratio (110.24) is considerably higher than the 20X1 actual current ratio (16.56) because of the small amount of accounts payable expected at the end of 20X2. C&F must carefully manage its current assets and current liabilities to meet this projection.

Figure 8.1
**Financial leverage reveals
how much debt a company
uses to finance its assets.
Retailers and manufacturers
often rely on debt to manage
the high costs of real estate,
buildings, and significant
inventories.**

Financial Leverage. Financial leverage indicates what proportion of a company's assets are funded by creditors rather than by owners. Higher financial leverage suggests that a company is relying more on debt than on owner financing. For C&F, financial leverage is projected to be slightly lower (1.11) in 20X2 than in 20X1 (1.19). This modest decrease suggests a more stable balance sheet and that owners are increasing their share of rights to the company's assets through retained earnings.

Asset Turnover. Asset turnover measures a company's ability to generate revenue from its assets. Exhibit 8.3 shows an increase in this ratio from 3.95 in 20X1 to 4.94 in 20X2, suggesting that on a relative basis C&F will generate an additional 99 cents in sales revenue for every dollar invested in assets. This increase in asset turnover arises because sales are projected to grow at a faster rate (37.0 percent in Exhibit 8.2) than assets (9.5 percent in Exhibit 8.1).

Profit Margin Ratio. The profit margin ratio shows how much net income a firm generates from each dollar of sales revenue. This ratio measures a company's ability to manage costs. Profit margin is projected to be 7.5 percent in 20X2 versus 5.3 percent in 20X1. This positive increase suggests sales will grow faster than expenses in the coming year. To meet these goals, Keith and Dale must control expenses in addition to growing sales.

Return on Assets. Return on assets (ROA) measures a firm's operating efficiency by showing how much net income is generated for each dollar of assets. For C&F, ROA is projected to be considerably higher in 20X2 (37.2 percent) versus 20X1 (20.9 percent). This very favorable increase (16.3 percent) is driven by both the increase in asset turnover and improving profit margin. As demonstrated in Chapter 3, multiplying asset turnover by profit margin yields ROA. Keith and Dale expect ROA to increase during 20X2 because they anticipate higher sales per dollar of assets and increased net income relative to sales.

Return on Equity. Many analysts and investors consider return on equity (ROE) to be the ultimate measure by which to evaluate a firm's performance. By dividing net income by owners' equity, ROE indicates the extent to which returns have been generated for owners. ROE in 20X2 (41.3 percent) is budgeted to be much higher than in 20X1 (24.8 percent). This highly favorable increase is driven by the considerable increase expected in ROA. Overall, this ratio suggests that C&F Enterprises, Inc. will generate positive and generous returns for its owners.

Overall, Keith and Dale were quite satisfied with the results of their analysis of the 20X2 budgeted financial statements. They understood that a lot of hard work lay ahead if they were to realize their ambitious projections. After talking things over, they felt confident that the underlying budget assumptions were both reasonable and attainable and that they could make the projected financial statements a reality.

C&F Enterprises, Inc.: Using Industry Averages to Assess Budget Credibility

Keith and Dale's accounting advisors encouraged them to compare their numbers to industry averages for companies of similar size to assess the credibility of their budget. The accountants specifically recommended BizStats.com since this website provided actual performance data for small businesses in a wide array of industries. Although the website did not have any data for partnerships or corporations, it did report the average results from over 270,000 proprietorships (that is, businesses owned by a single person). The data below compare some major expenses and net income (as a percentage of sales) for C&F Enterprises with the industry averages.

	C&F Enterprises, Inc. 20X2 Budget	BizStats Industry Average
Payroll	52.3%	10.3%
Rentals	15.7%	2.0%
Advertising	9.6%	0.8%
Depreciation	0.6%	6.5%
Interest	0.2%	1.1%
Net Income	7.5%	21.6%

At first, Keith and Dale were quite alarmed that some of their expenses were much higher than the industry average and that their projected net income was much lower than average. They brought these results to their accounting advisors, who quickly pointed out some important differences. First, Keith & Dale jointly

Figure 8.2
While many firms in the highly competitive retail industry have encountered financial difficulty in recent years, Nordstrom has consistently generated profits. Attention to industry financial ratio averages and past company performance enables managers to develop credible budgets.

owned their business whereas the data are based on sole proprietorships. For instance, at C&F, there were two owners working in the business and drawing salaries, explaining the major difference in payroll as a percentage of sales. Also, C&F had just completed its first of year of business. Therefore, advertising was critical to the success of the enterprise and was likely to be much higher than the marketing costs of existing businesses. In addition, since Keith and Dale started with relatively little financial capital, they decided to rent rather than buy their

Management Accounting: A Business Planning Approach

equipment. As a result, their rental expense is much higher than the industry and depreciation is much lower. Finally, since they have little debt, their interest expense is consistent with the industry average. Collectively, these differences explain why C&F's net income as a percentage of sales is lower than the industry average.

With the insight provided by their accounting professionals, Keith and Dale were confident in the credibility of their budget and felt that as C&F grew, business performance would be closer to the industry averages.

Sensitivity Analysis Using Flexible Budgeting

Even budgets based on very credible assumptions will not perfectly predict future results. Therefore, managers also test the reasonableness of budgets using sensitivity analysis (or "what-if" analysis). This technique is so named because it allows managers to determine how *sensitive* budgets are to changes in core assumptions, such as sales price, sales volume, and/or cost estimates.

Learning Objective 2
Illustrate the development of flexible budgets.

The budget that Keith and Dale prepared in Chapter 7 is often referred to as a static budget, since it is based on a specific (fixed or static) expected sales level. To assess budget credibility using sensitivity analysis, managers create flexible budgets to allow changes in key assumptions (for example, sales level). Flexible budgets permit changes in operating assumptions and highlight the effects of these changes when compared to the static budget. Flexible budgets also can be used to evaluate performance when actual activity levels differ from an original plan. For example, flexible budgeting shows how a budget would differ if activity levels or prices are higher or lower than originally planned.

To create a flexible budget, managers must decide how they believe costs will change across different levels of activity. As we learned in Chapter 5, variable costs change as activity levels change, but the fixed costs remain constant across different activity levels. Therefore, managers can create new budget projections to reflect expected levels of activity.

The first step in flexible budgeting is to identify what assumptions to test and to calculate their effect. For example, Keith and Dale know that their success in 20X2 will depend on the growth of the commercial services customer base. While they are confident that sales will materialize, they want to see how changing their assumptions about the number of customers (sales activity) will affect total revenue. Exhibit 8.4 shows C&F's sales budget for commercial services under three different scenarios. The static budget reflects Keith and Dale's original assumptions, which are documented in Chapter 7. Two new flexible budgets also are presented. In the first flexible budget, C&F estimates two fewer customers per quarter than in the static budget: a low estimate. The other flexible budget assumes that C&F has two more customers per quarter than in the static budget: a high estimate. However, each flexible budget assumes the same sales price and average quarterly demand per customer used in the static budget.

Exhibit 8.4
Commercial Sales Revenue Static and Flexible Budgets

Static Budget	Q1	Q2	Q3	Q4	Total
Number of commercial customers (A)	9	12	14	11	—
Average quarterly demand per customer (B)	1	10	12	2	—
Estimated total customer demand (A × B)	9	120	168	22	319
Average $ price per customer (C)	$ 250	$ 250	$ 250	$ 250	$ 250
Estimated total commercial revenues	$2,250	$30,000	$42,000	$5,500	$79,750
(A × B × C)					

Flexible Budget (2 fewer customers per quarter)	Q1	Q2	Q3	Q4	Total
Number of commercial customers (A)	7	10	12	9	—
Average quarterly demand per customer (B)	1	10	12	2	—
Estimated total customer demand (A × B)	7	100	144	18	269
Average $ price per customer (C)	$ 250	$ 250	$ 250	$ 250	$ 250
Estimated total commercial revenues	$1,750	$25,000	$36,000	$4,500	$67,250
(A × B × C)					

Flexible Budget (2 more customers per quarter)	Q1	Q2	Q3	Q4	Total
Number of commercial customers (A)	11	14	16	13	—
Average quarterly demand per customer (B)	1	10	12	2	—
Estimated total customer demand (A × B)	11	140	192	26	369
Average $ price per customer (C)	$ 250	$ 250	$ 250	$ 250	$ 250
Estimated total commercial revenues	$2,750	$35,000	$48,000	$6,500	$92,250
(A × B × C)					

The differences among all three budgets can be seen by comparing the total customer demand and estimated total revenue. For example, the static budget shows total customer demand of 319 service jobs resulting in commercial revenues of $79,750 for the year. The low estimate shows that losing two customers per quarter will reduce total customer demand to 269 jobs and $67,250 in revenue. Conversely, if Keith and Dale realize the high estimate, C&F will service 369 commercial jobs and generate $92,250 in revenue. These schedules show just how sensitive total revenue is to a change in the number of commercial customers.

The data in Exhibit 8.4 also can be used to analyze how the contribution margin changes under each customer demand assumption. Exhibit 8.5 reports contribution margin under all three scenarios: the static budget, as well as high and low flexible budget conditions (that is, greater or fewer customers per quarter). In all three cases, C&F assumes that variable costs for the commercial services business

Management Accounting: A Business Planning Approach

Exhibit 8.5
Commercial Revenue
Contribution Margin
Analysis

Flexible Budget Analysis			
	Low Flexible	Original Static	High Flexible
Estimated Sales Revenue	$ 67,250	$79,750	$92,250
Variable Costs	46,519	55,166	63,813
Contribution Margin	$ 20,731	$24,584	$28,437
Change in Contribution Margin from Static Budget	$ (3,853)	—	$ 3,853

will change with sales activity at the constant percentage of 69.17 percent of sales originally forecast in Exhibit 7.8.

Exhibit 8.5 indicates that if C&F had two fewer commercial customers per quarter, contribution margin (and net income) would decline by $3,853. Alternatively, if C&F had two more commercial customers per quarter, contribution margin (and net income) would be higher by $3,853. Since net income was originally budgeted to be $7,719 (Exhibit 8.2), it is clear that changing customer demand by just two units per quarter will significantly impact net income in 20X2. Therefore, flexible budgets help managers see just how sensitive projected profits are to changes in key assumptions. It is possible to construct similar analyses for changes in assumptions for sales price, variable cost percentages, and/or fixed costs.

C&F Enterprises, Inc.: The Results for 20X2 Are In!

With their analysis of budgeted financial statements complete and their flexible budgets appearing to confirm the reasonableness of commercial service assumptions, Keith and Dale embarked on their second year of operations. The year proved to be a busy one, passing very quickly and presenting new challenges, some planned as well as some that were unforeseen. Nevertheless, Keith and Dale felt that business had gone reasonably well based on the periodic reports that their bookkeeping service had provided. However, they were worried because their end-of-year bank account balance did not reflect the cash balances they had forecast at the beginning of the year. It was time to see how C&F Enterprises, Inc. really had done!

Keith and Dale called their bookkeeper, Frances Chan, to see when they could expect their 20X2 annual financial reports. She assured them that she would run the reports that day and deliver them the next. The anticipation was almost too much to bear.

Variance Analysis

Learning Objective 3

Discuss how financial statement variances are computed and interpreted.

In addition to planning, companies also use budgets to evaluate *actual* performance. In fact, most companies compare actual year-end financial statements to their budget projections for the same year. Differences between actual and budgeted amounts are known as financial statement variances. When managers investigate the reasons for these differences, they perform variance analysis. This analysis provides clues as to why actual performance exceeded or failed to meet budgeted expectations.

Comparing Balance Sheets
(Current Actual vs. Budgeted Performance)

C&F's bookkeeping service prepared and delivered the 20X2 financial statements as promised. Exhibit 8.6 presents a report that compares the actual 20X2 balance sheet to the originally budgeted forecasts made in Chapter 7. The last column of Exhibit 8.6 also shows each financial statement dollar variance as a percentage of its respective 20X2 budgeted line item. Managers are expected to know why actual results vary from budget. With reports in hand, Keith and Dale began to analyze their operations for 20X2.

Exhibit 8.6 highlights two notable variances on the comparative balance sheets. Cash and retained earnings are both more than 10 percent lower than expected. No other variances are significant in either dollar amounts or percentages. The shortfall in cash and retained earnings suggests that C&F probably did not earn as much income as expected in 20X2. However, to confirm this, a comparative income statement for 20X2 must be analyzed next.

Comparing Income Statements
(Current Actual vs. Budgeted Performance)

Exhibit 8.7 shows the 20X2 income statement in contribution margin format comparing each actual result to the 20X2 budgeted amount.

Keith and Dale were in shock! Although they felt all along that they had grown the business considerably in 20X2, Exhibit 8.7 indicated that they had exceeded even their own ambitious sales goal of $102,490 by $1,360, or 1.3 percent. Yet, somehow income was $825, or 10.7 percent, under budget. They thought for sure that growing sales would increase net income. Although fuel was well over budget, it was not enough to explain why net income did not meet its target. They could not understand why salaries and wages also were over budget, as they had not authorized much overtime and no one had received a raise. Looking at these results, they realized that they needed their accountants' advice on how to determine what happened. The accountants told them to first examine sales mix and then to investigate cost variances.

Exhibit 8.6

C&F Enterprises, Inc. Actual and Budgeted Comparative Balance Sheets December 31, 20X2				
Assets	**Actual**	**Budgeted**	**Variance**	**Percentage Variance**
Cash	$ 6,957	$ 7,767	$ (810)	(10.4%)
Accounts Receivable	919	941	(22)	(2.3%)
Supplies	262	250	12	4.8%
Prepaid Advertising	—	—	—	—
Current Assets	$ 8,138	$ 8,958	$ (820)	(9.2%)
Equipment	$13,000	$13,000	$ —	—
Less Accumulated Depreciation	(1,200)	(1,200)	—	—
Equipment (net)	$11,800	$11,800	$ —	—
Total Assets	$19,938	$20,758	$ (820)	(4.0%)
Liabilities and Owners' Equity				
Accounts Payable	$ 86	$ 81	$ 5	6.2%
Long-Term Note Payable	2,000	2,000	—	—
Common Stock	12,000	12,000	—	—
Retained Earnings	5,852	6,677	(825)	(12.3%)
Total Liabilities and Owners' Equity	$19,938	$20,758	$ (820)	(4.0%)

Revenue Variances

When total sales differ from budget, the difference is called a **revenue variance**. This amount represents the extent to which actual sales are greater or less than budgeted sales. Revenue variance can arise from changes in sales price, sales volume, and/or sales mix. Since C&F has three lines of business, their accountants advised them to examine each service separately.

The total revenue variance is computed by subtracting budgeted sales from actual sales. Exhibit 8.8 shows the revenue variance for each line of C&F's business. The total revenue variance of $1,360 is consistent with the data presented earlier in Exhibit 8.7.

When actual sales exceed budgeted sales, companies have a favorable revenue variance because the outcome is generally considered positive. Conversely, when actual sales are less than budget, a company is said to have an unfavorable revenue variance. As we can see from Exhibit 8.8, actual commercial services sales revenue exceeded budgeted expectations by $6,250. This revenue variance is considered to be favorable. However, much of this favorable variance was offset by unfavorable variances in the two other service line offerings. The three variances "net" to the combined total revenue variance of $1,360. Keith and Dale were

Learning Objective 4
Explain the use of revenue variance analysis.

Exhibit 8.7

C&F Enterprises, Inc.
Actual and Budgeted Comparative Income Statements
For the Year Ended December 31, 20X2

	Actual	Budgeted	Variance	Percentage Variance
Service Revenue	$103,850	$102,490	$ 1,360	1.3%
Variable Costs:				
Wages	45,184	44,111	1,073	2.4%
Rentals	16,111	16,120	(9)	(0.1%)
Supplies	3,932	3,803	129	3.4%
Fuel	1,768	1,126	642	57.0%
Taxes	2,835	2,798	37	1.3%
Other	2,176	2,213	(37)	(1.7%)
Contribution Margin	$ 31,844	$ 32,319	$ (475)	(1.5%)
Fixed Costs:				
Salaries	$ 9,500	$ 9,500	—	0.0%
Depreciation	600	600	—	0.0%
Advertising	9,900	9,800	100	1.0%
Bookkeeping Services	3,250	3,000	250	8.3%
Interest	200	200	—	0.0%
Other	1,500	1,500	—	0.0%
Net Income	$ 6,894	$ 7,719	$ (825)	(10.7%)

eager to learn what caused their revenue variances. Were they due to differences in price or sales volume?

Computing Revenue Volume and Price Variances. There are two primary types of revenue variances: revenue volume variances and revenue price variances. Exhibit 8.9 shows how these variances are computed. The **revenue volume variance** shows the change in total revenue that can be attributed *solely* to a change in sales volume, measured in the number of units or services sold.

Exhibit 8.8
20X2 Sales Revenue
Variances

	Actual	Budgeted	Variance	
Commercial	$ 86,000	$ 79,750	$6,250	Favorable
Residential	12,600	14,940	(2,340)	Unfavorable
Other	5,250	7,800	(2,550)	Unfavorable
Total	$103,850	$102,490	$1,360	Favorable

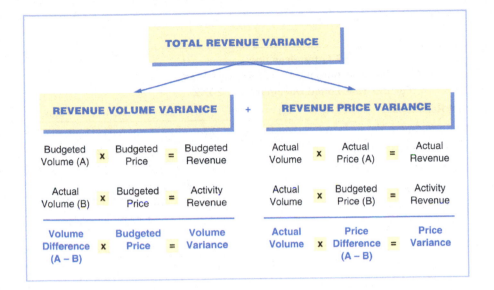

Exhibit 8.9
Computing Revenue
Variances

This variance compares the number of actual units or services sold to budgeted units or services sold, while keeping selling price constant at the budgeted level (that is, budgeted price). Therefore, the revenue volume variance is computed by comparing activity revenue to budgeted revenue. Activity revenue is computed by multiplying actual sales volume by budgeted sales price. Alternatively, *budgeted revenues* are calculated by multiplying budgeted sales volume by budgeted sales price. The revenue price variance shows the change in total revenue that is due *solely* to a change in sales price. The revenue price variance is calculated by multiplying the difference between actual and budgeted prices by the actual sales volume.

Revenue price and volume variances are described as favorable when actual prices or volumes exceed budgeted amounts. Conversely, these variances are said to be unfavorable if budgeted amounts exceed actual prices or volumes. Since either the revenue price or volume variance may be favorable while the other is unfavorable, it is important to compute both to determine what drives the total revenue variance.

We will illustrate these revenue variances as we explore each of C&F's service offerings in greater detail.

Revenue Variance—Commercial Services. Since commercial lawn services are C&F's largest line of business, Keith and Dale decided to start by investigating variances in this business line using data provided by their bookkeeper, Frances Chan. Upon reviewing the revenue report shown in Exhibit 8.10, Keith and Dale were quite happy to see that they exceeded their targeted number of customers even though it was by only one in each quarter. This single commercial customer accounted for an annual increase in demand of 25 jobs over four quarters, causing C&F to deliver a total of 344 jobs compared to the budgeted goal of 319. They were able to collect their projected $250 price per job from customers, so the revenue increase appears to result from sales volume alone.

Exhibit 8.10

Budgeted Commercial Revenues	Q1	Q2	Q3	Q4	Total
C&F Enterprises, Inc.					
Budgeted and Actual Commercial Revenues					
For the Year Ended December 31, 20X2					
Number of commercial customers (A)	9	12	14	11	—
Average quarterly demand per customer (B)	1	10	12	2	—
Estimated total customer demand (A × B)	9	120	168	22	319
Average $ price per customer (C)	$ 250	$ 250	$ 250	$ 250	$ 250
Budgeted total commercial revenues (A × B × C)	$2,250	$30,000	$42,000	$5,500	$79,750

Actual Commercial Revenues	Q1	Q2	Q3	Q4	Total
Number of commercial customers (A)	10	13	15	12	—
Average quarterly demand per customer (B)	1	10	12	2	—
Actual total customer demand (A × B)	10	130	180	24	344
Average $ price per customer (C)	$ 250	$ 250	$ 250	$ 250	$ 250
Actual total commercial revenues (A × B × C)	$2,500	$32,500	$45,000	$6,000	$86,000

Exhibit 8.11 uses the revenue volume variance formula provided in Exhibit 8.9 and the data from Exhibit 8.10 to compute the revenue volume variance for commercial services. This calculation confirms that the entire revenue variance can be attributed to the favorable volume variance. The favorable volume variance of 25 jobs at a budgeted price of $250 per job explains the favorable revenue variance of $6,250 (the extent to which activity revenue exceeded budgeted revenue) for this service offering.

We also can compute the revenue price variance for commercial services to illustrate how it confirms our volume variance results. Exhibit 8.12 applies the price variance formula from Exhibit 8.9 to compute the revenue price variance for commercial services. Since the actual price equals the budgeted price and activity revenue equals actual revenue, the total revenue price variance is zero.

Combining the results from Exhibits 8.11 and 8.12 confirms that the total revenue variance of $6,250 for C&F's commercial lawn service can be explained solely by the increase in sales volume.

Revenue Variance—Residential Services. As for C&F's residential service line, Keith and Dale knew that their national competitor had taken some of their business. In fact, according to Exhibit 8.13, they completed just 450 jobs compared to their budgeted goal of 498. To stay competitive in the residential service line during the year, they had lowered their average price from $30 to $28 per job. These results suggest that the unfavorable revenue variance in the residential segment reported in Exhibit 8.8 was driven by *both* unfavorable revenue price and revenue volume variances.

Budgeted Volume (A)	×	Budgeted Price	=	Budgeted Revenue
319 (Exhibit 8.10)	×	$250 (Exhibit 8.10)	=	$79,750 (Exhibit 8.10)
Actual Volume (B)	×	Budgeted Price	=	Activity Revenue
344 (Exhibit 8.10)	×	$250 (Exhibit 8.10)	=	$86,000
Volume Difference (A – B)	×	Budgeted Price	=	Favorable Volume Variance
25	×	$250 (Exhibit 8.10)	=	$6,250

Exhibit 8.11
Revenue Volume Variance— Commercial Services

Exhibit 8.14 uses the revenue volume variance formula presented in Exhibit 8.9 and data from Exhibit 8.13 to compute C&F's revenue volume variance for residential services. The un favorable revenue volume variance of 48 jobs at a budgeted price of $30 results in a $1,440 unfavorable revenue volume variance for residential services. Since the total unfavorable revenue variance for residential services was $2,340, there also must be an unfavorable price variance to account for the remaining unexplained difference.

Exhibit 8.15 uses the revenue price variance formula presented in Exhibit 8.9 and the data from Exhibit 8.13 to compute the revenue price variance for residential services. The actual price of residential services ($28) was two dollars less than the budgeted price. Multiplying this job price variance ($2) by the actual residential service volume (450 jobs) results in the $900 unfavorable revenue

Actual Volume	×	Actual Price (A)	=	Actual Revenue
344 (Exhibit 8.10)	×	$250 (Exhibit 8.10)	=	$86,000 (Exhibit 8.10)
Actual Volume	×	Budgeted Price (B)	=	Activity Revenue
344 (Exhibit 8.10)	×	$250 (Exhibit 8.10)	=	$86,000
Actual Volume	×	Price Difference (A – B)	=	Price Variance
344 (Exhibit 8.10)	×	$0	=	$0

Exhibit 8.12
Revenue Price Variance— Commercial Services

Exhibit 8.13

C&F Enterprises, Inc. Budgeted and Actual Residential Revenues For the Year Ended December 31, 20X2					
Budgeted Residential Revenues	Q1	Q2	Q3	Q4	Total
Number of residential customers (A)	15	20	21	23	—
Average quarterly demand per customer (B)	—	10	12	2	—
Estimated total customer demand (A × B)	—	200	252	46	498
Average $ price per customer (C)	$30	$ 30	$ 30	$ 30	$ 30
Budgeted total residential revenues (A × B × C)	$—	$6,000	$7,560	$1,380	$14,940
Actual Residential Revenues	Q1	Q2	Q3	Q4	Total
Number of residential customers (A)	13	18	19	21	—
Average quarterly demand per customer (B)	—	10	12	2	—
Actual total customer demand (A × B)	—	180	228	42	450
Average $ price per customer (C)	$28	$ 28	$ 28	$ 28	$ 28
Actual total residential revenues (A × B × C)	$—	$5,040	$6,384	$1,176	$12,600

price variance shown in Exhibit 8.15. In this case, Keith and Dale had expected activity revenue to be $900 higher than actual revenue.

Combining the results from the Exhibits 8.14 and 8.15 shows that the unfavorable total revenue variance ($2,340) for C&F's residential service can be explained by combining the unfavorable revenue volume variance ($1,440) with the unfavorable revenue price variance ($900).

Exhibit 8.14
Revenue Volume
Variances—Residential
Services

Budgeted Volume (A) 498 (Exhibit 8.13)	×	Budgeted Price $30 (Exhibit 8.13)	=	Budgeted Revenue $14,940 (Exhibit 8.13)
Actual Volume (B) 450 (Exhibit 8.13)	×	Budgeted Price $30 (Exhibit 8.13)	=	Activity Revenue $13,500
Volume Difference (A – B) (48)	×	Budgeted Price $30 (Exhibit 8.13)	=	Unfavorable Volume Variance ($1,440)

Actual Volume 450 (Exhibit 8.13)	×	Actual Price (A) $28 (Exhibit 8.13)	=	Actual Revenue $12,600 (Exhibit 8.13)
Actual Volume 450 (Exhibit 8.13)	×	Budgeted Price (B) $30 (Exhibit 8.13)	=	Activity Revenue $13,500
Actual Volume 450 (Exhibit 8.13)	× ×	Price Difference (A – B) ($2)	= =	Unfavorable Price Variance ($900) (Exhibit 8.13)

Exhibit 8.15
Revenue Price Variance—
Residential Services

Revenue Variance—Other Services. The remaining portion of C&F's revenue variance shown in Exhibit 8.8 can be found in Other Service Revenue (that is, snow removal and weed control and fertilization). The actual and budgeted sales data for this service offering is reported in Exhibit 8.16. Other revenues proved to be $2,550 less than budget, an unfavorable variance.

With the help of their accountants, Keith & Dale found this variance to be completely due to a volume shortfall. On all of their snow and weed control jobs, they had achieved the desired prices. The decline in residential services previously discussed contributed to a shortfall in the weed control and fertilization business, which led to the unfavorable variance of $2,550. Since other services represented less than 10 percent of C&F's total revenue, Keith and Dale felt

Exhibit 8.16

C&F Enterprises, Inc. Budgeted and Actual Other Service Revenues For the Year Ended December 31, 20X1					
Budgeted Other Revenues	Q1	Q2	Q3	Q4	Total
Snow removal	$1,030	$ —	$ —	$ 430	$ 1,460
Weed control and fertilization	900	1,240	2,100	2,100	6,340
Budgeted total other revenues	$1,930	$1,240	$2,100	$2,530	$ 7,800
Actual Other Revenues	Q1	Q2	Q3	Q4	Total
Snow removal	$ 850	$ —	$ —	$1,000	$ 1,850
Weed control and fertilization	700	800	900	1,000	3,400
Budgeted total other revenues	$1,550	$ 800	$ 900	$2,000	$ 5,250
				Unfavorable variance	$(2,550)

further investigation was unnecessary. They agreed that the focus in future years would be on growing the commercial and residential customer bases.

Exhibit 8.17 summarizes the data presented in Exhibits 8.10 through 8.16. Notice that the favorable total revenue variance, $1,360, can be explained by both revenue volume and price variances across C&F's three lines of business. Keith and Dale must next determine why they did not meet their profit expectations despite exceeding their total sales target by $1,360. To answer this question, they need to investigate cost variances for both fixed and variable costs.

Cost Variance Analysis

Resources used by business processes are commonly called inputs. Inputs may include such human and physical capital resources as labor, supplies, and fuel. As we learned in Chapters 1 and 2, business processes convert these inputs into a company's services or goods (that is, outputs). Cost variances arise when the quantity or price of inputs does not meet budgeted expectations. When costs exceed budget, these variances are considered unfavorable. When costs are below budget, favorable variances result.

Once again, following the instructions provided by C&F's accounting advisors, the bookkeeping service prepared the cost schedule presented in Exhibit 8.18. This exhibit compares the actual and budgeted amounts for each of C&F's fixed and variable costs. Since fixed and variable costs behave differently, it is necessary to investigate each type of variance separately.

Variable Cost Variances. Variable cost variances—the differences between actual and budgeted variable costs—arise from changes in activity or input prices. As demonstrated in Chapter 5, when sales volume increases, total variable costs usually increase because of the increased quantity of products or services sold.

Learning Objective 5
Demonstrate the use of cost variance analysis.

Exhibit 8.17

	Actual Revenue	Budgeted Revenue	Volume Variance	Price Variance	Total Variance
	C&F Enterprises, Inc. **Total Revenue Variances** **For the Year Ended December 31, 20X2**				
Commercial	$86,000	$79,750	$6,250	$—	$6,250
	(Exhibit 8.10)	(Exhibit 8.10)	(Exhibit 8.11)	(Exhibit 8.12)	(Exhibit 8.8)
Residential	12,600	14,940	(1,440)	(900)	(2,340)
	(Exhibit 8.13)	(Exhibit 8.13)	(Exhibit 8.14)	(Exhibit 8.15)	(Exhibit 8.8)
Other	5,250	7,800	(2,550)	—	(2,550)
	(Exhibit 8.16)	(Exhibit 8.16)	(Exhibit 8.16)		(Exhibit 8.8)
Total	$103,850	$102,490	$2,260	$(900)	$1,360

Figure 8.3
ExxonMobil, one of the world's largest manufacturers and retailers of petroleum products, uses variance analyses to explain to its investors why earnings performance changes between reporting periods. This information provides insight into how operations have changed in oil and drilling operations, as well as in its refining and retail sales segments.

Exhibit 8.18

	C&F Enterprises, Inc.						
	Actual Versus Budgeted Costs by Type						
	For the Year Ended December 31, 20X2						
	Actual Fixed Costs	**Actual Variable Costs**	**Total Actual Costs**[a]	**Budgeted Fixed Costs**[b]	**Budgeted Variable Costs**[b]	**Total Budgeted Costs**[b]
Salaries and Wages	$ 9,500	$45,184	$54,684	$ 9,500	$44,111	$53,611
Rentals	—	16,111	16,111	—	16,120	16,120
Supplies	—	3,932	3,932	—	3,803	3,803
Fuel	—	1,768	1,768	—	1,126	1,126
Depreciation	600	—	600	600	—	600
Advertising	9,900	—	9,900	9,800	—	9,800
Bookkeeping Services	3,250	—	3,250	3,000	—	3,000
Interest	200	—	200	200	—	200
Taxes	—	2,835	2,835	—	2,798	2,798
Other	1,500	2,176	3,676	1,500	2,213	3,713
Total	$24,950	$72,006	$96,956	$24,600	$70,171	$94,771

[a] Total actual costs from Exhibit 8.7 in this chapter.
[b] Budgeted cost data from Exhibit 7.10 in Chapter 7.

Variable costs like labor, supplies, and fuel also may differ from budget if the prices of such inputs rise or fall. Input prices frequently are expressed in terms of dollars, as a percentage of sales dollars, or both.

Variable cost variances arising from quantity differences are known as **variable cost volume variances**, while those arising from input price changes are referred to as **variable cost price variances**. Similar to revenue variances, combining cost volume and price variances accounts for the total variance in variable cost.

Exhibit 8.19 compares actual and budgeted amounts for each of C&F's variable costs and presents variances for the difference between actual and budgeted amounts. When actual costs exceed budgeted amounts, the variance generally is considered unfavorable. For example, wages exceeded budget by $1,073 yielding an unfavorable variance. When actual costs are less than those budgeted, the variance is thought to be favorable. Since rentals were $9 less than expected, a favorable variance results.

Exhibit 8.20 further disaggregates the variable cost variances across C&F's three service lines. Commercial services represented over 80 percent of sales volume (Exhibit 8.8), and it was the only service line with a net unfavorable variable cost variance (Exhibit 8.20) in 20X2. Therefore, Keith and Dale decided to investigate variable cost variances for commercial services only.

Computing Variable Cost Volume and Price Variances. Like revenue variances, variable cost variances can arise for several reasons: differences in volume, differences in price, or both. Exhibit 8.21 illustrates the formulas for computing variable cost volume and price variances.

As we can see from Exhibit 8.21, we compute variable cost volume variances by multiplying the difference between actual and budgeted volume by the budgeted cost expected to be paid. Volume can be measured either in terms of total sales dollars, total units or services sold, or total units of resource inputs used. We compute variable cost price variances by multiplying the difference between actual cost and budgeted cost by the actual volume. We calculate the **activity cost** by multiplying actual volume by budgeted cost. This amount shows managers what level of cost they should have expected at the actual level of input usage.

After reviewing Exhibit 8.20 Keith and Dale thought it would be useful to examine why two major variable costs, wages and fuel, were over budget in the commercial service line of business. They knew that gasoline prices had increased in the summer of 20X2, but they were somewhat perplexed as to why they had an unfavorable wages variance.

Wages Variance—Commercial. Exhibit 8.22 shows the wages volume variance for commercial services. As noted in Chapter 7, Keith and Dale's salaries are fixed costs. All other employees are paid wages based on jobs completed, making these costs variable in nature. Therefore, the majority of C&F's salary and wage costs are variable and directly related to business volume (that is, sales). Therefore, total sales and employee wage cost as a percentage of total sales are used to compute the wages volume variance. Multiplying budgeted variable wage cost (44.79 percent from Exhibit 7.8) by the increase in sales ($6,250) yields a $2,799 wage volume variance. Since activity cost exceeds budgeted cost, this variance

	Actual Variable Costs	Budgeted Variable Costs	Variable Cost Variance	
Wages	$45,184	$44,111	$1,073	Unfavorable
Rentals	16,111	16,120	(9)	Favorable
Supplies	3,932	3,803	129	Unfavorable
Fuel	1,768	1,126	642	Unfavorable
Taxes	2,835	2,798	37	Unfavorable
Other	2,176	2,213	(37)	Favorable
Total	$72,006	$70,171	$1,835	Unfavorable

Exhibit 8.19
20X2 Variable Cost Variances

Commercial Services	Actual Variable Costs	Budgeted Variable Costs	Variable Cost Variance	
Wages	$38,516	$ 35,717	$ 2,799	Unfavorable
Rentals	12,647	11,728	919	Unfavorable
Supplies	3,449	3,199	251	Unfavorable
Fuel	1,376	746	630	Unfavorable
Taxes	2,348	2,177	171	Unfavorable
Other	1,725	1,599	125	Unfavorable
Total	$60,061	$ 55,166	$ 4,895	(A)
Residential Services	Actual Variable Costs	Budgeted Variable Costs	Variable Cost Variance	
Wages	$ 5,040	$ 5,976	$ (936)	Favorable
Rentals	2,520	2,988	(468)	Favorable
Supplies	378	448	(70)	Favorable
Fuel	265	224	41	Unfavorable
Taxes	344	408	(64)	Favorable
Other	189	224	(35)	Favorable
Total	$ 8,736	$ 10,268	$(1,532)	(B)
Other Services	Actual Variable Costs	Budgeted Variable Costs	Variable Cost Variance	
Wages	$ 1,628	$ 2,418	$ (790)	Favorable
Rentals	944	1,404	(460)	Favorable
Supplies	105	156	(51)	Favorable
Fuel	127	156	(29)	Favorable
Taxes	143	213	(70)	Favorable
Other	262	390	(128)	Favorable
Total	$ 3,209	$ 4,737	$(1,528)	(C)
Total Variable Cost Variances	(A) + (B) + (C)	=	$ 1,835	Unfavorable

Exhibit 8.20
Variable Cost Variances by Service Offering

Exhibit 8.21
Computing Variable Cost
Variances

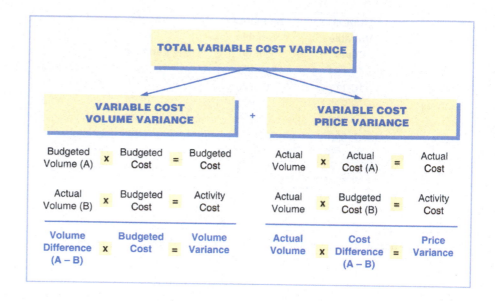

is unfavorable. This total variable cost volume variance fully accounts for the wage cost variance reported in Exhibit 8.20. Since commercial sales were greater than expected, C&F apparently incurred additional employee wages to support the new business. Thus, sales volume drove the entire variable cost employee wage variance.

We also can compute the variable wage cost price variance to illustrate how it confirms our variable wage cost volume variance results. As indicated in Exhibit 8.23, this is done by multiplying the cost difference by the actual sales volume.

Exhibit 8.22
Variable Commercial Wage
Cost Volume Variance

Budgeted Volume (A)	×	Budgeted Cost	=	Budgeted Cost
$79,750 (Exhibit 8.8)	×	44.79% (Exhibit 7.8)	=	$35,717 (Exhibit 8.20)
Actual Volume (B)	×	Budgeted Cost	=	Activity Cost
$86,000 (Exhibit 8.8)	×	44.79% (Exhibit 7.8)	=	$38,516 (Exhibit 8.20)
Volume Difference (A – B)	×	Budgeted Cost	=	Unfavorable Volume Variance
$6,250 (Exhibit 8.8)	×	44.79% (Exhibit 7.8)	=	$2,799

Actual Volume $86,000 (Exhibit 8.8)	× ×	Actual Cost (A) 44.79% (Computed)[a]	= =	Actual Cost $38,516 (Exhibit 8.20)
Actual Volume $86,000 (Exhibit 8.8)	× ×	Budgeted Cost (B) 44.79% (Exhibit 7.8)	= =	Activity Cost $38,516 (Exhibit 8.20)
Actual Volume	×	Cost Difference (A – B)	=	Price Variance
$86,000 (Exhibit 8.8)	×	0.00%	=	$0

[a] Actual price as a percentage of sales is computed by dividing actual variable cost (Exhibit 8.20) by actual sales revenue (Exhibit 8.8).

Exhibit 8.23
Variable Commercial Wage
Cost Price Variance

Since actual costs equal budgeted costs, the variable wage cost price variance equals zero.

Combining the total volume and price variances from Exhibits 8.22 and 8.23 fully explains the variable wage cost variance (Exhibit 8.20) for the commercial services line of business. This variance can be completely explained by increased sales volume. This example illustrates how increasing sales of a particular product or service can demand more inputs and increase variable costs.

Budgeted Volume (A) $79,750 (Exhibit 8.8)	× ×	Budgeted Cost 0.94% (Exhibit 7.8)	= =	Budgeted Cost $746 (Exhibit 8.20)
Actual Volume (B) $86,000 (Exhibit 8.8)	× ×	Budgeted Cost 0.94% (Exhibit 7.8)	= =	Activity Cost $804 (Exhibit 8.20)
Volume Difference (A – B)	×	Budgeted Cost	=	Unfavorable Volume Variance
$6,250 (Exhibit 8.8)	×	0.94% (Exhibit 7.8)	=	$58

Exhibit 8.24
Variable Commercial Fuel
Cost Volume Variance

Exhibit 8.25
Variable Commercial Fuel
Cost Price Variance

Actual Volume	×	Actual Cost (A)	=	Actual Cost
$86,000	×	1.6%	=	$1,376
(Exhibit 8.8)		(Computed)[a]		(Exhibit 8.20)
Actual Volume	×	Budgeted Cost (B)	=	Activity Cost
$86,000	×	0.94%	=	$804
(Exhibit 8.8)		(Exhibit 7.8)		
Actual Volume	×	Cost Difference (A – B)	=	Unfavorable Price Variance
$86,000	×	0.66%	=	$572
(Exhibit 8.8)				

[a] Actual price as a percentage of sales is computed by dividing actual variable cost (Exhibit 8.20) by actual sales revenue (Exhibit 8.8).

Fuel Variance—Commercial. Exhibit 8.24 illustrates the fuel variable cost volume variance for the commercial services that C&F provided during 20X2. As with salaries and wages, we again use total sales and fuel costs as a percentage of total sales to compute the variance. Multiplying the budgeted cost (0.94 percent from Exhibit 7.8) by the difference in budgeted and actual sales ($6,250) results in an unfavorable $58 variance, since sales were higher than expected. C&F had to use more fuel than expected to service its additional customers.

The variable cost volume variance for fuel only accounted for part of the **total** fuel cost variance, $630, shown in Exhibit 8.20. Therefore, the variable cost price variance for fuel must also be computed. The actual input price of 1.60 percent (commercial fuel variable cost in Exhibit 8.20 divided by actual commercial sales in Exhibit 8.8) was 0.66 percentage points higher than the budgeted cost of 0.94 percent from Exhibit 7.8. Multiplying the cost difference of 0.66 percent by actual sales, $86,000, results in a $572 unfavorable variable cost price variance for fuel, as shown in Exhibit 8.25. Combining the unfavorable variable cost volume and price variances from Exhibits 8.24 ($58) and 8.25 ($572) fully explains the variable fuel cost variance of $630.

This example illustrates how economic changes beyond managers' control can affect a firm's profits. Other companies such as airlines, mail delivery services, and taxi services also can be affected greatly by fuel price changes.

Fixed Cost Variances. As discussed in Chapter 5, fixed costs normally do not vary across activity levels. In practice, however, price changes or additional spending often cause fixed costs to vary from budget, resulting in a fixed cost variance. As noted in Chapter 7, C&F's fixed costs consist of Keith and Dale's salaries, depreciation, advertising, bookkeeping, interest, and other expenses. In 20X2, the company's depreciation and interest equaled budgeted amounts;

Figure 8.4
**When investigating cost vari-
ances, managers must con-
sider environmental factors
that affect business processes.
A shortage of nurses may lead
to higher salaries or unexpected overtime that yield
unfavorable budget variances.
Understanding why a variance
occurs enables managers
to effectively evaluate past
performance and project
future financial results.**

however, advertising and bookkeeping costs exceeded projections (Exhibit 8.18). After reviewing their records, Keith and Dale discovered that advertising was $100 over budget because they had advertised in the local high school football team's weekly game programs. On top of that, the bookkeeping service charged $250 for overtime on some of C&F's special reporting projects.

Issues to Consider When Analyzing Variances

When investigating why variances occur, managers must consider several important issues. First, they must decide what size of variance warrants their attention. For example, it may not be practical or particularly insightful to determine why paper clip usage may have increased during the fiscal year. In contrast, reviewing the costs and service provided by office supply vendors may yield significant cost savings.

Second, managers must recognize that variances can be related and often may offset each other. For example, a particular expense may show a zero (or near zero) total variance due to offsetting volume and price variances. In other cases, variances may be driven by business decisions that yield opposite effects. For example increased phone costs may be offset by reductions in travel expense if a business decides to rely on teleconferencing rather than face-to-face meetings with out-of-town clients. Clearly, managers must understand business processes and their interrelationships.

Finally, as discussed in Chapter 1, managers must understand how the business environment affects budget variances. Competition, supplier demands, and changes in customer preference all may cause operating results to differ from budget.

Therefore, understanding the environment in which a company competes is critical to accurately analyzing past performance and planning future operations.

Summary

Managers use budgets to plan activities and evaluate performance. It is critical that the assumptions underlying a firm's budget are reasonable and believable. Managers can assess the credibility of their budgets by comparing them to past performance as well as to industry benchmarks. Financial results can vary from budget projections for a variety of reasons including changes in economic conditions, customer demand, and costs. Variance analysis allows managers to determine whether differences from budget resulted from price changes, volume changes, or both. This tool helps managers to investigate the business conditions and events that created these variances to determine what (if any) adjustments must be made to achieve their firm's strategy. The next chapter shows how financial measures can be integrated with nonfinancial measures to more completely evaluate and understand a company's operating performance.

Summary of Learning Objectives

1. **Demonstrate how budget credibility can be assessed.** To assess the credibility of budgets, managers frequently compare projected outcomes to past performance. Comparative financial statements and ratio analysis are

Net Gains

Budget Analysis Resources

There are many online resources that managers can use to assess budget credibility. For example, managers frequently use industry ratios to determine whether a budget is reasonable. If elements of a firm's budget are considerably above or below industry averages, managers often review and evaluate assumptions underlying the budget. The websites listed below provide resources that are valuable in analyzing and evaluating budgets across a wide range of industries.

- **BizStats (http://www.bizstats.com).** This site offers "instant and easy access to useful business statistics and effective online analysis of businesses and industries." The content is split into two sections. *National Business Statistics* provides general insights into business performance. *Small Business Industries* reports comprehensive small business operating statistics sorted by industry. Another valuable feature is the option to compare a budget to the average financial statements of similar businesses with various levels of sales.

- **Strategic Advantage (http://www.strategy 4u.com).** This website offers useful analysis tools that can assist a company in evaluating its competitive position. It provides information and interactive questionnaires that help firms define their strategic advantage. The site has a unique strategy quote archive and spotlights the business advantages of budget analysis, performance improvement, and mistake avoidance.

common techniques used to evaluate assumptions and calculations underlying final budget projections. Using these assessment techniques, managers can examine their projections for reasonableness and identify items requiring possible revision.

2. **Illustrate the development of flexible budgets.** To create a flexible budget, managers must identify how costs react to changing levels of activity. Specifically, managers must determine how sensitive their budgets are to changes in core assumptions like sales price, sales volume, and/or cost estimates. Changing core assumptions and their estimated values will provide managers with information about the sensitivity of projected profits at different estimated activity levels. Flexible budgeting creates a new set of budgeted expectations that more accurately reflect actual levels of activity.

3. **Discuss how financial statement variances are computed and interpreted.** Financial statement variances are computed by comparing actual to budgeted results for each amount on the company's financial statements. These variances are expressed as the difference between the actual and budgeted dollar amounts. A percentage variance is the dollar difference expressed as a percentage of the original budget amount. Financial statement variances help managers investigate why actual performance exceeded or failed to meet budgeted expectations.

4. **Explain the use of revenue variance analysis.** Revenue variance analysis is used to assess why actual sales are greater or less than budgeted sales. Total revenue variances can be computed by subtracting budgeted sales from actual sales. Favorable revenue variances occur when actual sales exceed budget expectations. The two primary types of revenue variance are revenue volume variance and revenue price variance. Managers must examine each of these revenue variances separately to fully understand the effects of volume and price on business performance.

5. **Demonstrate the use of cost variance analysis.** Fixed and variable cost analysis evaluates the variances that arise when the price or quantity of inputs does not meet budget expectations. Favorable cost variances occur when costs fall below budget expectations. Since fixed and variable costs behave differently, managers must investigate each type of variance separately.

Glossary of Terms

Activity cost A component of cost variance analysis computed by multiplying actual volume by budgeted cost.

Activity revenue A component of revenue variance analysis computed by multiplying actual sales volume by budgeted sales price.

Financial statement variances Differences between budget projections and the actual operating results reported in the end-of-period financial statements.

Fixed cost variance The difference between actual and budgeted fixed costs.

Flexible budget A budget that permits changes in multiple key assumptions—expected sales levels, for example. This type of budget highlights how changes in assumptions will affect performance. Managers use flexible budgets to evaluate performance when actual activity differs from the original plan.

Inputs The resources used by business processes to create and deliver products and services to a firm's customers.

Revenue price variance The portion of the revenue variance that can be attributed solely to a change in sales price.

Revenue variance The difference between actual and budgeted sales revenue.

Revenue volume variance The portion of the revenue variance that can be attributed solely to a change in sales volume.

Sensitivity analysis A tool used by managers to determine how *sensitive* budgets are to changes in core assumptions, such as sales price, sales volume, and/or cost estimates. Sensitivity analysis also is known as "what-if" analysis.

Static budget A budget prepared using a specific and fixed sales level.

Variable cost price variance The portion of the variable cost variance that can be attributed to input price changes.

Variable cost variance The difference between actual and budgeted variable costs.

Variable cost volume variance The portion of the variable cost variance that can be attributed to input volume changes.

Variance analysis The investigation of differences between actual and budgeted amounts in financial statements for a specific fiscal period to determine why actual performance exceeded or failed to meet budgeted expectations.

Chapter Review Questions

1. How do comparative financial statements help managers assess the credibility or reasonableness of a budget?
2. How does ratio analysis help managers assess the credibility or reasonableness of a budget?
3. Name six ratios commonly used to assess the credibility of budgets.
4. What is sensitivity analysis?
5. Name three common assumptions that managers test using sensitivity analysis.
6. What is a static budget?
7. What is a flexible budget?
8. Why do firms prepare flexible budgets?
9. How will a change in sales volume affect total variable costs?
10. How will a change in sales price affect total variable costs?
11. How will a change in sales volume affect total fixed costs?
12. How will a change in sales price affect total fixed costs?
13. What are financial statement variances?

Management Accounting: A Business Planning Approach

14. What are the two primary types of revenue variances? Describe each.
15. How is a revenue volume variance computed?
16. How is a revenue price variance computed?
17. What is an input?
18. Name three types of inputs a business is likely to use.
19. What are the two primary types of variable cost variances? Describe each.
20. How is a variable cost volume variance computed?
21. How is a variable cost price variance computed?
22. What is a fixed cost variance?
23. How do fixed cost variances occur?
24. Name three business issues managers must consider when investigating variances.

Exercises and Problems

1. Here is a partially completed comparative balance sheet for Snow Cones Company for the year ended December 31, 20X2.

Snow Cones Company Comparative Balance Sheets				
	20X2	20X2		Percentage
Assets	**Actual**	**Budgeted**	**Variance**	**Variance**
Cash	$ 7,500	$ 7,800	(a)	(3.85%)
Accounts Receivable	9,200	9,000	200	2.22%
Inventory	1,000	720	280	(b)
Current Assets	$17,700	$17,520	$ 180	1.03%
Equipment (net)	(c)	11,000	1,000	9.09%
Total Assets	$29,700	(d)	$1,180	4.14
Liabilities and Owners' Equity				
Accounts Payable	$ 3,000	$ 2,500	$ 500	20.00%
Long-Term Note Payable	1,000	(e)	(1,000)	(50.00%)
Common Stock	20,000	17,000	3,000	17.65%
Retained Earnings	5,700	7,020	(1,320)	(g)
Total Liabilities and Owners' Equity	$29,700	(f)	$1,180	4.14%

Required: Compute the following missing amounts:
a. Cash variance (in dollars)
b. Inventory percentage variance
c. 20X2 actual equipment (net) balance
d. 20X2 budgeted total assets
e. 20X2 budgeted long-term note payable
f. 20X2 budgeted total liabilities and owners' equity
g. 20X2 retained earnings percentage variance

2. Valley Forge Company has prepared its budget. The company president compared financial statements and ratios to industry averages and prior-year company performance. For each of the following comparisons, comment on whether each is favorable or unfavorable and identify a credible reason to explain why such a difference may exist.
   a. Contribution margin is lower than the industry average.
   b. Current ratio is higher than the industry average and prior-year performance.
   c. Financial leverage is lower than the industry average.
   d. Cash on hand is projected to be lower than the cash on hand at the end of the prior year.
   e. Asset turnover is higher than the industry average and prior-year performance.

3. Glenn Martin is the owner of the GM Car Wash. The company sells car washes for $10. The variable cost (water, soap, and labor) per wash is $4. The company incurs $100,000 of fixed costs per year. The company expects to deliver 25,000 washes in the coming year.
   a. Based on these data, prepared a static budget for the coming year.
   b. How would net income differ if 15,000 washes were delivered?
   c. How would net income differ if 30,000 washes were delivered?

4. Joe's Airport Cafe sells sandwiches for $5. The variable cost per sandwich is $3. The company incurs $50,000 of fixed costs per year. The company expects to sell 40,000 sandwiches in the coming year.
   a. Based on these data, prepare a static budget for the coming year.
   b. Holding all other factors constant, how would net income differ from the static budget if fixed costs were 10 percent higher than expected?
   c. Holding all other factors constant, how would net income differ from the static budget if fixed costs were 10 percent lower than expected?
   d. Holding all other factors constant, how would net income differ from the static budget if variable costs were 10 percent higher than expected?
   e. Holding all other factors constant, how would net income differ from the static budget if variable costs were 10 percent lower than expected?

5. The Tired Traveler Motel rents rooms for $50 per night. The variable cost per room rental is $10. The company incurs $300,000 of fixed costs per year. The company expects to rent 10,000 rooms in the coming year.
   a. Based on these data, prepare a static budget for the coming year.
   b. Holding all other factors constant, how would net income differ from the static budget if sales price was 10 percent lower than expected?
   c. Holding all other factors constant, how would net income differ from the static budget if sales volume (number of room rentals) was 10 percent lower than expected?
   d. Holding all other factors constant, how would net income differ from the static budget if variable costs were 10 percent higher than expected?
   e. Holding all other factors constant, how would net income differ from the static budget if fixed costs were 10 percent higher than expected?
   f. Which scenario (b, c, d, or e) would result in the lowest net income?

6. Broad Brush Painting Company has prepared the following projections for its residential painting business for 20X5:

Budgeted number of customers: 1,000
Budgeted average contract price: $800
Budget variable costs per job: $300
Budgeted annual fixed costs: $200,000

Compute the following (consider each independently):

a. Budgeted contribution margin
b. Budgeted net income
c. Net income if sales volume is 10 percent lower than expected
d. Net income if sales volume is 10 percent higher than expected
e. Net income if sales price is 10 percent lower than expected
f. Net income if sales price is 10 percent higher than expected
g. Net income if variable costs per job are 10 percent lower than expected
h. Net income if variable costs per job are 10 percent higher than expected
i. Net income if fixed costs are 10 percent lower than expected
j. Net income if fixed costs are 10 percent higher than expected
k. What will have the greatest effect on net income: a 10 percent increase in sales price, a 10 percent decrease in variable costs, or a 10 percent decrease in fixed costs? Why?

7. Speedy Sandwich Shoppe delivers box lunches to busy executives in a major metropolitan area. Speedy has prepared the following projections for its business for June 20X2:

Budgeted number of meals: 10,000
Budgeted average price per meal: $12
Budget variable costs per meal: $5
Budgeted annual fixed costs: $50,000

a. Compute budgeted contribution margin.
b. Compute budgeted net income.
c. Prepare a flexible budget for sales of 8,000, 12,000, and 15,000 box lunches. How does net income change from the static budget?

8. Visit a small local business and arrange to meet with the store's manager or owner. Ask this person the following questions about budgeting at his or her enterprise and prepare a memo to your instructor summarizing your findings.

a. How often does the company compare actual results to its budget?
b. Who prepares this comparison? Is it someone internal or external to the business?
c. Are variances investigated?
d. What dollar or percentage threshold does the company use when deciding whether or not to investigate a variance?
e. How does variance analysis affect evaluation of employee performance?
f. How does variance analysis affect future planning?

9. LA Tour Guides sells maps to the homes of Hollywood stars. Assume that the actual number of maps sold exceeded the budgeted sales volume. Also, assume that actual sales price per map exceeded the budgeted sales price per map. Actual variable cost per map equaled the budgeted cost. Indicate whether each of the following items is *true* or *false*.

a. LA Tour Guides would have an unfavorable revenue volume variance.
b. LA Tour Guides would have a favorable revenue price variance.

c. LA Tour Guides would have a favorable total revenue variance.

d. LA Tour Guides would have an unfavorable variable cost volume variance.

e. LA Tour Guides would have a favorable variable cost price variance.

f. LA Tour Guides would have an unfavorable total variable cost variance.

10. Old Vermont Furniture Maker Company reported the following values for the most recent month:

Total revenue variance:	$500 favorable
Revenue price variance:	$100 unfavorable
Variable cost volume variance:	$150 unfavorable
Variable cost price variance:	$100 favorable

Compute the following and indicate whether each is favorable or unfavorable:

a. Revenue volume variance

b. Total variable cost variance

c. Total contribution margin variance

11. Professional Uniform Company sells uniforms to various food service companies. Here are the actual and budgeted results for a recent year:

Actual number of uniforms sold:	10,000
Budgeted number of uniforms to be sold:	11,000
Actual average variable cost per uniform:	$20
Budgeted average variable cost per uniform:	$18

Compute the following:

a. Total variable cost variance

b. Variable cost price variance

c. Variable cost volume variance

12. Sweet Tooth Candy Company sells candy boxes for local fundraising groups. Here are the actual and budgeted results for a local fundraiser;

Actual number of boxes sold:	1,000
Budgeted number of boxes to be sold:	900
Actual average selling price per box:	$5.00
Budgeted average selling price per box:	$4.80
Actual average variable cost per box:	$3.00
Budgeted average variable cost per box:	$3.20

Compute the following:

a. Total revenue variance

b. Revenue price variance

c. Revenue volume variance

d. Total variable cost variance

e. Variable cost price variance

f. Variable cost volume variance

13. Lime Sports sells T-shirts to campus organizations (clubs, sororities, honor societies, etc.). Here are the actual and budgeted results for a recent year;

Actual number of shirts sold:	12,000
Budgeted number of shirts to be sold:	15,000
Actual average selling price per shirt:	$10.00
Budgeted average selling price per shirt:	$12.00
Actual average variable cost per shirt:	$5.00
Budgeted average variable cost per shirt:	$4.60

Management Accounting: A Business Planning Approach

Compute the following:
a. Total revenue variance
b. Revenue price variance
c. Revenue volume variance
d. Total variable cost variance
e. Variable cost price variance
f. Variable cost volume variance

14. Susie's Sushi sells sushi to the campus student center. Sushi is sold fresh each day in prepackaged boxes. Here are the actual and budgeted results for a recent year:

Actual number of boxes sold:	9,000
Budgeted number of boxes to be sold:	8,000
Actual average selling price per box:	$5.00
Budgeted average selling price per box:	$5.00
Actual average variable cost per box:	$3.00
Budgeted average variable cost per box:	$3.10

Compute the following:
a. Total revenue variance
b. Revenue price variance
c. Revenue volume variance
d. Total variable cost variance
e. Variable cost price variance
f. Variable cost volume variance

15. Select a public company (one whose stock is actively traded on any major exchange) in which you are interested (or that your instructor has assigned). Do not pick a bank, insurance company, brokerage firm, any type of financial services entity, or a firm that operates in a regulated industry. It is very important that the company you select reports accounts receivable, inventory, and debt on its balance sheet. Once you have selected a company that meets these criteria, perform the following:

a. Download the company's balance sheet and income statement from the Securities and Exchange Commission's EDGAR data site: http://www.sec.gov/edgar.shtml. Using EDGAR, search for the company's filings using the Search for Company Filings link. Click Companies and Other Filers and simply enter the company's name. Then click OK to view the company's filings. Once you have a listing of filings, select the *most current* 10-K filing. Note that the 10-K filing could be listed simply as 10-K or 10-K could be followed by other letters and numbers, e.g., 10-KT405. Click on the filing and then search the 10-K filing for the balance sheet and income statement. Once you have found them, print them out, as you will be required to attach these to your assignment.

b. Enter the balance sheet and income statement information for the two most recent years into an Excel spreadsheet. Compute the change in each item on the balance sheet and income statement in terms of dollar amounts and percentages. Provide a brief discussion of the major changes on each financial statement. What information can you find in the company's 10-K to explain why each major change occurred?

University Backpacks (Part 1)

You are the owner-manager of University Backpacks, a company that you started this year (20X1). The company sells backpacks to students attending several local colleges in the area. Your company sells two types of backpacks: those for transporting laptop computers and smaller ones not intended for laptop storage. The latter type comes in two styles, with dividers and zippered pockets and without. All backpacks carry the unique logos of the colleges in the community. For this right, University Backpacks pays a licensing fee on a percentage-of-sales basis. You order only enough inventory to meet immediate sales, so there is no inventory at year end. Few alterations or adjustments are made to the backpacks received from your wholesaler. However, in addition to affixing the local college emblems, customers sometimes request special stitching or the addition of extra patches to meet their own unique tastes. During its first year of business, University Backpacks sold 3,800 backpacks (almost evenly split between laptop and non-laptop styles) and reported the following operating results:

University Backpacks		
Actual Income Statement		
For the Year Ended December 31, 20X1		
Sales		$152,000
Cost of Sales		113,256
Gross Profit		$ 38,744
Expenses:		
Advertising	$ 5,000	
Licensing fee	6,200	
Depreciation	2,500	
Insurance	2,700	
Miscellaneous	1,688	
Payroll Taxes (on owner's salary)	2,000	
Owner's Salary	20,000	
Storage	1,000	
Income Taxes (Refund)	(2,503)	
Telephone	2,500	
Travel and Entertainment	3,500	
Total Expenses		44,585
Net Loss		$ (5,841)

Requirements

1. Review the above income statement (prepared in accordance with generally accepted accounting principles) and determine which costs are fixed and which are variable.
2. Using the information provided above and in the income statement, answer the following questions:
   a. What is the contribution margin per unit?
   b. What is the breakeven point in units?
   c. What is the contribution margin ratio?
   d. What is the breakeven point in sales dollars?
   e. How many units must be sold to produce a target profit of $25,000?
   f. How many dollars of sales must be generated to produce a target profit of $25,000?
   g. What is the margin of safety with a target profit of $25,000?

University Backpacks (Part 2)—Budget Analysis

Although you didn't really expect to make much money during your first year of business, you were somewhat shocked when you realized just how much money your company lost. A friend suggested that you should have prepared a budget to manage your operations before you started business. It had been several years since your last exposure to budgeting, so you asked your friend to prepare a budget based on the 20X1 amounts and operations. Your friend presented you with the following budget based on a review of your records and discussions with you:

University Backpacks First-Year Budget January 1 – December 31, 20X1	Unit Amount	Number of Units	Annual Budget
Sales (backpacks)	$40.00	5,000	$200,000
Computer storage (large)	$30.00	2,500	$ 75,000
Regular storage (folders, no pockets)	$25.00	2,500	62,500
Patches, logos, etc.	$ 1.00	5,000	5,000
Wages	$ 1.00	5,000	5,000
Payroll taxes	10%		500
Licensing fee	3%		6,000
Total variable costs	$30.80		$154,000
Contribution margin	$ 9.20		$ 46,000
Depreciation			4,000
Insurance			3,800
Owner's salary			20,000
Payroll taxes (owner)			2,000
Storage			2,500

Telephone	3,000
Total fixed costs	$ 35,300
Sales commissions	$ 10,000
Advertising	5,000
Travel and entertainment	1,300
Income taxes	(1,680)
Other expenses	$ 14,620
Total fixed and other costs	$ 49,920
Net loss	$ (3,920)

Requirements

1. Using the information provided above answer the following questions:
   a. What was the expected monthly sales volume?
   b. Do all the backpacks sell for the same price? Do all have the same cost?
   c. How did licensing costs affect the per-unit cost of each backpack? Was this cost reasonable? Was this cost necessary?
   d. How many people would it take to perform the labor needed to embroider and sew "extras" on the backpacks?
   e. Do all the costs appear to be categorized correctly in the budget? Why or why not?
   f. How are payroll taxes estimated?
   g. What is the equation of the line that estimates the budgeted costs?
   h. What is the contribution margin for the laptop backpacks?
   i. What is the contribution margin for the non-laptop backpacks?
   j. How many potential customers does the company have?
2. Using this information and the contribution margin income statement completed for University Backpacks (Part 1), prepare University Backpacks' budget variance report for 20X1. Be prepared to discuss the potential reasons for any variances you identify and what can be done about these in the future.
3. Prepare a flexible budget and a budget variance report for 20X1. How do your results compare with what you found with the static budget (2 above)?

Assessing Budget Credibility

The financial statement budget is a central element of the business plan. The budget shows investors whether a good business idea will generate financial returns. It is important that your business plan include sensitivity analysis and ratio analysis to provide readers with insight into the credibility of the financial projections. These analyses and accompanying discussion should clearly identify and communicate any major assumptions and their effects on operating results.

Sensitivity Analysis

Sensitivity analysis allows readers to see the effects of changes in key operating assumptions. Developers of the business plan should include multiple scenarios to assess the effects of changing assumptions on projected outcomes. Common "what-if" analyses include increasing and decreasing some of the following variables:

1. Sales price
2. Sales volume
3. Variable costs
4. Fixed costs
5. Cash flow timing

Typically, start-up enterprises are fairly optimistic about their projections. However, investors and creditors often are more critical, looking to see if more conservative estimates also yield desired returns before they invest or lend money to the new enterprise. Your business plan should provide "what-if" statements (sensitivity analyses) that address any alternative approaches that may be reasonable. Explain why your breakeven point is achievable and why the assumptions on which it is based are reasonable. Each number in your budget must be justified and supported by some credible source or assumption.

Ratio Analysis

Ratios provide readers of business plans with a tool to easily compare firms of different sizes and across industries. Your business plan should include a section that computes each of the major ratios presented in Chapter 3. You also should consult with industry guides or trade associations to see if there any specific or special ratios that are particularly important in your industry. After computing each ratio, compare it to some industry benchmark. Industry ratios can be obtained from one of the following sources (check your library for the most recent editions):

1. www.bizstats.com (online resource)
2. *Dun & Bradstreet Industry Norms and Key Business Ratios*
3. *Risk Management Associates (RMA) Annual Statement Studies*
4. *Standard & Poor's (S&P) Industry Guides*
5. *The Almanac of Business and Industrial Financial Ratios*

Each of these resources will have up-to-date ratios for your company's industry. You should prepare a schedule that compares each of your ratios to the industry average. Be careful to compare your firm to others with similar sales and assets. Your text describes ratio analysis and how this comparison should be done. Be sure to explain in detail why any of your ratios differs from the industry. If most of your ratios are very different from the industry, you may want to reconsider some of the key assumptions in your budget. Sensitivity analysis and a ratio comparison will greatly enhance the credibility of your business plan.

Image Credits

Fig. 8.1: Copyright © Ildar Sagdejev (CC by 2.0) at https://commons.wikimedia.org/wiki/File%3A2008-11-10_Lowe's_Home_Improvement_Warehouse_in_Chapel_Hill.jpg.

Fig. 8.2: Copyright © Vrysxy (CC by 2.0) at https://commons.wikimedia.org/wiki/File%3ANordstrom.jpg.

Fig. 8.3: Copyright © Michael Rivera (CC by 4.0) at https://commons.wikimedia.org/wiki/File%3AExxon%2C_Flash_Foods_Dr%2C_Glynn_County.JPG.

Fig. 8.4: Copyright © Depositphotos/monkeybusiness.

Chapter 9

LEARNING OBJECTIVES

1. Explain the purpose and benefits of performance evaluation.

2. Define and explain the use of responsibility centers.

3. Demonstrate how firms evaluate responsibility center performance.

4. Illustrate the use of cost-benefit analysis for business decision making.

5. Describe and illustrate the use of the balanced scorecard for performance measurement and evaluation.

Performance Evaluation and Decision Making

Previous chapters illustrated how managers use profit planning and forecasting techniques to manage business processes. While those chapters focused on planning for the future, this chapter shows how companies evaluate performance at the end of a fiscal period. It begins by reviewing the most common financial performance evaluation techniques in use today and discusses their benefits and limitations. Then it illustrates how the balanced scorecard approach (BSA) introduced in earlier chapters uses financial and nonfinancial performance data to improve decision making as managers work toward achieving their organization's strategy. In doing so, this chapter integrates many key concepts discussed throughout the book.

Evaluating Performance and Creating Accountability

Managers need feedback to assess how well they have executed business strategy and managed business processes. This management accounting information also helps them with their future planning and decision making. **Performance evaluation** is the system of feedback that companies develop and use to assess progress, evaluate employees, and guide future decision making. Such a system allows a company to evaluate its progress in attaining its strategic objectives. It also helps individual employees to see exactly how their decisions and actions affect the company's operating results. In fact, to motivate managers to meet business objectives, many companies offer stock options, pay raises, and other forms of bonus compensation (for example, a free car or vacation) when the firm meets or exceeds performance targets. Therefore, performance evaluation offers three potential benefits: accountability, feedback, and decision guidance.

Accountability

An organization's stakeholders (especially its employees, managers, and owners) often possess different amounts of performance data about the organization. Consequently, the information that each of these parties holds is not *symmetric* or *balanced*. Such differences, known as **information asymmetry**, may benefit some stakeholders while harming others. For example, employees may have private information that they use to make decisions that benefit themselves at the expense of the company

Learning Objective 1
Explain the purpose and
benefits of performance
evaluation.

and its owners. Therefore, companies need performance evaluation systems to compensate for information asymmetries that inevitably arise.

Periodic performance evaluation in a business is very similar to a student's report card. Knowing that one's performance will be reviewed generally creates incentives to take the proper actions. Top performers often are rewarded with pay increases, promotions, and/or greater responsibility. In contrast, most companies first counsel and then terminate those individuals who consistently fail to meet expectations. Companies also use performance evaluation to determine whether to continue a company segment, a product, or a service offering. For example, airlines frequently eliminate or reduce travel routes that do not generate enough ticket sales.

Feedback

A good performance measurement system provides timely feedback that enables managers to take corrective action, if necessary. As we saw in Chapter 8, a variance report that compares budgeted with actual sales can provide insight as to why budget projections are not being met and what operating changes may be required. If sales are below expectations, managers may develop and execute strategies to promote certain products. Alternatively, they may use such feedback to initiate cost-cutting to help the company meet its goals. Therefore, to best use the feedback gained from performance evaluation systems, managers need a solid understanding of how business processes affect financial results.

Decision Guidance

Understanding how performance is evaluated can help managers make routine business decisions. Periodic, systematic performance evaluation provides

Figure 9.1
Purchasing a pre-owned car highlights the concept of information asymmetry. The salesperson usually has more information about a vehicle's condition than the potential buyer does. To reduce the possibility that dealers will exploit this information imbalance, buyers rely on dealer reputation, governmental regulation, and their own inquiry to enforce dealer accountability.

Figure 9.2
Disney operates its famous
theme parks and other entertainment units around the
world. Companies like Disney
that possess different business
segments, often delegate the
authority to make business
decisions. When decision
making is decentralized
this way, managers of each
business segment are held
accountable by information
systems that compare
financial performance across
business segments.

managers with the decision guidance they need to manage business processes throughout a fiscal period. Such performance evaluation is often based on budgets similar to those discussed in Chapters 7 and 8. Budgets provide specific, quantifiable objectives that help managers make business decisions. Basing performance evaluation on managers' ability to meet budget motivates them to carefully consider the costs and benefits of their actions and business decisions. For example, a salesperson rewarded for overall total sales may act differently from another who is rewarded for selling a firm's most profitable product. Likewise, a manager responsible for a company's travel and entertainment budget would likely be encouraged to seek economical ways to control these costs. Further, a manager held responsible for cash flow management and company financing will carefully consider targets (such as expected financial leverage) when making capital budgeting, investment, and borrowing decisions. We will discuss other examples of such common business decisions later in this chapter.

Using Responsibility Centers to Assess Performance

Learning Objective 2
Define and explain the use of responsibility centers.

In Chapter 8, we used variance analysis to evaluate a company's *overall* performance. Management accounting information also can provide insight into how various departments or operating units *within* the firm are performing. Through a process known as decentralization, many companies delegate authority to independent operating groups in the organization. Each of these operating units is known as a business segment and its manager controls its daily operations.

To evaluate performance in these autonomous business segments, firms often use a technique known as responsibility accounting. Responsibility accounting is a performance assessment approach that provides periodic comparisons of a business segment's actual performance against its budget. The term responsibility center frequently is used to describe any point in an organization where managers are responsible for and control revenues, costs, and/or assets. Four types of responsibility centers commonly are found in companies today: revenue, cost, profit, and investment centers.

Responsibility Center Characteristics

In a revenue center, managers are held accountable for and control *only the revenues* that the operating unit generates. Performance usually is evaluated by comparing actual revenues to some budget target. Revenue center managers are not held responsible for any of the costs of products or services sold, although they may be held accountable for sales and marketing costs if they exercise some degree of control over these costs. Examples of revenue centers can be found in retail department stores and in regional sales offices of most corporations. A major disadvantage of these centers is that rewarding personnel solely based on revenue can create incentives to promote products with higher sales prices, not necessarily the most profitable products.

Cost centers are responsibility centers in which managers are held accountable for and asked to control *only costs*. Cost center managers are not responsible for revenues, profits, or assets of a business segment. Organizations evaluate the performance of cost centers by comparing the unit's actual costs with target cost levels for the amount and type of work done. Examples of cost centers can be found in both manufacturing operations (for example, the production department of a mill) and service firms (for example, the items processing department in a bank). A potential danger of exclusively using cost centers to measure performance is that they may ignore other critical issues closely related to cost. For example, a company should be careful to consider such issues as product or service quality, response time, employee motivation, and environmental safety as it minimizes costs. Managers must ask how cutting costs will affect these and other critical dimensions.

In **profit centers**, managers are responsible for *both* the revenues and the costs of a product or service delivered by their operating unit. Comparing segment profit to some budgeted profit target is the most common way to assess performance. These centers operate similarly to independent businesses, except that senior management (not the profit center manager) determines the amount of assets invested in the centers and how resources will be used. Most retail chain operating units (hotels, restaurants, and stores for example) are considered profit centers by their firms. Since the profit reported by these units is a broad performance measure that reflects both center and higher-level firm decisions, it cannot be solely relied on as a perfect measure of the unit's performance. Firms must evaluate additional measures, including quality, resource utilization, and service measures that the business segment can control.

Finally, **investment centers** are responsibility centers in which managers are held accountable for revenues, costs, and the level of investment in the operating unit. Since managers are held responsible for the level of investment in their units, investment centers are even more similar to independent business units than profit centers are. Management generally evaluates performance using some return on investment criteria set by the firm. This allows performance to be easily disaggregated and analyzed using the *DuPont system* ratios described in Chapter 3. The next section discusses how each type of responsibility center can be evaluated.

Evaluating Responsibility Centers

Chapter 8 illustrated how managers use budget variances and ratio analysis to assess budget credibility for the firm as a whole. This section demonstrates how firms evaluate the performance of individual business segments within the company. Given the differences in operational responsibility found in revenue, cost, profit, and investment centers, we also can expect dissimilarities in how management assesses performance in these business segments.

Learning Objective 3
Demonstrate how firms evaluate responsibility center performance.

Evaluating Revenue and Cost Centers

Revenue and cost centers generally are evaluated using the variance analysis techniques illustrated in Chapter 8. Revenue centers are expected to meet sales targets, and revenue variances indicate the extent to which actual sales differ from budgeted sales. As discussed in Chapter 8, revenue variances can arise from changes in sales price, sales volume, and/or sales mix. Managers use variance analysis to determine why negative variances occur and what remedial actions are needed to successfully generate future revenue.

Exhibit 9.1
Business Segment
Performance Report

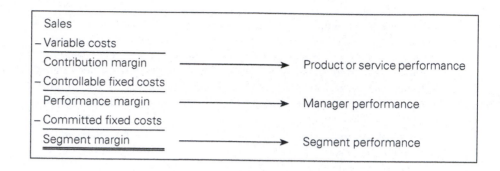

Conversely, cost center managers are expected to control only expenses. Cost centers are evaluated using the fixed and variable cost variance analysis techniques illustrated in Chapter 8. As we saw, variable cost variances can arise from changes in activity or input prices. Variable cost variances arising from quantity differences are known as variable cost volume variances, while those arising from input price changes are referred to as variable cost price variances. If sales volume increases, total variable costs increase simply because the quantity of products or services sold increases. Variable costs may differ from the budget if the input prices increase or decrease. By definition, fixed costs are not expected to change across activity levels. However, in practice, additional spending for new equipment or other operating assets can often cause fixed costs to differ from budget. Regardless of cost behavior, cost center managers are responsible for meeting cost targets.

Evaluating Profit Centers

Profit center managers are responsible for managing both revenues and expenses. As discussed in Chapter 5, managers often create a special income statement that considers cost behavior, allowing them to see the relationships underlying CVP analysis. This special income statement, known as the contribution margin income statement, highlights the differences between variable and fixed expenses and is used for profit planning. Managers commonly use another special income statement, called a business segment performance report, to evaluate profit centers. This report compares the performance of different segments of a business.

Exhibit 9.1 reveals that the business segment performance report is very similar to the contribution margin income statement. Both start by calculating contribution margin, the amount by which total sales exceed variable costs. The only major difference between these two reports is that the business segment performance report further separates fixed costs into two new categories: controllable and committed.

As introduced in Chapter 6, controllable fixed costs are those that a manager has the authority and the discretion to change. Controllable fixed costs can include expenses like advertising, insurance, and the fixed portion of utilities. These costs are controllable because a segment's manager can choose either to incur or avoid these costs. In contrast, committed fixed costs cannot be controlled or changed by a segment manager. Depreciation and long-term leases (for example, rent) are examples of committed fixed costs.

By categorizing a company's costs in this manner, the segment performance report presents three different types of profit margins: contribution margin, performance margin, and segment margin. Disaggregating performance into these three margins allows companies to independently evaluate products and/or services (contribution margin), segment managers (performance margin), and individual segments (segment margin).

As discussed in Chapter 5, contribution margin is the difference between selling prices and variable costs. Not only is contribution margin used in breakeven analysis, it also is useful for evaluating a segment's product or service line. If a firm or its segments cannot sell a product or service at a price above its variable costs, it will not be able to cover fixed cost or generate a profit.

Contribution Margin = Sales – Variable Costs

Performance margin equals contribution margin less controllable fixed costs. This margin considers all costs controllable by an individual manager. Since performance margin deducts all variable and fixed costs that a manager is responsible for and controls, it is useful in evaluating individual managers and comparing them across segments.

Performance Margin = Contribution Margin – Controllable Fixed Costs

The third margin in Exhibit 9.1, **segment margin** equals performance margin less committed fixed costs.

Segment Margin = Performance Margin - Committed Fixed Costs

Segment margin generally is used to compare profit center segments with each other or with a budgeted profit margin. We will use C&F's three service lines (commercial, residential, and other) to illustrate the use of a segment performance report.

Because they had failed to meet their 20X2 profit target, Keith and Dale were eager to analyze their operations using responsibility accounting performance tools. The starting point of the analysis is the contribution margin report. Exhibit 9.2 shows 20X2 sales, variable costs, and contribution margin for each of C&F's segments.

The next step in preparing the business segment performance report is to separate each segment's fixed costs into controllable and committed categories. Keith and Dale were not sure how to properly categorize each cost, so they again turned to their accounting advisors for help in preparing the schedule presented in Exhibit 9.3 from C&F's 20X2 records. Advertising and fixed costs for other services were classified as controllable in each segment, while salaries were the only committed cost.

The accountants then informed Keith and Dale that some costs simply could not be attributed to any of C&F's three operating segments. Such costs, which do not relate to any one segment but are shared by the company as a whole, are called **common costs**. Common costs include such items as the owners' salary, shared services (accounting and bookkeeping, for example), and income taxes. While

Exhibit 9.2
Contribution Margin
Performance Data

C&F Enterprises, Inc. 20X2 Contribution Margin				
	Commercial	Residential	Other	Total
Sales (Exhibit 8.8)	$86,000	$12,600	$5,250	$103,850
– Variable costs (Exhibit 8.20)	60,061	8,736	3,209	72,006
Contribution margin	$25,939	$ 3,864	$2,041	$ 31,844

such costs affect the company's net income, they often cannot be assigned to a particular business segment. Exhibit 8.18 in Chapter 8 reported C&F's total fixed costs for 20X2. With the help of their accounting advisors, Keith and Dale used these data to identify common costs. Exhibit 9.4 details these common costs and reconciles them to C&F's total fixed costs. As we can see, Keith and Dale agreed that $7,300 of C&F's total fixed costs were common and shared across all three segments. Common costs included depreciation, bookkeeping, interest on loans, and a portion of their salaries and advertising. All other costs were assigned to each segment.

After identifying common costs and separating each segment's fixed costs into controllable and committed categories, C&F's accounting advisors prepared C&F's 20X2 business segment performance report. This report appears in Exhibit 9.5. The report begins with sales, from which variable costs are deducted to yield contribution margin both in dollars and as a percentage of sales. C&F's contribution margin is 30.7 percent; other services reports the highest contribution margin of the three segments (38.9 percent). Despite its large contribution margin percentage, Keith and Dale recognized that other services accounted for a very minor percentage of sales and contributed the smallest amount of contribution margin dollars to company profits. This example suggests that managers must consider both the relative (percentage) and absolute (dollar) contribution of a segment's products and services when evaluating performance.

Although the commercial segment has the highest controllable fixed costs ($6,175), it also has the highest performance margin in dollars ($19,764). The

Exhibit 9.3
Controllable and
Committed Fixed Costs

C&F Enterprises, Inc. December 31, 20X2 Controllable and Committed Fixed Costs				
	Commercial	Residential	Other	Total
Controllable Fixed Costs				
Advertising	$ 5,000	$3,500	$ 150	$ 8,650
Other	1,175	325	—	1,500
Total	$ 6,175	$3,825	$ 150	$10,150
Committed Fixed Costs				
Salaries	$ 4,500	$2,000	$1,000	$ 7,500
Total segment fixed costs	$10,675	$5,825	$1,150	$17,650

| C&F Enterprises, Inc. | |
Reconciliation of Common Costs to Total Fixed Costs	
Salaries	$ 2,000
Depreciation	600
Advertising	1,250
Bookkeeping	3,250
Interest	200
Total common costs	7,300
Total segment fixed costs (Exhibit 9.3)	17,650
Total C&F fixed costs (Exhibit 8.18)	$24,950

Exhibit 9.4
Reconciliation of Common
Costs to Total Fixed Costs

residential service line reports the highest percentage of controllable fixed costs (30.4 percent) but contributes only $39 of performance margin. Apparently, the $3,500 spent on advertising (see Exhibit 9.3) did not generate much in the way of residential sales. These findings provided Keith and Dale with answers as to why C&F's profits were not as high as expected and identified the residential segment as an operating unit warranting further attention and analysis. As owner-managers, Keith and Dale will have to reconsider their marketing decisions in the residential service line.

The commercial service line reports the highest segment margin both in percentage (17.8 percent) and dollars ($15,264). The residential segment was unable to cover its committed fixed costs of $2,000 and showed a net loss for the year ($1,961). Keith and Dale looked at the segment margin numbers and knew they had a tough decision to make in 20X3. Should they abandon residential lawn care services and focus solely on commercial and other services, or should they attempt to improve the residential segment's performance? The segment performance report is a valuable tool for identifying such critical decisions.

Finally, it is important to note that the sum of the individual segment margins does not equal the company's net income for the period. Common costs must be deducted from total segment margin ($14,194) to evaluate C&F as a whole. Deducting $7,300 of common fixed costs yields net income of $6,894.

Evaluating Investment Centers

As we have illustrated, the business segment performance report is useful for evaluating profit centers. However, one issue that companies must address when evaluating business segment performance is that these units often operate with different sets of resources. It is not surprising that a segment with a large amount of assets (relative to another unit) has the potential to generate higher sales, margins, and profits. A supermarket, for example, is much larger than a convenience store and would be expected to sell more inventory and yield higher dollar margins and profits in a given fiscal period. To account for differences in resource use, both in quantity and efficiency, many companies evaluate business

Exhibit 9.5

Business Segment Performance Report

	C&F Enterprises, Inc. 20X2 Business Segment Performance Report							
	Total		**Commercial**		**Residential**		**Other**	
Sales[a]	$103,850	100.0%	$86,000	100.0%	$12,600	100.0%	$5,250	100.0%
−Variable costs[b]	72,006	69.3%	60,061	69.8%	8,736	69.3%	3,209	61.1%
Contribution margin	$ 31,844	30.7%	$25,939	30.2%	$ 3,864	30.7%	$2,041	38.9%
−Controllable fixed costs[c]	10,150	9.8%	6,175	7.2%	3,825	30.4%	150	2.9%
Performance margin	$ 21,694	20.9%	$19,764	23.0%	$ 39	0.3%	$1,891	36.0%
−Committed fixed costs[c]	7,500	7.2%	4,500	5.2%	2,000	15.9%	1,000	19.0%
Segment margin	$ 14,194	13.7%	$15,264	17.8%	$ (1,961)	(15.6%)	$ 891	17.0%
−Common costs[d]	7,300	7.0%						
Net income[e]	$ 6,894	6.7%						

[a] Sales data from Exhibit 8.8.
[b] Total variable costs from Exhibit 9.2.
[c] Fixed costs from Exhibit 9.3.
[d] Common costs from Exhibit 9.4.
[e] Net income from Exhibit 8.7.
Note: All numbers have been rounded.

segments as investment centers using a ratio called return on investment (ROI). Dividing segment margin by the assets used by the segment (that is, that segment's asset base) yields ROI.

Return on Investment (ROI percentage) = Segment Margin Segment ÷ Assets

Similar in concept to return on assets (discussed in Chapter 3), ROI can be used to compare the performance of segments with different amounts of assets. For example, assume that a firm has two divisions (A and B), and each earned $10,000 in segment margin. If segment A has $100,000 of assets and segment B has assets of only $50,000, then B's ROI (20 percent) would be twice as large as A's ROI (10 percent). Using ROI allows management to make relative comparisons of segment margins. In this case, B would be considered the better-performing segment since it generated the same margin as A with half as many assets. In C&F's case, ROI does not yield much insight into the performance of each business segment, since the company rents (rather than owns) most of its equipment. However, ROI can be useful to Keith and Dale in the future, as they purchased equipment at the end of 20X2.

Limitations of ROI. Although ROI is a simple and common tool used to evaluate business operations, it does have several drawbacks. As indicated in Chapter 7's capital-budgeting discussion, managers use *several* different techniques to evaluate investments in physical capital. Generally, managers favor investments in assets that provide returns that exceed the cost of financing the asset's acquisition. As discussed in Chapter 3, some companies have adopted economic value added (EVA) analysis to measure the value created for owners during a fiscal year. Essentially, EVA represents a company's profits *after* deducting its costs of raising financial capital (for example, notes payable and common stock). Also, ROI does not consider the time value of money.

A related method commonly used to evaluate business segments is the residual income approach. Residual income equals a segment's margin less a computed interest "charge" for the use of the company's financial capital. A segment's interest charge is calculated by multiplying the company's borrowing rate by the segment's assets; therefore, a positive residual income value for a segment indicates that it has earned more than it costs the company to finance the segment's operations. In C&F's case, if Keith and Dale purchased an asset financed by the bank at an interest rate of 10 percent, their investment would *not* positively contribute to the company's earnings unless the asset generated an ROI greater than the 10 percent borrowing rate.

Since it is possible for a segment to report both a positive ROI and negative residual income, companies frequently supplement ROI with EVA or residual income to gain a more complete picture of investment center performance. Further discussion of residual income and EVA is beyond the scope of this text; it can be found in more advanced finance and cost accounting courses.

Firms also review a variety of other factors when evaluating an asset investment. These factors include the expected life of the asset, possible maintenance costs, and cash flow requirements. As discussed in Chapter 7, businesses also should consider the time value of money when making capital use decisions. The net present value (NPV) method encourages managers to invest in assets that yield cash flow streams with positive NPVs. However, managers whose performance is evaluated using ROI alone may be tempted to reject positive NPV investments if they have a negative short-term effect on ROI. For example, those managers might reject an asset that produces relatively low cash flow levels in its early years, even though it has a very favorable net present value over its useful life. Such an investment will increase assets (the denominator) in the ROI calculation in the short run without a commensurate increase in segment margin (the numerator), causing the segment's ROI percentage to decrease. Companies must recognize such ROI limitations when making investment decisions and evaluating performance.

Insights from Responsibility Accounting

Responsibility accounting helps managers evaluate performance. If managers know they are responsible for revenues, costs, profits, and/or asset use, they have incentives to make decisions consistent with the firm's objectives. For example, a cost center manager will seek out ways to control costs, while the sales force would be motivated to increase revenue. Performance evaluation often leads managers to take corrective action with regard to some business process. However, this is only one of the many types of decisions that managers make. We will discuss some other common business decisions next.

Cost-Benefit Analysis

When managers face new business opportunities, they must determine how decisions will affect profitability. In doing so, managers frequently compare the benefits and costs of each new activity. This process is called cost-benefit analysis. These analyses show the extent to which benefits exceed costs (in dollars) or vice versa. In Chapter 5, we demonstrated why contribution margin analysis is critical to decision making. However, the contribution margin's focus on cost behavior (that is, fixed versus variable) is only one decision making consideration. Managers also must evaluate the importance of a cost to the cost-benefit decision. Therefore, managers also must classify costs as an incremental, opportunity, or sunk costs when making business decisions.

Decision Cost Issues

An incremental cost is any additional expenditure that a decision alternative incurs or requires. These costs can either be fixed or variable in nature. For example, if company plans to expand its sales territory, it might incur incremental fixed costs for a new monthly lease and/or for insuring delivery vehicles. An example of an incremental variable cost would be the commissions paid to the expanded sales force. Companies also frequently decide to reduce or eliminate costs. For example, companies frequently transfer the processing of employee payroll, a highly automated function, to a contract service firm outside the organization. This decision eliminates avoidable costs, since the company no longer pays its own employees to process payroll. An opportunity cost, on the other hand, is a forgone benefit that managers give up by choosing a particular decision alternative. For example, many firms rent out unused warehouse or factory space to other companies. If a particular decision alternative requires a firm to reclaim that space and end the rental agreement, any forgone rental revenue is an opportunity cost of that decision alternative. A sunk cost is a cost that has already been incurred and cannot be changed or eliminated in the short term. Most fixed costs are considered to be sunk and will not affect future decisions. For example, depreciation resulting from the acquisition of a long-term asset cannot be avoided in the short term as the assets are used.

To appreciate these concepts, consider the following examples. Assume that a friend asks you to go to the beach for the weekend. If you go to the beach, your incremental costs would include travel, hotel lodging, food, entertainment, and the cost of a new bathing suit. If going to the beach also means missing two days of work and you earn $50 per day, your opportunity cost (forgone wages) would be $100 (2 days @ $50 per day). Other costs that you might incur would not be relevant to your decision to take a beach vacation. For example, if you live in a

Management Accounting: A Business Planning Approach

rented apartment, its cost would be considered a sunk cost and would not affect your decision to go the beach.

Only incremental and opportunity costs are relevant to cost-benefit analysis. These costs sometimes are called *relevant costs*. A **relevant cost** is a cost that is different under the decision alternatives. Sunk costs are *not* relevant to decision making because they remain constant under the decision alternatives. Relevant costs equal the sum of incremental and opportunity costs.

Relevant Costs = Incremental Costs + Opportunity Costs

Managers use cost-benefit analysis to make business decisions. Most decisions that managers face offer several alternatives. To make appropriate decisions, managers compare the relevant costs and benefits for each decision alternative. Cost-benefit analysis is best demonstrated through two common management decisions: make-or-buy and "special offers."

The Make-or-Buy Decision

As discussed in Chapter 8, firms use resources, known as inputs, to successfully execute key business processes. Inputs may include goods and services such as labor, supplies, and materials for production processes. A routine business decision related to such inputs is commonly referred to as the make-or-buy decision. As the name implies, this decision requires managers to determine whether the firm should produce certain goods or services on its own or pay a supplier to deliver them. For example, a restaurant may elect to make its own desserts or, alternatively, buy cakes and pastries from a bakery. Likewise, many firms choose to have vendors provide technology support or janitorial services rather than employing and supporting their own staff. To make such decisions, managers carefully compute and compare the relevant costs of the available make-or-buy alternatives. They must also carefully consider the relevant business risks of producing the good or service within the firm versus relying on a supplier.

C&F Enterprises, Inc.: Exploring a New Opportunity. Keith and Dale were pleased with their 20X2 performance, but they were looking for ways to improve profits. One day, while reading the local newspaper, Keith noticed that a local garden center was offering classes on growing flowers—it was even selling greenhouse space to interested parties. He shared the ad with Dale and suggested that maybe they could save money if they grew the flowers used in their landscaping projects rather than buying them.

C&F typically plants about 1,000 flower beds each spring for its commercial and residential customers. Each flower bed includes a strip of eight to ten flowers. The flower beds are quite popular, but C&F does not make much money on them. The market price is $10 per bed and the lowest price that C&F pays its supplier is $8 per bed, yielding a $2 per bed profit margin. Of course, C&F also incurs labor costs to plant and water the flower beds. However, C&F is able to recoup some

Figure 9.3
Make-or-buy is a
common decision faced
by many businesses. For
example, should a pizza shop
make its own dough or buy
frozen crusts prepared by a
supplier? When making such
decisions, managers must not
only consider the relevant
financial costs, but also
such important qualitative
factors as employee training,
customer satisfaction, and
supplier reliability.

of these costs by selling "excess" planting soil that protects the flowers during shipment. A local farmer pays them $250 for this soil each year.

Although neither Keith nor Dale had any horticultural experience, they thought the nursery's offer was worth considering. After attending the class at the nursery, Keith and Dale realized that growing their own flowers was a possibility, so they decided to inquire about the greenhouse rental fees and material costs. The manager told them that the seasonal rental and storage fees would be $2,000. He also told Keith and Dale that they could buy the necessary disposable pottery, soil, and seeds for $4 per bed. He informed them that the greenhouse would maintain the proper temperatures, but that C&F would be responsible for watering the flowers and that C&F would bear the risk of successfully growing the flowers.

Exhibit 9.6
Make-or-Buy
Cost-Benefit Analysis

Alternative 1: Buying the Flower beds	
Incremental variable costs (1,000 beds @ $8 per bed)	$ 8,000
Total relevant cost of buying flower beds	$ 8,000
Alternative 2: Growing the Flower beds	
Incremental variable costs (1,000 beds @ $4 per bed)	$ 4,000
Incremental fixed costs	2,000
Opportunity cost (forgone sale of unused soil)	250
Total relevant cost of growing flower beds	$ 6,250
Net benefit (cost) of growing flower beds	**$1,750**

To determine whether they should grow or buy the flowers, Keith and Dale asked their accounting advisors to help them to conduct a cost-benefit analysis.

The accountants helped C&F determine the relevant costs for each alternative: growing or buying the flower beds. Their analysis is shown in Exhibit 9.6. Calculating the cost of buying the flower beds was fairly straightforward. One thousand beds purchased from suppliers at $8 per bed equals total relevant costs of $8,000. Growing the flowers results in incremental variable costs of $4,000 ($4 per flower bed) and incremental fixed costs of $2,000 for the greenhouse rental. In addition, the $250 opportunity cost of not selling "excess" soil to the local farmer must be included in calculating the relevant cost of growing the flowers. All other fixed costs that C&F incurs (that is, salaries, bookkeeping, and advertising) are sunk costs and would not be relevant to this decision, since these costs are not affected by C&F's decision to grow or buy the flower beds.

When Keith and Dale compare the relevant costs of each alternative, they find that the cost of growing the flowers is $1,750 less than buying them. If they base their decision on this quantitative analysis alone, C&F should choose to grow the flowers, because this decision will save the company $1,750. However, Keith and Dale should consider several risk-related *qualitative* factors before making their final decision. How reliable is the greenhouse? How likely is it that C&F will grow the flowers successfully? Is additional training necessary? How much time must Keith and Dale dedicate to caring for the flowers? Will this time commitment draw them away from other important business activities? Does the nursery stock the same types of flowers that they currently buy from suppliers? If the flowers do not grow, will they have enough time to place an order with their current supplier? If such an emergency order is needed, how will it affect their purchase costs? If they need more than 1,000 beds in future years, will the greenhouse be able to offer such capacity?

These qualitative questions are representative of those that managers ask when confronting a make-or-buy decision. Other issues that can affect the decision relate to the adequacy of employee training, reliability of suppliers, risk of waste or spoilage in the new process, safety hazards, and the potential effects of the decision on other operations. Clearly, make-or-buy decisions should not be based on numeric calculations alone. Managers must carefully assess the risks inherent in the make-or-buy decision and evaluate their effect on business processes and related costs.

Special Offers

Cost-benefit analysis also helps managers when they contemplate accepting special offers. When ordering large amounts of a product or service, a customer or group of customers sometimes will approach a business for either a group or quantity discount. For example, the American Institute of CPAs and the Institute of Management Accountants commonly request such discounts from hotels and airlines when scheduling and hosting the annual meeting of their members. These transactions are usually for one-time purchases, but they are sometimes used for longer-term contracts. These arrangements benefit the seller by guaranteeing a large volume of sales, and they benefit the buyer by offering a discount off the regular price of a product or service.

Exhibit 9.7

Special Offer Cost-Benefit
Analysis

		Percentage of Sales
Sales revenue (150 servicings @ $225 each)	$33,750	100.0%
Incremental variable costs	(23,570)	69.8
Net benefit (cost) of special offer	$10,180	30.2%

C&F Enterprises, Inc.: The Cost of a Quantity Discount. In early 20X3 a local corporate park, a potential new client, approached Keith and Dale with a request for a quantity discount. The corporate park was home to ten well-known corporations. The companies wished to contract for lawn care services as a group. The ten corporations each offered to commit to 15 lawn cuttings and servicings over the course of the year. Since they collectively were committing to 150 cuttings, the corporate park's association manager asked Keith and Dale if they could provide a 10 percent discount per cutting. In other words, he sought a price of $225 per cutting and servicing ($250 regular price less $25 discount).

C&F never had offered discounts before. Although Keith and Dale recognized that the offer had the potential to bring in a lot of new business, they wondered if they could still make a profit at that price. C&F did have the time and labor available to accommodate these new customers, so why not offer the discount?

Keith and Dale could foresee no additional fixed costs to accepting this engagement; therefore, only variable costs were incremental to their decision. Based on this assumption, they prepared the cost-benefit analysis shown in Exhibit 9.7. Servicing ten new clients would generate an additional $33,750 in sales revenue at the discounted price. If C&F variable costs remained at 69.8 percent of sales revenue for commercial customers (Exhibit 9.5), C&F would incur an additional $23,570 in incremental variable costs. Since incremental revenues exceed incremental costs, accepting this deal appears to improve C&F's net income by $10,180.

However, Keith and Dale also must consider several qualitative and strategic questions before offering the discount. How will this discount affect C&F's normal pricing structure? Will other customers now demand a discount? Will C&F be able to meet profit targets by offering all commercial customers service at $225 per job? Does the company really have enough capacity (time and resources) to deliver the services? Will the additional 150 cuttings and servicings place a strain on existing resources? Is any long-term relationship possible with customers who are so price conscious? Will the customers contract for services beyond one year?

Questions like these again reinforce the importance of considering both quantitative and qualitative factors in cost-benefit analysis. These two examples of cost-benefit analysis demonstrate the value of understanding fundamental cost concepts. They also show why knowledge of the business and market are so critical to long-term strategic decision making.

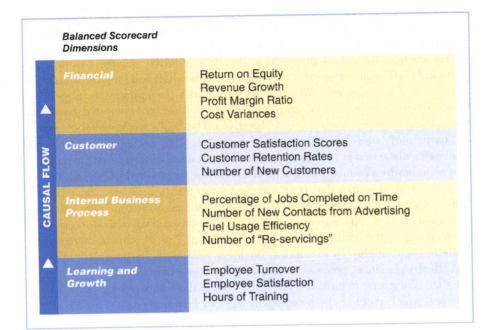

Exhibit 9.8
C&F Enterprises, Inc.
Balanced Scorecard
Measures

Balanced Scorecard Dimensions

CAUSAL FLOW		
▲	Financial	Return on Equity Revenue Growth Profit Margin Ratio Cost Variances
	Customer	Customer Satisfaction Scores Customer Retention Rates Number of New Customers
	Internal Business Process	Percentage of Jobs Completed on Time Number of New Contacts from Advertising Fuel Usage Efficiency Number of "Re-servicings"
▲	Learning and Growth	Employee Turnover Employee Satisfaction Hours of Training

The Balanced Scorecard: A Performance Measurement Framework

Managers generally rely on both financial and nonfinancial performance measures to guide the company to its business goals. As discussed in Chapter 3, a variety of stakeholders use financial statement data and ratios to evaluate a company's performance. These **financial performance measures** (for example, sales growth, return on assets, and financial leverage) are operating indicators that can be drawn directly from a company's financial statements and other reports. Chapter 4 introduced you to the factors that actually *drive* these financial performance measures. However, companies also use a variety of other measures not found in the financial statements to evaluate performance. These are referred to as **nonfinancial performance measures** and generally are designed to capture outcomes associated with customer satisfaction, process effectiveness and efficiency, and resource utilization.

As you learned in the early chapters of this book, the balanced scorecard is a strategic management framework that helps organizations communicate strategic goals to employees by linking them to relevant performance measures. An increasing number of companies are using the balanced scorecard approach (BSA) to evaluate company performance because it incorporates both financial

Learning Objective 5
Describe and illustrate the use of the balanced scorecard for performance measurement and evaluation.

and nonfinancial measures along four business dimensions: financial, customer, internal business process, and learning and growth.

For each of these four dimensions, the BSA requires managers to develop goals and performance measures that reflect both the short and long-term strategic objectives of the company. Management determines the appropriate targets for these performance measures, and employees often are compensated based on their ability to meet these goals and objectives. The BSA's nonfinancial measures are particularly useful in interpreting financial results. For example, declining customer satisfaction or increased product defect rates (both nonfinancial metrics) may explain why a company fails to meet its revenue targets. Exhibit 9.8 illustrates a basic set of measures that Dale and Keith can use to evaluate C&F's performance along each BSA dimension. The causal relationships found in the balanced scorecard are one of its major features. When employers train their workers, they are focusing on the learning and growth dimension. They do this to increase the skills of their employees to improve business processes. By operating efficient and effective business processes, companies are more likely to satisfy customers. Satisfied customers, in turn, will be willing to buy the company's products and/or services, which should help the company meet its financial goals.

Learning and Growth Dimension

The first dimension of the BSA relates to learning and growth. This dimension deals with how well a company supports the human capital necessary to delivering the value chain processes. This dimension helps managers focus on the people that run the business. Keith and Dale realized that without their helpful and well-trained staff of lawn-care providers they would not be able to meet customer needs.

Companies can use many employee-related measures to assess the competence and satisfaction of their staff. One of them, employee turnover, shows how many employees left the organization during the past year. High employee turnover may indicate unsatisfactory work conditions, pay, or advancement opportunities. Firms seek to minimize employee turnover because replacing and training employees can be very costly. For example, a major telecommunications firm once reported that it saved more than $23 million just by reducing employee turnover. They relied on an aggressive growth campaign to successfully hire, manage, and retain employees during a period of low industry unemployment. The company implemented the balanced scorecard to analyze turnover statistics, calculate their financial impact, prescribe solutions, and track improvement trends.

Keith and Dale similarly realized that it is important to keep their staff intact. Their accounting advisors suggested that they survey or interview their employees each year to judge their level of job satisfaction and to identify ways to improve employee morale and productivity. In addition to employee job satisfaction, the BSA encourages firms to monitor the professional development of their workers. Hours of training or number of new certifications are indicators of employee learning and growth. Collectively, these measures help company owners maintain a well-trained, highly motivated work force that will to be able to run the business and execute business strategy.

Internal Business Process Dimension

The internal business process dimension focuses managers on the elements of the value chain that are most critical to meeting customer demands. As discussed in Chapter 2, the value chain is the interrelated set of business processes necessary to execute business strategy. In the case of C&F Enterprises, customer satisfaction is driven by the consistency and quality of their key business process—lawn-care services. Therefore, measuring the number of jobs completed on time and the number of re-servicing requests due to customer complaints may be good indicators of customer satisfaction.

The value chain also includes marketing and promotion, so Keith and Dale may want to monitor the number of new customers generated by their marketing activities to determine the effectiveness of their annual advertising expenditures. Likewise, as discussed in Chapter 8, fuel expenses were higher than expected in 20X2. So Keith and Dale may wish to track fuel usage to identify equipment that needs to be replaced or repaired by the rental company and to identify ways to operate more efficiently. Collectively, the internal business process measures provide information critical for evaluating and interpreting financial performance.

Customer Dimension

This set of BSA nonfinancial measures addresses customer issues. The customer dimension focuses managers on what customers want and whether or not they are satisfied. Possible measures include customer satisfaction, customer retention rates, and number of new customers. For example, C&F could conduct surveys, interviews, or focus groups with key customers to assess their level of satisfaction and to identify areas for possible service improvement. Customer referral activity is also an excellent indicator of customer satisfaction. Other indicators are customer retention rates and the number of new customers. Keith and Dale can easily review their customer lists to calculate the number of new customers as well as those they have retained from prior years. These indicators will give them insight into how well they are growing the business and also can help them with forecasting future sales.

Financial Dimension

The financial perspective identifies measures that can be used to assess whether strategy has been successfully executed from the perspective of shareholders. We have discussed financial measures extensively throughout this book. As discussed in Chapter 3, shareholders look to several key financial ratios (return on equity, profit margin, and financial leverage) to evaluate how well a firm has performed. Chapters 7 and 8 described several budget-based measures (that is, revenue and cost variances) that provide specific feedback on various elements of financial performance. For C&F Enterprises, Keith and Dale were particularly concerned with sales growth and profit margin, in addition to return on equity.

Measures that Matter: An Interview

Financial measures such as profit and loss do not give employees much information on how to improve in their daily jobs. "If you choose the right performance measures, each employee should know when they leave the job every day if they have done well," according to Swedish researcher, professor, and business consultant Eric Giertz. The following is an excerpt from a CIO Magazine interview with Giertz. CIO Magazine is distributed to Chief Information Officers and technology managers across the world.

CIO: Are financial measures becoming less important than nonfinancial measures like customer satisfaction?

Giertz: The financials are still important to some people, like managing directors, but individual workers cannot understand how to improve their operations just by looking at financial ratios. They can't connect their work to these numbers. In retailing it would be more helpful to look at things like average purchase per customer.

If you really want to improve the processes, you have to involve management and employees in the discussion. Then you shouldn't try to compare different units but look at how you can manage each unit to improve its business. Too many people want to take the easy way and say there is only one set of indicators for measuring every kind of operation all over the world. If that's the approach you take, then you will fail.

CIO: How would these new indicators work at, say, an auto manufacturer?

Giertz: You have capital-intensive processing-machines that work twenty-four hours a day, seven

days a week, making single parts within the motor. In that kind of operation you'd need to measure equipment availability and production quality. Then you have people assembling cars, which is where labor productivity is a priority—so you'd look at the number of cars assembled per month.

In the repair shop at the dealer, you must look not only at the time it takes to perform a service but also how to classify the time, such as billable time versus total time. You should also try to understand customer satisfaction through questionnaires. Then you should conduct spot checks to see if the jobs that you charged the customer for really got done. You may get some kind of objective quality index indicating that you have a lot of recalls for jobs that are not well done. Or, let's say there's a lot of wasted supplies—4.8 percent, for instance.

To get it down to less than 1.8 percent, you can measure it each day for six months. So you can use recall job ratio, quality index, customer attitudes, capacity utilization and labor productivity as performance measures. If you perform well on all five, probably you will have great revenues, customer return, and high productivity.

As this interview illustrates, performance measurement is gaining global attention and must be carefully tailored to match the needs of the organization. Technology is playing an increasing role in tracking data. Managers in turn are expected to develop the necessary insight to act on these analyses.

Source: "Measures that Matter" by Polly Schneider. *CIO Magazine*, January 2000. (http://www.cio.com/archive/010100/qanda.html) Reprinted through the courtesy of CIO. Copyright © 2004 CXO Media Inc.

Exhibit 9.9

Sample Balanced Scorecard Measures by Industry

Industry	Financial Dimension	Customer Dimension	Internal Business Process Dimension	Learning and Growth Dimension
Airlines	Return on assets	Frequent flier program participation rates	Percentage of on-time takeoffs and arrivals	Labor contract length
Consumer retail banks	Ratio of assets to debt	Number of new accounts opened	Number of new branches	Hours of employee training completed
Accounting, consulting, and law firms	Profit margin	Client retention rate	Percentage of projects completed on time	Certification and education levels of professionals
Mobile device manufacturers	Sales growth from new products	Number of corporate customers	Number of product defects	Percentage of factory employees who completed quality control training
Supermarkets	Inventory turnover	Customer satisfaction	Product spoilage rates	Employee turnover rates

The analytical tools presented in this and earlier chapters can provide insight into whether a company has met its financial objectives. The balanced scorecard enhances this insight by highlighting the critical *nonfinancial* measures that drive financial performance. These nonfinancial measures explain changes in financial results and help to forecast and manage future performance.

Balanced Scorecard Measures by Industry

The BSA's measures vary with a firm's strategy and industry. Exhibit 9.9 lists examples of performance indicators for each BSA dimension across a wide range of industries.

Airlines. Commercial airlines operate with heavy fixed costs and large investments in expensive equipment. Their success depends on their ability to sell tickets and maximize the number of passengers per flight. The variable cost per passenger is usually relatively small and includes costs such as providing on-board food and beverage service. Therefore, from a financial perspective, airlines focus closely on

Figure 9.4
Many companies rely on the balanced scorecard to measure performance. For example, banks monitor financial measures like revenue from loans and interest paid on customer deposits. They also review nonfinancial metrics such as the number of new customers and branches, ATM and website usage, and employee training levels. All of these measures provide companies with insight into whether business processes are meeting their strategic goals.

profit margins and return on assets. In terms of the customer dimension, frequent flier participation rates provide the airlines with data about the frequency and extent of travel of their most loyal customers.

Since the industry is so competitive, the airlines need to be attentive to internal business process dimension issues such as on-time takeoff and arrival rates. Frequent delays or cancellations may drive customers to competitors. To ensure that the airline operates efficiently, they also must focus on the learning and growth dimension. Airlines typically employ unionized labor; the length and continuity of labor contracts is critical to keeping a satisfied and committed workforce in place. Employee strikes can interrupt service and affect customer perceptions of the airline. Measures that capture the continuity and length of employee contracts are useful to airline managers. Collectively, these measures demonstrate how the balanced scorecard may be used by an airline.

Consumer Retail Banks. The success of consumer retail banks depends on their ability to generate enough revenue from investments, loans, and customer fees to offset interest paid to customers. Customer deposits provide the financial capital that banks use to issue loans and make investments. These deposits also represent obligations on the part of the bank to have money available on demand and to pay a stated rate of interest each period. From a financial perspective, retail banks closely monitor the ratio of assets to debt to assess solvency and capital strength. In terms of the customer dimension, new accounts mean access to funds and the potential to generate fee revenue. Banks frequently measure the number of new accounts opened. To encourage customers to open new and different types of accounts, banks today are allowed by law to offer many financial services including life insurance, retirement planning, and stock brokerage accounts. Banks seek

Management Accounting: A Business Planning Approach

to attract customers by offering multiple financial services, a practice known as cross-selling. Accordingly, banks also measure the extent to which its customers demand multiple services.

To maximize customer participation, many consumer retail banks open numerous branch locations within a geographic region. The number of new branches is an example of an internal business process measure that consumer retail banks use to assess progress toward strategic goals. It is important for bank managers to understand how the number of new branches drives the number of new accounts, which in turn drive financial results. Last, of course, opening new branches requires significant amounts of staffing. A learning and growth measure that banks commonly use is hours of staff training. Such training should lead to higher quality of delivered services and higher levels of customer satisfaction. All of these measures are reflected in the BSA.

Many retail banks now encourage customers to use online services. Recently, Wells Fargo implemented a balanced scorecard in its online financial services group, a division that enables customers to conduct transactions online. From an internal business process perspective, they found that the BSA decreased website malfunctions (downtime) by 71 percent. They also attracted 250,000 additional online customers who reported high levels of satisfaction. As an added bonus from a financial perspective, their average cost per customer dropped 22 percent. The balanced scorecard clearly helped Wells Fargo to successfully implement and evaluate online banking.

Accounting, Consulting, and Law Firms. Professional service firms rely on highly educated individuals to deliver services to clients. For example, Saatchi & Saatchi, an international advertising agency, relies on employee creativity for its success. They implemented the balanced scorecard throughout their global offices, and as a result, they have won a record number of new clients. The balanced scorecard helped them monitor the success of new products as well as employee and customer satisfaction.

As discussed in Chapter 6, since accounting, consulting, and law firms rely on their human capital to execute strategy, a primary cost to these firms is the salary of their professional staff. Salaries for these professionals are functions of education (degrees and institution quality), experience, and certifications (for example CPA licenses, licenses to practice law). Typically, these professionals are highly competitive, quality individuals who command premium compensation. Therefore, in terms of the financial perspective, professional service firms focus on profit margin. They encourage employees to identify projects that will generate enough revenue to cover employees' significant hourly rates.

These firms typically offer highly tailored and personal services to a limited set of clients. Unlike major retailers, professional service firms invest a lot of time and effort to get to know their clients. A common customer measure is client retention rates. Retaining clients, in many cases, ensures renewable fees from year to year and eliminates the need to identify and develop relationships with new clients. To maximize client retention, these firms focus on the number of projects completed on time. The timeliness and quality of the services delivered have tremendous bearing on a client's decision to retain the firm for future services. To deliver quality services on time, the firms rely on people who possess the proper abilities, skills, and backgrounds to meet their clients' needs. Therefore, it is important for these firms to recruit and retain quality employees. From a learning and growth perspective, these firms frequently monitor the education level and number of professional certifications of their employees.

Mobile Device Manufacturers. Unlike the service firms discussed in the three preceding examples, mobile device manufacturers, such as Apple, produce and deliver physical products to customers. Since technology industries experience rapid change and innovation, one financial measure that these firms use is sales growth generated by new products. While overall sales growth is important, this financial indicator provides insight into the extent to which the sales base is growing from the firm's latest market releases. To maximize this element of sales, these companies must carefully identify customer needs and develop solutions to meet those demands.

One customer measure that mobile device manufacturers frequently use is number of corporate clients. Contracts with big companies can result in the sale of thousands of devices in a single order that carries with it the opportunity to sell replacements and accessory products over time. To meet customer expectations, manufacturers closely monitor production operations. They use internal business process measures such as the number of product defects to ensure quality and improve production. To maximize quality, these companies invest heavily in employee training and often measure the number of hours of training that each employee completes each year. These measures work together to help mobile device manufacturers develop and deliver leading technology products in today's competitive marketplace.

Supermarkets. Retailers, such as supermarkets, also use the balanced scorecard. Supermarkets often occupy very large retail spaces and offer an incredibly wide range of food, home, and personal products. Therefore, the two largest assets of these firms will usually be merchandise inventory and property, plant, and equipment. Supermarkets typically sell products at a relatively low profit margin and rely on high sales volume to generate returns for investors. As discussed in Chapter 3, asset turnover represents the sales generated relative to a firm's investment in its assets. Supermarkets monitor asset turnover to measure the financial performance of the business. It is critical that perishable inventory turn quickly to cover the costs of operating the store.

Supermarkets frequently measure customer satisfaction through surveys, focus groups, and analysis of "frequent buyer" purchases. Customer satisfaction is critical to maintaining and growing sales. From an internal business process measure, one action that supermarkets take to ensure customer satisfaction is minimizing spoilage of food. Unsold or spoiled foods can represent tremendous costs to a supermarket and may impair customer perceptions of the quality of a store's offerings. To minimize spoilage rates and maximize customer satisfaction, supermarkets try to create a friendly work atmosphere for employees. Since supermarkets

Management Accounting: A Business Planning Approach

The Balanced Scorecard Hall of Fame

The Palladium Group, a major consulting firm operated by the developers of the balanced scorecard, has created a Hall of Fame to honor organizations that successfully implemented and benefited from this innovative management approach. The Hall of Fame includes a well-known group of global companies across a wide range of industries. Some recent inductees include BMW automobile company, Hilton Hotels, AT&T Canada, Wendy's Hamburgers, and UPS. The Hall of Fame recognizes each company's unique accomplishments in improving its business processes and financial performance by using the balanced scorecard.

Mexico's PlayCity Casino launched the Balanced Scorecard in 2011, seeking to differentiate themselves from their competitors and grow market share through outstanding operations and outstanding service. Their efforts paid off: they saw revenue growth of 30 percent by 2014 and they nearly doubled average revenue per user. Soft benefits also abound: they are consistently recognized in written media, by their customers, and by their competitors as the best-operated casino in Mexico, and they have slashed their employee turnover in an industry that usually sees around 100 percent turnover annually.

You can learn more about the Hall of Fame organizations that have benefited from the balanced scorecard by visiting the following website: http://thepalladiumgroup.com/

rely heavily on part-time workers, such as clerks, cashiers, and shelf-stockers, it is critical that supermarkets focus on employee retention rates. Employee retention can greatly enhance the reputation and perceived quality of a store. Together, these measures help supermarket managers deliver quality products and services to customers in a manner that meets the expectations of investors and creditors.

As illustrated in the preceding examples, the BSA is adaptable across industries and provides a good capstone to many of the topics discussed in this textbook. It helps managers to communicate strategic goals and assess progress toward objectives along multiple dimensions. The balanced scorecard provides a consistent basis for measurement by which employees can assess progress toward many interrelated targets. The use of both financial and nonfinancial measures reminds managers of the role of business activities in driving financial results. The adaptability of this performance measurement tool highlights the commonalities in executing strategies, managing business processes, and measuring results regardless of firm size. In all cases, it is the insight and skill of management to use such tools that ultimately determines a firm's long-term success.

Summary

This chapter discussed the benefits of performance evaluation and illustrated several techniques that managers use to evaluate company performance. Effective performance evaluation is important because it provides managers with accountability, feedback, and decision guidance. The chapter also emphasized that business decisions and performance evaluation cannot be based on financial indicators alone. Firms use frameworks such as the balanced scorecard to integrate financial and nonfinancial performance indicators so as to provide managers with the critical insights necessary to execute strategy. In many cases performance evaluation results highlight business processes that may be under-performing and that warrant further management attention. This chapter also focused on the performance of individual responsibility centers and the company as a whole. The next chapter extends this discussion and introduces the most common techniques that managers use to analyze costs at the customer and product level.

Net Gains

Performance Measurement Resources on the Web

There are many Web resources that you can use to learn more about performance evaluation. For example, managers frequently look to industry "best practices" or examples of successful implementations at other firms when developing measurement programs. The websites listed below provide valuable resources for evaluating performance and business decision making across a wide range of industries.

- **The Balanced Scorecard Institute (http://www.balancedscorecard.org).** The Balanced Scorecard Institute is an educational group that provides training and guidance to assist government agencies and companies in applying balanced scorecard concepts to strategic management. Their website provides background information about implementing the balanced scorecard and the proper selection of nonfinancial measures. It also provides several examples of past successes.

- **American Productivity and Quality Center (http://www.apqc.org).** This is the homepage for the American Productivity & Quality Center (APQC). APQC has a membership of over 450 prestigious global firms including 3M, AT&T, Cisco Systems, and Ernst & Young. The objective of this collaborative center is to "Understand how innovative organizations create succession management programs to identify and cultivate potential leaders who will provide a sustainable business advantage." The Best Practices and Free Resources links lead to many useful resources.

Summary of Learning Objectives

1. **Explain the purpose and benefits of performance evaluation.** It is important for companies to develop measures that guide the organization to successful strategy execution. These measures may be either financial (drawn directly from the financial statements) or nonfinancial (qualitative indicators that drive performance). Performance measurement systems provide three primary benefits: accountability, feedback, and decision guidance.

2. **Define and explain the use of responsibility centers.** Responsibility centers describe any point in an organization where control (and the related responsibility) resides over revenues, expenses, or both. Four types of responsibility centers generally are recognized: revenue, cost, profit, and investment centers. A manager of a revenue center would be responsible only for the revenues generated by his or her unit, while a manager of a cost center would be responsible only for the costs. Profit center managers are evaluated on both revenues and costs, whereas investment center managers are responsible for all of these as well as for the level of invested assets in their unit.

3. **Demonstrate how firms evaluate responsibility center performance.** A performance report for operating segments typically includes three types of margins: contribution margin, performance margin, and segment margin. Each is useful in a different way. Contribution margin is used to evaluate a segment's product or service line. When comparing individual managers across segments, performance margin is used. Segment margin facilitates comparisons of operating units to each other or to a budgeted segment profit margin. Return on investment (ROI) also can be used to compare segments with different-sized asset bases.

4. **Illustrate the use of cost-benefit analysis for business decision making.** Understanding costs and performance evaluation expectations helps managers to make routine business decisions. This chapter illustrates two common decision contexts: make-or-buy and special offers. To make such decisions, managers use cost-benefit analysis. Cost-benefit analysis compares incremental benefits to relevant costs. In addition to quantitative analysis, managers must consider qualitative strategic factors regarding a decision that also may affect the firm.

5. **Describe and illustrate the use of the balanced scorecard for performance measurement and evaluation.** The balanced scorecard is a model that integrates financial and nonfinancial measures to help managers implement strategy and measure performance. The balanced scorecard translates the organization's strategy into an integrated, balanced set of performance measures that cut across traditional functional areas. Management determines the appropriate targets for these measures and frequently compensates employees based on their ability to meet these objectives.

Glossary of Terms

Avoidable costs Costs that companies no longer incur by making a particular decision.

Business segment An independent operating unit within an organization.

Business segment performance report A special income statement used to evaluate profit centers.

Committed fixed cost A cost that cannot be changed by the segment manager.

Common cost A cost that is not directly attributable to any particular segment because it is not under the direct control of any segment manager.

Controllable fixed cost A cost that a manager has the authority and the discretion to change.

Cost-benefit analysis A decision-making tool used by managers to compare the benefits and costs of various decision alternatives.

Cost center Point in an organization where managers control and are held accountable only for the costs incurred by the operating unit.

Decentralization The delegation of authority to independent operating groups in the organization.

Financial performance measure An indicator of a company's operating performance that can be drawn directly from the financial statements.

Incremental cost In cost-benefit analysis, any cost that represents an additional outlay of a firm's resources that is required by the decision alternative.

Information asymmetry A condition that exists when an organization's stakeholders possess different amounts of performance data about the organization. This informational imbalance often can lead to situations that may benefit some stakeholders while harming others.

Investment center Point in an organization where managers are held accountable for revenues, costs, and the level of investment in the operating unit.

Nonfinancial performance measure Indicators used to evaluate performance that generally cannot be found in the financial statements. They are generally designed to capture outcomes associated with customer satisfaction, process effectiveness and efficiency, and resource utilization.

Opportunity cost In cost-benefit analysis, any cost of forgone business opportunities related to a particular decision alternative.

Performance evaluation The system of feedback that companies develop and use to assess progress, monitor employees, and guide future decision making.

Performance margin A margin that accounts for all costs under a manager's control. It is computed by deducting controllable fixed costs from contribution margin and is useful for comparing individual managers across segments.

Profit center Point in an organization where managers control and are held accountable for both the revenues and the costs of the product or service delivered by their operating unit.

Quantity discount Lower prices provided to buyers who order goods or services in bulk.

Management Accounting: A Business Planning Approach

Relevant cost A cost that is different under various decision alternatives; includes both incremental and opportunity costs.

Residual income An evaluation technique that reports segment margin after deducting the cost of financing a segment's margin.

Responsibility accounting A performance assessment approach that provides periodic comparisons of a business segment's actual performance against its budget.

Responsibility center Any point in an organization where managers are responsible for and control revenues, costs, and/or assets.

Revenue center Point in an organization where managers control and are held accountable only for the revenues that the operating unit generates.

Segment margin A margin calculated by subtracting committed fixed costs from performance margin. It is useful for comparing segments with each other or with a budgeted profit margin.

Sunk cost Past expenditures that are not relevant to business decision making.

Chapter Review Questions

1. What is performance evaluation?
2. Identify three benefits of performance evaluation.
3. What are financial performance measures?
4. Give three examples of financial performance measures.
5. What are nonfinancial performance measures?
6. Give three examples of nonfinancial performance measures.
7. What is responsibility accounting?
8. What is decentralization and why do firms decentralize?
9. What is a responsibility center?
10. What is a revenue center? Identify an example of a revenue center.
11. What is a cost center? Identify an example of a cost center.
12. What is a profit center? Identify an example of a profit center.
13. What is an investment center? Identify an example of an investment center.
14. How are revenue centers typically evaluated?
15. How are cost centers typically evaluated?
16. How are profit centers typically evaluated?
17. What is a business segment performance report?
18. What are committed fixed costs?
19. What are controllable fixed costs?
20. What is meant by contribution margin?
21. What is meant by performance margin?
22. What is meant by segment margin?
23. What are common costs?
24. How are investment centers typically evaluated?
25. Identify two uses for return on investment.
26. Identify two limitations of using return on investment.

27. What is residual income?
28. What is cost-benefit analysis?
29. What is a relevant cost?
30. Define incremental, opportunity, avoidable, and sunk costs.
31. Give an example of a make-or-buy decision.
32. Give an example of "special offer" decision.
33. What are the four dimensions of the balanced scorecard?
34. How is the balanced scorecard used for performance evaluation?
35. Name one metric commonly used for each dimension of the balanced scorecard.

Exercises and Problems

1. Classify each of the following as a revenue, cost, profit, or investment center.
    a. Payroll processing department
    b. Sales team
    c. Production department for a furniture manufacturer
    d. Part-time hotel manager responsible for food sales and costs
    e. Regional department store manager responsible for store assets, sales, and costs
    f. Janitorial services
2. Categorize each of the following items incurred by a local grocery store as a variable cost, controllable fixed cost, or committed fixed cost.
    a. Advertising
    b. Cost of goods sold
    c. Manager's salary
    d. Depreciation
    e. County sales license
    f. Property tax
    g. Janitorial staff
    h. Wages paid to cashiers
3. Listed below are several balanced scorecard measures that might be used by a company. Classify each as a measure of the financial, customer, internal business process, or learning and growth dimension.
    a. Return on equity
    b. Employee turnover
    c. Product defects
    d. Customer satisfaction ratings
    e. Fuel usage efficiency
4. Listed below are several measures that might be used by a company using the balanced scorecard. Classify each as a measure of the financial, customer, internal business process, or learning and growth dimension.
    a. Cost variances
    b. Number of projects completed on time

c. Number of certified professional employees

d. Percentage of on-time shipments and deliveries

e. Number of new stores opened

5. Brigade Corporation operates with a central headquarters and three regional divisions: North, South, and West. Categorize each of the following fixed costs as common, controllable, or committed.

a. The CEO's salary

b. The salaries of each divisional president

c. Depreciation on the corporate headquarters building

d. Depreciation on a machine used by the North Division.

e. Cost of an advertising campaign in the South Division.

6. Poppy's Popcorn, a small vendor in the mall, is adding the sale of cotton candy to its operation. In order to do this, the owner needs to purchase a cotton candy machine and secure the use of an additional cart. Currently, Poppy rents out two other carts within the mall to similar vendors, one of which (under the proposed plan) will no longer be rented but will be used for the sale of cotton candy. Poppy's lease payments for space in the mall will remain the same. Classify each of the following items as an opportunity, incremental, avoidable, or sunk cost.

a. Cost of cotton candy ingredients

b. Forgone revenue from cart rental

c. Cost of cotton candy machine

d. Lease payments

e. Cost of advertising flyers distributed earlier in the year

7. Union Grille operates three restaurants. It reported the following data for the most recent fiscal year for Campus Café, its largest restaurant:

Sales	$100,000
Cost of sales	50,000
Advertising	2,000
Depreciation	5,000
Salaries	30,000
Property tax	1,000

a. What is Campus Café's contribution margin?

b. What is Campus Café's performance margin?

c. What is Campus Café's segment margin?

d. If Campus Café utilizes $35,000 of assets, compute return on investment (ROI) for the most recent year.

8. Donny's Motorcycle Repair operates three shops. It reported the following data for the most recent fiscal year for Main Street Shop, its largest operating unit:

Sales	$120,000
Cost of sales	10,000
Advertising	1,000
Depreciation	15,000
Salaries	60,000
Rent	20,000

a. What is Main Street's contribution margin?
b. What is Main Street's performance margin?
c. What is Main Street's segment margin?
d. If Main Street utilizes $56,000 of assets, compute return on investment (ROI) for the most recent year.

9. Microcom Company has two segments: hardware and software. The product lines reported the following data:

	Software	Hardware
Sales	$450,000	$650,000
Variable costs (as a percentage of sales)	30%	58%
Total direct fixed costs:	$189,000	$168,000
Controllable fixed costs	89,000	68,000
Committed fixed costs	?	?

In addition, common administrative costs amount to $31,500. The software manager suggests that these costs should be allocated based on segment revenues. The hardware manager disagrees and supports allocation based on segment margins.

Required:

a. Compute committed fixed costs for each business segment. Remember that total direct fixed costs equal the sum of controllable and committed fixed costs.

b. Prepare a business segment performance report for Microcom.

c. Should common costs be allocated? Comment on how each manager's common cost allocation suggestion would affect reporting.

10. Hot Bun Bakeries operates two segments: North and South. The business segment performance report for 20X2 follows:

	Total	Percentage of Sales	North	Percentage of Sales	South	Percentage of Sales
Sales	$152,000	100.0%	$90,000	100.0%	$600,000	100.0%
−Variable costs	97,000	63.8%	57,000	63.3%	378,000	64.5%
Contribution margin	$ 55,000	36.2%	$33,000	36.7%	$222,000	35.5%
−Controllable fixed costs	31,000	20.4%	19,000	21.1%	102,000	19.4%
Performance margin	$ 24,000	15.8%	$14,000	15.6%	$120,000	16.1%
−Committed fixed costs	11,000	7.2%	8,000	8.9%	66,000	4.8%
Segment margin	$ 13,000	8.6%	$ 6,000	6.7%	$ 54,000	11.3%
−Common costs	11,000	7.2%				
Net income	$ 2,000	1.4%				

Based on the data, answer the following questions:

a. Which segment performed better? Why?

b. Which division manager performed better? Why?

c. Suppose that the company would like to spend $3,000 in advertising in only one of the segments and that advertising would increase sales by 10 percent. Which segment should receive the advertising funds? Why?

11. Drexel Company operates three convenience stores. Here is the 20X2 business segment performance report for Drexel Company.

	Total	Percentage of Sales	Store 1	Percentage of Sales	Store 2	Percentage of Sales	Store 3	Percentage of Sales
Sales	$1,800,000	100.0%	$600,000	100.0%	$600,000	100.0%	$600,000	100.0%
–Variable costs	1,080,000	60.0%	372,000	62.0%	378,000	63.0%	330,000	55.0%
Contribution margin	$ 720,000	40.0%	$228,000	38.0%	$222,000	37.0%	$270,000	45.0%
–Controllable fixed costs	432,000	24.0%	120,000	20.0%	102,000	17.0%	210,000	35.0%
Performance margin	$ 288,000	16.0%	$108,000	18.0%	$120,000	20.0%	$ 60,000	10.0%
–Committed fixed costs	180,000	10.0%	48,000	8.0%	66,000	11.0%	66,000	11.0%
Segment margin	$ 108,000	6.0%	$ 60,000	10.0%	$54,000	9.0%	$ (6,000)	(1.0%)
–Common costs	36,000	2.0%						
Net income	$ 72,000	4.0%						

All three Drexel stores are similar in size, carry similar products, and operate in similar neighborhoods. Store 1 was established first and was built at a lower cost than Stores 2 and 3. The lower cost results in less depreciation expense for Store 1. Store 2 follows a policy of minimizing both cost and sales price. Store 3 follows a policy of quality customer service and charges slightly higher prices than the other stores. Based on these data, answer the following questions:

a. From the viewpoint of the company as a whole, which store is the most profitable?

b. Which store manager seems to be performing best? Why?

c. Suppose that spending $15,000 per year in advertising at a particular store can increase that store's sales by 10 percent, which store warrants the additional expenditure? Justify and explain your response.

12. Heart & Soul Coffee Emporium typically sells customized coffee mugs for $10 each. The mugs cost Heart & Soul $5 each. Assume that Heart & Soul is approached by a new coffee shop that would like to make a one-time purchase of 200 mugs. Suppose that the coffee shop offers to pay $9 per mug.

a. Should Heart & Soul accept the offer even though the selling price is below its normal price?

b. What are the advantages and disadvantages of offering an initial discount?

c. Identify at least three qualitative and strategic factors that management should consider. Explain each factor that you suggest.

13. Somerset Sluggers is a minor league baseball team. The team currently buys peanut bags from a local distributor for $1.00 per bag. The team sells peanuts for $1.50 per bag. They sell 1,000 bags per game and play 20 home games. The chief vendor suggested that they could roast their own peanuts. After investigating the costs, the team realized that peanuts and roasting oils will cost them an average of 75 cents per bag. The annual cost of renting and maintaining peanut roasters will be $3,000.

    a. What is the annual net benefit/cost of buying peanuts from the distributor?

    b. What is the annual net benefit/cost of roasting the peanuts themselves?

    c. Should Somerset roast or buy the peanuts?

    d. What other nonfinancial factors should the team consider when making this decision?

14. Anywhere Company has three divisions: Northeast, West, and South. Each segment had the following assets and generated the following margins last year:

	Northeast	West	South
Segment assets	$10,000	$50,000	$30,000
Segment margin	5,000	17,000	10,000

Return on investment (ROI) allows companies to compare segments of different sizes.

    a. Compute ROI for each segment.

    b. Which segment performed the best?

    c. Identify one benefit and one limitation of using ROI as a performance measure.

15. Elsewhere Company has three divisions: Atlantic, Central, and Pacific. Each segment had the following assets and generated the following margins last year:

	Atlantic	Central	Pacific
Segment assets	$100,000	$150,000	$320,000
Segment margin	45,000	17,000	80,000

Return on investment (ROI) allows companies to compare segments of different sizes.

    a. Compute ROI for each segment.

    b. Which segment performed the best?

    c. Identify one benefit and one limitation of using ROI as a performance measure.

16. A local pizza shop is considering adopting the balanced scorecard. Identify three relevant performance measures for each of the four dimensions of the balanced scorecard: financial, customer, internal business processes, and learning and growth. Explain how your nonfinancial measures represent drivers of financial performance.

Make-or-Buy Decision—Huskerhenge Pizza Company

You recently decided to trade your hectic, fast-track job in corporate finance in a major East Coast metropolitan city for that of a small business owner in a small Midwestern town. During the past year, you visited Huskerhenge, a major international tourist site known for its artistic replication of Stonehenge (in England) using rusting automobiles.

This unusual attraction attracts thousands from all over the world each year to Friendly, Nebraska, a small town of approximately 1,500 people. Naturally, tourism is the primary business for the community and good international cuisine is in high demand. During your two-week visit to Huskerhenge, you quickly noticed the absence of a quality pizzeria. Although microwave pizzas were available at the Dairy Princess, a "real" pizza could not be found within 500 miles of Friendly. So you decided to meet this market demand.

During your first year of operation, you decided to use frozen pizza crusts that were shipped to you monthly from a Chicago supplier. While first-year sales were considered acceptable, you wondered whether they could be higher if you used fresh pizza crusts in your pizzas. You fondly reflected on watching artisans toss their hand-crafted doughy delights in the windows of pizzerias in your home town. You decided that making your own pizza crusts might be a great way to increase sales. Also, the aroma of your pizza shop will become even more tempting when you start baking your own crusts. However, you are very concerned about whether it makes financial sense to make your own pizza crusts versus buying them already prepared (that is the classic make-or-buy decision). You definitely do not want to increase sales at the expense of higher costs that then reduce your bottom line. You have decided to determine what it would cost to make your own crusts versus buying them.

Required

1. Think about all of the possible benefits and costs associated with both alternatives: buying the prepared pizza crusts or making your own crusts.

2. Review the possible benefits and costs identified in response to the preceding question and determine how you will measure them. For example, can you measure the financial benefits and costs of each alternative? Which specific nonfinancial measures would be appropriate to assess business activity?

3. Compare the relevant benefits and costs for both alternatives. Prepare a recommendation for what you believe is the best decision for your business and be ready to discuss it in class.

4. Is your decision to make or buy crusts affected by the type of benefit/cost information that you have at your disposal? If so, why? If not, why not?

5. What additional data may be valuable? How would you obtain such data?

Deciding on an Online Strategy

In today's technology-intensive environment, one critical business decision facing all firms is the role that an internet presence will play in their operations. A business enterprise must carefully determine how technology will impact its business. There are several different models a start-up business might follow in order to get a business online. A start-up business might consider one of three models for adoption:

1. The company might outsource its online endeavor, allowing a service provider to design, build, and maintain its internet presence and mobile access presence. Under this model, the entrepreneur(s) would receive only reports of goods to ship and payments collected.

2. Alternatively, the start-up firm may choose to have a site hosted by a service provider that provides only the website and online transaction processing capabilities. The start-up firm would be responsible for designing and maintaining the content of the site in addition to receiving reports of goods to ship and payments collected.

3. Finally, the start-up firm might choose to build their own site, leasing a high-speed connection and purchasing the necessary computer equipment and online transaction processing software.

In choosing a strategy, it is essential to consider the costs and benefits of each alternative. Further, it is essential to understand performance measurement and thereby be able to communicate how the selection of a particular alternative will contribute to the overall success of the firm.

Assignment

For your start-up enterprise, identify the relevant costs of each of the three alternatives mentioned above. After carefully considering relevant qualitative factors, select an online strategy that is most appropriate for your business. Prepare a discussion of the advantages and disadvantages of each approach and justify your selection. This discussion is a pivotal part of a business plan in today's technology-enabled business environment.

Image Credits

Chapter 10

Analyzing Costs at the Customer and Process Level

In previous chapters, Keith and Dale relied on estimates based on averages (average quarterly demand and average price per customer, for example) to forecast revenues and expenses. They then compared these estimated or budgeted amounts with actual operating results to evaluate C&F's performance. Variance analysis allowed Keith and Dale to identify potential problem areas in their company's business.

However, fixing problems may not always be as easy as finding them. In fact, developing solutions frequently requires more detailed product or service cost information than the aggregate data commonly reported in most financial statements (see Chapter 3) and other performance reports (see Chapter 9). Companies increasingly want to know how profitable specific customers are or how much these patrons are costing them. Therefore, in this chapter, we introduce the terminology, tools, and structure needed to more fully evaluate the profitability of a company's product or service.

To evaluate whether a product or service is profitable, companies must be able to completely and accurately assess the costs incurred in producing and/or delivering it to the customer. The difficulty of assessing product or service costs varies with the type of business a company pursues. If a company is a merchandising firm, it buys completed inventory items from suppliers; it then sells those items to customers. For example, national chains like Target and Wal-Mart purchase the goods on their shelves from a variety of wholesale suppliers. Determining their product cost (both in the aggregate and individually) is relatively easy. It consists of the inventory item's purchase cost including shipping charges less any returns, allowances, and pricing discounts.

However, for firm's that make products for resale to customers, product costing can be very complex. These manufacturing firms convert raw materials into finished goods that then are sold to consumers. Assigning raw material resources to the individual items created increases the complexity of product costing. Service firms, such as hospitals, attorneys, and landscaping service providers, also often find it difficult to determine unit cost of their products because of the variety of resource inputs used to provide a service. Therefore, the rest of this chapter will address the tools and techniques manufacturers and service providers use to assess and assign costs to the products they create or services they deliver.

C&F Enterprises, Inc.: Addressing a Customer's Dissatisfaction with Price

Keith and Dale were beginning their third year in the lawn services business. They admitted to having learned quite a lot (some of it the hard way) and openly acknowledged that starting and operating a business was far more difficult than they had imagined. Nevertheless, the two entrepreneurs appreciated watching the fruits of their hard work, and the future seemed bright. Bright, that is, until they received an unexpected call from one of their biggest commercial customers.

Jim McGill, the office manager for a local luxury car dealer, called to let Keith and Dale know that he was going to put his lawn care and landscaping work "out for bid." Jim indicated that C&F's main competitor, Tru-Lawn Care (TLC), had approached him offering to perform lawn-maintenance services for $175 a cutting, a substantially lower price than the $250 rate C&F was currently charging. He further noted that since C&F had done such wonderful work for him in the past, he felt a little guilty considering another provider, but the potential cost savings to the dealership were too large to ignore. Jim hoped that C&F could find some way to lower their price, so that he could remain a customer.

Figure 10.1
Firms that produce goods for resale to customers are called manufacturing firms. For companies that manufacture very complex products like prosthetic limbs, assigning raw material resources and other costs of production can be a very complex process.

The news did not catch Keith and Dale completely by surprise, since they had heard from other commercial clients that TLC was becoming unusually aggressive on pricing. However, they were a little disappointed to learn that Jim was so "price-sensitive," particularly given TLC's reputation for providing poor service. Nevertheless, since commercial services accounted for so much of C&F's business, TLC's aggressive pricing behavior could not be ignored. Should they simply match TLC's price? How would this impact the bottom line? How would this affect C&F's future relationship with Jim's company? If they matched TLC, would Jim think C&F had been overcharging them all along? Would other commercial clients expect a similar price reduction? The more Keith and Dale thought about the situation, the more concerned they became. They quickly realized that a call to their accountants was in order.

After calming the two entrepreneurs down, the accountants advised Keith and Dale to first assess the reasonableness of the price they were charging their commercial customers, in particular Jim McGill. To do this, Keith and Dale needed to understand just how much it cost C&F to perform each lawn maintenance job. The accountants recommended that they start with last year's income statement, contribution margin data, and segment information, taking care to consider as many of the service delivery costs as possible in their analysis. With these data, they could then make a more informed decision on whether C&F needed to lower its price, reduce its costs, or both. Armed with this advice and increased confidence in their ability to create and use management accounting information, Keith and Dale plunged into this new service-costing exercise.

Understanding the Composition of Product and Service Costs

When a firm produces its products or delivers its services, it typically incurs costs that can be categorized as either directly or indirectly related to each unit. Some costs related to human and physical capital, such as worker time or food ingredients, can be directly traced to the production of an item or delivery of a service. Other necessary production costs, such as equipment maintenance or factory rent, are not directly traceable to a product or service. In addition, firms incur many nonproduction costs, such as marketing expenditures and administrative salaries, to run their businesses. This section introduces the classification and treatment of the costs that companies incur when manufacturing products or delivering services.

Learning Objective 1
Identify the types of costs firms incur when producing goods or services.

Manufacturing Costs

Firms incur three types of **manufacturing costs** when producing goods and providing services: direct materials, direct labor, and manufacturing overhead.

Figure 10.2
Because direct labor and direct materials are often the primary costs incurred in creating a product or delivering a service, they are known as prime costs. A bakery's prime costs can include product ingredients (direct materials) and wages paid to employees (direct labor) who prepare cakes and pastries. Other production costs like equipment and building rent, insurance, and utilities are categorized as manufacturing overhead.

Direct Materials. Direct materials cost is the cost of all raw materials that can be traced directly to a manufactured product or delivered service. For an automobile manufacturer, direct materials include body frames and bumper assemblies, engines and transmissions, tires, and a variety of other items. In the case of a service enterprise, a hospital for example, direct materials might include disposable surgical instruments, bandages, and medicines. In the case of C&F Enterprises, Inc., few of their costs are for direct materials since clients currently provide most of the lawn care supplies (fertilizer, weed killer, and other lawn care products) that Keith and Dale need to maintain their properties. However, any fuel or rental charges for special equipment needed on a particular job are counted as direct materials costs.

For many minor material costs, it simply may not be practical (in terms of time and effort) to trace costs to specific jobs. Also, it may not be cost efficient to try to match small dollar costs or infrequently occurring charges to specific jobs. Finally, manufacturing and service companies incur some material costs that relate to multiple products. Therefore, any materials that are not directly traced or applicable to a single product or service are called indirect materials. In C&F's case, any fuel, supplies, or rental costs that cannot be identified with a specific service line or job would be considered indirect costs.

Direct Labor. The labor costs that can be directly traced to items produced and services delivered are called direct labor costs. In the case of the automobile maker, the labor charges of the workers who make each vehicle are direct labor costs. For the hospital that delivers medical services, direct labor would include the cost of doctors and nurses directly involved in providing a patient's care.

Management Accounting: A Business Planning Approach

Labor Related	Building or Equipment Related
Indirect labor	Utilities (power, heat, light, etc.)
Overtime premium	Depreciation
Vacation and holiday pay	Property insurance
Payroll taxes	Repair and maintenance
Health insurance	Property taxes

Exhibit 10.1
Common Manufacturing
Overhead Costs

In C&F Enterprises, Inc., the employee salaries related to the actual delivery of lawn care services are direct labor costs.

However, none of Keith or Dale's salary related to supervising employees in the field are direct labor costs. It generally is not possible or practical to trace such supervisory costs to each job performed. Therefore, as with indirect materials, any production or service labor costs that are not directly traced to a particular product or service are called indirect labor costs.

Manufacturing Overhead. Since direct materials and direct labor represent the primary costs of production or service delivery, they frequently are referred to as prime costs. Any other costs that a company incurs in the manufacture of a product or delivery of a service are called manufacturing overhead. Historically, such costs also have been referred to as factory overhead, burden, or simply overhead. Recently more companies have begun calling them *indirect manufacturing costs*. Direct labor and manufacturing overhead together are frequently referred to as conversion costs. In addition to indirect materials and labor costs, manufacturing overhead includes other costs related to the production process, such as depreciation on a production facility and its equipment; rental charges for equipment common to multiple products, processes, and clients; property taxes for a manufacturing facility; and utility costs. Manufacturing overhead costs that are assigned to products or services are commonly referred to as applied overhead.

For an automobile manufacturer, manufacturing overhead might include depreciation and electricity costs for robots used in a production facility. For a hospital, building depreciation and rental charges for general-purpose medical equipment could be considered overhead. In C&F's case, overhead would consist of officers' salaries as well as depreciation costs for equipment used on most jobs. Exhibit 10.1 summarizes common overhead costs found in businesses.

Classifying Manufacturing Costs. Despite the apparent clarity of these three types of production cost, classifying costs in each category often is not easy. Complicating the task is the fact that costs frequently may be split between two cost classes: overhead and either direct materials or direct labor. Using the variable and fixed cost data in Exhibit 10.2, we can calculate C&F's costs of services sold for 20X2 in Exhibit 10.3. These costs include the use of direct materials, direct labor, and overhead to deliver lawn maintenance services to its customers.

Exhibit 10.3 finds total costs of services sold to be $77,095 and illustrates how each of C&F's service delivery costs potentially relates to a particular type

Exhibit 10.2
Contribution Margin
Income Statement

C&F Enterprises, Inc. Contribution Margin Income Statement For the Year Ended December 31, 20X2		
Service revenue	Exhibit 8.7	$103,850
Variable costs:		
Wages	Exhibit 8.7	45,184
Rentals	Exhibit 8.7	16,111
Supplies	Exhibit 8.7	3,932
Fuel	Exhibit 8.7	1,768
Taxes	Exhibit 8.7	2,835
Other	Exhibit 8.7	2,176
Total variable costs	Exhibit 8.18	$ 72,006
Contribution margin		$ 31,844
Fixed costs:		
Salaries	Exhibit 8.7	9,500
Depreciation	Exhibit 8.7	600
Advertising	Exhibit 8.7	9,900
Bookkeeping	Exhibit 8.7	3,250
Interest	Exhibit 8.7	200
Other	Exhibit 8.7	1,500
Total fixed costs	Exhibit 8.18	$ 24,950
Net income	Exhibit 8.7	$ 6,894

of production cost. Not surprisingly, since service businesses are labor intensive, the largest component of C&F's product cost is salaries and wages. The materials used in performing services (for example, equipment rental, supplies, and fuel) generally are considered incidental charges (that is, direct materials). In C&F's case, these materials were quite minor and could easily be traced to specific jobs or clients. As is true for many manufacturing firms, C&F's depreciation is an example of indirect manufacturing or overhead costs.

The Flow of Product Costs in a Manufacturing Firm

Learning Objective 2
Describe the flow of production costs in a manufacturing firm.

Given the short-term nature of most service-oriented businesses, cost of services sold is almost certain to equal the cost of services produced in a given time period. Although it is possible for service contracts to span several months (auditing, consulting, and legal services frequently entail long-term engagements), fees for such engagements generally are billed periodically and matched against the costs that generate them in the period's income statement. C&F's 20X2 income statement (shown in Exhibits 8.7 and 10.2) provides an example of such a treatment.

Exhibit 10.3
Cost of Services Sold

C&F Enterprises, Inc.
Cost of Services Sold
For the Year Ended December 31, 20X2

Salaries and Wages Variable: $45,184 Fixed: $9,500	$54,684	Most salary costs relate to employee performance of actual lawn care services, making them *direct labor costs*. However, any of Keith and Dale's time devoted to general employee supervision on the job would be an *indirect labor cost* or *overhead*.
Rentals All variable costs	16,111	Any equipment lease or rental costs associated with a *specific* job or *type of* service would be a *direct materials cost* (for example, hydraulic lifts for tree trimming). Any rental charges that cannot be traced to a specific engagement or type of service would generally be considered *indirect materials costs* or *overhead*.
Supplies All variable costs	3,932	Since C&F customers currently supply most (if not all) of their own lawn-maintenance supplies, any minor supply costs (lubricating oil, trimming line, small hand tools, etc.) can easily be traced to the job for which they are needed. They represent *direct materials cost*.
Fuel All variable costs	1,768	Fuel consumed by mowers, trimmers, and weeders can be traced to specific jobs. Therefore, it is considered a *direct materials cost*.
Depreciation All fixed costs	600	Depreciation costs for lawn-maintenance equipment is an *overhead cost*.
Total	$77,095	

However, the flow of product costs in manufacturing firms is quite different. Unlike service companies, it is highly improbable that a manufacturing company will start, finish, and sell all of its production in one reporting period. Consequently, manufacturing companies use several balance sheet and income statement accounts to report costs associated with their production activities. The balance sheet accounts commonly include three inventory asset accounts: raw materials, work-in-process, and finished goods. **Raw materials inventory**

Exhibit 10.4
Product Cost Flow in a
Manufacturing Firm

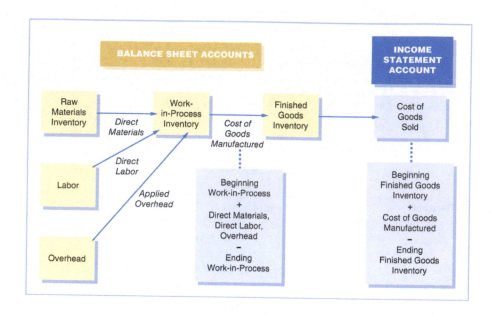

consists of the cost of materials that have been purchased but that have not yet entered the production process. Work-in-process inventory includes the costs of products that have entered the production process but that are not yet complete. The direct materials, direct labor, and overhead incurred so far in the production process for these units constitute their work-in-process cost. Finished goods inventory are those products that are complete and ready for sale. Included in this account are all the direct materials, direct labor, and overhead costs accumulated for completed units that have not yet been sold.

As direct materials are used in the manufacturing process, they decrease raw material inventory and work-in-process inventory increases. Work-in-process inventory also increases as direct labor is used in production. However, indirect materials and indirect labor are not directly added to work-in-process inventory. Instead, these two overhead costs are temporarily accumulated in a Manufacturing Overhead account with other overhead costs, which then are added to work-in-process inventory. Once a product is finished, its costs are transferred from work-in-process inventory (decrease) to finished goods inventory (increase).

The total cost of the finished goods completed during a reporting period is called the cost of goods manufactured for that period. Cost of goods manufactured can be easily computed using the following formula. It is equal to the work-in-process balance at the beginning of the reporting period, plus total manufacturing costs (direct materials, direct labor, and overhead) for the period, minus the work-in-process balance at the end of the reporting period.

When finished goods are ultimately sold, their cost is finally transferred from the balance sheet (where they appear as finished goods) to the income statement, where they appear as cost of goods sold. The formula for calculating cost of goods sold is similar to that for cost of goods manufactured. Cost of goods sold is equal to the finished goods inventory balance at the beginning of the reporting period, plus the cost of goods manufactured during the period, minus the finished goods

inventory balance at the end of the reporting period. Exhibit 10.4 illustrates the flow of product costs in a manufacturing firm.

Nonmanufacturing Costs

All costs not specifically related to the production of goods or the delivery of a service are referred to as nonmanufacturing costs. Such costs commonly are divided into two categories: selling costs and general and administrative costs.

Selling Costs. Selling costs consist of all costs incurred to find and attract customers, convince them to buy, store a product prior to its sale (if necessary), and transport it to the buyer. Such costs commonly include advertising and marketing costs, salaries for personnel directly involved in sales, depreciation on any equipment used by marketing personnel, and any finished product storage or shipping costs. As reported in Exhibit 10.2, C&F's actual 20X2 selling costs were $9,900 consisting of newspaper and online advertising and marketing services provided by a local consulting firm.

General and Administrative Costs. General and administrative costs include all costs that are neither product or service related nor selling costs. These costs generally are associated with the general management of a business and its support functions (they include accounting, finance, human resources, etc.) and consist of such items as administrative and clerical salaries, depreciation on office equipment, interest, and taxes. As reported in Exhibit 10.2, during 20X2 C&F reported $9,961 in general and administrative costs for bookkeeping ($3,250), interest ($200), taxes ($2,835), and other costs ($3,676).

C&F Enterprises, Inc.: Accumulating Service Costs by Type of Service

Keith and Dale began their product-costing exercise by preparing a schedule that matched revenues to their related service delivery costs. Using information from their 20X2 income statement, variance analyses, and segment performance reports, they prepared a summary of production costs by type of service. They were particularly careful to make sure that their schedule accounted for all reported costs and matched the income statement totals for both cost of services sold, gross profit, and net income. The schedule is illustrated below.

	References	Commercial	Residential	Other	Overhead	Total
Service revenue	Exhibit 8.8	$86,000	$12,600	$5,250	—	$103,850
Cost of services sold:						
Salaries and wages						
Variable	Exhibit 8.20	38,516	5,040	1,628	—	45,184
Fixed	Exhibits 9.3 & 9.4	4,500	2,000	1,000	2,000	9,500
		$43,016	$ 7,040	$2,628	$2,000	$ 54,684
Rentals						
Variable	Exhibit 8.20	12,647	2,520	944	—	16,111
Supplies						
Variable	Exhibit 8.20	3,449	378	105	—	3,932
Fuel						
Variable	Exhibit 8.20	1,376	265	127	—	1,768
Depreciation						
Fixed	Exhibit 9.4	—	—	—	$ 600	600
Cost of services sold	Exhibit 10.3					$ 77,095
Gross profit						$ 26,755
Nonmanufacturing costs:						
Selling						9,900
General & administrative						9,961
Net income	Exhibit 8.7					$ 6,894

Their most difficult task was determining which production costs were overhead. However, their prior work with costs (Exhibits 8.7 and 9.4) eventually helped them classify costs into overhead ($2,600), selling ($9,900), and general and administrative costs ($9,961).

With this schedule complete, Keith and Dale could easily separate their total service delivery costs of $77,095 into direct labor and direct materials for each service line, with overhead accounting for the balance. For commercial customers specifically, direct labor was $43,016 and direct materials totaled

Figure 10.4
**United Parcel Service (UPS)
ships over 18 million packages around the world each
day using a mix of ground
and air transportation. UPS
relies on activity-based
costing to evaluate the
profitability of its various
delivery services. Activity-
based costing allows UPS
to appropriately price its services, identify cost-reduction
opportunities, manage its
distribution centers, and
plan future operations.**

$17,472 (sum of rental, supplies, and fuel costs). Total overhead remaining to be allocated among the three service lines was $2,600: $2,000 in salaries and $600 in depreciation. Keith and Dale's next task was to assign the overhead to each service line and estimate how much it cost C&F to deliver commercial services to its customers.

Assigning Overhead to Product and Service Costs

Although tracing raw material and direct labor costs to products and services is a relatively straight-forward process, assigning the overhead incurred in creating goods and services is more complex. By definition, overhead costs cannot be directly traced to specific goods and services. Therefore, some method of assigning or allocating overhead to products and services is needed. Two such methods are traditional overhead allocation and activity-based costing.

Traditional Overhead Allocation

In traditional overhead allocation, overhead is allocated to products or services based on some characteristic that the products or services have in common. This common characteristic is known as the allocation base. Since this base is used to distribute overhead costs proportionately to each product made or service rendered, it should be strongly associated (that is, positively correlated) with overhead cost. In other words, increases (or decreases) in overhead cost should be accompanied by increases (or decreases) in the allocation base.

Learning Objective 3
Explain the traditional method of overhead allocation.

Historically, many manufacturing firms used direct labor hours or direct labor cost as an allocation base for overhead. This base was chosen because most production processes were very labor intensive prior to the dramatic technical innovations of the last quarter century. It simply made sense (and still does today) to use labor hours or direct labor cost to allocate overhead when large quantities of labor were used to create a product or deliver a service. However, as machines increasingly replace labor and production processes become more mechanized, the use of machine hours as an allocation base is gradually becoming more prevalent. Nevertheless, direct labor hours, direct labor cost (in dollars), direct materials cost (in dollars), and machine hours are the most common allocation bases used to allocate overhead.

Once an allocation base has been selected, an overhead allocation rate is used to assign overhead to a product or service.

$$\frac{\text{Overhead Cost}}{\text{Allocation Base}} = \text{Overhead Allocation Rate}$$

If a company incurred $100,000 of overhead cost in manufacturing its product and used 25,000 machine hours during the year in its production process, its overhead allocation rate would be $4 ($100,000 ÷ 25,000) per machine hour. Therefore, if a particular product or service required 200 machine hours, traditional overhead allocation would assign $800 in overhead cost (200 hours at $4 per hour) to the product or service.

C&F Enterprises, Inc.: Allocating Overhead Using the Traditional Method

After a quick call to their accountants, Keith and Dale decided to assign the entire $2,600 in overhead to their three service lines using direct labor cost as an allocation base since $2,000 of the overhead represented salaries related to employee supervision. Since C&F's total direct labor cost was $52,684 (total salaries and wages less $2,000 assigned to overhead), the overhead allocation rate would be 4.935 cents ($2,600 divided by $52,684) per direct labor dollar. Overhead could then be assigned to each service line based on the relative usage of direct labor. Using this approach, commercial lawn care services would be allocated $2,123 in overhead cost (.04935 times its $43,016 in direct labor cost).

Now, Keith and Dale were ready to calculate the total amount it cost C&F to deliver commercial lawn care services during 20X2. When the previous totals for direct labor of $43,016 and direct materials of $17,472 (sum of rental, supplies, and fuel costs) were added to the overhead allocation of $2,123, the total cost of delivering commercial lawn care services in 20X2 was computed to be $62,611. This meant that C&F earned a gross profit of $23,389 (revenues of $86,000 less related costs of $62,611) on its commercial services line. This translated into a commercial gross profit percentage of 27.2 percent ($23,389 divided by $86,000).

Activity-Based Costing

Although some overhead costs may relate to a single allocation base, it is quite likely that many do not. In fact, overhead costs generally result from many activities, and the activity that drives one overhead cost (for example, indirect labor) may be completely different from the activity that affects another cost (for example, indirect materials). Therefore, using the traditional overhead allocation approach with its reliance on a single base will probably result in some products being overcosted and others being undercosted.

Recently, activity-based costing has been suggested as a possible solution to the single-allocation-base dilemma. **Activity-based costing (ABC)** allocates overhead to products or services based on the activities that cause the overhead cost. Unlike the traditional approach that relies on single allocation base to assign all overhead costs (that is, uses a single cost pool), ABC assigns the overhead costs of major production or service activities to multiple cost pools. Next, multiple overhead allocation rates are computed by dividing the amount in each cost pool by a measure of the activity that "drives" the overhead cost in each pool. This measure is called a **cost driver**. Overhead is then assigned to a product or service based on how much of each activity (or cost driver) it caused. Exhibit 10.5 summarizes several common manufacturing activities that produce overhead and their related cost drivers.

Exhibit 10.6 highlights the principal difference between traditional overhead allocation and activity-based costing. Assume that a company incurs total overhead costs of $702,500. The traditional approach accumulates total overhead costs in six financial statement accounts (salaries, technology, depreciation, repairs and maintenance, utilities, and supplies). These are then allocated to products or services using a single allocation base. In this case, total overhead of $702,500 would simply be allocated to a product or service using a single cost driver, such as direct labor hours or cost, direct materials cost, or machine hours.

In contrast, ABC assigns the total overhead to the *activities* that generated the overhead. In this example, the $702,500 in overhead was caused by six different activities: purchasing, setup, special orders, tooling design, training, and quality testing. Next, the overhead assigned to each activity is allocated to a product or service using allocation rates based on that activity's cost driver. Exhibit 10.7 illustrates this process.

Once a cost driver for each activity is identified, allocation rates for each overhead-producing activity can easily be computed by dividing the activity's overhead by the total activity for the related cost driver. Note that the cost drivers represent process activities that actually "cause" the overhead cost to increase or decrease in a given activity. Exhibit 10.7 lists the allocation rates for each of the six activities, which then are used to allocate total overhead to a single product or service (Product X). The final overhead allocation under both the traditional and ABC methods is compared in Exhibit 10.8.

When the allocation rates computed in Exhibit 10.7 are multiplied by each of the actual activity units (that is, the number of orders, etc.) used by Product X in Exhibit 10.8, the result is the amount of overhead incurred by the product

Learning Objective 4
Illustrate how activity-based costing is used in assigning overhead.

Exhibit 10.5
Production Activities,
Related Overhead, and
Cost Drivers

Activity	Overhead Cost	Cost Driver
Purchasing of materials and supplies	Indirect labor associated with processing of purchase orders	Number of orders
Material handling	Indirect labor and equipment-related expenses (depreciation, maintenance, rent, etc.)	Number of material requests
Material inspection	Indirect labor and equipment-related expenses (depreciation, maintenance, rent, etc.)	Number of inspections
Equipment setup	Indirect labor and equipment-related expenses (depreciation, maintenance, rent, etc.)	Number of setups
Automated production	Equipment-related expenses (depreciation, maintenance, rent, etc.)	Machine hours or number of production runs
Quality control and testing	Indirect labor and equipment-related expenses (depreciation, maintenance, rent, etc.)	Number of components tested or number of inspections
Customer order processing	Indirect labor for coordinating delivery, invoicing, and collection.	Number of customer orders
Shipping and delivery	Costs of shipping products to customers (UPS, overnight priority, etc.)	Number of shipments or pounds of products shipped
Facility security	Indirect labor and equipment-related expenses (depreciation, maintenance, rent, etc.)	Direct labor hours or direct labor cost

Exhibit 10.6
Traditional vs. ABC View of
Overhead Cost

Costs	Traditional View	Activities	ABC View
Salaries	$500,000	Purchasing	$132,500
Technology	125,000	Machine setup	125,000
Depreciation	30,000	Special orders	77,500
Repairs and maintenance	25,000	Tooling design	200,000
Utilities	17,500	Training	47,500
Supplies	5,000	Quality testing	120,000
Total overhead	$702,500	Total overhead	$702,500

Exhibit 10.7
Allocating Overhead Costs to Activities

Activities	ABC View	Cost Driver	Total Activity	Allocation Rates per Cost Driver	
Purchasing	$132,500	Number of orders	10,000	$13.2500	per order
Machine setup	125,000	Number of setups	5,000	25.0000	per setup
Special orders	77,500	Number of orders	800	96.8750	per order
Tooling design	200,000	Machine hours	100,000	2.0000	per hour
Training	47,500	Direct labor dollars	2,000,000	0.0238	per labor dollar
Quality testing	120,000	Number of inspections	4,000	30.0000	per inspection
Total overhead	$702,500				

Exhibit 10.8
Allocating Overhead: ABC vs. Traditional Method

ABC Allocation Approach			
Cost Driver	Product X Activity	Allocation Rates* (Exhibit 10.7)	Allocated Overhead
Number of orders (Purchases)	2,000	$13.2500	$ 26,500
Number of setups	250	$25.0000	6,250
Number of orders (special)	100	$96.8750	9,688
Machine hours	25,000	$ 2.0000	50,000
Direct labor dollars	$100,000	0.0238	2,375
Number of inspections	250	$30.0000	7,500
Total overhead for Product X			$102,313

Traditional Allocation Approach			
Single Cost Pool	Product X Activity	Allocation Rates	Allocated Overhead
$702,500	$100,000	5.0000%	$ 35,125

*Rates have been rounded to four decimals.

for each activity. When the six allocated overhead amounts are summed, they yield $102,313, the total overhead for the product under an activity-based costing approach. How would this compare with the traditional method?

Assume that direct labor dollars were believed to be an appropriate allocation base. Since all production processes used direct labor costing $2 million (see Exhibit 10.7), the current product only accounted for 5 percent of total direct labor dollars ($100,000 divided by $2,000,000). Therefore, when the traditional allocation rate of 5 percent is applied to total overhead costs of $702,500, the product is assigned only $35,125 in overhead using the traditional approach.

Analyzing the Differences: ABC vs. Traditional Overhead Allocation

How could the results for ABC and the traditional approach be so different? The reason that ABC allocates a much larger amount of overhead to the product is quite simple. In using direct labor cost as an allocation base, the traditional approach assumed that labor played a major role in the manufacture of the product being analyzed. However, this was not case. Exhibits 10.7 and 10.8 reveal that the item's production process was very automated and actually consumed 25,000 machine hours, 25 percent of those used by all production activities. Given this automation, little physical labor was required in the product's manufacture, and total direct labor cost for this product was only 5 percent of the labor used by all production activities. Since direct labor cost played such a minor role in production, using it as an allocation base resulted in an *underallocation* of overhead.

Would the traditional approach have performed better if machine hours had been used as the allocation base? Under this scenario, the product would have been allocated 25 percent (25,000 product machine hours divided by 100,000 total machine hours) of the total overhead, or $175,625. Therefore, using just machine hours, while dramatically increasing the allocation, would have resulted in an *overallocation* of overhead to the product. This example highlights the importance of tracing overhead costs to the various activities that cause them to be incurred.

ABC or Traditional Overhead Allocation: Which to Use?

As illustrated by the preceding example, using the traditional overhead allocation approach with its single allocation base can result in *either* the under- or over-allocation of overhead to a product or service. The weaknesses of the traditional method are most glaring in complex products or services whose manufacturing and delivery processes include a wide variety of activities. For such products, ABC may be more accurate because it uses more cost drivers to allocate overhead. ABC also can help managers control costs better since they view costs by activity rather in a single cost pool.

However, for a relatively simple product or service whose manufacturing process consists of few activities, like the landscaping service that C&F Enterprises Inc. offers, the traditional costing system may continue to be useful. A major advantage of the traditional approach is its simplicity, which translates into a lower cost of implementation. In fact, a major disadvantage of ABC is its expense, a direct result of having to gather, analyze, and allocate data over numerous production activities.

Types of Costing Systems

Product and service cost information is critical when making pricing and sales decisions. To successfully plan and control such costs, managers must understand how specific value chain production activities transform human capital (that is, labor) and physical capital (that is, materials) into products and services. In fact, this is a major theme of Chapter 2. In order to measure and record the cost of the products or services produced, companies commonly use one of two costing systems: job order costing or process costing. Deciding which system to use depends on whether the goods or services produced consume similar enough amounts of resources (direct materials, labor, and overhead) that an average cost per unit would accurately reflect the product or service's cost. If so, process costing should be used. Conversely, if the units produced or services delivered consume very different amounts of resources, an average cost per unit is probably meaningless, and job order costing should be used.

Learning Objective 5
Discuss two systems used to measure the cost of products or services.

Job Order Costing

A job order costing system accumulates manufacturing or service costs for each job performed, each unit produced, each order received, or simply each product or service. The method generally is used when a company produces goods or delivers services to a customer's unique requirements. Job order systems commonly are used by construction companies, airplane and ship builders, and custom furniture manufacturers. When this method is used, managers monitor each job's material, labor, and overhead by tracking the costs accumulated for each job. When the job's units or items are completed and sold, managers can determine the job's gross profit by matching its cost with the revenue it produced.

Process Costing

In a process costing system costs are accumulated by each operation, rather than by each job, with the unit cost of items determined by dividing the operation's total production costs for a process by the number of identical items produced. This method is commonly used by manufacturers whose products are subjected to a uniform set of operations. Examples of such products include metals, chemicals, paints, and plastics.

$$\frac{\text{Total Production Cost}}{\text{Number of Units Produced}} = \text{Average Cost per Unit}$$

When products or services produced are very similar, there is little need to trace costs to specific jobs or items produced. Assigning each unit produced an average cost of production is more than adequate for such products or services.

Unfortunately, the above formula does not consider that some units may be only partially complete (that is, they may still be work-in-process) at the end of a reporting period. If units in work-in-process inventory are included in the denominator, the average cost per unit will be understated. If they are excluded from the denominator, the average cost will be overstated. Therefore, partially completed units must be converted to a comparable number of completed units. These are called equivalent units of production. For example, if 200 units of a particular product are 20 percent complete at the end of a reporting period, then they are equivalent to 40 completed units (200×20 percent). Consequently, the average unit cost in a process costing system is referred to as the cost per equivalent unit, and is computed using the following formula:

$$\frac{\text{Cost in Beginning Work-in-Process Inventory} + \text{Current Period Total Manufacturing Cost}}{\text{Units Completed} + \text{Equivalent Units in Ending Work-in-Process Inventory}} = \frac{\text{Cost per}}{\text{Equivalent Unit}}$$

The numerator consists of the total production cost for which a processing department is responsible during the reporting period. The denominator represents the number of units for which those production costs were incurred. Actually determining the cost per equivalent unit in a process costing system can be quite complex in practice; more advanced cost accounting courses address this subject.

C&F Enterprises, Inc.: The Process vs. Job Order Costing Debate

Despite the healthy 27.2 gross profit percentage earned in 20X2 on the commercial business line, C&F's two owners soon were at odds over how to calculate the cost of servicing Jim McGill's auto dealership. Dale argued that the commercial jobs were all similar enough that one simply needed to divide the total cost of commercial services ($62,611) by the total number of service engagements (344), as shown in Exhibit 8.10, to determine Jim McGill's cost. Keith, on the other hand, believed that McGill's job was *not* the same as all the others, but unique on a number of dimensions. Specifically, Keith believed less labor was used on the dealership because the property had fewer obstacles (utility poles, trees, and so on) than most of their other commercial clients. This made mowing and trimming much easier and less time-consuming. In addition, the auto dealership had on-site fueling capability and frequently offered C&F free fuel for their mowers and trimmers. Finally, McGill's job did not require any special rental equipment. Given these factors, Keith believed that the dealership's individual job costs should be lower than that of the "average" commercial client. Their debate resulted in yet another call to their accounting advisors.

The accountants informed them that they were engaging in a classic process-costing-versus-job-order-costing debate. They advised the two to first compute the

Management Accounting: A Business Planning Approach

unit cost of delivering the service using Dale's approach (process costing). Although this unit cost likely would be overstated (given the issues raised by Keith), it could provide a useful benchmark when performing a more detailed job order analysis later. Dale quickly computed the average cost of each commercial job under the process costing method. This approach yielded an average servicing cost of $182.01 as illustrated.

	Commercial
Direct labor	$43,016
Direct materials	17,472
Allocated overhead	2,123
Total cost of services sold	$62,611
Actual customer demand (Exhibit 8.10)	344
Average cost per job	$182.01
Avg. direct labor per job	$125.05
Avg. direct materials per job	50.79
Avg. overhead per job	6.17
	$182.01

After thumbing through 20X2's employee time sheets for the commercial jobs performed, Keith was more convinced than ever that the process costing approach overestimated the cost of doing Jim McGill's work. In fact, Keith found, that "on average," the dealership required only 75 percent of the labor and materials needed for most of the other commercial engagements. However, he did note that the amount of supervision remained relatively constant regardless of the commercial job. Given these developments, Keith recomputed the dealership's unit cost of service to be $138.05. This revised cost was based on direct labor of $93.78 (75 percent of $125.05), direct materials of $38.09 (75 percent of $50.79), and allocated overhead of $6.17 (same as under process costing). Dale was stunned to see that his approach had overestimated the dealership's service costs by $43.96 or 31.84 percent ($43.96 divided by $138.05). The job costing results indicated that C&F had been earning a much higher percentage of gross profit on the dealership (44.8 percent based on unit revenues of $250) than on its other clients. Clearly, Keith and Dale had room to lower the price they had been charging Jim McGill. But by how much should they lower it?

As illustrated below, if they lower their price by 30 percent to match TLC's rate of $175 per cutting, C&F's gross profit margin would fall below the 27.2 percent recognized for commercial clients as a whole. Equally troubling is the kind of message such a price reduction might send to Jim McGill and the rest of C&F's commercial customers.

Service price	$250.00	$190.00	$175.00
Estimated job cost	138.05	138.05	138.05
Gross profit	$111.95	$ 51.95	$ 36.95
Gross profit percentage	44.78%	27.34%	21.11%

After looking at the numbers, Keith and Dale decided to drop the price they charged the dealership to $190. This rate would provide C&F a gross profit margin that approximates that for the service line as a whole. Equally important, it would signal to the market that C&F was not going to engage in vicious price competition that completely disregarded the quality of the service rendered.

Keith and Dale drove over to Jim McGill's dealership to deliver their bid. They explained that their proposed rate was based on the dealership continuing to provide free fuel as well as the assumption that no major obstacles to cutting and mowing would be constructed on the property to be serviced. The two entrepreneurs also emphasized their commitment to high quality and timely customer service. They concluded by pointing out that their new price would save the dealership $1,500 per year based on an estimated 25 cuttings per year. A broad smile crept across Jim McGill's face as he said, "You boys have got a deal!"

As they left the dealership, Keith asked Dale if he thought they needed to revisit the prices C&F was charging their other commercial customers. Dale thought that was probably a good idea because if they had been overcharging Jim Murphy, then they must have been undercharging one or more of their other commercial customers. Keith agreed and suggested they start with those clients that required special equipment rentals. As they drove off to celebrate the retention of one of their major commercial customers, Keith and Dale could not help but appreciate how much they had learned in the past few years about the importance of management accounting information to good business decision-making.

Management Accounting: A Business Planning Approach

Summary

Understanding how much a particular product or service costs is critical to managing profitability. Although aggregate budget and segment data is useful in assessing operating performance, detailed product or service cost data can provide significant insights into whether value chain activities are operating as intended and resources are being allocated as planned. Companies generally use one of two systems to accumulate product or service cost data: job order costing or process costing. Manufacturing costs include direct materials and direct labor, as well as indirect production costs called overhead. How overhead is assigned to a product or service can dramatically impact the product's total cost. Many firms use the traditional method of allocation and assign overhead using a single base (direct labor cost, direct labor hours, direct materials cost, machine hours, and the like). Increasingly, however, companies have recognized the benefits of assigning overhead based on the activity that causes it; these companies have adopted the activity-based costing method of overhead allocation. The costing techniques introduced in this chapter complete the inventory of fundamental management accounting tools you will need to complete your remaining business education.

Summary of Learning Objectives

1. **Identify the types of costs firms incur when producing goods or services.** Firms that produce goods and services commonly incur three types of manufacturing costs: direct labor, direct materials, and overhead. Direct labor and direct materials are the human and physical resources whose use can be directly traced to the production of an item or delivery of a service. Since direct materials and direct labor represent the primary costs of production or service delivery, they frequently are referred to as prime costs. Overhead includes other indirect costs of production not directly traceable to a product or service.

2. **Describe the flow of production costs in a manufacturing firm.** As a manufacturing firm begins the production process, it acquires raw materials inventory. To these resources, direct labor and overhead are applied to create work-in-process inventory. When the production process is complete, the work-in-process items become finished goods inventory. The total cost of the items produced in a fiscal period is referred to as the cost of goods manufactured. The cost of any finished goods inventory actually sold in a fiscal period is called the cost of goods sold. The cost of goods manufactured will only equal the cost of goods sold when all of the items produced in a fiscal period are sold in the same period, a situation more common for service companies that manufacturers.

3. **Explain the traditional method of overhead allocation.** Traditional overhead allocation assigns overhead to products or services based on some

characteristic that the products or services have in common (that is the allocation base). Since the allocation base is used to proportionately distribute overhead costs to each product made or service rendered, it should be strongly associated with overhead cost. Direct labor hours, direct labor cost (in dollars), direct materials cost (in dollars), and machine hours are the most common allocation bases used to allocate overhead using the traditional method.

4. **Illustrate how activity-based costing is used in assigning overhead.** Activity-based costing (ABC) allocates overhead to products or services based on the activities that cause the overhead cost. Unlike the traditional approach that relies on single allocation base to assign all overhead costs (that is, using a single cost pool), ABC assigns the overhead costs of major production or service activities to multiple cost pools. Next, multiple overhead allocation rates are computed by dividing the amount in each cost pool by a measure of the activity that "drives" the overhead cost in each pool. Overhead is then assigned to a product or service based on how much of each activity it caused.

5. **Discuss two systems used to measure the cost of products or services.** Companies commonly use one of two systems to measure and record the cost of products or services produced: job order costing or process costing. A job order costing system accumulates manufacturing or service costs for each job performed, each unit produced, each order received, or simply each product or service. The method generally is used when a company delivers goods or services to a customer's unique requirements. In a process costing system costs are accumulated by each operation, rather than by each job, with the unit cost of items determined by dividing the operation's total production costs by the number of identical items produced. This method is commonly used by manufacturers whose products are subjected to a uniform set of operations.

Glossary of Terms

Activity-based costing (ABC) An overhead allocation approach that allocates overhead to products or services based on the activities that cause the overhead cost.

Allocation base The common characteristic shared by products or services that is used to assign overhead.

Applied overhead Manufacturing overhead costs that are specifically assigned to products or services.

Conversion costs A term used to describe the sum of direct labor and manufacturing overhead.

Cost driver The measure of an activity that causes or "drives" the overhead cost in a given cost pool.

Cost of goods manufactured The total cost of finished goods completed during a reporting period.

Cost of goods sold The total production cost of finished goods that are sold and reported in the income statement.

Direct labor costs The labor cost that can be directly traced to items produced or services delivered.

Direct materials cost The cost of all materials that can be traced directly to a manufactured product or delivered service.

Equivalent units of production The number of units that could have been completed if they had been worked on from start to finish.

Finished goods inventory The inventory of products that are complete and ready for sale. Included in this account are all the direct materials, direct labor, and overhead costs accumulated for completed units that have not yet been sold.

General and administrative costs Costs that are neither product- or service-related nor selling costs.

Indirect labor costs Any production or service delivery labor costs that cannot be directly traced to a particular product or service.

Indirect materials Any materials that cannot be directly traced or that are not applicable to a single product or service.

Job order costing system A costing system that accumulates manufacturing or service costs for each job performed, each unit produced, each order received, or simply each product or service.

Manufacturing costs The costs incurred in producing goods and delivering services, including direct materials, direct labor, and overhead.

Manufacturing firm A company that converts raw materials into finished goods that are then sold to customers.

Manufacturing overhead Any costs other than direct materials and direct labor that a company incurs in the manufacture of a product or delivery of a service.

Merchandising firm A company that buys completed inventory items from suppliers that it then sells to customers.

Nonmanufacturing costs All costs incurred by a business not specifically related to the production of goods or the delivery of a service.

Prime costs A term used to describe the sum of direct materials and direct labor used in the manufacturing or service delivery process.

Process costing system A costing system that accumulates costs by each operation, rather than by each job, with the unit cost of items determined by dividing the operation's total production costs for a process by the number of identical items produced.

Raw materials inventory Inventory consisting of the cost of materials that have been purchased, but which have not yet entered the production process.

Selling costs All costs incurred to find and attract customers, convince them to buy, store a product prior to its sale (if necessary), and transport it to the buyer.

Traditional overhead allocation An overhead allocation method that assigns overhead to products or services based on some characteristic that the products or services have in common.

Work-in-process inventory Inventory consisting of the costs of products that have entered the production process but that are not yet complete.

Chapter Review Questions

1. Explain how a merchandising firm does business.
2. How does a merchandising firm determine its product costs?
3. Explain how a manufacturing firm does business. Is product costing in a manufacturing company easier or more difficult than in a merchandising enterprise? Justify your answer.
4. Name the three types of costs manufacturers incur when producing goods and services.
5. What is meant by direct materials cost? Provide several specific examples for both a manufacturing firm and a service enterprise.
6. Define indirect materials cost. Provide several specific examples for both a manufacturing firm and a service enterprise.
7. What is meant by direct labor cost? Provide several specific examples for both a manufacturing firm and a service enterprise.
8. Define indirect labor cost. Provide several specific examples for both a manufacturing firm and a service enterprise.
9. What are prime costs?
10. What is meant by manufacturing overhead? Provide several specific examples for both a manufacturing firm and a service enterprise.
11. What three balance sheet accounts do manufacturing firms use to record their inventory assets?
12. What types of costs are included in raw materials inventory?
13. What types of costs are included work-in-process inventory?
14. What types of costs are included in finished goods inventory?
15. How does cost of goods manufactured differ from cost of goods sold? How is each computed?
16. Describe the flow of product costs in a manufacturing firm.
17. What is meant by nonmanufacturing costs? List the two major categories of such costs.
18. What are selling costs? Provide several examples.
19. What are general and administrative costs? Provide several examples.
20. How is overhead assigned to products or services when the traditional method of overhead allocation is used?
21. What is an allocation base? How is it used?
22. What is activity-based costing? How does it differ from the traditional method of overhead allocation?
23. What is a cost driver? How does it affect overhead allocation when using activity-based costing?
24. Under what conditions is the traditional method of overhead allocation likely to perform as well as activity-based costing?
25. Under what conditions will activity-based costing result in a more accurate allocation of overhead than the traditional method?

Management Accounting: A Business Planning Approach

26. What two information systems are commonly used to measure and record the cost of products or services produced? Under what conditions is it appropriate to use each of these?
27. What is job order costing? When is it normally used? Which industries commonly use this system?
28. What is process costing? When is it normally used? Which industries commonly use this system?
29. What is meant by equivalent units of production? Why is this concept important?
30. Define cost per equivalent unit. What system of costing relies on this concept?

Exercises and Problems

1. Several costs commonly incurred by manufacturing companies are listed. For each of the costs, indicate what type of manufacturing cost (direct labor, direct materials, or overhead) or nonmanufacturing cost (selling or general and administrative cost) the particular cost is.
   a. Materials used in production
   b. Supplies used in sales activities
   c. Supplies used in production
   d. Alarm company charges for a production facility
   e. Security guards hired for grand opening event for new plant
   f. Wages paid to employees involved in production process
2. Several costs commonly incurred by manufacturing companies are listed. For each of the costs, indicate what type of manufacturing cost (direct labor, direct materials, or overhead) or nonmanufacturing cost (selling or general and administrative cost) the particular cost is.
   a. Depreciation on the accounting department's Xerox machine
   b. Depreciation on plant supervisor's Xerox machine
   c. Automobile rental charges incurred by marketing personnel
   d. Production supervisor salaries
   e. Production equipment rental costs
   f. Senior executive salaries
   g. Overtime wages paid to the company president's secretary
3. Several costs commonly incurred by manufacturing companies are listed. For each of the costs, indicate what type of manufacturing cost (direct labor, direct materials, or overhead) or nonmanufacturing cost (selling or general and administrative cost) the particular cost is.
   a. Health insurance costs for plant security guards
   b. Roof repairs on an executive office building
   c. Depreciation on equipment used in the production process
   d. Payroll taxes for production plant workers
   e. Factory insurance charges
   f. Cost of mobile phones used by sales personnel
   g. Property taxes on a production facility

4. For each of the products listed, indicate whether a job order costing system or a process costing system would be most appropriate. Explain your answer.
   a. Container cargo ship
   b. Can of beer, cola, or other beverage type
   c. Commercial airliner
   d. Toothpaste
   e. Advertising campaign
   f. Antibiotic medicine
   g. Commercial office building
   h. Manufactured home builder

5. For each of the products listed, indicate whether a job order costing system or a process costing system would be most appropriate. Explain your answer.
   a. Fuel oil
   b. Wedding invitations
   c. Dog food
   d. Custom window molding
   e. Billboard advertising
   f. Bread
   g. Laptop computer or tablet
   h. New hotel construction

6. H&R Manufacturing Corporation provided the following cost data for its most recent fiscal year end. The company manufactured 100,000 units of its product during the past fiscal year.

Beginning work-in-process inventory	$ 70,000
Ending work-in-process inventory	90,000
Beginning finished goods inventory	124,000
Ending finished goods inventory	100,000
Total manufacturing costs	700,000

   a. Compute the cost of goods manufactured during the year
   b. Compute the cost of goods sold for the year
   c. Why are your answers to questions (a) and (b) different?

7. Joshua Manufacturing Corporation provided the following cost data for its most recent fiscal year end. The company manufactured 75,000 units of its product during the past fiscal year.

Beginning direct materials inventory	$ 48,000
Ending direct materials inventory	54,000
Beginning work-in-process inventory	90,000
Ending work-in-process inventory	99,000
Beginning finished goods inventory	124,000
Ending finished goods inventory	139,000
Direct materials purchased	856,000
Indirect materials used in production	10,000
Supplies used in the manufacturing process	13,000
Plant facility depreciation	70,000

Depreciation on sales office	11,000
Depreciation on executive office building	25,000
Salaries for marketing personnel	100,000
Labor costs for production personnel	900,000
Plant facility security costs	25,000
Depreciation on production equipment	450,000
Depreciation on office equipment	32,000

Required: Compute the following amounts.
a. Cost of direct materials used during the year
b. Cost of direct labor used during the year
c. Cost of manufacturing overhead incurred during the year
d. Total manufacturing cost incurred during the year
e. Cost of goods manufactured during the year
f. Cost of goods sold for the year

8. Quick File tax preparation service began its operations on January 1. Quick File specializes in preparing personal income tax returns. Quick File's owner is very concerned about covering all costs and making a reasonable profit. During its first year of operations, the company prepared 450 individual income tax returns. Its information system contained the following additional data as of December 31.

Tax preparation service revenue	$100,000
Salaries paid to tax return preparers	50,000
Office rent	15,000
Depreciation on equipment used in preparing tax returns	2,500
Supplies used in preparing returns	850
Advertising	1,000
Receptionist salary	12,000

Required: Answer each of the following questions.
a. What is the total cost of the tax services provided?
b. What average cost did Quick File incur for each individual tax return that it prepared during the year?
c. What was Quick File's net income for the year? Did it differ from the cost of services provided? If so, why?
d. What information would you recommend that Quick File collect to better manage costs and more accurately bill its clients? How would this information ensure that costs are covered and profitability achieved?

9. The president of Brooklyn Brewers forecasts the company will incur $1,000,000 of manufacturing overhead in the coming year. The company also expects the following results for its operations in the coming year:

Direct labor hours	100,000
Direct labor cost	$2,000,000
Machine hours	20,000

Compute overhead allocation rates based on the following bases:
a. Direct labor hours
b. Direct labor dollars
c. Machine hours
d. If the company decides to use direct labor hours as it basis for overhead allocation, how much overhead would be allocated to a product that requires 25,000 hours of direct labor?

10. Custom Computers reported the following data for its most recent fiscal year's manufacturing operations:

Direct labor hours	40,000
Direct labor cost	$500,000
Machine hours	30,000
Material cost	$800,000
Manufacturing overhead	$600,000

Required: Complete each of the following requirements.
a. Compute overhead allocation rates using each of the four potential allocation bases provided.
b. One of Custom Computers' custom jobs uses $5,000 of direct materials, $3,000 of direct labor (150 hours at $20 per hour), and 200 machine hours. Calculate the total cost of this job using each of the overhead rates.

11. Melbourne Industries reported the following data about its production process for the current month

Cost of beginning work-in-process	$ 60,000
Total manufacturing cost	$700,000
Units completed	30,000
Units-in-process (40% complete)	20,000

a. Compute the equivalent units of production for the month.
b. Compute the average cost per unit.

12. Tropical Delights Canned Fruit Company reported the following data about its production process for the current month:

Cost of beginning work-in-process	$ 200,000
Total manufacturing cost	$1,000,000
Units completed	1,000,000
Units-in-process (50% complete)	200,000

a. Compute the equivalent units of production for the month.
b. Compute the average cost per unit.

13. Paradise Professional Services, a local accounting and consulting firm, employs 10 full-time professionals (certified public or management accountants) as well as 20 noncertified associates. Each CPA and CMA earns an average of $90,000, while each associate is paid $35,000. Indirect (or

overhead) costs total $320,000 and consist of such items as rent, secretarial support, temporary help, and copying. The firm traces the cost of each professional and associate to each client and uses total salaries to assign overhead.
Required: Answer each of the following questions.
a. How much overhead would be allocated to a client that required $20,000 of professional cost and $10,000 associate cost?
b. How much would you bill this client if you wanted to cover your costs and earn a 150-percent profit?

14. Cellcom Communications Products uses the same machinery to produce multiple products. Given the technological nature of these products, the company periodically modifies the products to meet market expectations. Engineering costs incurred to make these product changes total $260,000 per year. Each production run also requires a unique setup for each product. Total setup charges of $520,000 are included in manufacturing overhead. Total overhead for the company including setup and engineering changes is $1,750,000. During the year, 70,000 direct labor hours were used. The following additional information was found in the company's records.

	Product A	All Other Products
Units produced	1,000	100,000
Direct materials cost	$240,000	$2,400,000
Direct labor cost	$ 36,000	$ 480,000
Machine hours used	6,000	800,000
Direct labor hours used	3,000	67,000
Number of engineering changes per year	6	24
Number of production setups	50	120

Required: Complete each of the following requirements.
a. Calculate the cost of Product A using the traditional method of overhead allocation. Estimate the product's cost using each of the following four possible allocation bases: direct materials cost, direct labor cost, machine hours, and direct labor hours.
b. Calculate the cost of Product A using activity-based costing. Use machine hours to allocate any overhead not identified with a specific activity.
c. How does the cost of Product A under the traditional allocation method differ from that computed using activity-based costing? Using the data provided in this problem, explain why this difference occurs?
d. Write a short memo explaining why you believe activity-based costing would or would not help this company.

Keystone Academy (Part 3)

In Chapters 4 and 5, two mini-cases introduced you to Keystone Academy, a private college preparatory school serving grades 9 through 12. In Chapter 4, you were asked to identify activities and related cost drivers for nine separate costs. In Chapter 5, you were asked to evaluate these same costs to determine whether their behavior was fixed, variable, or mixed. The school superintendent is now interested in how each cost contributes to the cost of educating the academy's students.

Required:

1. For each item listed below, specify whether the costs associated with each activity represent direct labor, direct materials, or overhead costs of teaching students.
   a. Wages and fringe benefits for the academy's administrative staff.
   b. Academic materials (e.g., books and laptop computers) provided to students by the academy at no charge.
   c. Wages and fringe benefits for the academy's full-time faculty.
   d. Repairs to student laptop computers.
   e. Fee charged by a local public accounting firm to audit the academy's financial records.
   f. Wages for the school's part-time athletic coaches (baseball, football, basketball, tennis, and ice hockey). These coaches are hired on a temporary basis.
   g. Depreciation on the academy's recently completed performing arts pavilion.
   h. Rent for the buses the academy uses to transport its students to and from school.
   i. Electricity to operate the academy's facilities.
2. Based on your knowledge of Keystone's operations, would you expect the academy to use job order costing or process costing to monitor its cost of serving students? Explain your answer fully.
3. Based on your knowledge of Keystone's operations, would you advise the academy to use the traditional method of overhead allocation or activity-based costing to assign overhead to its cost of serving students? Explain your answer fully.

University Backpacks (Part 3)

In Chapter 8, the University Backpacks mini-cases (Parts 1 and 2) place you in the role of owner of a start-up company that sells backpacks to local university students. These mini-cases required you display your knowledge of contribution margin analysis and flexible budgeting. Since the budget for your second year of operations (Part 2) continues to show an operating loss, you decided to investigate the relative profitability of each of University Backpacks' products (the large computer storage backpack and the regular storage backpack). Use the cost data provided in the first-year budget in Part 2 of the Mini-Case to complete the following requirements.

Required:

1. For each of the variable and fixed costs and other expenses listed in the first-year budget:
   a. Specify whether the cost is a manufacturing or nonmanufacturing cost.
   b. If a manufacturing cost, specify whether it represents direct labor, direct materials, or overhead.
   c. If a nonmanufacturing cost, specify whether it is selling or general and administrative.
2. Assume that the total fixed costs of $35,300 are overhead. Allocate this amount to each product using each of the following methods: direct labor cost and direct materials cost.
3. Given the nature of University Backpacks' business, which of these allocation bases would you recommend for allocating overhead between the two products sold? Explain your answer fully.
4. Calculate the gross profit percentage for each product under both overhead allocation scenarios (direct labor cost and direct materials cost). Does this analysis provide any insight into the preferred allocation base or possible reasons why the business continues to lose money?
5. Given what you know about the company's business, do you think activity-based costing would offer any advantage over the traditional method in assigning costs? Explain your answer fully.

Analyzing Planned Product and Service Costs

Just as readers of business plans use sensitivity and ratio analysis to evaluate the credibility of a budget (see Chapter 8), they frequently also like to see what each product or service that is being offered will contribute to the bottom line. Specifically, investors may wish to know the gross profit percentage that each product or service line will earn for the business.

To compute this percentage, however, a company must know what each of its products or services costs. Using the tools and techniques described in this chapter, estimate the unit cost of each product or service that your start-up company sells or delivers to its customers. Prepare a detailed product or service cost schedule for the next twelve-month operating period. Your schedule should include the following features:

1. Separates each product or service cost into one of five categories: direct labor, direct materials, overhead, selling, and general and administrative costs.
2. Discusses which costing system is most appropriate for your start-up business (job order or process costing).
3. Assigns overhead using a method of overhead allocation appropriate for the business, given the nature and complexity of its operations. You must fully justify the method selected.
4. Calculates the gross profit percentage for each product or service offered based on its estimated selling price.
5. Evaluates the appropriateness of each gross profit percentage given the company's mission and business strategy.

Be sure that all of the costs reflected in your budgeted income statements are captured in the costing analysis performed above. After completing your analysis, you again may wish to compare its results to industry benchmarks for your business. Explain in detail why the profitability of your product or service differs from the industry. Preparing such a cost analysis will not only provide you with key insights about the product or service you intend to deliver, but it also will provide potential investors with confidence in your ability to manage the business.

Image Credits

Appendix

Preparing and Presenting the Business Plan

This textbook introduces a variety of management accounting topics in a business planning context. The Business Planning Application in each chapter encourages the use of management accounting tools and techniques to create a realistic, market-quality business plan. This simulation personalizes the value of management accounting information throughout a company's operations and at the same time prepares you for subsequent courses in the business curriculum. This appendix summarizes and expands on the business planning processes discussed in the text chapters. It concludes with a detailed business plan checklist and business plan presentation guidelines.

Preparing a Business Plan

As we learned in Chapter 1, a business plan is a formal document that describes how a company intends to compete. As such it details the resources that a company requires to execute its strategy. A good business plan provides managers and employees with a clear understanding of the company's future direction and, therefore, shapes business process decisions that ultimately affect stakeholders. Internally, the business plan helps managers to:

- Identify strengths and weaknesses of the business

- Communicate expectations about a firm's future objectives and performance

- Coordinate resource use across departments and divisions

- Evaluate performance over time

The business plan also benefits external stakeholders. For example, creditors and equity investors rely on business plans to evaluate a company's funding requests.

As noted in Chapter 1, a business plan generally contains five main parts:

1. Analysis of the company's current and future business operations
2. Mission statement that describes company goals

3. Action plan
4. Description of resource requirements
5. Financial projections

However, most plans also include an executive summary to introduce readers to the information in these five sections.

1.0 Executive Summary

The executive summary may be the *most important part* of a business plan because it is the first section that a reader sees. Many who read business plans never go beyond this summary. Investors and busy financial executives, for example, often have too many plans to review and too little time to read them all thoroughly. Therefore, a well-crafted executive summary is crucial. If the plan summary is not convincing and interesting, business executives will simply move on to the next plan. It is estimated that only 10 percent of all business plans are read thoroughly, meaning that 90 percent are rejected based solely on the executive summary.

The executive summary should review the most important points in the business plan. Although this section appears first in the formal business plan, it should always be written last. It should be no longer than two pages and should include the following information:

- *Company name and contact information.*

- *Company overview:* Describe the business and explain the potential for successful operations. Rely on facts and logic, rather than jargon, buzzwords, and unsubstantiated claims. Since some investors will not invest in particular industries, save time for everyone by clearly describing the firm's industry (ten words or less). Provide a thumbnail sketch of the firm's history and background. Emphasize the positive and be brief (generally 150 words or less). State what the company's primary product or service is, but do not overcomplicate matters by listing product extensions or auxiliary services. Stress the uniqueness of the company's product or service. If it is not unique, discuss why it will succeed.

- *Description of the management team and their qualifications:* Usually, it is sufficient to list and discuss the industry experience of the top three or four people in the firm. Potential investors are very interested in knowing about the firm's key employees, as well as any special skills that will be needed to run the business.

- *Summarized market analysis:* Briefly discuss the nature and size of the target product or service market, identify existing competition, and describe the niche that your firm will occupy. Clearly explain why the company will be able to compete successfully in the marketplace. Specifically identify the company's competitive advantage. This section of the executive summary should be no longer than 150 words in length.

- *Financial forecast summary:* This section should discuss only the highlights of the detailed financial schedules contained in the business plan. It is not uncommon to see a table that summarizes assets, liabilities, revenue, and net income for the first three years of operation in this section of the executive summary. This section also should clearly state the amount and expected source of any funds needed to successfully execute the plan, including a brief discussion of how creditors will be repaid and investors rewarded. Funding needs and payback plans are critical pieces of data that allow potential investors to quickly screen business opportunities.

In short, the executive summary should clearly reflect the goals of the plan and highlight what is most exciting about the business (for example, market growth rates, competitive edge, special managerial talent, or access to/use of an exciting new technology). Explain the fundamentals of the business: what is the product or service, who are the customers, who are the owners and key managers, and what does the future hold for the business and its industry? Make the executive summary enthusiastic, professional, complete, and concise. A sample executive summary is provided in Exhibit A.1.

Exhibit A.1
Sample Executive Summary
for Moonlighters Diner

Company Name and Contact Information

Moonlighters Diner
David Bowie
1234 Lancaster Ave.
Collegetown, PA 19085
999.555.0315

Company Overview

Moonlighters Diner will provide evening and late-night dining for residents in the Ivory Tower University area. The restaurant's strategy is to provide students and faculty with an establishment that is solely dedicated to their need for convenient food in a social and safe environment. Moonlighters will be a late-night eatery that serves delicious food at reasonable costs with service from 2 p.m. until 6 a.m. Monday through Saturday and until 12 p.m. on Sunday. It will also offer an ample brunch on Sunday mornings. These hours will best serve a target market seeking a unique restaurant that is open later than competing businesses. We will market our diner as a stay-up-late spot that provides two distinct

(continued)

Management Accounting: A Business Planning Approach

atmospheres. The first will be an atmosphere conducive to studying. This will attract students and faculty looking for a place to work late while they get a cup of coffee. The other area will be designed to attract those customers looking for a place to go with friends to relax, converse, and eat. Our competitive advantage lies in our effort to fulfill the need for a late-night dining venue in this town.

Ownership Management Team

The three primary owners of Moonlighters are David Bowie, Samantha Hagar, and Edina Simmonds. Each of these owners received a business degree from Ivory Tower University within the last ten years. Mr. Bowie is a certified public accountant. Ms. Hagar spent seven years as menu designer and marketing director for an international restaurant chain. Ms. Simmonds served as a regional sales director at a national technology company. The ownership has secured a commitment from Mr. Carey Fergus, a chef with twelve years of experience, to oversee the kitchen operation.

Market and Competition

Moonlighters Diner targets the market attending Ivory Tower University and living in the communities surrounding Collegetown, Pennsylvania. Research has shown that this age group has an increasing amount of disposable meals-and-entertainment income that averages $75.00 per week. Our surveys suggest most students and faculty at Ivory Tower would visit our diner at least twice per month. This market has been previously unsatisfied with the options available for late-night eating venues and social spots.

Our three major competitors are Western Diner, Sunshine Diner, and Smokey Tomato's Grille. Our fiercest competition comes from the Western Diner, whose low prices and quality food attract a similar demographic. However, we plan to distinguish our diner by its accessible location and trendy appeal to younger adults. Smokey Tomato's is another source of competition. However, it appeals more to children and is a considerable drive for residents of Collegetown. The Sunshine Diner is competitive with Moonlighters because it is located in the most convenient area. A notable difference, however, is that it targets the senior population of Collegetown through price deals and atmosphere.

Financial Overview

Funds Requested: The three primary owners—David, Samantha, and Edina—will invest $90,000 each. Moonlighters is seeking $100,000 of additional equity investment as well as $85,000 in bank loans. These funds will be used for start-up expenses and the purchase of fixed assets.

Financial Projections:

	First Year	Second Year	Third Year
Revenues	$880,000	$915,200	$951,808
Net income	100,098	109,693	117,747
Assets	294,112	325,207	374,762
Liabilities	111,871	113,371	124,871

Future and Growth

We project a 4 percent increase in sales every year. This rate is consistent with the industry growth average reported by Standard & Poor's. The owners of Fun Times envision further expansion if this venue proves successful and profitable in the first few years. Options for growth include franchising in nearby college areas.

2.0 Current and Future Business Operations

This section of the business plan should evaluate the current state of the company's operations, as well as its future prospects. As we learned in Chapter 1, it should describe the business and products, its markets, and the risks that could influence the plan's success.

2.1 Company Description. Describe the business and the industry in which the company intends to operate. Clearly identify product and/or service offerings. For each product or service, offer a description of its value-adding features, its costs, and its value to the customer. Discuss those factors that the company believes will put it at a competitive advantage or disadvantage (for example, quality or unique features).

Also include a paragraph that describes the ownership structure of the company. Is the company a corporation, partnership, or sole proprietorship, and to what extent do outside parties share in the ownership of the business? The business plan should justify the form of business selected. A sample company description is provided in Exhibit A.2.

2.2 Market Analysis. A convincing business plan includes an analysis of the environment in which the company chooses to compete. It is imperative to address industry, customers, competitors, and critical success factors. This section should be as specific as possible and should reference relevant statistics and their sources. Chapter 2's Business Planning Application provides guidance on performing customer and competitor analyses.

All-Star Sports Bar and Grill will offer a fun, sports-oriented atmosphere for young adults. The restaurant's commitment to providing the latest sports video games and state-of-the-art audio/visual equipment places All-Star ahead of the local competition. Weekly live musical performances will entertain the customers while they enjoy the restaurant's quality cuisine and innovative beverages. All-Star Sports Bar and Grill will target young adults in the Mainville area by catering to their dining and entertainment needs.

The restaurant will sell moderately priced all-American fare, including hamburgers, chicken fingers/wings, soup, sandwiches, nachos, steak, fries, and salads. The bar will offer a wide variety of imported and domestic beer and liquor. These entrees and drinks are popular with younger people, especially in a sports bar atmosphere. Prices will be slightly lower than comparable franchise restaurants in the area. In addition to the moderate food prices, a unique dining experience that revolves around sports, video games, and music will differentiate All-Star from the competition.

The key to our business's success is the ability to draw customers into our restaurant. We plan to draw these customers in with an aggressive advertising campaign and attractive promotional offers (such as student discounts, happy hours, and two-for-one deals). In addition we hope to benefit from a well-earned stellar reputation generated by great word-of-mouth advertising from our restaurant patrons. Management is confident that our pricing and enjoyable restaurant and bar atmosphere will attract young adults, especially during premier televised sporting events like the Super Bowl and the Stanley Cup Playoffs.

All-Star Sports Bar and Grill is a privately held limited liability corporation (LLC). This type of company combines the corporate advantage of limited liability with the pass-through tax advantage of a partnership. Limited liability appeals to the owners because it reduces their risk should a default occur. Five local investors will hold 87 percent of the company stock. The founders plan to seek other investors to contribute a total of $90,000 to the business. These investors will control no more than 13 percent of All-Star's equity. However, the shareholders will have voting privileges representative of their stock holdings and will earn any declared dividends in proportion to their investment percentage. The company intends to borrow an additional $100,000 of funds from an area bank.

2.2.1 Industry The business plan should assess the industry in which the company plans to operate. It should include data about the size and profitability of the company's industry. It should specifically address industry growth or decline, as well as trends in consumer preferences and product development. This section should also describe any potential barriers to entering the industry and discuss how they will be overcome. These barriers could include such hurdles as licenses, international trade restrictions, high costs (start-up capital, production, marketing, and the like), consumer acceptance/brand recognition, training/skills, unique technology/patents, and labor unions. Finally, the plan should discuss changing forces in the industry that might impact the company's success. Several such factors include changes in technology, governmental regulations, and economic conditions. A sample industry analysis is provided in Exhibit A.3.

Exhibit A.3
Industry Analysis for a
Commercial Printer

The commercial printing segment represents all printers that produce commercial products on a custom basis, from annual reports to business cards, menus, brochures, and catalogs. Overall, commercial printing is the fourth largest manufacturing employer in the United States, comprising around 35,000 companies, employing 567,200 workers, and generating $89.7 billion in annual sales in 20X0. Commercial printing ranks among the top ten employers in 47 states. The large majority of commercial printers are small- or medium-sized businesses that operate one production plant, employ fewer than twenty people, and have annual revenue less than $3 million (although a substantial number have revenues over $20 million).

Small printers can compete effectively with large ones because the small size and high variability of most printing jobs means that few economies of scale are achieved by having larger presses. The high degree of personal attention that most print jobs require, such as client approvals of proofs and press checks during actual printing, means that customers prefer to use a local printer. Price is often a secondary consideration to quality and timeliness. Some types of printing, such as magazines and catalogs with large print runs, are more effectively handled by large printers. Large companies are often consolidators who have bought, and now operate, numerous local businesses.

The volume of commercial printing is closely tied to the health of the U.S. economy. Advertising, in the form of newspaper inserts, magazines, directories, product catalogs, and direct-mail pieces, is the mainstay of commercial printing. Financial printing has also grown rapidly in the past decade, as financial management customers have required larger volumes of annual reports, prospectuses, and proxy materials for stocks and other financial instruments. Both advertising and financial management are sharply affected by the economy and the stock market. After benefiting from a long period of economic expansion, commercial printers may face a more difficult climate. Total print shipments rose 2.2 percent in the first two quarters of 20X2 compared to the same period in 20X1, according to the Graphic Arts Technical Foundation and Printing Industries of America (GANT/PIA).

Printers feel the impact of cost fluctuations of paper and ink prices. Paper, a printer's single biggest recurring expense, represents about 23 percent of printers' cost of sales, according to industry estimates (more for printers specializing in long

(continued)

runs, less for those producing mainly short runs). Pending environmental issues in paper manufacture may raise paper prices. Ink prices are affected by fluctuations in oil and resin prices. Despite a slight recovery in the commercial printing industry, ink prices remain depressed by earlier weak demand from commercial printers. Ink prices could rise as advertising volume and printers' demand increase. Ink prices have been hit hard by weak advertising, cuts in magazine printing volume, and cost-cutting shifts to black-and-white from pricier color printing.

A growing percentage of commercial printers expect "excellent" conditions in the next two years, according to TrendWatch Graphic Arts (TWGA). Commercial printers plan to invest in computer hardware and software, work more closely to "train" customers, expand digital printing capabilities, and make their websites more interactive. TWGA suggests that commercial printers incorporate more value-added services, including personalization, cross-media capability, short-run color services, and new technology.

Source: Adapted from First Research Industry Profile Commercial Printing. © Copyright 2003, First Research, Inc. All rights reserved. www.1stresearch.com (accessed May 27, 2004).

2.2.2 Customers Since customer satisfaction is key to long-term success in business, the market analysis should clearly and thoroughly define the target customer or groups of customers. Many businesses may have multiple target markets. Distinct customer groups are known as market segments. Market segments may be defined by age, income, product type, geography, buying patterns, customer needs, geographic location, or other classification. For example, a coffee shop may appeal to working commuters in the morning hours and college students in the evenings. Since sales forecasts are based on the market analysis, it is essential to clearly identify such market segments.

A complete customer analysis documents and analyzes the demographics, spending habits, preferences, and size of the target customer base. New businesses typically rely on surveys and credible, publicly available data to address these issues. A wealth of information can be found in the library and on the Internet. While free Web-based resources may provide you with timely, aggregate industry and market data, the subscription, fee-based resources housed in the library will generally be the most useful. Many companies hire marketing consultants to collect firm-specific data to support their customer analyses.

Once a target customer base has been identified, the company must decide what goods and/or services to deliver and what not to offer. In other words, what competitive strategy will the business adopt? Which segment or segments of the market will the business pursue? Every business must define its market and determine whether consumer demand will be strong enough to support operations. A sample customer analysis is provided in Exhibit A.4.

Our business targets young adults and families. According to the 20X0 U.S. Census, 9,840 people ages 15 to 18 are residents in the local area towns, along with 14,610 college students in the community's seven colleges. The number of college-student customers, however, will be significantly lower from May to August due to summer vacation. We will market to upper/middle class families, primarily to parents ranging from 30 to 50 years of age and children 5 to 18 years of age. The median household income for Durango County is $60,829 and $50,092, respectively. Most individuals living in the area will have the disposable income to afford miniature golfing. In addition, about 70 percent of area residents live in a family. Thus, this large market segment will form the preponderance of our customer base.

We surveyed 100 local citizens in our target market concerning their movie-going experience. There were an equal number of males and females surveyed. The number of times subjects went to the movie theaters ranged from only once a year to every week without exception (fifty-two times a year) and averaged about sixteen visits per year. The median and mode of visits were both twelve visits per year, or monthly. The number of visits to the cinema was surprisingly high, showing that we have many people who go to the movies frequently.

When we asked respondents to identify their favorite movie genres, comedy took the lead with 29 percent of the vote, followed by romantic comedy with 20 percent and drama with 17 percent. Other genres, such as historical, action, murder/mystery, and epics, were preferred by 4 percent to 6 percent of those surveyed. The fact that most people in the area were drawn to standard movie genres seemed to be discouraging at first, but when asked if they would be interested in going to a movie theater that showcased foreign or independent films, 76 percent of the respondents said they thought it was an interesting concept and they would go "at least once to check it out."

When queried about price, 58 percent of those surveyed thought that $8.00 to $9.00 was close to what they would pay for a movie ticket. Eleven percent said they would pay a maximum of $5.50 to $7.00. A surprising 24 percent were willing to pay $10.00 or more (up to as much as $15.00) for their movie ticket. These figures were strongly encouraging because of the 76 percent of people more than willing to spend between $8.00 and $9.00.

When asking for suggestions about how to make the movie-going experience more attractive, the most common comments focused on better food options, pricing, seating, and parking. Since so many people were concerned with the lack of food options, this was a great opportunity to follow up by asking their opinions about a movie theater that included a restaurant or alternative dining facility. Of those questioned, 89 percent were interested in this idea, and most suggested that this eating facility should be similar to a chain family restaurant, a fast food chain, or a health food eatery. Our plans for food services will cater to all of these requests.

(continued)

Our survey provided interesting results that motivated us to revise our business plan to satisfy more customers. While some of the results caused us to reevaluate our business, most of the responses were positive and signaled to us that our business was sufficiently interesting and different to succeed in this area.

2.2.3 Competition This section should describe the concentration of competing businesses in the area to be served, discuss the way current market competitors are servicing consumers, and list specific competitors with their addresses.

- Who are three to five of the nearest direct competitors? A search of the online market directories can often yield this information.

- Are there any other products and services that have the potential to compete *indirectly* for your customers? For example, a movie theater competes, not only with other cinemas, but also with alternative forms of entertainment in the area (for example, sports, clubs, and the like).

Once identified, the strengths and weaknesses of each of the company's competitors must be evaluated and discussed.

- How does the competition's product or service differ from the company's planned offering? Get a feel for the pricing strategy that competitors are using to determine if planned prices are in line with competitors in the market area as well as with industry averages.

This section of the business plan should clearly state why the company will be able to succeed against existing competition. Existing competitors in the marketplace have an established reputation. What will the company do to promote awareness and the credibility of its product or service offering? For example, a new restaurant must explain how it will differentiate itself from existing enterprises and build a customer base. Does the firm expect to compete on the basis of price, location, availability, personalized service, or some other dimension? A new enterprise must explain how it will overcome the lack of reputation to fill a void in the market.

Finally, evaluate the general growth rate of business in the target market area. Are similar businesses opening or closing? Do these businesses seem to be popular? Visiting an existing competitor's business can yield considerable insight into these and other questions. A sample competitor analysis is provided in Exhibit A.5.

2.2.4 Critical Success Factors. After thoroughly analyzing the company's industry, customers, and competition, the business plan should outline those

The food industry is highly competitive. Sandwiches constitute a large percentage of restaurant market share, as shown in the chart below.

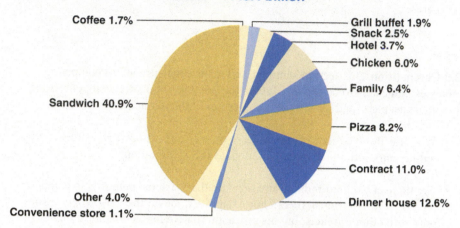

**Restaurant Market Shares
20X1 — 145.4 billion**

Coffee 1.7%
Grill buffet 1.9%
Snack 2.5%
Hotel 3.7%
Chicken 6.0%
Family 6.4%
Sandwich 40.9%
Pizza 8.2%
Contract 11.0%
Dinner house 12.6%
Other 4.0%
Convenience store 1.1%

Source: S&P Industry Surveys

The sandwich business is very competitive with large national chains holding a more than 55 percent market share. According the most recent Gale Market Share Reporter, Subway holds the largest share of the healthy "fast-casual" market with 29.1 percent. Our local market is highly competitive as well, with over 180 food service establishments in the area. According to the most recent Census Bureau statistics for the Parkway District of Philadelphia, there are 180 establishments in the "accommodation and food services" industry, 71 of which are "full-service restaurants," 41 of which are "limited-service restaurants," 17 of which are "snack and nonalcoholic beverage bars," and 3 of which are "caterers."

Fresco's competitors possess brand equity—people's awareness and perception of the quality of a product or service. They have established reputations and benefit from strong customer awareness. This factor will influence our potential customers' choice of our product versus our competitors. Our marketing strategy will be designed to differentiate our business and establish our brand equity—catering to the needs of the business professional—along with our dedication to freshness and quality.

factors considered to be most critical to its success. Commonly known as critical success factors (CSFs), these elements reflect what a company must do to execute its strategy. CSFs commonly include such factors as creating or retaining market share, promoting product awareness, improving customer service, increasing or maintaining product quality, distributing goods or services in a timely manner, or recruiting and retaining talented employees. In the case of a new premier restaurant, for example, the most critical success factors might be the ability to hire top chefs and ensure dining quality so as to create an experience that customers will value. It is important to note that CSFs will be different for every business. A sample of CSFs is provided in Exhibit A.6.

2.3 Business Risk Assessment. Because a business plan is based on a company's expectations for the future, it is filled with assumptions about the risks that a firm bears today and will confront tomorrow. Therefore, it is very important to disclose to interested parties the major risks that may affect the business plan's success. At first, this might seem counterintuitive, since no company wants to discourage potential investors. Nevertheless, such disclosure demonstrates the thoroughness with which a plan has been developed, as well as the honesty and integrity of the company's management.

Three critical factors will allow Crunch Time to be a success in its industry and with its customers. The following is a breakdown of our keys to success:

- *Customer Service and Satisfaction:* In order to differentiate Crunch Time from our competitors, customer service must be a priority. Since several full-time personal trainers and staff members will interact with customers, we feel that can attain a more personal relationship with our clients. Each customer will receive a monthly personal fitness plan as part of his or her membership. This will enable us to gain a competitive edge over other fitness facilities in the area. We will measure our success by the number of memberships and by the customer retention ratio. We are targeting 700 memberships during the first year of operation, 910 memberships in year two, and 1,040 memberships by year five. We will address any complaints in a timely fashion and survey our customers quarterly for valuable feedback.

- *Convenience:* Since Crunch Time customers will have a wide variety of lifestyles and goals, we have created a facility that accommodates each person's needs. Included in this facility are a juice bar, nutritional shop, multipurpose gym, nursery, and several different exercise classes. These elements allow for one-stop-shopping where a member can get a great workout and supplements all at the same time. We will closely monitor the sales of each product line to best meet our customers' needs.

- *Customer Safety:* We will seek to minimize and will closely monitor the number of accidents and injuries. As a significant part of our safety effort, we will provide an exceptionally well-maintained exercise environment for our customers. We will make sure that adequate staff are available to help members use the equipment safely. We will strictly limit children's access to the equipment area. Failure to maintain our equipment and facilities, train staff, and provide first-aid care may undermine the success of our enterprise.

Exhibit A.6
Critical Success Factors for Crunch Time Fitness Facility

If a firm currently exists, the business plan should summarize management's analysis of its strengths, weaknesses, opportunities, and threats (SWOT). This planning tool was introduced in Chapter 1. If the company has not performed a SWOT analysis or is in the idea or start-up phase, the business plan should discuss the following three types of risks: environmental risk, process risk, and information for decision-making risk. Chapter 4's Business Planning Application will help you assess the business risk issues that should be included in this section of the business plan.

2.3.1 Environmental Risk As we learned in Chapter 4, environmental risks relate to forces external to the company that can affect is ability to achieve its objectives or threaten its existence. Chapter 2 discussed three structural forces that continue to impact many companies today: technology, globalization, and the customer value imperative. This section of the business plan should discuss any natural, economic, political, and/or social risks that are beyond the direct control of managers but that may affect strategic success.

2.3.2 Process Risks Chapter 4 defined process risk as the risk that a company's operating processes do not perform efficiently or effectively in meeting business objectives or do not protect the physical, financial, intellectual, or information resources that a company uses. These risks occur within the organization and can be prevented, detected, corrected, and managed through an effective system of internal control. This section should specifically address what controls, policies, and procedures have been put in place to manage the potential process risks found in a company's value chain.

2.3.3 Information for Decision-Making Risk Finally, a company should address those factors that will prevent it from creating the information that it will need to manage strategic, operating, and financial decisions. Specifically, how will a company collect and analyze information? What types of information does it consider to be particularly critical? What are the potential hazards that the business may face if information is not properly collected, processed, and utilized? These are just a few of the questions related to information that must be addressed when assessing and evaluating business risk.

2.3.4 Strategies and Plans for Managing Major Risks In addition to listing the company's most critical environmental, process, and information risks, the business plan also should address management's strategies for mitigating these uncertainties. As we learned in Chapter 4, risk management strategies generally fall into one of four broad categories: avoidance, transference, mitigation, and acceptance. Discuss in this section which of these strategies or combination of strategies the company intends to use to manage its business risks. A sample business risk assessment is provided in Exhibit A.7.

Any start-up business will face various types of business risk, including environmental risk, process risk, and information for decision-making risk. The first step in avoiding business risks is to be able to identify the specific risks that can affect your company or industry and prepare for ways to prevent certain risks before they occur or plan ways to overcome risks that you cannot control. Dinner and a Game is a start-up business that combines a pizza shop with a board game delivery service. This combination of offerings raises risks that many manufacturing and service firms face.

Environmental Risks

The biggest environmental risk we will encounter is succeeding over our competitors. Because other companies are already well established in this area, we will need to take market share from them. Cyclical changes in the economy will also directly affect our company. During times of prosperity, consumers have more disposable income and are more willing to spend money on leisure activities and entertainment like movies. Periods of economic growth will directly correlate with increased sales and higher profits. The opposite holds true during economic recessions. If decreased demand diminishes our industry's health, Dinner and a Game will be affected more adversely than a nationwide chain. Our business is at a higher risk from economic downturns than the industry as a whole as individuals may spend less on entertainment and delivered foods.

Numerous regulatory factors will affect our market. In addition to taxes, which affect profits, our kitchen must meet standards set by the Board of Health and other state regulatory agencies. To avoid potential liability, we will limit our drivers to those with excellent safety records.

Other environmental factors that may affect our market are the possibility of periods of snow or heavy rain that may curb foot and automobile traffic and curtail deliveries at times during the winter. Our commitment will be to safety first.

Process Risks

Our most important process risk will be gaining a positive reputation from the start. Without a positive reputation, we will be unable to attract customers and sell products. We plan to overcome this risk by providing an upbeat and effective advertising campaign that will inform, persuade, and remind our customers of our presence, creating a positive perception of our business.

Other process risks that we may encounter are employee safety, employee theft, and employee carelessness that results in shrinkage; customers not returning games; legal liability; and equipment quality. It will also be crucial to make sure our employees are properly trained and well suited for their positions in order to avoid process risk.

The most important part of our business value chain is production, procurement, and distribution. We will need to stand by the reputation that we are trying to make for ourselves, so we must provide a quality product and friendly, prompt service. In order to manage these risks, we will constantly evaluate our employees and give them incentives to perform well and deliver our product as quickly and efficiently as possible.

Information for Decision-Making Risks

Some types of information for decision-making risks that will affect our business are the credibility of our accountants, the utilization of our website, methods of measuring the implementation of our marketing strategy, and inventory selection. We plan to have our financial statements audited in order to ensure that they are completed correctly and ethically. We will initiate an ambitious research program to identify the technological needs of our customers in order to make sure our website is user friendly and appropriate for our target market. We will periodically update our marketing research in order to create sales and promotion campaigns to attract the specific target market that we wish to retain. We will also initiate a program of continuously analyzing trends in the movie and entertainment industry in order to determine which games we should purchase. The information that we gain from this analysis will also help us decide which games we need to purchase additional copies of and which games in our current inventory can be sold or recycled.

3.0 Mission Statement

Next, the business plan should define the company's mission and the goals needed to achieve it. As we learned in Chapter 1, a mission statement is intended to clearly document a company's vision for the future. The mission statement presented in the business plan should:

- Be understandable: simple, clear, concise, and free of jargon

- Define the business the company wishes to pursue, not necessarily the business in which the firm is currently engaged

- Differentiate the company from other firms in the "same" business

- Identify broad objectives and directions for the long term

- Be relevant to all stakeholders

Sol Day Spa seeks to be the leading provider of convenient, life-enhancing spa services for men and women in the San Diego metropolitan area. Our company is committed to offering a relaxing and informal atmosphere with a range of quality treatments performed by our highly trained and personable staff. To ensure a soothing and stress-free environment for customers, we are dedicated to a safe and rewarding workplace and competitive pay for our employees. To deliver future success and financial returns to our owners, we dedicate ourselves to developing long-term relationships and meeting the relaxation needs of our clients.

The mission of most companies as to increase owner wealth over the long term by providing a reasonable rate of return to investors, quality service to customers, and a favorable work environment to employees. A sample mission statement is provided in Exhibit A.8.

4.0 Action Plan

After documenting the company's mission statement and goals, the business plan should describe in detail how the company will move from where it is now to where it would like to be in the future. As we learned in Chapter 1, action plans outline the specific activities and tasks that help a company allocate resources in order to meet its goals. Ideally, the business plan should summarize all major action plans, but at a minimum, it should describe the company's *marketing* action plan. How does the company plan to promote the sale of its products and/or services and price them? Have customer service issues been considered?

4.1 Promotion. After identifying a market need for its product or service, a company must have a *promotion plan:* a plan to build customer awareness. This plan should be designed to reach the company's target market segments. It also should describe creative ways to attract customers. For example, promotion strategies might include alliances with other businesses, giveaways, direct mailings, or discounts. The promotion plan also should provide specific examples of print advertisements, brochures, online ads, social media presence, direct mail pieces, catalogs, and similar marketing materials. The following questions should prove useful when evaluating the adequacy of a company's promotion plan:

- What image does the company wish to project to its customers?

- How will the company get the word out to customers?

- What media will be used for advertising? Why and how often?

- Has the company identified low-cost methods to get the most out of its promotional budget?

- Will methods other than paid advertising, such as trade shows, catalogs, dealer incentives, word of mouth, and a network of friends or professionals, be used?

- In addition to advertising, what plans does the company have for logo design, cards and letterhead, brochures, signage, and the interior design of its stores?

4.2 Pricing. The marketing plan also should explain how the company intends to set its prices. For most businesses, particularly smaller one, having the lowest product or service price may not be a good policy. Customers may not care as much about price as one might think, and a low-price policy can rob a company of needed profit margins. If possible, it is usually better to have average prices and compete on quality and service. The marketing plan should compare the company's prices along product lines to those of each of its competitors. The following questions raise issues that should be addressed when crafting a pricing policy:

- Does the company's pricing strategy make sense given the conclusions in the market analysis (section 2.2.3)?

- How do the company's prices compare with those of the competition? Are they higher, lower, the same? Why?

- Is price an important competitive factor? Do your intended customers really base their purchase decisions mostly on price?

4.3 After-Sale Customer Service. A final section of the marketing plan should discuss what the company intends to do about customer service after a sale has occurred. Other key customer-related issues that must be addressed include how the company plans to handle returns, requests for assistance, and complaints. Does the company plan to monitor customer satisfaction? If so, how? Are there any plans to identify repeat customers and then systematically contact them to assess customer satisfaction? A sample marketing plan is provided in Exhibit A.9.

5.0 Resource Requirements

This section of the business plan describes the resources that will be needed to support the products and services that a company intends to deliver to customers. The business plan should describe the company's value chain and the processes that will consume resources. At a minimum, this section should address the human resource, physical, and technology requirements. Financial capital resource needs are detailed later in the business plan when financing is discussed.

5.1 The Company's Value Chain. As we learned in Chapter 4, the company's value chain can provide significant insight into resource requirements. The value

We plan to introduce a multilevel marketing campaign to bring in customers. A key part of our strategy includes securing a location within walking distance of La Bella Moda, a local gown shop. Our bride can walk directly out of La Bella Moda, where she purchases her high-end designer wedding dress, and into Wedding Belles to purchase all of her designer accessories. The close proximity makes it much easier for brides to shop conveniently for their dress and accessories. The amount of time needed to gain a customer base will decrease by half, at a minimum, because of cross-marketing with La Bella Moda. Some general strategies include promotion, pricing, and after-sale customer service.

Promotion

We will begin our advertising campaign with signage, business card distribution, and verbal recommendations from La Bella Moda. Outside marketing will include advertising in local telephone directories. We will place advertisements in the form of graphics and text in local business/high-end publications. These publications will include, but are not limited to, local magazines and newspapers and *The Knot,* a national bridal magazine and website that offers area-specific advertising. Another form of marketing will be to advertise at area bridal showcases, such as the Annual Bridal Expo in January. We will rent a booth at these events displaying signage explaining our services and bringing in one of our expert wedding employees to display our items of the month. We will give away coupons, literature including directions to our store and online location, and business cards for all brides that attend the event.

Pricing

Our products will be premium goods priced at competitive levels. We will sell our designer products at a premium price, so as not to detract from the customer's perception of quality and to maintain our high-class image in the market. Occasionally single items may be discounted to move inventory that is not selling well. Shoes will have an average price of about $100, but they will range from $50 for a set of decorative bridal footwear to about $400 for a pair of heels by Badgley Mishka. Vera Wang shoes are typically priced at about $250 and Richard Tyler shoes fall into the more modest $100 range. The jewelry that we will be selling will consist of necklaces, earrings, bracelets, and tiaras. All our jewelry will have a wide range of pricing so that we will be able to accommodate a range of budgets and needs. The necklaces will range between $25 and $350; the earrings will sell for between $15 and $100. Bracelets will have a price range of $25 to $75 and the tiaras will run between $50 and $150. Perfumes range in price from $35 to over $150, depending on scent and quantity.

After-Sale Customer Service

Wedding Belles will not accept returned merchandise. We will contact the bride after her wedding to make sure that all went as planned and to make sure that she was happy with our product. We will also follow-up to see if we can help customers with galas or parties in the future. Customer retention is limited because of the nature of bridal purchases—most women only plan on getting married once. Nevertheless, we expect they will return for accessories for other formal occasions. The relationships we form with our customers will support customer acquisition through word-of-mouth recommendations. Brides look to family and friends to point them in the right direction when selecting items for their wedding day. The customer service and personal attention we give to our brides will ensure that they will, at minimum, refer one friend and/or relative, thus maintaining our primary customer base.

chain starts with understanding what customers want and ends with customer satisfaction. The intervening internal business processes focus on the business operations needed to make the customer value imperative a reality. A review of the value chain, therefore, will help managers determine what human, physical, and financial capital will be consumed by the company's business processes. Therefore, this business plan section should describe and illustrate the value chain for the company. A sample value chain is illustrated in Exhibit A.10.

5.2 Management and Human Resources. People are an essential part of any business. This section should list the management team and provide a brief biography of each team member. The biography should highlight education, as well as relevant professional credentials and experience. Potential creditors and equity investors must be convinced that their monies will be managed by capable individuals. This section also should describe the company's other human resource requirements. In addition to the management team, what types of employees does the company require? This business plan section should discuss how these employees will be organized, their opportunities for advancement, and any performance incentives planned. If more than ten employees will work for the company, create an organizational chart showing the management hierarchy and who is responsible for key functions. A sample discussion of management and human resources is provided in Exhibit A.11.

5.3 Location and Facilities. In this section, the business plan should describe offices, storefronts, production facilities, and locations planned for the company. For companies that rely on mobile locations (a food delivery service, for example), outline the required equipment here. It may be helpful to include maps and data about the cost of properties and facilities. Exhibit A.12 contains a sample location and facility plan.

Sample Value Chain for Paradise Miniature Golf Course

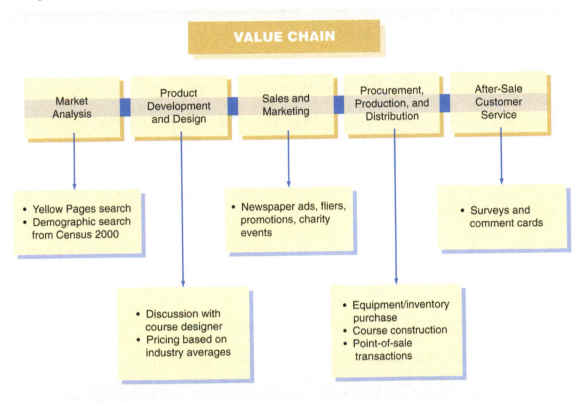

The value chain for Paradise Miniature Golf Course will consist of the following sets of activities.

Market Analysis

To verify that there is sufficient demand for a miniature golf course in the local market, we relied on telephone listings of miniature golf courses in the area and recent demographic information about local residents. We first found that there was limited competition in the Oceantown area. Though our services and price levels are similar to those of other miniature golf courses in the area, our location is much more convenient for our target market segments: tourists, students, and families. Because of our location, we will more closely meet their need for easily accessible recreation. Secondly, local demographic statistics from the U.S. Census 20X0 proved that there is a sufficient customer base in the area. Specifically, there is an abundance of tourists in addition to local high school and college students and families residing in Oceantown.

Product Development and Design

Paradise Miniature Golf provides its customers with reasonably priced miniature golf entertainment services. Our price per round will be $8.00 for adults and $5.00 for children. These prices are in line with industry averages. We will also offer snack foods in our snack shop at midlevel prices. The miniature golf course itself will be specially designed by Charles Hugh Miniature Golf Courses, Inc. to include eighteen holes surrounded by natural landscapes. This type of course is most attractive to customers. Basic equipment rental will be included in the price. The price, service, and quality levels that we have set satisfy the customer's needs while allowing us to hit our company's profit target.

Sales and Marketing

We will reach our customers by placing ads online and in local newspapers. We will distribute fliers around local campuses and residential areas. Paradise Miniature Golf will offer other promotional incentives, including, we hope, a charity event that will provide a way of giving back to the community.

Procurement, Production, and Distribution

Paradise Miniature Golf's equipment and inventory represent the procurement phase of the value chain. This includes the initial purchase of putters, golf balls, scorecards, pencils, snack shop equipment, furniture, and snack food. Charles Hugh Miniature Golf Courses, Inc, the premier miniature golf course builder in the Northeast with forty years of experience, will build the course. It will take six weeks to complete construction. To fulfill the production phase of the value chain, Paradise Miniature Golf will be prepared to offer a miniature golf experience at the time (our operating hours) and place (our convenient location) preferred by our customers. Preparation will include having a safe, clean, and well-equipped miniature golf course for customers to use at any point during our hours of operation. Due to the nature of our business, Paradise Miniature Golf requires a point-of-sale transaction. This transaction comprises the distribution phase of the value chain.

After-Sale Customer Service

To encourage repeat business from customers, Paradise Miniature Golf will distribute post-service questionnaires and comment cards. Customer responses will help us identify and address any areas that might need improvement. We will meet routinely to address these matters.

Exhibit A.11
Sample Management and Human Resources Plan for Dinner and a Movie Delivery Shop

Four owners will equally manage the business. Donny Smith, Christopher Columbus, Andrea Klapowitz, and Ivanna Lottacash are all qualified for this position. They each possess strong leadership skills and have significant experience working in restaurants. We will hire two full-time managers and fifteen workers. The workers will be high school and college age students who will work six-hour shifts making pizza, delivering products, cleaning the store, etc., at a rate of $10.00 an hour. The managers will each make a salary of $45,000 a year, not including benefits.

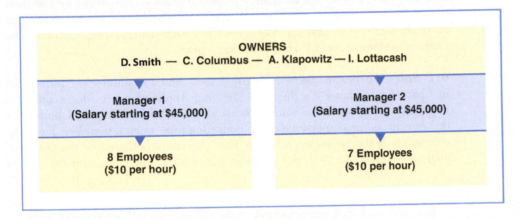

Located adjacent to the intersection of Hamilton and Franklin Roads, our movie theater will be located on the factory site formerly used by the now-bankrupt Worldwide Textile Industries. The estimated cost for our facilities and real estate totals $245,000. This amount is primarily comprised of the property cost and construction of ramping, which are all estimated values based on research through local commercial real estate agents and the industry data from United Drive-In Theaters Owners Association. Our facilities include a concession stand ($5,000) and two drive-in movie theater screens ($25,000 each). We will also require outside lighting that will cost an additional $30,000. The appendices to our business plan include maps of location and preliminary architectural designs of our facilities.

Exhibit A.12
Sample Location and Facility Plan for Pine Valley Drive-In Movie Theater

5.4 Technology. All businesses today use technology in some way. This business plan section should describe the specific ways that the company will employ technology in its business operations. It should list the names of technology vendors used, as well as the anticipated benefits of using specific technologies. For some companies, technology *is* the business. For example, Internet-based firms rely solely on technology for success. Other firms may incorporate technology into production and delivery processes, inventory tracking, or customer communications. Chapter 9's Business Planning Application describes several business models that a company might consider when planning for its technology needs. Exhibit A.13 provides a sample technology plan.

6.0 Financial Plan

The financial plan reflects all of the discussions in preceding sections of the business plan and presents the company's projected financial results, as well as their underlying assumptions. The financial plan also should include accompanying narrative that clearly and concisely describes each figure, table, schedule, and financial statement included in the business plan.

6.1 Sales Forecast. Sales forecasting tools and techniques are introduced in Chapter 6. Chapter 6's Business Planning Application provides a series of important questions that a sales forecast should address. Chapter 7 notes that this forecast is the cornerstone of the budgeting process and, therefore, a critical component of the business plan. This forecast should be based on the customer analysis section (2.2.2) of the business plan and should document the size of

Exhibit A.13
Sample Technology Plan
for Berry Good Smoothie
Drink Shop

Use of current technology will encourage sales in several ways. We can take advantage of programs that monitor customer purchases in a data-base and then tailor marketing campaigns based on these results. We can keep track of which items are most popular and what time is the busiest, which will help us better forecast sales, stock sufficient inventory, and staff the shop appropriately. To accomplish these goals, regular cash registers will not suffice. We will need to use computers specifically designed to track these data. Our company will use the Internet primarily as a way to make customers aware of our products and services. At this moment we do not believe it will be profitable to give customers the ability to make transactions online, since all we are offering are fruit smoothies.

After serious consideration of our e-business options, we have decided that iBizHelp would be the best provider for our purposes. For only $274, iBizHelp would not only set up and host our website, they would also allow us to communicate with our customers and provide us with website traffic analysis and an e-mail address. Finally, for an extra fee of $29.95 a month, they offer a mass marketing e-mail option that would allow us to send up to 10,000 e-mails a month to potential customers in our target market. iBizHelp is an extremely reliable corporation to support our e-commerce needs.

Management Accounting: A Business Planning Approach

the customer base, customer preferences, and the expected level of demand. In short, the sales forecast quantifies key assumptions about demand, price, and sales mix. The amounts reported in the sales forecast are used to create revenue and expense forecasts that drive a company's cash flow and financial statement budgets. A short text narrative that summarizes the highlights of the sales forecast should accompany the numerical schedule. A sample sales forecast is provided in Exhibit A.14.

6.2 Operating Budget. The operating budget was introduced in Chapter 7. It reports the projected financial results expected to arise from a company's business processes; it is, therefore, an integral part of a company's business plan. It is based on both sales and cost forecasts, as well as on other assumptions about purchases and operating cash flows; it provides the basis for a firm's budgeted financial statements. For start-up enterprises, business plans often include monthly operating budgets for the first year of operations and annual budgets for two years thereafter (a total of three years). Existing companies generally provide only annual operating budgets for a three- to five-year period. A short text narrative that summarizes the highlights of the operating budget should accompany the numerical schedule. Company's also may wish to include a schedule that reports what each product or service offered will contribute to the bottom line. Chapter 10's Business Planning Application describes how such a schedule can be prepared. Exhibit A.15 shows a sample operating budget for the first four months of KAAS Home Gourmet's in-home catering and grocery delivery service. Notice that the schedule shows amounts both in dollars and as a percentage of sales. Detailed discussion of the assumptions underlying the totals and percentages that appear in the table commonly accompany operating budgets.

6.3 Breakeven and Sensitivity Analysis. As noted in Chapter 5, managers used breakeven analysis to determine the level of sales needed to earn a profit. Chapter 8 showed how sensitivity analysis can be used to test the reasonableness of budget assumptions. Both tools provide information critical to a credible business plan.

6.3.1. Breakeven Analysis When screening investment opportunities, potential creditors and equity investors frequently use breakeven analysis to evaluate a firm's cost structure and the sales volume needed to generate profits. Therefore, all business plans must include a breakeven analysis. This analytical tool was introduced in Chapter 5 in the context of planning profitable operations, and the chapter Business Planning Application actually provides a detailed walk-through of a basic breakeven analysis. A short text narrative that summarizes the highlights of the breakeven analysis should accompany the numerical schedule. In this discussion identify which costs have been considered as well as their assumed cost behavior, which was discussed in Chapter 5. This brief written analysis will provide those reading the business plan with a glimpse behind your calculations and enhance the credibility of the breakeven analysis. A sample breakeven analysis is provided in Exhibit A.16.

Exhibit A.14

Sales Forecast for Sky Nightclub

We developed our sales forecast primarily through studies based on company profiles in our market analysis. We visited several competitors to determine the prices they set for their products and services, as well as to gauge the approximate quantity sold at various points in the year. From our market analysis, we learned that the college community in the area comprises approximately 25 percent of the customer base in our industry. However, during college breaks, the target market for companies such as Sky changes. Our competitors draw an older crowd to their establishments during holiday vacations, spring break, and summer months, which allows the business to continue its normal operation. We gained additional insights from the industry website (www.NightClubBiz.com).

By analyzing menu prices of competitors in our industry, we calculated the average meal is priced at $11. The average sale of meals is approximately 250 plates, spanning lunch and dinner. Our competition review and industry analysis indicate that food makes up 40 percent of sales, while beverages make up the other 60 percent. However, based on our unique competitive advantage combining a bar, restaurant, and nightclub in one facility, we then had to factor in information from different sources.

We estimate that 350 guests will visit the nightclub each night of operation (Thursday, Friday, and Saturday). A $10 cover charge will be levied for anyone wishing to enter the upstairs club. With the addition of this cover charge, the sales mix changed. Sky will have the following sales mix: 31.9 percent from food sales, 47.8 percent from beverage sales, and 20.3 percent from admission sales. Because of regulations in Radnor Township, Sky will be able to operate on Sundays with a special permit. In order to be granted a *Sunday Permit*, at least 40 percent of sales must come from food, and Sky only obtains 31.9 percent of its revenue from this source.

Based on these estimates, we expect total sales to equal $2,691,000 in 20X1 (comprised of $858,425 in food sales, $1,286,300 in beverage sales, and $546,275 in cover charges). Of course, the restaurant and bar business is seasonal in nature and we have accounted for these fluctuations based on changes in the size of our target market, which is made up largely of college students. Therefore, there are slight variations from month to month, depending on the time of college breaks. Our monthly sales forecast is depicted in the graph below.

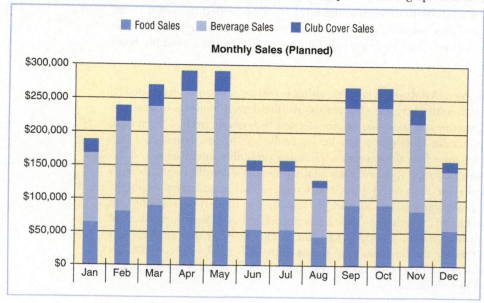

Management Accounting: A Business Planning Approach

Exhibit A.15

Sample Operating Budget for KAAS Home Gourmet's In-Home Catering/Grocery Delivery Service

	Jan	%	Feb.	%	Mar.	%	Apr.	%
Revenue (Sales)								
Meal prep	$4,200	87.5	$4,200	87.5	$4,200	87.5	$5,880	87.5
Grocery shopping	600	12.5	600	12.5	600	12.5	840	12.5
Total revenue (sales)	$4,800	100.0	$4,800	100.0	$4,800	100.0	$6,720	100.0
Expenses								
Accounting and legal	$ 285	5.9	$ 485	10.1	$ 85	1.8	$ 85	1.3
Advertising	170	3.5	170	3.5	170	3.5	170	2.5
Car, delivery, and travel	300	6.3	300	6.3	300	6.3	300	4.5
Depreciation	63	1.3	63	1.3	63	1.3	63	0.9
Home office—rent/utilities	50	1.0	50	1.0	50	1.0	50	0.7
Insurance/membership fees	25	0.5	25	0.5	25	0.5	25	0.4
Supplies	76	1.6	76	1.6	76	1.6	76	1.1
Technology expenses	20	0.4	20	0.4	20	0.4	20	0.3
Telephone	18	0.4	18	0.4	18	0.4	18	0.3
Training	200	4.2	200	4.2	200	4.2	200	3.0
Wages	1,600	33.3	1,600	33.3	1,600	33.3	2,240	33.3
Total expenses	$2,807	58.5	$3,007	62.6	$2,607	54.3	$3,247	48.3
Net profit before taxes	$1,993	41.5	$1,793	37.4	$2,193	45.7	$3,473	51.7

Note: All percentages have been rounded to one decimal place.

KAAS Home Gourmet's only variable costs are wages. Customers will pay for the cost of all meal ingredients and provide cooking utensils. Each chef will be paid at a rate of $10 an hour. All other costs are fixed. They include accounting and legal, advertising, car/delivery and travel, depreciation, home/office expenses, rent/utilities, insurance/membership fees, supplies, taxes, technology expenses, telephone, and training.

Breakeven analysis is used to determine the number of customers that are needed monthly and annually for a business to break even; that is, to recoup expenses with no profit or loss. KAAS estimates that the average job size will be 4 hours. Total revenue per job is $120: 1 hour shopping charged at $15 per hour, and 3 hours of cooking charged at $35 per hour. The variable cost per unit (job) is $40. This number reflects our single variable cost: wages. The chef working the job will be paid $10 an hour for four hours, a total of $40. The contribution

Exhibit A.16

Sample Breakeven Analysis for KAAS Home Gourmet's In-Home Catering/ Grocery Delivery Service margin is $80, calculated as total revenue per unit minus variable cost per unit ($120–$40). KAAS does not have a weighted contribution average because although we have two services (cooking and grocery shopping), these services will be sold as a combined standard service. Each job will include one hour of shopping and three hours of cooking. To find our breakeven point in units (jobs), we divided total fixed costs by contribution margin. In order for the company to exactly break even, we need to have 159 jobs a year or $19,080 in total sales.

> Average revenue per job (unit): $120.00
> Variable cost per unit: $40.00
> Contribution margin: $80.00
> Contribution margin ratio: 66.67%
> Total variable expenses: $6,360.00
> Total fixed expenses: $12,684.00
> Breakeven by number of jobs: $12,684 ÷ $80 = 159 jobs (units)
> Sales volume in dollars at breakeven point: $19,080

The breakeven analysis reinforces the idea that KAAS is a low-risk enterprise. Our research shows that there is a great demand for the services we would be offering and that there are also a significant number of families that will be able to afford our services. Our conservative projected demand for our services is 768 jobs in the first year. We believe that we can comfortably achieve this level of sales; because we are a service business with few assets, our costs are very low. The highest cost we face is the wages of the chefs. This low breakeven number underscores how profitable our business has the potential to be, especially as our projected sales are approximately 80 percent higher than our breakeven level of sales. After we complete 159 jobs, we will have covered our fixed costs and will be making a significant profit.

6.3.2 Sensitivity Analysis As noted in Chapter 8, sensitivity analysis allows users of information to assess how sensitive budgets are to changes in core assumptions, such as sales price, sales volume, and/or cost estimates. The chapter's Business Planning Application describes some common variables included in sensitivity analyses. Potential creditors and equity investors often use this tool to critically examine business plan estimates before putting their money into a company. At a minimum, this section of the business plan should examine how sensitive revenues, expenses, net income, and the breakeven point are to the changes in the sales forecast assumptions for price, demand, and sales mix. A short text narrative that summarizes the highlights of the sensitivity analysis should accompany the numerical schedule. A sample sensitivity analysis is provided in Exhibit A.17.

In performing our sensitivity analysis, we will look at the effects from changes in sales price, expected quantities of sales, and sales mix assumptions.

Sales price. If we were not attracting enough customers, we might be forced to drop our ticket price by $1 to $6 to stimulate sales. In this case, revenues would decline by $11,080, an 8.3 percent drop in sales revenue. If we decided to raise the prices of all our products, tickets, snacks, and memorabilia, by $1 for each item, the price rise would generate a 13.3 percent increase in sales revenue if the number of customers held constant. If we also decided to raise prices of our tickets to $8.75 to match those of indoor movie theaters, we would see a drastically large increase in sales revenue, assuming the expected number of customers remained the same. Sales revenue would rise by 14.6 percent for this 25 percent increase in price. Therefore, we conclude that sales revenue is very sensitive to price changes.

Sales volume. If we gained just one additional customer every night, we would have sixteen more customers for each our six operating months and ninety-six more customers for that fiscal year. This would have a substantial impact on sales revenue because we would earn $13,152 more in sales, increasing revenue by 9.9 percent. If we lost one customer for every business night, we would lose $23,120 in sales revenue—a 17.4 percent decrease. Thus, every customer is valuable, and losing one customer has a greater adverse impact on sales revenue than the positive impact of gaining a single extra customer.

Sales mix. If we changed sales mix assumptions by assuming that every person, rather than every other person, who bought a ticket also bought snacks, our sales mix would be 47 percent (tickets), 40 percent (snacks), 13 percent (memorabilia). This would increase sales revenue by 25 percent to $166,200. This change would increase profits by $20,300. If we decided not to sell any memorabilia at all, our sales mix would be 70 percent ticket sales and 30 percent snack sales. With this new sales mix, we would make only $110,800 in sales revenue, which is a 16.7 percent decrease. This change would decrease profits by $7,500. We must carefully monitor changes in our sales mix.

6.4 Start-up Costs. For new companies that have yet to begin operations, the business plan should also include a start-up budget to tell creditors and equity investors just how much financial capital is necessary to start the business. As discussed in Chapter 7's Business Planning Application, the start-up budget is a financial schedule that lists all of the expenditures and reserve funds believed necessary to begin operations. It includes the cost of facilities, equipment, supplies, starting inventories, licenses, and utility deposits, as well as a cash reserve to fund the business until it can rely on operating cash flows to pay the bills. A short text narrative that summarizes the highlights of the start-up budget should accompany the numerical schedule. Exhibit A.18 illustrates a sample start-up budget.

6.5 Financing Sources. This section of the business plan should describe in detail the financial resources that the company will require to finance its growth, as well as the expected sources of these funds (that is, debt or equity capital). For borrowed funds, the company should provide estimates of loans and their repayment terms. For equity issues, the company should report how much it expects each investor will be able to contribute and what percentage of ownership these investors will have in the company. Finally, the company should include a detailed discussion of its plan for paying back creditors and investors. Exhibit A.19 shows a sample schedule of financing sources for the start-up needs of the dinner theater illustrated in Exhibit A.18.

Exhibit A.18
Start-Up Budget for a
Dinner Theater

Start-Up Expenses	
Bar supplies	$ 5,500
Deposits on utilities	5,000
Fees and permits	20,000
Initial marketing and advertising	90,000
Manuals/handbooks/recipes	2,420
Office/miscellaneous expenses	5,500
Paper products	2,500
Training and hiring cost	10,000
Uniforms	3,450
Total start-up expenses	$ 144,370
Start-Up Assets	
Point of sale system (5 stations)	$ 2,045
Construction cost	45,000
Film projector	2,000
Furniture (chairs, tables, etc.)	13,200
Kitchen/architectural plans	75,000
Projector screen	1,390
Plumbing and electricity	19,000
Sound system	5,500
Tableware (glasses, silverware, plates)	9,500
Cash reserve	75,000
Start-up inventory and supplies	17,500
Total start-up assets	$ 265,135
Total Start-Up Requirements	**$409,505**

Management Accounting: A Business Planning Approach

Investors:	
Investor 1, Ron Lamonica	$ 75,000
Investor 2, Buddy Ryan	75,000
Investor 3, Tony Mendez	75,000
Investor 4, Susanne Oltz	75,000
Total investment	$300,000
Loans:	
Southwestern Bank, 5-year note	$ 75,000
Seventeen National Bank, 7-year note	25,000
Tammie Starnes	9,505
Total loans	$109,505
Total Financing	**$409,505**

Exhibit A.19
Schedule of Financing
Sources for a Dinner Theater

6.6 Pro Forma Financial Statements.   As noted in Chapter 3's Business Planning Application, the financial statements presented in a business plan generally include the balance sheet, the income statement, and the statement of cash flows. For start-up companies, it is common to include monthly pro forma financial statements for the first twelve months of operations and annual pro forma financial statements for the following two years. For established companies, the

KAAS HOME GOURMET Pro Forma Balance Sheets On December 31			
	20X1	20X2	20X3
Assets			
Current Assets:			
Cash	$ 42,019	$ 95,753	$ 158,299
Supplies	100	300	600
Total Current Assets	$ 42,119	$ 96,053	$ 158,899
Fixed Assets:			
Computer	$ 1,600	$ 1,600	$ 1,600
Cooking Equipment	1,060	1,060	1,060
Less Accumulated Depreciation	(756)	(1,512)	(2,268)
Net Fixed Assets	$ 1,904	$ 1,148	$ 392
Total Assets	**$ 44,023**	**$97,201**	**$159,219**
Liabilities			
Accounts Payable	$ 4,089	$ 8,965	$ 15,119
Owners' Equity			
Investment Capital	$ 8,800	$ 8,800	$ 8,800
Accumulated Retained Earnings	31,134	79,436	135,371
Total Owners' Equity	$ 39,934	$ 88,236	$ 144,171
Total Liabilities and Owners' Equity	**$ 44,023**	**$97,201**	**$159,291**

Exhibit A.20
Sample Pro Forma Balance
Sheets for KAAS Home
Gourmet's In-Home Caterer/
Grocery Delivery Service

business plan usually contains annual pro forma financial statements for three to five years of future operations. The business plan section should disclose any important accounting and financial reporting assumptions. A short text narrative should accompany each financial statement presented. This discussion should summarize the operating highlights reported in each financial statement presented. The formatting and development of financial statements was discussed extensively in Chapters 3 and 7 of this text. Sample pro forma financial statements for KAAS Home Gourmet's in-home caterer/grocery delivery service are provided in Exhibits A.20, A.21, and A.22.

6.7 Ratio Analysis. The last piece of the business plan is a schedule that compares the company's financial ratios (based on the operating budgets and pro forma financial statements) to those for its industry and/or major competitor. Chapters 3 and 8 include Business Planning Applications that provide several useful resources for performing this analysis. Be careful to compare your firm to others with similar sales and assets. The ratios included in this analysis are those profitability ratios, liquidity ratios, debt ratios, and performance ratios reviewed in Chapter 3. Any unusual or significant differences between the business plan's

Exhibit A.21
Sample Pro Forma Income Statements for KAAS Home Gourmet's In-Home Caterer/ Grocery Delivery Service

KAAS HOME GOURMET Pro Forma Income Statements For the Years Ended December 31			
	20X1	**20X2**	**20X3**
Sales Revenue	$ 92,160	$ 155,520	$ 201,600
Operating Expenses:			
Accounting & Legal	(1,790)	(1,000)	(1,000)
Advertising	(2,380)	(2,081)	(2,122)
Car, Travel, & Delivery	(3,600)	(3,600)	(3,600)
Depreciation	(756)	(756)	(756)
Home Office/Utilities	(600)	(612)	(624)
Insurance/Fees	(300)	(300)	(300)
Salaries	(31,680)	(51,840)	(67,200)
Start-Up Costs	(3,000)	—	—
Supplies and Equipment	(720)	(530)	(349)
Technology	(240)	(245)	(250)
Telephone	(216)	(220)	(225)
Training	(2,400)	(2,400)	(2,400)
Total Operating Expenses	$ (47,682)	$ (63,584)	$ (78,826)
Operating Income	$ 44,478	$ 91,936	$ 122,774
Taxes (at 30)	13,343	27,581	36,832
Net Income	$ 31,135	$ 64,355	$ 85,942

Management Accounting: A Business Planning Approach

KAAS HOME GOURMET Pro Forma Statements of Cash Flows For the Years Ended December 31			
	20X1	20X2	20X3
Cash Flows from (Used by)			
Operating Activities:			
Net Income	$31,134	$ 64,355	$ 85,942
Adjustments to reconcile net income to cash flows from operating activities:			
Depreciation	756	756	756
Changes in assets and liabilities that provided (used) cash:			
Supplies	(100)	(200)	(300)
Accounts Payable	4,088	4,877	6,154
Cash Flows from **Operating Activities**	$ 35,879	$ 69,788	$ 92,552
Cash Flows from (Used by)			
Investing Activities:			
Cash Paid for Computer	$ (1,600)		
Cash Paid for Equipment	(1,060)		
Cash Flows Used by **Investing Activities**	$ (2,660)	—	—
Cash Flows from (Used by)			
Financing Activities:			
Cash Provided by Owners	$ 8,800		
Cash Dividends Paid to Owners	—	$ (16,054)	$ (30,006)
Cash Flows from Financing **Activities**	$ 8,800	$ (16,054)	$ (30,006)
Increase in Cash During Year	$ 42,019	$ 53,734	$ 62,546
Cash Balance at Beginning **of Year**	—	42,019	95,753
Cash Balance at End of Year	$ 42,019	$ 95,753	$ 158,299
Summary			
Cash Provided by Operating Activities	$ 35,879	$ 69,788	$ 92,552
Cash Used by Investing Activities	$ (2,660)	—	—
Cash Provided by (Used by) Financing Activities	$ 8,800	$ (16,054)	$ (30,006)

Exhibit A.22

Sample Pro Forma Statements of Cash Flows for KAAS Home Gourmet's In-Home Caterer/Grocery Delivery Service

ratios and those for the industry or the competition should be explained, as they may signal problems with the assumptions underlying the plan. Chapter 8 provides guidance on how ratios can be used to evaluate budget or business plan credibility and reasonableness. A short text narrative should accompany this ratio analysis. The discussion should address any significant differences noted in the ratio analysis, particularly their impact on the business plan's assumptions. A sample ratio analysis is provided in Exhibit A.23.

After the business plan is completed, it should be carefully reviewed before it is distributed to potential investors and lenders. The next section details how to review a business plan.

Exhibit A.23

Sample Ratio Analysis for
KAAS Home Gourmet's
In-Home Caterer/Grocery
Delivery Service

	20X1	20X2	20X3	Industry Average
Profitability				
Profit margin	33.8%	41.4%	42.6%	**5.6%**
Return on assets	0.71%	0.66%	0.54%	**6.8%**
Return on equity	0.78%	0.73%	0.60%	**9.9%**
Liquidity				
Financial leverage	1.10	1.10	1.10	**1.46**
Current ratio	10.30	10.71	10.51	**2.30**
Efficiency				
Asset turnover	0.48	0.63	0.79	**1.21**

In our analysis, we compared our ratios to industry averages found in the 20X3 editions of Almanac of Business and Industrial Financial Ratios and Dun & Bradstreet's industry reports for financial data for SIC 2099 (food preparation). Our profit margin is excellent in all years and far higher than the industry average. Our average far exceeds the industry due to low overhead—we prepare meals in client's homes.

Our current ratio is much better than the industry average, meaning that KAAS Home Gourmet is in a good financial position because it has far more assets that can be converted to cash than it has liabilities. KAAS exceeds the industry average because of its limited payables, as KAAS holds no inventory. KAAS has minimized receivables by requiring payment in advance.

Our financial leverage is lower than the industry, due to the fact that we have a little debt. Also, most businesses in this industry have much higher fixed assets, including property, which we do not have.

Our asset turnover fixed ratio is lower than the average, primarily due to our relatively low asset balance. KAAS Home Gourmet is maintaining a high balance of cash in hopes of future expansion possibilities. Although comparable data are not entirely accurate, our ratios are favorable and show that our company is well-positioned for a prosperous future.

Management Accounting: A Business Planning Approach

Business Plan Review

The final step in creating a market-quality business plan is to thoroughly review its contents for accuracy, completeness, and consistency. Exhibit A.24 presents a checklist of sixty questions that will enable you to systematically and efficiently review and revise your business plan before sharing it with potential investors and creditors.

Exhibit A.24
Business Plan
Review Checklist

After completing your business plan, use this sixty-question checklist to be sure that you have addressed all of the critical issues and concerns facing potential stakeholders.

1.0 Executive Summary

1. Does your executive summary include company name and contact information?
2. Does your executive summary include a clear business description?
3. Does your executive summary identify your product and service offerings?
4. Does your executive summary *clearly and concisely* identify your competitive advantage?
5. Does your executive summary include a description of management and their qualifications?
6. Does your executive summary include a market analysis summary (including target market and competitors)?
7. Does your executive summary specifically state the amount of funding that you are seeking?
8. Does your executive summary include financial projections (sales, income, assets, and liabilities)?
9. Does your executive summary include clearly titled subheadings to separate the major sections?

2.0 Current and Future Business Operations

Business Description

10. Does your plan include a clear description of the company's business strategy and source of competitive advantage?
11. Does your plan clearly describe the company's intended product and service offerings?
12. Does your plan discuss and justify the company's form of ownership?

Market Analysis

13. Does your plan convincingly analyze the industry in which the company plans to operate?
14. Does your industry analysis address important economic, legal, and regulatory issues affecting your firm?

15. Does your plan clearly identify your target market and its demographics?

16. Does your plan document important trends in your market (income, demand, growth potential)?

17. Is your target market analysis supported with data from credible, publicly available sources and/or surveys?

18. Does your plan clearly identify competitors (names, addresses, descriptions)?

19. Does your plan convincingly discuss the degree of competition in your marketplace?

20. Does your plan clearly and credibly discuss your firm's strengths and weaknesses relative to those of your competitors?

21. Does your plan identify the critical success factors for your firm (that is, what your company will need to do well to succeed)?

Risk Assessment

22. Does your plan credibly discuss the major environmental, process, and information for decision-making risks facing your firm?

23. Does your plan discuss strategies to manage each of these risks?

3.0 Mission Statement

24. Does your plan include a mission statement that clearly documents the company's vision for the future?

25. Does the mission statement clearly state the firm's competitive advantage?

26. Does the mission statement address the needs of various stakeholders?

27. Is the mission statement clear, concise, and free of jargon?

4.0 Action Plan

Promotion

28. Does your analysis include a thorough and convincing promotion and marketing plan (brand image, use of media, advertising plans)?

29. Does the business plan discuss how the firm plans to set prices of products and services?

30. Does the marketing plan discuss what the company intends to do about customer service after a sale has occurred?

31. Does the plan discuss how the firm plans to measure and monitor customer satisfaction?

5.0 Resource Requirements

Value Chain

32. Does the business plan include a description and diagram of the firm's value chain activities?

(Continued)

Management and Human Resources

33. Does the plan discuss the management team and their experience?
34. Does the plan discuss any special required skills or employee certifications?
35. Does the plan identify how the firm plans to recruit, train, and retain its employees?

Location and Facilities

36. Does your proposal clearly identify the location and nature of facilities that will be required to start the business?

Technology

37. Does the proposal discuss the effects of current and future technology on your business?
38. How will your company incorporate technology into its business processes?

6.0 Financial Plan

Sales Forecast

39. Does your sales forecast clearly identify reasonable product/service prices?
40. Does your sales forecast outline expected quantities of sales (based on your market analysis)?
41. Does your sales forecast credibly address sales mix assumptions?
42. Does your sales forecast include clear and credible what-if analyses for changes in any key assumption?

Operating Budget

43. Does your submission include a credible and easy-to-follow monthly operating budget for the first year of operation?

Breakeven and Sensitivity Analysis

44. Does your discussion explain why your breakeven point is achievable and why the assumptions on which it is based are reasonable?
45. Does your discussion provide what-if statements (sensitivity analyses) that address any alternative approaches that may be reasonable?

Start-Up Budget and Financing

46. Is your start-up budget complete?
47. Does your start-up budget include current assets (inventories, cash, etc.)?
48. Does your start-up budget address fixed assets (equipment)?
49. Does your start-up budget identify necessary fees, deposits, and legal costs?
50. Do your balance sheets and related discussion identify and explain your initial source of equity and/or debt capital?

51. Have you demonstrated and explained how you will finance the growth of the business?

Pro Forma Financial Statements

52. Does your business plan include pro forma financial statements for at least three fiscal years?
53. Are your financial statements properly labeled and formatted?
54. Do your balance sheets include all significant items?
55. Do your relevant numbers (cash, net income, retained earnings) accurately tie out across income statements, balance sheets, and statements of cash flows?
56. Do your cash flow schedules include all significant items and tie to the change in cash for each fiscal year?
57. Are your financial statements clearly supported by text discussion that describes the numbers in the financial statements and any key assumptions affecting these data?

Ratio Analysis

58. Have you presented a schedule showing all financial ratios relevant to your business and industry?
59. Does your business plan report the source of industry averages?
60. Do you compare your ratios to industry averages and discuss and explain all significant differences?

Presenting a Business Plan

"Here's how I define a business plan: It's a document that convincingly demonstrates that your business can sell enough of its product or service to make a satisfactory profit and be attractive to potential backers. In other words, a business plan is a selling document."

—David E. Gumpert, *How to Create a Really Successful Business Plan*

A business plan is really a selling tool, particularly when a company shares it with its stakeholders. When firms use business plans to introduce new products and services to the markets, their value as marketing tools grows. In these instances, companies rarely rely on the formal document to "sell" itself. Instead, they call on their managers to make formal presentations to potential creditors and equity investors. What follows are some general tips to consider when preparing for a formal business plan presentation.

Be Creative in Presenting the Plan   Use any professional tool at your disposal to gain and maintain the attention of your audience. The business plan document

Management Accounting: A Business Planning Approach

itself should look professional (binding, printing, ordering, labeling, etc. should meet the highest standards), but do not sacrifice content for appearance. Consider creating handouts to accompany the plan that address commonly asked questions or highlight particularly innovative ideas in the plan. When making a business plan presentation, employ the highest level of technology available (video, sound, Internet, charts, PowerPoint, etc.). However, be careful not to lose the message in the communication media. In short, the communication tools used should be tailored to the unique message being delivered.

Sell the Plan's Benefits   A significant amount of presentation time should be devoted to discussing why the business plan *must* be executed. Clearly articulate the plan's expected benefits vis-à-vis the company's current financial position. The audience should leave the presentation believing that there is only one course of action possible: the one outlined in the business plan.

Acknowledge the Risks of Pursuing the Plan   Potential creditors and investors understand that business is not a risk-free endeavor. Therefore, fully disclose the *major* risks to the plan's success, but be careful not to destroy the excitement created when presenting the plan's benefits. The audience must leave the presentation believing that the plan's risks are both reasonable and manageable, particularly given the resources the company has at its disposal.

Apply Common Financial Analysis Tools   When convincing the audience of the plan's credibility and worth, use tools and techniques with which the audience is familiar (breakeven analysis, common ratios, etc.). Do not introduce "cutting-edge" methods or unusual reporting formats whose validity can be argued.

Support All Claims with Data   Business plan presentations should never include any unsubstantiated claims. Any such benefits or claims must be supported by data from credible sources. Potential creditors and equity investors find financial data particularly compelling, and it should be used to support presentation arguments whenever relevant. Present only that amount of data needed to make a case for accepting the plan. Be careful not to inundate the audience with facts and figures or they will soon lose interest in the venture. When presenting financial data to support the plan, do not rely on the data to explain itself. Be sure to explain the financial results in very simple terms. When in doubt, keep it simple!

Avoid Industry Jargon and Other Potentially Sensitive Issues   Buzzwords and jargon can alienate members of an audience who might feel intimidated or inferior when such terms are used. Therefore, a formal presentation should avoid such language (both in writing and verbally), as well as any other topic whose discussion might bias the audience against the business plan being presented.

Speak with Confidence and ENTHUSIASM!   The audience must have confidence in the presenter's understanding and belief in the plan. The presentation should begin by focusing on the key selling points of the business plan. Start with a convincing reason why the plan must be adopted. Throughout the presentation, show enthusiasm and entice potential investors up front with "what's in the deal for them." Keep the presentation simple and focus only on what is most important. After all, the details are in the written plan. Do not distract listeners with irrelevant or confusing anecdotes. Close by reinforcing the nature of the business opportunity.

Plan Group Presentations   When presenting with a team of individuals, be sure to integrate ideas and themes across speakers. Be sure to introduce the presentation team and discuss their qualifications and topical areas. Plan for questions and decide how the team will address them. It may be useful to prepare in advance for questions that might arise. Be sure to rehearse the presentation—practice makes perfect!

This appendix provides the framework for integrating the tools and techniques discussed in this textbook to create a successful business plan and its presentation. For additional information and guidance, the U.S. Small Business Administration (SBA) offers useful and valuable tools. We describe some of the resources available from the SBA in the next section.

Additional Resources: U.S. Small Business Administration

Each chapter has provided several web sites and resources that are helpful for business planning. Additional information and resources are available through the SBA. Exhibit A.25 describes how to contact the SBA and obtain some its valuable resources.

Exhibit A.25
U.S. Small Business
Administration

The Small Business Administration (SBA) offers an extensive selection of information on most business management topics, from how to start a business to exporting products. You may learn more about the SBA by visiting its web site (www.sba.gov) or by obtaining a copy of its *Resource Directory for Small Business Management* available at no cost from your nearest SBA office. Consult the U.S. Government section in your telephone directory for the office nearest you. It is also available by writing to the agency's Consumer Information Catalog or by downloading through the SBA Online Bulletin Board System. The SBA offers a number of programs and services, including training and educational programs, counseling services, financial programs, and contract assistance including:

- Service Corps of Retired Executives (SCORE), a national organization sponsored by SBA of over 10,000 volunteer business executives who provide free counseling, workshops, and seminars to prospective and existing small business people.

(Continued)

- Small Business Development Centers (SBDCs), sponsored by the SBA in partnership with state and local governments, the educational community, and the private sector. They provide assistance, counseling, and training to prospective and existing businesspeople.

- Business Information Centers (BICs), offering state-of-the-art technology, informational resources, and on-site counseling for start-up and expanding businesses to create business, marketing, and other plans; do research; and receive expert training and assistance.

For more information about SBA business development programs and services, call the SBA Small Business Answer Desk at 1-800-U-ASK-SBA (827-5722).

CPSIA information can be obtained
at www.ICGtesting.com
Printed in the USA
BVOW07s1635090318
509997BV00004B/76/P